ECONOMIES AND THE TRANSFORMATION OF LANDSCAPE

SOCIETY FOR ECONOMIC ANTHROPOLOGY (SEA) MONOGRAPHS
Dolores Koenig, American University
General Editor, Society for Economic Anthropology

Monographs for the Society for Economic Anthropology contain original essays that explore the connections between economics and social life. Each year's volume focuses on a different theme in economic anthropology. Earlier volumes were published with the University Press of America, Inc. (#1–15, 17), Rowman & Littlefield Publishers, Inc. (#16). The monographs are now published jointly by AltaMira Press and the Society for Economic Anthropology (http://anthropology.tamu.edu/sea).

No. 1 Sutti Ortiz, ed., *Economic Anthropology: Topics and Theories*
No. 2 Sidney M. Greenfield and Arnold Strickon, eds., *Entrepreneurship and Social Change*
No. 3 Morgan D. Maclachlan, ed., *Household Economies and Their Transformation*
No. 4 Stuart Plattner, ed., *Market and Marketing*
No. 5 John W. Bennett and John R. Brown, eds., *Production and Autonomy: Anthropological Studies and Critiques of Development*
No. 6 Henry J. Rutz and Benjamin S. Orlove, eds., *The Social Economy of Consumption*
No. 7 Christina Gladwin and Kathleen Truman, eds., *Food and Farm: Current Debates and Policies*
No. 8 M. Estelle Smith, ed., *Perspectives on the Informal Economy*
No. 9 Hill Gates and Alice Littlefield, eds., *Marxist Trends in Economic Anthropology*
No. 10 Sutti Ortiz and Susan Lees, eds., *Understanding Economic Process*
No. 11 Elizabeth M. Brumfiel, ed., *The Economic Anthropology of the State*
No. 12 James M. Acheson, ed., *Anthropology and Institutional Economics*
No. 13 Richard E. Blanton, Peter N. Peregrine, Deborah Winslow and Thomas D. Hall, eds., *Economic Analysis Beyond the Local System*
No. 14 Robert C. Hunt and Antonio Gilman, eds., *Property in Economic Context*
No. 15 David B. Small and Nicola Tannenbaum, eds., *At the Interface: The Household and Beyond*
No. 16 Angelique Haugerud, M. Priscilla Stone, and Peter D. Little, eds., *Commodities and Globalization: Anthropological Perspectives*
No. 17 Martha W. Rees and Josephine Smart, eds., *Plural Globalities in Multiple Localities: New World Border*
No. 18 Jean Ensminger, ed., *Theory in Economic Anthropology*
No. 19 Jeffrey H. Cohen and Norbert Dannhaeuser, eds., *Economic Development: An Anthropological Approach*
No. 20 Gracia Clark, ed., *Gender at Work in Economic Life*
No. 21 Cynthia Werner and Duran Bell, eds., *Values and Valuables: From the Sacred to the Symbolic*
No. 22 Lillian Trager, ed., *Migration and Economy: Global and Local Dynamics*
No. 23 E. Paul Durrenberger and Judith Martí, eds., *Labor in Cross-Cultural Perspective*
No. 24 Richard Wilk, ed., *Fast Food/Slow Food*
No. 25 Lisa Cliggett and Christopher A. Pool, eds. *Economies and the Transformation of Landscape*

ECONOMIES AND THE TRANSFORMATION OF LANDSCAPE

EDITED BY
LISA CLIGGETT AND CHRISTOPHER A. POOL

ALTAMIRA PRESS
A Division of Rowman & Littlefield Publishers, Inc.
Lanham • New York • Toronto • Plymouth, UK

AltaMira Press
A division of Rowman & Littlefield Publishers, Inc.
A wholly owned subsidiary of The Rowman & Littlefield Publishing Group, Inc.
4501 Forbes Boulevard, Suite 200, Lanham, MD 20706
www.altamirapress.com

Estover Road, Plymouth PL6 7PY, United Kingdom

British Library Cataloguing in Publication Information Available

Library of Congress Cataloging-in-Publication Data

Economies and the transformation of landscape / edited by Lisa Cliggett and Christopher A. Pool.
p. cm. -- (Society for Economic Anthropology monographs ; no. 25)
Papers from a conference on " 'Economies and the Transformation of Landscapes' ... the theme for the 2005 annual meeting of the Society, held at Dartmouth College"--P. .
Includes bibliographical references and index.

ISBN-13: 978-0-7591-1117-2 (pbk. : alk. paper)

1. Landscape changes--Congresses. 2. Landscape assessment--Congresses. 3. Nature--Effect of human beings on--Congresses. 4. Human geography--Economic aspects--Congresses. 5. Economic geography--Congresses. 6. Space in economics--Congresses. I. Cliggett, Lisa, 1965- II. Pool, Christopher A.
GF90.E36 2008
304.2'8--dc22

2007029199

Printed in the United States of America

™ The paper used in this publication meets the minimum requirements of American National Standard for Information Sciences—Permanence of Paper for Printed Library Materials, ANSI/NISO Z39.48-1992..

CONTENTS

Figures and Tables

Figures

Tables

1

Introduction
Economies and the Transformation of Landscapes

CHRISTOPHER A. POOL AND LISA CLIGGETT

IN THE WORLD OF ANTHROPOLOGY, THE REALMS OF ECONOMY and ecology are like two continents joined over a broad expanse—a Europe and an Asia whose inhabitants are separated by (and sometimes transcend) an arbitrary line imposed by history and culture far more than by the nature of the field's subject matters. Thus it is that students of hunter-gatherer subsistence strategies debate the application of models inspired by microeconomics while students of transnational commodity flows explore the flows' impacts on rainforest environments. Within this world of real but increasingly blurred and porous disciplinary boundaries, the concept of landscape offers a common ground, not only for the meeting of economic and ecological anthropologists, but for ethnographers, archaeologists, economists, historians, and of course, geographers. It was with the intention to offer a common ground for discussion among the disciplinarily diverse membership of the Society for Economic Anthropology that we proposed "Economies and the Transformation of Landscapes" as the theme for the 2005 annual meeting of the society, held at Dartmouth College, and this volume, which springs from it. Thirty-seven archaeologists, cultural anthropologists, geographers, economists, and historians shared case studies from their research that offered compelling and new perspectives on the ways humans, economies, and ecologies intersect to create powerful landscapes. From those presentations, twelve papers were selected, revised, and expanded to form a synthetic, though not conclusive, overview of current research on economy and landscape linkages. These papers appear in this volume.

Space, Environment, and Landscape in Anthropology

Anthropologists, including archaeologists, have a long engagement with the broadly geographical concepts of space and environment, going back at least as far as the various diffusionist and geographically determinist schools of the late nineteenth and early twentieth centuries (for detailed historical overviews see Anscheutz et al. 2001; Ashmore and Knapp 1999; Hirsch 1995; A. Smith 2003; Tilley 1994). Prior to the 1980s, however, anthropologists tended to conceptualize landscapes in ecological terms as a suite of resources distributed through space to which human populations adapted (e.g., Binford 1980; Flannery 1972; Sanders and Price 1968; Steward 1955), or in locational and physiographic terms as factors that distorted ideal spatial distributions of economic and political central places (e.g., C. Smith 1976; see A. Smith 2003). In general, "the environment" was neatly divided between nature and culture, with the natural environment constituting the stage on which culture was acted, providing local detail to formal economic, social, and political relations (cf. Hirsch 2004: 437). When the natural environment was not treated as static, the relation between nature and culture tended to be viewed in one direction or the other—either as the effects of climate change and natural disaster on societies or the modification of the environment by society (usually the state). As the geographer Carl Sauer famously put it in 1925, "Culture is the agent, the natural area is the medium, the cultural landscape is the result" (Sauer 1963: 343). Rarely was the transformation of landscapes seen in mutualistic terms, and the capacity of stateless societies to significantly transform landscapes was often downplayed or denied (Denevan 1992; Fisher and Feinman 2005: 65).

Since the 1980s developments within and beyond the academy have dramatically changed how anthropologists view landscapes and use landscape and the related concepts of place and space as significant variables in their research (Low and Lawrence-Zúñiga 2003; Winslow 2002: 157). In the social sciences, "space" is no longer an independent entity separate from the objects and actions that exist within its measured confines. Rather, space is understood as a fundamentally relational phenomenon defined by and arising from the positions of subjects and objects with respect to one another (A. Smith 2003: 69), and it is given meaning by the sensual experiences of the actors who inhabit it and move through it (Ingold 1993; Low 2000; Richardson 1982; Tilley 1994). Specific locations invested with meanings as a consequence of human experience and practice in and through time are "places," which, with the stretches between them, are embraced by "landscapes" (A. Smith 2003: 32). In the words of Adam Smith (2003: 32), "Landscapes assemble places to present more broadly visions of the world."

As a consequence of these shifts in perspective, "landscape" now implies a mutually constitutive relationship between the practices of humans and the physical environment, which itself is as much a product of culture as of nature (Smith 2004: 72; de Certeau 1984: 102). As Kurt Anschuetz and his associates (2001: 160–61) emphasize, landscapes "are synthetic . . . with cultural systems structuring and organizing peoples' interactions with their natural environments" and they "are worlds of cultural product" in which "communities transform physical spaces into meaningful places" not just through physical constructions of the "built environment" but also by means of the ways they perceive and imagine the world (see also Ashmore and Knapp 1999: 20; Jackson 1984: 156). Other significant qualities of landscapes identified by Anscheutz and others (2001: 161) are that they constitute the arenas of activities through which communities sustain and reproduce themselves, and that they are dynamic constructions.

Nevertheless, definitions of landscape that encompass all of its natural, cultural, material, perceptual, conceptual, recursive, and dynamic elements are difficult to construct (Layton and Ucko 1999: 2). Instead, individual researchers tend either to lean toward a definition that emphasizes the material existence of the landscape (e.g., Crumley's [1994: 6] oft-cited "the material representation of the relation between humans and the environment"; see Pérez in this volume) or toward one that portrays landscape as "a cultural image, a pictorial way of representing, structuring, or symbolizing surroundings (Daniels and Cosgrove 1988: 1; see Layton and Ucko 1999: 1–2). Cosgrove (1993: 8–9) points a way toward the integration of these concepts by observing that landscape refers to "the totality of the external world as mediated through subjective human experience" (A. Smith 2003: 10). In constructing his actor-based "dwelling perspective," Ingold clarifies that place is not just constructed or represented, but inhabited, and "the landscape, in short, is not a totality that you or anyone else can look at, it is rather the world *in* which we stand in taking up a point of view on our surroundings" (Ingold 1993: 171; emphasis in original). Similarly, A. Smith (2003: 10) distills from Cosgrove's observation a definition of landscape as "land transformed by human activity or perception": that is, "land that humans have modified, built on, traversed or simply gazed on." What these definitions share is an understanding that, at a fundamental level, "landscape" implies the active engagement of humans. In Knapp and Ashmore's words (1999: 20–21), "The environment manifests itself as landscape only when people create and experience space as a complex of places."

In considering economies and the transformation of landscapes, the contributors to this volume lean toward material, social, and political perspectives, as opposed to the purely symbolic. The definitions of landscape they employ are intended less as general theoretical statements than as operationalizations of landscape geared toward the particular studies. Thus, for example, Pérez and Trawick draw on historical ecology and Crumley's definition of landscape as material representation of human-environmental relationships, while Bolender, Steinberg, and Durrenberger acknowledge the range of meanings from "highly subjective, multifaceted, and transient experience of individuals . . . to the structured products of these individuals in spatial practice and the built environment." In their varying use of "landscape" the contributors also highlight particular aspects and extend the concept in interesting ways. For example, in operationalizing landscape for the Andean case he analyzes, Trawick includes the productive activities that take place within the irrigated terrain belonging to a community, while Matejowsky refers to a "commercial landscape" consisting of the "linked commercial activities, institutions, and patterns that define trade in a given locale," both ideas resonating with Hirsch's characterization of the landscape as "cultural process" (1995: 5). Earle and Doyel remind us that *landscape* is not just a noun, but also a verb, and that humans have landscaped their environments in various ways throughout history. On the other hand, Håkansson's observation that "landscape is both the result of human regional interaction and a force that shapes land use over time" resonates with Tsing's (2001: 5) discussion of "nature's agency" with respect to the humanly created "environments that then become stubborn or willing agents in human schemes and dreams." In a different vein, Crothers views the development of an agricultural landscape as "fundamentally an institutional change in the way humans perceive resources, negotiate rights of access or ownership, and organize the social relations of production." Little pushes the conception of landscape even further by characterizing the Maya street vendors of Antigua not just as observers and creators, but as critical elements of the landscape, valued by tourists for the exotic flavor they impart to the setting and reviled by Ladinos, who associate the vendors' presence with filth and disorder.

Recent reconceptualizations of landscape open many avenues for analysis of economies, although economic anthropology has not explored them to the extent they merit (Hirsch 2004). Why is not entirely clear, although A. Smith's (2003: 73–75) discussion of practical "dimensions of landscape" suggests some possibilities. Building on Lefebvre (1991: 38–46) and Harvey (1989: 220–21), Smith constructs a framework for investigating landscapes that distinguishes spatial experience, spatial perception, and spatial imagination. Although Smith correctly observes that these dimensions "must ultimately be understood in relation to one another," we think it is fair to say that his dimensions of spatial perception (concerning the sensual interaction between actors and physical spaces) and imagination (revealed in representations of, and discourse about, space) have received the lion's share of attention in the anthropological literature that presents itself as concerned with space, place, and landscapes (e.g., Appadurai 1992, 1996; Ashmore and Knapp 1999; Gupta and Ferguson 1992; Low 1996, 2000; Tilley 1994). Smith, however, assigns most economic practices to the dimension of spatial experience, described as "the flow of bodies and things through physical space" and "the techniques and technologies" by which spaces are constructed. Thus spatial experience "attends most closely to distribution, transport, communication, . . . land use, resource exploitation," but also to "property rules . . . and administrative, economic, or cultural divisions in physical space."

Obviously, such practices are the subject matter of economic anthropology, and they have received a great deal of attention in archaeology, but they are usually discussed in terms of economy or ecology without explicit recourse to landscape as a theoretical concept (cf. Winslow 2002). Moreover, in the course of abstract economic analysis of transactions, commodity flows, or capital accumulation, the particulars of environment and landscape often become "figure" to the "ground" of economic relations with little attention to their mutual connections (Hirsch 2004: 437; see also Hirsch 1995). While we do not disagree with Smith that economic practices are critical to the experience of space, we would also emphasize that exchanges give meaning to the places in which they occur and that those places and exchanges contribute fundamentally to the "sensual interaction between actors and physical spaces" (A. Smith 2003: 73). The sights, smells, and sounds of the market, the wharf, or the trading floor are every bit as evocative as the plaza, the palace, or the cathedral. Moreover, as Helms (1993) convincingly shows in *Craft and the Kingly Ideal*, the associations of exchanged and crafted items with other places, times, and spiritual realms contribute strongly to their imagining, just as the objects acquire power from those imagined spaces. Further, the definition of rules of territory, property, and usufruct, and their representation via maps, descriptions of meets and bounds, or recountings of historical claims are all conceptualizations, which are negotiated, enacted to varying degrees, and expressed in various ways, on the ground (see, e.g., Erazo, this volume). Thus economic practice is implicated across the material, perceptual, and conceptual dimensions of landscape.

Landscape, Transformation, and Economy

The theme of transformation in this volume springs from the recognition of the recursive relationship between physical and cognized landscapes and the role of economic practice in shaping them. By focusing on transformations we highlight the dynamic qualities of interaction between economic and ecological, sociopolitical, and ideological factors as they are influenced by individual and group decision making played out within and across different temporal spans and geographical scales.[1] Here we expand on the *recursive*, multiscalar, and historical qualities of landscapes in relation to economies as represented in the various contributions to this volume.

The recursivity of landscapes operates in at least two senses. One involves the interaction between the mental and the material. All landscapes are in some sense imagined, in that they are conceived and debated. For all the academic discourse about imagined landscapes and for all the rhetoric about abstract political and social landscapes, there is nevertheless a fundamental materiality to the idea of landscape, which is what gives the term its metaphorical power. On the one hand, the physical particulars of experienced landscapes shape general conceptualizations of landscape; on the other hand, mental constructions of landscape expressed in custom, law, and policy, and materialized through construction and use, have undeniable effects—which may be both profound and persistent—on the physical landscape. Moreover, the recursive interaction between the material and the mental is generally mediated by culturally filtered perceptions of landscape, which respond to intentional efforts to shape those perceptions (e.g., through the marking of boundaries and the construction of buildings, monuments, and roads) as well as the incidental consequences of particular forms of land use (e.g., the effects of tilling, deforestation, or strip mining). Especially as concerns property rights, this recursivity of the mental (imagined) and the material (experienced) in shaping landscapes is implicated in most of the chapters in this volume. It is especially evident, however, in George M. Crothers's model of changing property rights among prehistoric hunter-gatherers and the transition to agriculture in eastern North America, in Carol MacClennan and Christa Walck's history of land use in the southwestern United States, and in economist Paul A. Rivera's analysis of how the abolition of slavery and changing property law transformed the Brazilian landscape.

The other sense in which landscapes are recursive phenomena—closely intertwined with the first sense—concerns the interaction between the physical environment and human society and culture. As Fisher and Feinman (2005: 64) underscore, "Environment and culture change in tandem, and . . . this relationship is continually renegotiated at a variety of temporal and spatial scales" as humans "modify the environment in pursuit of social, political, and economic goals." By means of their economic focus, all of the chapters in this volume examine the recursive interaction of society with the physical environment in the transformation of landscapes. However they might be imagined, rights and access to land and resources cannot be divorced from their social contexts, as Crothers, Rivera, and MacClennan and Walck show in their chapters. For the delicate environmental context of northern Iceland's grasslands and forests, Bolender, Steinberg, and Durrenberger draw on historical sagas and archaeological settlement patterns to describe how a stratified social system and changing household demographics created a hierarchical propertied landscape in a series of stages from the initial settlement through the later division of farmsteads. Settlement, in this case of nomadic pastoralists rather than seafaring Vikings, is also a focus of the chapter by Elliot Fratkin, who turns our attention to sedentarization as an unfortunate consequence of population growth, political conflict, and economic encroachment. Fratkin concludes that pastoralist livelihoods may be increasingly unsustainable as grazing territories are lost. Similarly, N. Thomas Håkansson's examination of the agricultural economy in northern Tanzania emphasizes how the precolonial political economy, geared toward the accumulation of wealth through intensive agriculture, imprinted the landscape with a patchwork of irrigation furrows, fields, marketplaces, and grassland savanna, and how the inception of colonialism initiated a shift toward landscape deterioration and declining resources. Taken together, Fratkin's and Håkansson's chapters set in broadly similar environments provide an illustration of how social factors affect the resilience of economies and landscapes (see Redman 2005).

Several chapters in this volume describe engineered landscapes; *engineered landscapes* is a term used in Tim Earle and David Doyel's chapter. Among the most spectacular are the terraced mountains of the Andes, like those in the Cotahuasi valley that Paul Trawick discusses. Framed in terms of the "drama of the commons" under the contrasting social organizations and moral economies of indigenous, colonized, and hacienda-dominated communities, Trawick's analysis of water management systems provides an excellent example of the variable effects of social systems on intensively cultivated landscapes. As Trawick's example illustrates, even spectacularly engineered landscapes can be successfully constructed and run through cooperation at the local level. Verónica Pérez Rodríguez's study of ancient lama-bordo terraced irrigation systems in the Mixteca Alta of Oaxaca, Mexico, offers a further example of how the decisions and actions of households and communities can produce complex irrigated landscapes without state intervention, and in fact, preceded the appearance of states (see also Hunt 1988). The engineered landscapes of prestate societies is also the focus of the chapter by Earle and Doyel, who compare the irrigation systems of historically documented chiefdoms in Hawaii and the prehistoric Hohokam culture of the southwestern United States. Like Håkansson, Earle and Doyel employ the concept of *landesque capital* (Brookfield 1984)—human alterations to the landscape designed to yield long-term gains in productivity (Fisher and Feinman 2005: 64). Whereas Håkansson highlights the degradation of Tanzanian landesque capital under colonial demands, Earle and Doyel incorporate landesque capital in an evolutionary model. Eschewing Wittfogel's managerial argument that extensive irrigation systems required central administration, Earle and Doyel argue that with the emergence of sociopolitical ranking in chiefdoms, "highly intensified landscapes of water management created an artificial world" that allowed the imposition of new hierarchies of property ownership, and new opportunities for elite control to generate surpluses that could be employed toward political ends.

With its emphasis on cross-generational maintenance of irrigation systems, terraces, raised fields, stone walls, anthropogenic soils, and the like, the concept of landesque capital underscores the temporal dimension of landscapes. Transformative events and processes run the gamut of temporal scales, from brief but catastrophic eruptions, earthquakes, storms, floods, and fires to the millennia of Holocence climate change. Similarly, landscape transformations with human causes can happen in seconds when a bomb drops and in hours when a levee breaks, or they may transpire over centuries and millennia of harvesting shellfish, cultivating and grazing land, constructing terraces, or building cities. The imprints of human activities on the landscape persist long after the activities have ceased, with the result that landscapes are historically contingent entities that have recursively shaped human activities in the past and continue to do so in the present. Such imprints tell stories over time of social, political, and economic relations. In those stories we learn how humans create landscapes and produce the places that give meaning to their social worlds.

The chapters in this volume offer examples of landscape transformations at a variety of temporal scales. At the shorter end, Walter E. Little examines the events in the years leading up to the relocation by municipal fiat of Maya vendors in Antigua, Guatemala, and the consequent reconceptualization and negotiation of public space. At decadal scales, Ty Matejowsky discusses changes wrought by retail "modernization" in the urban landscape of San Fernando City, the Philippines, and Juliet S. Erazo discusses the negotiation of land titling in the Ecuadorian Amazon. Elliot Fratkin's chapter on sedentarization of pastoralists in Kenya likewise examines a span of decades, while Håkansson provides a historical analysis of intensive agriculture and landscape transformation over the course of more than a century. Temporal scales of one century to several are also employed by McClennan and Walck; Rivera; Trawick; Bolender, Steinberg, and Durrenberger; Earle and Doyel; and Pérez, whereas Crothers's discussion of changing property rights among prehistoric hunter-gatherers extends the scale of analysis to the order of millennia (although the proposed transformation to a delayed return economic system and exclusive property rights itself may have occurred more rapidly). Taken as a whole, the various contributions make a compelling case for the importance of history in the analysis of landscapes, modern as well as ancient.

Just as landscapes operate over a variety of temporal scales, they are also multiscalar in spatial and structural terms. This point is driven home with particular force in the chapters that examine the effects on landscapes of interactions across local, national, and global scales. Erazo's analysis of the development of land-titling systems in a community in the Ecuadorean Amazon offers an excellent example of the negotiation of how landscapes are perceived and property rights are conceived across local and national scales, as well as among traditionalists and others locally. Negotiation of interests between household and state are also implicated in Pérez's analysis of the construction of ancient lama-bordo systems in Mexico's Mixteca Alta, and state intervention in land-use practice is a key component of MacClennan and Walck's chapter. Interaction at scales beyond the national are introduced in Håkansson's discussion of the landscape effects of colonial extraction in Tanzania and Rivera's analysis of colonial and global demands for sugar and coffee and their transformative effects on property rights and slavery in Brazil. In the contemporary setting, international tourism backgrounds disputes between Maya vendors and Ladino municipal authorities in Little's study, while global commercialism frames Matejowsky's study of the San Fernando cityscape.

Themes and Organization of the Volume

In this collection we have brought together varied timescales and perspectives to create a synthesized understanding of economical-ecological transformations, and what such transformations reveal about human culture. At the core, examining landscape transformation reveals social, political, and economic transformation. Issues of rights, both as practiced and as perceived, permeate all chapters in the volume, as do issues of landscape definition. As the foundational work of Steward (1955) and more recent ecological and economic anthropologists documents (e.g., Netting 1981, 1993; Wilk 1991; Guyer 1997), societies, communities, kin groups, and individuals negotiate livelihoods and social relations through access to physical and perceived landscapes. Changing access and use have recursive links to changing economies, ecologies, and social worlds, and ultimately, a focus on changing landscapes provides a window on transformations in other aspects of culture.

While each chapter stands on its own, offering detailed insight on particular case studies, the cumulative understanding we gain from this volume challenges us to consider a set of ideas that interlinks economies and ecologies. Foremost is the point that humans imprint the landscape, and those imprints, in turn, influence human action. Ultimately, these imprints reveal the dynamics of social, political, and economic relations. All chapters in the volume agree that landscapes are produced by human action, but the mechanisms of production differ in relation to economic, ecological, and social histories.

It is a daunting task to bring together a body of work that has such rich interlinkages of ideas. The organization of the volume could take shape around any number of factors—varied time and spatial scales are two obvious points that emerge from each chapter. As the previous section indicates, each chapter speaks to a variety of cross-cutting scales and themes, creating valuable resonances with each other, as well as presenting valuable case material on particular places and topics. We wanted to resist the tempting option to group chapters by the subdisciplines of archaeology, cultural anthropology, and history. One of our goals in organizing the conference and subsequently coediting this volume was to demonstrate that theories and concepts can cross the artificial boundaries of disciplines to offer synthesized views of landscape and economic change. In fact, our understanding is enhanced by integrating the varying methodologies and time scales presented through archaeology, cultural anthropology, and history.

Resisting the disciplinary organization, we chose instead to organize the volume around a political-economy framework. Using such an organizational lens highlights the social complexity of landscapes and economic system linkages. Each case illustrates an element of power, politics, and societal linkages on the landscape. Within the broad theme of the political economy of landscape transformation, we address three content areas in particular.

Part I, "Domesticated Landscapes in Historical Frames," provides four unique cases of how humans have left their imprint through "domesticating" or "engineering" landscapes over time. Earle and Doyel's chapter examines Hawaiian and Hohokam irrigation systems, revealing how rights over engineered landscapes provide the base for financing new institutional complexity over extended time frames. Trawick's chapter on the history of irrigation in a Peruvian mountain region explores the ways that the engineering of landscapes can determine sustainability of water use, and ultimately the sustainability and autonomy of those communities. Pérez's discussion of household and community-level construction of terraced landscapes in the Mixteca Alta (Oaxaca, Mexico) indicates that complex agricultural systems can exist *without* state-level interventions, and that local-level actors can and do effect, in institutional ways, large ecosystems. MacLennan and Walck's chapter documents the transformations in industrial uses and rights over vast expanses of the southwestern United States, ultimately resulting in an overextraction of resources.

Part II brings together a group of chapters highlighting the complexity of "Transformations, Political Strategies, and Decision Making" in landscape change. Crothers's chapter succinctly links the profound shift from hunter-gatherer livelihoods to agricultural production in the U.S. Green River valley region by suggesting instrumental changes in land tenure rights and associated ecological shifts from the Archaic to the Early Woodland period. Fratkin's chapter demonstrates how changing grazing rights and state intervention in Kenyan pastoralists' (Rendille and Ariaal) settlement practices have recursive links to degrading ecology in the region. Erazo's chapter on one community's efforts to establish formal land titling in the Ecuadorean Amazon eloquently captures the complex social maneuverings as a group of Kichwa Indians form an agricultural cooperative, and subsequently negotiate among themselves, and with the government, on what such a cooperative should "look like." Rivera's examination of nineteenth-century Brazilian coffee production persuasively documents how slavery, and its demise, relate to land grabbing as a wave of European immigration brought new tenure systems to the country. Taken together these four chapters provide a multifaceted view of the ways that choice and intentionality have recursive links to ecological and social landscapes.

Part III, "Political Economy and Institutional Interactions," presents four cases from divergent time frames that document the ways local actors, social institutions, and ecosystems produce politically shaped landscapes. The chapter by Bolander, Steinberg, and Durrenberger employs a creative and compelling combination of archaeological and ethnohistorical data to unveil northern Iceland's complex socioeconomic and natural landscape, and the emergence of inequality during the Viking era. Håkansson's thorough study of political-economic history and landscape transformation in Tanzania prior to colonialism offers detailed evidence for a highly dynamic African landscape, and perhaps more importantly, for highly complex *precolonial* economic systems that thrived on that dynamic landscape. Little's chapter on Maya handicraft vendors takes us from Guatemalan households to the town markets where exchange occurs between local populations and global tourists—while producers and policymakers negotiate what the proper "landscape" for such exchanges should be. Matejowsky's study of a Philippine city documents transformations in the retail economy tied to Western market forces that intersect with the sociophysical landscape of the area, and threatens small-scale industries that previously defined the urban landscape. This collection of chapters reveals the multifaceted relationships between landscapes, economies, and institutions, and the ways in which these interactions produce political-ecological outcomes.

Conclusion

When anthropologists comment on the value of a landscape perspective, they unfailingly point to its ability to integrate a variety of stubborn oppositions. For anthropology in general and economic anthropology in particular these oppositions include the insidious divide between culture and nature (Håkansson) as well as that between the inhabited settlement or archaeological site and the meaningfully constructed, productively utilized, and historically understudied countryside (Knapp and Ashmore 1999). Similarly, a landscape perspective can help span the gulf between the transience of individual experience and the structure of its persistent products (Bolender, Steinberg, and Durrenberger) and between the "*here* and *there*" of local and larger frames of reference (Winslow 2002: 156).

The idea of landscape therefore provides many points of departure for discussions of human society. Focusing the kaleidoscope of landscape on the interactions of economy and society brings us to a common grounding—and the goal of this volume. The twelve cases presented here offer a baseline for understanding the dialectical relationship between economy and landscape transformation. Key aspects of these relationships include the fundamental concern of rights over resources; the power dynamics inherent in the production, perception, and use of landscapes; and the multiscalar nature of interactions relating to landscapes. Although the case studies presented here emerge from a variety of academic disciplines and subdisciplines, the volume as a whole, with its focus on landscape, offers a crystal through which to cast our gaze—shedding light from different angles so that the outcome of our vision is more complete than it would be from our individual disciplines. Indeed, it is through our cross-disciplinary conversations that we gain greater ability to synthesize our understanding, and to make sense of our world.

Note

1. This is a near quote from our original proposal. We are grateful to Timothy K. Earle for reminding us of these dimensions of landscape in his remarks as discussant in our session at the American Anthropological Association meetings of 2005. Almost simultaneously with the SEA conference Fisher and Feinman (2005) published an article that similarly highlighted the recursive, historical, multiscalar, and dynamic qualities of landscapes.

References

Anscheutz, Kurt F., Richard H. Wilshusen, and Cherie L. Scheick. 2001. "An Archaeology of Landscapes: Perspectives and Directions," *Journal of Archaeological Research* 0: 157–211.

Appadurai, Arjun. 1992. "Global Ethnoscapes: Notes and Queries for Transnational Anthropology." In *Recapturing Anthropology: Working in the Present*, ed. Richard G. Fox, 191–210. Santa Fe: School of American Research Press.

———. 1996. *Modernity at Large: Cultural Dimensions of Globalization*. Minneapolis: University of Minnesota Press.

Ashmore, Wendy, and A. Bernard Knapp, eds. 1999. *Archaeologies of Landscape: Contemporary Perspectives*. Oxford: Blackwell.

Binford, Lewis R. 1980. "Willow Smoke and Dogs' Tails: Hunter-Gatherer Settlement Systems and Archaeological Site Formation." *American Antiquity* 45:4–20.

Brookfield, Harold C. 1984. "Intensification Revisited." *Pacific Viewpoint* 25:15–44.

Cosgrove, D. E. 1993. *The Palladian Landscape: Geographical Change and Its Cultural Representation in Sixteenth-Century Italy*. Leicester: Leicester University Press.

Crumley, Carole L. 1994. "Historical Ecology: A Multidimensional Ecological Orientation." In *Historical Ecology: Cultural Knowledge and Changing Landscapes*, ed. C. L. Crumley, 1–16. Santa Fe: School of American Research Press.

Daniels, S., and D. E. Cosgrove. 1988. "Introduction: Iconography and Landscape." In *The Iconography of Landscape: Essays on the Symbolic Representation, Design, and Use of Past Environments*, ed. D. E. Cosgrove and S. Daniels, 1–10. Cambridge: Cambridge University Press.

de Certeau, Michel. 1984. *The Practice of Everyday Life*. Berkeley: University of California Press.

Denevan, William M. 1992. "The Pristine Myth: The Landscape of the Americas in 1492." *Annals of the Association of American Geographers* 82:369–85.

Fisher, Christopher T., and Gary M. Feinman. 2005. "Introduction to 'Landscapes Over Time.'" *American Anthropologist* 107 (1): 62–69.

Flannery, Kent V. 1972. "The Cultural Evolution of Civilizations." *Annual Review of Ecology and Systematics* 3:399–426.

Gupta, A., and J. Ferguson. 1992. "Beyond 'Culture': Space, Identity, and the Politics of Difference." *Cultural Anthropology* 7 (1): 6–23.

Guyer, Jane I. 1997. *An African Niche Economy: Farming to Feed Ibadan, 1968–88*. Edinburgh: Edinburgh University Press.

Harvey, David. 1989. *The Condition of Postmodernity*. Oxford: Blackwell.

Helms, Mary W. 1993. *Craft and the Kingly Ideal*. Austin: University of Texas Press.

Hirsch, Eric. 1995. "Landscape: Between Place and Space." In *The Anthropology of Landscape: Perspectives on Place and Space*, ed. E. Hirsch and M. O'Hanlon, 1–30. Oxford: Oxford University Press.

———. 2004. "Environment and Economy." *Anthropological Theory* 4 (4): 435–53.

Hunt, Robert. 1988. "Size and Structure of Authority in Canal Irrigation Systems." *Journal of Anthropological Research* 44:335–55.

Ingold, Tim. 1993. "The Temporality of Landscape." *World Archaeology* 25 (2): 152–74.

Jackson, J. B. 1984. *Discovering the Vernacular Landscape*. New Haven, CT: Yale University Press.

Knapp, A. Bernard, and Wendy Ashmore. 1999. "Archaeological Landscapes: Constructed, Conceptualized, Ideational." In *Archaeologies of Landscape: Contemporary Perspectives*, ed. W. Ashmore and A. B. Knapp, 1–30. Oxford: Blackwell.

Layton, Robert, and Peter J. Ucko. 1999. "Introduction: Gazing on the Landscape and Encountering the Environment." In *The Archaeology and Anthropology of Landscape: Shaping Your Landscape*, ed. P. J. Ucko and R. Layton, 1–30. London: Routledge.

Lefebvre, Henri. 1991. *The Production of Space*. Oxford: Blackwell.

Low, Setha M. 1996. "Spatializing Culture: The Social Production and Social Construction of Public Space in Costa Rica." *American Ethnologist* 23:861–79.

———. 2000. *On the Plaza: The Politics of Public Space and Culture*. Austin: University of Texas Press.

Low, Setha M., and D. Lawrence-Zúñiga, eds. 2003. *The Anthropology of Space and Place: Locating Culture*. Cambridge, MA: Blackwell.

Netting, Robert. 1981. *Balancing on an Alp: Ecological Change and Continuity in a Swiss Mountain Community*. Cambridge: Cambridge University Press.

———. 1993. *Smallholders, Householders: Farm Families and the Ecology of Intensive, Sustainable Agriculture*. Stanford, CA: Stanford University Press.

Redman, Charles L. 2005. "Resilience Theory in Archaeology." *American Anthropologist* 107 (1): 70–77.

Sanders, William T., and Barbara Price. 1968. *Mesoamerica: The Evolution of a Civilization*. New York: Random House.

Sauer, Carl O. 1963. "The Morphology of Landscape." In *Land and Life: A Selection of the Writings of Carl Sauer*, ed. J. Leighly, 315–50. Berkeley: University of California Press.

Smith, Adam. 2003. *The Political Landscape: Constellations of Authority in Early Complex Polities*. Berkeley and Los Angeles: University of California Press.

Smith, Carol A., ed. 1976. *Economic Systems.* Vol. 1 of *Regional Analysis.* New York: Academic Press.
Steward, Julian. 1955. *Theory of Culture Change: The Methodology of Multilinear Evolution.* Urbana-Champaign: University of Illinois Press.
Tilley, Christopher. 1994. *A Phenomenology of Landscape: Places, Paths, and Monuments.* Oxford: Berg.
Tsing, Anna Lowenhaupt. 2001. "Nature in the Making." In *New Directions in Anthropology and Environment*, ed. C. L. Crumley, 3–23. Walnut Creek, CA: AltaMira.
Wilk, Richard. 1991. *Household Ecology: Economic Change and Domestic Life among the Kekchi Maya in Belize.* Tucson: University of Arizona Press.
Winslow, Deborah. 2002. "Space, Place, and Economic Anthropology: Locating Potters in a Sri Lankan Landscape." In *Theory in Economic Anthropology*, ed. J. Ensminger, 155–81. Walnut Creek, CA: AltaMira.

I

ENGINEERED LANDSCAPES IN HISTORICAL FRAMES

The Engineered Landscapes of Irrigation 2

TIMOTHY EARLE AND DAVID E. DOYEL

THE THEME OF THE 2005 SOCIETY FOR ECONOMIC Anthropology annual meeting asked a deceptively simple question: how are landscapes and human economies related one to another? As archaeologists, we provide a long-term perspective on this question. As materialists, we conceive of the relationship in fairly straightforward terms, involving the productivity of the land, the organization of human labor working on the land, and property rights in the land. We want to consider how people constructed and maintained landscapes, how property rights determined rights to land, and how ownership structured social stratification and political control. Productivity, labor, and property rights provide a first-order understanding of the variability in human economies and societies that then offers a foundation for detailed studies of meaning, values, and relationships that emerge in other chapters of this volume.

A compelling lesson from archaeology is that across history, humans have extensively modified their environments. All environments are more or less "landscaped" and the extent of this landscaping has increased dramatically across human history. Ten thousand years ago, much of the world was heavily forested. Humans may have altered habitats using fire, but the world was essentially "natural." Since adopting agriculture in the Neolithic, however, humans have increasingly transformed the land quite purposefully. They have cleared forests for animals and crops, channeled rivers, terraced hills, and drained swamps.

Brookfield (1984; Blaikie and Brookfield 1987) describes environmental improvements as *landesque capital*, meaning that human labor has manufactured special soils and built facilities like drainage ditches, terraces, and irrigation canals that substantially increase the productivity of the land. Unevenly spread over the globe, this landesque capital of human alterations "is a carpet of investment for future agricultural production" (Widgren n.d.). With proper maintenance, such improvements continue to raise productivity of the land for generations, and as such the improvements represent substantial fixed capital, the ownership, transfer, and inheritance of which become of major concern. Landscaping thus increases the consequence of property systems, giving rights to some against others. At the same time, marking the land with permanent facilities helps associate the land with groups or families who built them.

Landscapes also have been subjected to massive unintended changes that can be severe and devastating to food production. Forest clearing, for example, can increase erosion, flooding, desertification, and species extinctions. Many have argued that population growth and required intensification are unsustainable, thus causing environmental degradation. But, despite long-term intensification, devastating environmental losses are not inevitable or uniform across the globe. As illustrated by Asian irrigated rice agriculture, farmers can develop specialized skills for cultivating and maintaining highly intensive agriculture (Bray 1986). In an *American Anthropologist* special section, archaeologists describe how human population growth, sociopolitical organization, and environmental degradation interact to create individual landscapes (Fisher and Feinman 2005). They argue that banking of labor as landesque capital acts to buffer production systems against degradation, because careful maintenance of soils, terraces, embankments, and canals creates a productive infrastructure for sustainable agriculture. Regarding the question of the relationship between landscapes and economies, we can conclude that environmental disasters and environmental stability are to a large measure both products of human action.

We focus on extreme examples of Brookfield's landesque capital called *engineered landscapes* (Lansing 1991). Engineered landscapes are cultural artifacts, built up across generations to contain permanent facilities, including fields, terraces, canals, dams, and reservoirs for agriculture and walls, roads, buildings, monuments, villages, and eventually cities. They are notable in the extent and variety of change to the physical appearance and sustained productivity of the landscape. An engineered landscape has some of the characteristics of an urban world, in which many aspects are "man made" and maintained. Engineering is a quantitative variable that can be measured across time by the labor invested in the construction and modification of improved facilities, and, by determining the uses of the engineering, archaeologists can describe how the human goals of landscaping may have changed over time (Kolb 1997). Across generations, building on the land creates a palimpsest that meets the shifting needs and expectations of the people.

Heavily engineered landscapes, like the Balinese countryside described by Lansing, are topographically altered in impressive and permanent ways, changing production functions and social uses. Most important perhaps is how the creation of engineered landscapes played into the building of complex societies. Although complex societies arise for many and complicated reasons, all must develop means to finance their newly created political institutions. Typically this finance requires the mobilization of wealth that can be used to pay for the events and personnel associated with new ruling institutions. Our thesis is that engineered landscapes, especially those with irrigation, were both highly productive *and* controllable, and so could be used to generate a reliable surplus to finance many (perhaps most) precapitalist chiefdoms and nonmercantile states.

Does Irrigation Matter in Its Need for Central Management?

Anthropologists know that human labor transforms a region's look and its productivity through landscaping, and we have often discussed the organization of the labor involved and whether particular forms of engineering, such as large-scale irrigation or massive pyramidal mounds, required central management for their construction. Interest in the organization of labor is, of course, rooted in the writings of Karl Marx, and, for traditional economies, Karl Wittfogel argued that irrigation required central management in ways analogous to capital technologies. The management of irrigation continues to generate considerable interest, and a consensus has emerged that irrigation systems, even of large scale, can be managed in alternative ways.

The focus on irrigation's management derives from Wittfogel's (1957) influential book *Oriental Despotism*. While Marx had believed that village-based irrigation farming created a conservative, modular, and nondynamic economy (the Asiatic Mode of Production), Wittfogel argued that irrigation's complicated and large-scale technology required central management to construct and reconstruct its often impressive dams, levees, branching canals networks, terraces, and drainage ditches. He argued that a need for central management in these activities was the organizing function responsible for forming state bureaucracies. His theory gained favor, providing the basis for a comparative study of state origins (Steward 1955).

Following a trajectory common for general theories in our discipline, as soon as Wittfogel's hydraulic hypothesis gained favor, anthropologists began to assemble case material to show its inadequacies. Archaeologists argued that even the complex irrigation of the Hohokam in southwestern Arizona was built up progressively and did not require central management (Woodbury 1961; cf. Howard 1993). In both Mesopotamia and Mesoamerica, the construction of large-scale irrigation apparently followed the development of states and so could not have caused it (Adams 1966). Ethnographies of irrigation in both the new and old worlds were amassed to show that irrigation's management could be highly variable and often quite local (Fernea 1970; Hunt 1986; Hunt and Hunt 1976; Lansing 1991; Leach 1961; Lees 1973; Mitchell 1991; Mitchell and Guillet 1993; Sahlins 1962; Scarborough 2003; Spooner 1974).

As a graduate student at the University of Michigan, Tim Earle became involved in this debate when Marshall Sahlins asked him to join Sahlins's Hawaiian project (Earle 1978). In his treatise, Wittfogel (1957: 241–43) had used Hawaii to support the empirical generalization that irrigation and agrarian states were closely linked. At contact, Hawaiian chiefdoms were the most complex of Polynesian societies, verging on a state structure, and they depended heavily on intensive irrigation-based taro farming. Wittfogel focused on the position of the *konohiki*, a low-level chief assigned to administer the local economy. He argued that these managers were required by the complexity of the irrigation, and thus caused the exceptional development of Hawaiian political structures. In his dissertation, however, Sahlins (1958) took a different tack, explaining the complexity of Hawaiian society based on the gross productivity of its intensive agriculture, not on its irrigation systems' needs for central management. Wittfogel, a member of Sahlins's doctoral committee, aggressively questioned Sahlins's interpretation, and later, when setting up his historical project to study Hawaiian society, Sahlins remembered that attack and recruited Earle as a "hired gun" to demonstrate that Wittfogel's interpretation was mistaken.

Showing that Wittfogel was mistaken on the Hawaiian case proved to be empirically quite easy. Although much of the Hawaiian landscape had been extensively engineered to create highly productive irrigated agriculture and aquaculture, nothing about these facilities suggested a need for central management for either construction or maintenance (Earle 1978, 1980). Hawaiian irrigation systems were very small scale; all but a few were less than 10 ha, and virtually all were restricted to single-valley communities. After the nineteenth-century change in property law, without any central oversight, cooperating Hawaiian farmers provided all management themselves for their irrigation. As expressed in the nineteenth-century legal testimony by a native farmer, "Everybody, now that he has a kuleana [land allocation], is his own konohiki" (see Earle 1978: 137). Considering other well-documented ethnographic cases of small-scale irrigation showed that management was highly variable (local farmers, community officials, or chiefly managers), corresponding not to the needs of irrigation management but to the overarching political structure within which irrigation was embedded. In simplest terms, the political superstructure, not the requirements of such modest irrigation, determined the managerial style of small-scale irrigation.

One concern of irrigation is risk. Many scholars have mentioned the possibility that irrigation's design creates conditions particularly susceptible to disruption by flooding and drought. In the Hawaiian Islands, for example, the removal of upland forests made flooding a major threat, and the coastal locations of some systems occasioned their vulnerability to tidal waves (Earle 1978). As we discuss later, however, irrigation does not routinely lead to increased risk and the opposite may in fact be true. Risks that do exist, however, tend to be borne differentially by some farmers, especially those at the edges of irrigation systems. For example, in highland Peruvian communities, when water is abundant, farmers expand production by building new terraces, but when annual rainfall decreases, as it does cyclically, those terraced fields at the margins are cut off from water and must be abandoned (Guillet 1987). Irrigation creates a landscape that is fundamentally differentiated into better and worse land. Some soils are more productive and lower in risk. Ownership of the most productive and lowest risk lands can give substantial long-term advantage to an emerging elite.

Both archaeological and ethnographic cases now provide many good examples of how state management of irrigation was unnecessary; this consensus is well supported by Robert Hunt's (1988) cross-cultural study of fifteen cases in which state societies used larger-scale irrigation. While small-scale systems, like those in Hawaii, could be managed informally, many activities on larger irrigation systems (water allocation, head dam construction, ditch cleaning, and the like) require considerable social coordination. Such coordination, however, can be provided in alternative ways, classed roughly into self-organizing irrigation community and national government management. In Hunt's analysis, the scale of irrigation and the tasks of its management do *not* apparently require more centralized decision making. Ranking the cases by the size of irrigation systems shows a largely random mix of state versus local management options (Hunt 1988: table 1). Evidently, many large-scale systems are managed cooperatively by irrigation communities that are composed of smaller segments that self-organize to solve operational problems (see Scarborough 2003). Management of even large-scale irrigation does not require state bureaucratic oversight, and so it could not require the evolution of a state superstructure. We now have a detailed and refined understanding of how different communities around the world manage irrigation, and that variation well illustrates the social alternatives to organize productive labor. Even large-scale irrigation does not require state bureaucratic management.

Why Irrigation Does Matter

Wittfogel's hypothesis seems fatally flawed, except for the nagging fact that many (but not all) primary states and chiefdoms are evidently associated with irrigated agriculture. Wittfogel's emphasis on management has directed the attention of anthropologists away from other significant linkages. We develop a different line of argument: surpluses from engineered landscapes with irrigation, terracing, and/or drainage (see Scarborough and Isaac 1993) were essential to finance the emergence of complex political institutions. Although there exists a number of possibilities by which complexity can be financed, engineered landscapes of irrigation realize particularly high and sustainable productivity. The high productivity of irrigated agriculture simply makes possible the substantial surpluses that chiefdoms and states can mobilize (Hunt 2000). Most importantly, surplus production from irrigated landscapes can be easily controlled by elites to support their emergent institutions of rule.

High and Sustainable Productivity

The first requirement for the evolution of complex societies is to fashion a political economy to finance emergent institutions of order and control. The vast majority of chiefdoms and early states depended on agriculture, and their political development required highly productive and sustained agricultural intensification.[1] Many developing chiefdoms and states intensified agriculture with irrigation, progressively replacing the natural cycles with water flows from canals, soils embanked by terraces, and nutrient cycles closely managed and augmented. Unlike other forms of intensification, irrigation appears to increase substantially the productivity of labor on its fields compared to neighboring, nonirrigated lands (compare Boserup 1965). The contrast is most dramatic in dry lands like Peru, Mesopotamia, and the American Southwest where the canals often mark a line in the sand between the fertile and the sterile.

Irrigation systems seem to have an almost infinite potential for intensification, and remarkably high population densities can be sustained (Bray 1986). Geertz (1963) describes how laboring on Balinese irrigation is an "agricultural involution." The individual farmer can always work just a little harder—control water flow more carefully, weed another time, use more fertilizer, transplant seedlings, and the like. Each new input increases the farmer's output, allowing families to subsist on smaller plots and to provide more to the landlord or the taxman. The harder and more carefully they work, the better they can live and the more that elites can demand from them. In irrigation, the potential for self-exploitation and class exploitation seem almost inexhaustible.

Intensification by irrigation is also sustainable. Related to processes of degradation and resilience (Krech 2005), sustainability implies that agricultural production does not diminish long-term potential productivity. By what means and how much the environment is landscaped may mitigate its exposure to degradation. While all highly intensified landscapes are susceptible to loss, engineering and its regular maintenance substantially reduce that susceptibility when compared to nonengineered landscapes. Better dams, larger reservoirs, deeper wells, better drainage, and more terracing help control water availability, erosion, and salinization. In Hawaii, for example, increasing production by expanding swidden caused massive denuding of upland soils with resulting erosion and species extinction. The building of irrigation systems, however, provided an alternative highly productive agriculture that sustained long-term intensification without major degradation (Earle 1997). The irrigated pondfields in Hawaii proved to be productive year-round, and they were continuously farmed in some areas for more than a thousand years.

Each environment has distinct possibilities for intensification, but the long-term consequences vary significantly. On dryland landscapes without terracing and other engineering, intensification may cause increased erosion and decreased fertility that makes high levels of production unsustainable. On engineered landscapes with irrigation, although collapse is always a possibility, especially if maintenance is relaxed, productivity is less susceptible to degradation. Some intensification may be justified by family self-interest. Supporting their children and storing more output in order to offset future risks would seem reasonable justification to invest labor in land, but why would farmers be willing to produce further surplus to support ruling institutions? The answer seems self-evident: they had to.

Control through Enforced Property Rights

To finance emergent political systems of rule, surplus must be mobilized through a political economy, and families do not willingly surrender that which they have produced by much toil. To gain access to land or facilities owned by a ruling elite, peasants relinquish surplus as tax or tribute, what

Wolf (1966) calls a *fund of rent*. The origin of such hierarchical systems of property needs still to be considered. Although intensification of agriculture increases the importance of ownership, individual farming families can own land without strongly increasing stratification (Netting 1993). Irrigation systems, however, differentiate land based on productivity and inherent risk. Elites organize (or at least allege to have organized) landscape engineering and thus lay plausible claims to surplus from farmers. The irrigation system built by an elite can thus be the lever to extract surplus, while ownership of actual fields and responsibilities for management can still be vested in the hands of farmers. Furthermore, because irrigation creates lands of exceptionally high and concentrated productivity, a warrior retinue can enforce demands to rent. Monuments, buildings, and the agricultural facilities themselves mark these lands and persist through time to materialize ownership within the political economy.

The landscape of a Hawaiian community embodied a dynamic interplay between natural topographies, vegetation, and human facilities. Before colonization, forests blanketed the islands, but the Hawaiian settlers cleared the land for dryland farming and eventually for extensive irrigation. Communities were literally built up over hundreds of years by human labor to create the palimpsest of landesque capital investment and physical markings. The natural topography is physically dramatic, but it became progressively developed and associated with narratives of gods, chiefs, and commoners.

A typical community (*ahupua'a*) was a valley defined by mountainous cliffs, waterfalls, and knife-edge ridges. The valleys are often deeply entrenched and narrow, broadening out as they enter the coastal plain. Kolb (1997) describes how year after year a local community constructed the facilities of an engineered landscape. Irrigation canals, in particular, were built up wherever water was available to feed the pondfields that covered the valley floors and they provided the infrastructure for both subsistence and political economies. Although the irrigation systems were very small scale, they were highly productive and were owned and managed by chiefs. The paramount chief assigned a community to one of his high-ranking supporters, who then assigned a konohiki to manage its activities. The konohiki then allocated pondfields, house lots, and other resources to commoners, in compensation for their work on the chief's agricultural plots and on special projects such as digging new canals, making fishponds, and building shrines. The Hawaiian chiefdoms were a classic example of a political economy based on corvée labor and staple finance (Earle 1978, 1980), but the management of that economy by the konohiki was in no sense required by the simple irrigation technology.

Hierarchical property relationships that structured chiefly right to surplus from the engineered landscape were often kept by coercive force, an ability to restrict others from using landesque capital and making those who used it pay for that right. Farmers on irrigated land were easy marks, and they were reluctant to abandon long-term investments (Gilman 1981). Typically, only a small portion of the land was irrigated, and so these highly productive zones could be carefully monitored and controlled by a warrior elite. Michael Mann (1986) talks of these peasant farmers as being "caged" by irrigation, because they could not escape central control without losing use rights to the improved land. Farmers were locked into the engineered landscape.

The coercive superstructure is well illustrated by the Hawaiian case. Attached to the ruling chiefs was a retinue of trained and gifted fighters (Earle 1997). These warriors helped the chiefs gain power and enforce their rule. If he did not serve his corvée responsibilities, a farmer would be turned off his plots and denied subsistence use. During the annual ceremony of tribute collection, warriors accompanied the god-chief around the island territory (Malo 1951 [1898]: 141–59). They would stop at the boundary of an ahupua'a to collect tribute, and, if the "gifts" offered to the god-chief were considered paltry, more would be demanded, and warriors could ransack the community to obtain any shortfall.

The social nature of engineered landscapes also reinforced the hierarchical property relationships of irrigation. Lansing (1991; see also Mitchell 1991) describes how the daily operation and routine maintenance of irrigation were embedded within local ceremonial cycles. The irrigation communities were articulated with water temples whose priests helped manage patterns of cropping and water use. Participation was based on self-interest in water allocation, crop rotation, and pest management. Although operated without state direction, however, the irrigation systems in Bali, as elsewhere in Asia (Morrison and Lycett 1994), displayed memorial inscriptions that recorded the history, or purported history, of their construction by Balinese kings (Schoenfelder 2003). Rights to surplus rested on the organized events of construction that were used to co-opt a proportion of surplus production.

The role of the lord was formally recognized as the builder because he financed the construction and his managers put the people to work. The result was an overarching ownership that legitimized the lord's rights to surplus extraction. In Hawaii, labor crews were organized by the community's konohiki to construct and maintain irrigation systems and fishponds. In legal documents, farmers would describe a construction event with the name of the konohiki who organized it and his chief who financed it. These construction events were elaborate, with special foods and dress to make them memorable. A system was said to be built by the chief, who provided the food for the festive construction. The annual festivals that prepared pondfields for planting also reinforced the role of the chiefs in maintaining the fields' productivity. During a special ceremony, the god-chief of the island chiefdom went waist deep into the water of a ceremonial pondfield to begin the arduous task of treading its floor to make it watertight (I'i 1959: 68). By supporting the ceremonial events of construction and routine maintenance, chiefly action became infused into the most visible events associated with irrigation.

Irrigation facilities also provided the permanent physical markings of water flow and farmed plots that helped define property rights. We are familiar with how property is defined and transferred within a literate state; the transactions are recorded on deeds, contracts of sale, and wills that are held by the state or other legal representatives. But in nonliterate societies, an important device for determining property units was the physical marking of the land with walls and monuments that materialized the memory of their construction and prolonged use (Earle 2000, 2004).

The facilities of an engineered landscape were built to be permanent, and their walls and banks marked the embedded units of production and ownership across the generations. Ownership rights in irrigation are carefully measured and watched, as each square meter of land and liter of water matters for a farmer's total yield. Their physical divisions and connections are also all but impossible to alter surreptitiously, and their group construction and maintenance made them accepted intersubjectively. The physicality of an engineered landscape is well illustrated by the Hawaiian case (Earle 1997). The floor and lower slopes of each valley were a checkerboard of fields, each a pond surrounded by earthen bunds. In the 1850s, the property system was changed to a new system of private property modeled after the British one. To receive ownership of fields and house lots, each commoner had to come before the courts and describe his land allocation (*kuleana*) and its history. The farmer would testify to the physical elements that marked the kuleana's borders: the neighbor's pondfields, the chiefly plots, canals, and walls. A property's reality was the social memory of those involved in construction and allocation, and the everyday activities of the marked space (Earle 2000).

The engineered landscape of Hawaiian communities included the irrigated ditches and fields, patchworks of earth and stone walls, shrines, and paths that marked property, labor, and tribute responsibilities, and ceremonial cycles. Hawaiian chiefdoms and many other chiefdoms and agrarian states existed in such artificial landscapes that materialized the rights and obligations in their political economies (D'Altroy and Earle 1986). Irrigation systems both large and small formed the basis for staple finance, not because of any need for management, but because the intensified and engineered landscape provided the permanent structure for political domination.

Hohokam

To illustrate how irrigation was linked to the development of complexity, we turn to the prehistoric Hohokam culture, the archaeology of which documents long-term processes of social evolution for one of North America's most complex societies. The Hohokam of southern Arizona is an exceptionally well-documented case with which we can assess the relationships between irrigation, management, and the formation of complex polities. The Hohokam created the largest and most impressive irrigation systems in ancient North America and constructed landscapes with impressive public monuments and closely packed villages. These engineered landscapes were anthropogenic islands of green fields and canals in the desert that provided subsistence for dense populations and finance for complex political institutions. How did this happen? Major comparative scholars of irrigation have discussed the role of management (Hunt et al. 2005; Scarborough 2003; Wittfogel 1957), but we want to shift attention to changes in property and vertical mobilization of resources.

First of all, irrigation was necessary. The Hohokam occupied the arid and harsh Sonoran Desert, home to cacti, mesquite trees, and other xerophytic plants. Summer temperatures exceed 38°C (100°F), and annual precipitation is only 150 to 300 mm. Fed by mountain catchments to the north and east, however, the main rivers in the desert basins provided sufficient water to cultivate corn, beans, squash, cotton, and other crops. To access and maintain the supply of water, impressive irrigation complexes were constructed; for example, in the lower Salt River Valley, fourteen irrigation networks had an estimated aggregate length of 500 km of canals and encompassed 650 km^2 of agricultural land and settlement (Gregory 1991: 171; Masse 1981: 408; Nicholas and Feinman 1989: 199).

Wittfogel (1957: 20) used the Hohokam case to support his hypothesis that irrigation requires central management that results in the emergence of complex societies. Counter to Wittfogel, however, Woodbury (1961) argued that the impressive Hohokam canals could have been built incrementally through time and thus would not have required labor management or central authorities greater than those of the egalitarian

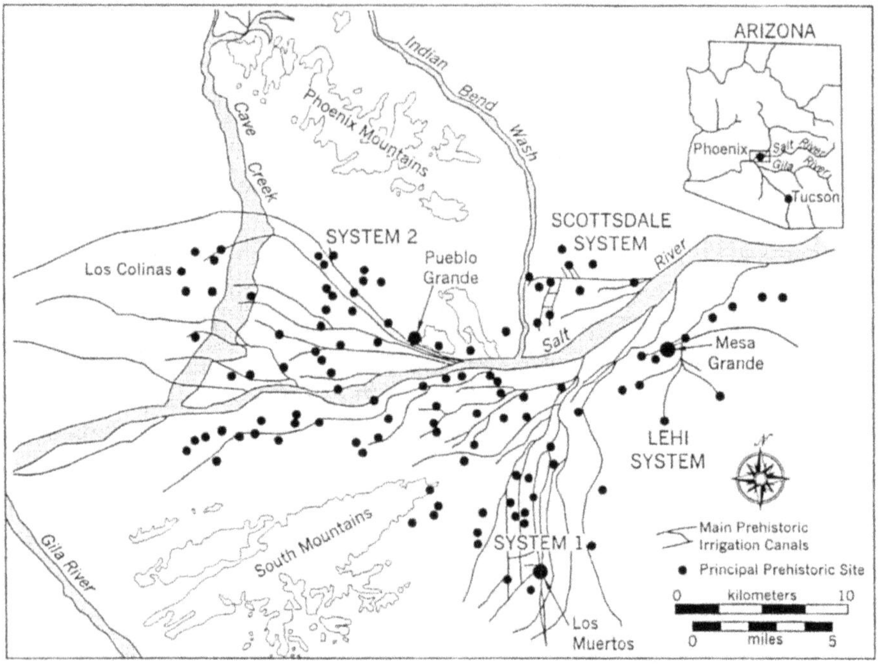

Figure 2.1 Map of the irrigation communities and Hohokam archaeological sites in the lower Salt River Valley located within the larger Hohokam area in southern Arizona.

social institutions recorded for historic ethnographic groups in the region. Haury (1962, 1976) believed that Hohokam society was organized according to the egalitarian principles of modern southwestern groups, such as the O'odham. But recent archaeological research appears to have reinvigorated interest in Wittfogel's ideas. The Hohokam were evidently more complexly organized than their living descendants; these prehistoric people had constructed and maintained irrigation systems and public architecture of vastly different scales than the historical tribes (Doyel 1991a). The engineering dynamics and logistical needs of construction for Hohokam irrigation suggest that these complexes were *not* built incrementally (Howard 1993: 267; Masse 1991; Nicholas and Feinman 1989). Howard (1993: 272) describes the growth of Hohokam irrigation systems as "a process of continual rebuilding and re-engineering," underscoring the need for a constant labor supply, and also notes that systems of this scale require relatively complex forms of organization such as chiefdoms (Howard 1993: 264; also see Scarborough 2003: 125–28; Hunt et al. 2005). Intermediate-scale polities are well documented for the Hohokam (Earle, Doyel, and Ravesloot n.d.).

Our synthesis of settlement patterns, population, monumental architecture, and prestige markers provide strong support for the expanding scale and hierarchy of Hohokam polities through time. The question is how the building of the irrigation systems related to emergent political complexity. To address this question, we summarize four periods of Hohokam irrigation history along with their changing political organizations and institutions. From earliest to latest, we discuss together the Pioneer and Colonial periods (AD 0–900); the Sedentary period (AD 900–1100); the Classic period (AD 1100–1450); and the Postclassic period after AD 1450. We find that Hohokam irrigated landscapes formed the basis of highly productive economies that initially were self-organized but changed progressively as new social and property relationships were instituted to create a political economy of staple finance that supported a chiefdomlike society.

The Pioneer and Colonial Periods

The Hohokam built extensive canals during the Pioneer and Colonial periods. Using a simple head dam, each ditch complex tapped a river and distributed water to fields through a network of main canals, primary and secondary distribution canals, and field laterals (Masse 1991). The earliest Hohokam ditch, a relatively small feature, has been radiocarbon dated to AD 50 (Ackerly and Henderson 1989), but earlier dates may be anticipated with recent research dating irrigation in the Tucson Basin to 1200 BC, well before the beginning of Hohokam culture as currently defined (Muro 1998). Some early systems were small, while others were comparatively large with more than 20 km of ditches and hundreds of hectares of irrigated land. Irrigation expanded rapidly in the Colonial period; for example, the large System 2 in central Phoenix on the north side of the Salt River expanded from an estimated 850 ha with three head dams in the Pioneer period (AD 0–650) to around 7,500 ha with 138 km of main canals and six to eight head dams in the Colonial period (AD 650–900) (Howard 1993: table 5, figures 6 and 7). Hunt (1988: 347) estimates that a threshold of between 1,200 and 1,600 ha (3,000–4,000 acres) defines large-scale systems, indicating that Hohokam constructed such systems early in the sequence.

To determine the scale and complexity of irrigation, the primary descriptive unit is the irrigation system in terms of such variables as length of ditches, numbers of farmers, area of farmed land, and numbers of dependent communities. Various scholars (e.g., Earle 1978; Hunt 1988) define an irrigation system as the ditch complex and agricultural fields watered from a single source, as for example one head dam. For the Hohokam, however, we will discuss multiple head dams on a single "system." This follows traditional archaeological terminology among Hohokam specialists, and it also recognizes the fact that these multiple-head dams share a particular location on the river. In terms of management, the multiple-head dams should be considered conceptually as a single system. Although the several head-dam sections could have been constructed separately originally, their operation in terms of water allocation and flood control would quickly have required close coordination.

During the Pioneer and Colonial periods, construction of large-scale irrigation systems was quite rapid. Despite the generally accepted wisdom that such "expansionist developments" are associated with states (Scarborough 2003: 13), Hohokam organization then was a mosaic of small-scale polities. The Colonial period settlement pattern consisted of multiple site clusters, referred to as *ball court communities*, each composed of one larger settlement with one or more ball courts and neighboring settlements without these features. These communities probably represented corporate groups materialized by ceremonies and marketplaces. Some social distinction is, however, evident in highly crafted display items (Haury 1976). Likely used by emerging leaders to mark status, prestige goods included fine objects of stone, clay, and marine shell, and exotic materials like turquoise.

Many ball court communities were distributed along the river valleys but their respective irrigation systems were apparently not hierarchically integrated into larger polities. As suggested by Hunt and others (2005), groups along a single ditch system must have been self-organized as an irrigation community for both construction and maintenance. Ritual calendars likely dictated ceremonies including those associated with ball courts to coordinate social relations and intergroup actions involving irrigation and trade (Abbott 2000; Doyel 1979, 2007a; Wilcox 1987). The strength of the leaders and the scale of political centralization were likely similar to the dynamics of New Guinea Big Men (Feil 1987), a political structure of minimal hierarchical centrality apparently adequate to support the construction and long-term maintenance of the Hohokams' extensive irrigation.

The Sedentary Period

During the Sedentary period the Hohokam maintained their engineered landscapes on a scale similar to the Colonial period, although changes are evident. The overall size of System 2, for example, appears to have been reduced to about 6,000 ha with six to eight head dams, but large facilities were built elsewhere including in the eastern Salt River Valley (Howard 1993: table 5, figure 8). To date, 238 ball courts have been reported at 194 sites distributed across the region, many built in the Colonial and most occupied into the Sedentary period (Marshall 2001: 120; Wilcox and Sternberg 1983: figure 10.2).

Within the Phoenix Basin, ball court villages were spaced at regular 5 km intervals along the rivers (Gregory 1991), and overall, ball court villages were usually less than 10 km (two to three hours' walk) from their nearest neighboring ball court village. Mostly dependent on irrigation, an interacting network of ball court communities was spread across the desert region and beyond.

If not present by the late Colonial period, political centralization of ball court communities on the level of an irrigation community is now evident. A good example is the central settlement of Snaketown (87 ha) with an estimated population of 1,000–2,000. With sixty mounds, a central precinct containing a large plaza, two ball courts, and a small platform mound surrounded by extensive residential areas, this site was a primary center for its area (Haury 1976: 37; Wilcox 1991). Two other ball court villages were located 6 km west along the same irrigation system, and another ball court village was 8 km farther west at the end of the canal (Ravesloot and Rice 2004). These secondary villages would have perhaps doubled the size of the Snaketown polity, making it then one of the largest in North America at that time. Long-distance imports (copper bells and pyrite mirrors from Mesoamerica, trade pottery, marine shell, etc.) were concentrated in large central villages, such as Snaketown, where they were most probably associated with an emergent social elite. At Snaketown, three of twenty-four cremation cemeteries contained the preponderance of prestige items at the site (Nelson 1981: 468).

At this time some Hohokam communities most likely became organized as chiefdoms, each with populations in the several thousands. This sociopolitical hierarchy, however, was formed well after the successful building and sustained maintenance of the largest irrigation complexes and thus was unlikely associated with their managerial needs. Motivated by principles of common interests, associations of farming communities organized by ceremonial cycles were apparently able to construct this substantial irrigation complex. The development of irrigation seems then to have created the productivity that allowed for surplus production and the ability to control its extraction.

Overall, for the Preclassic period, we conclude that Hohokam culture was organized as horizontal networks of communities with self-aggrandizing individuals supporting ceremonies within an arena of competitive networks. Some communities of several thousand people were consolidated into chiefdoms focused on primary villages of substantial size and ceremonial elaboration. Although much of the ideology emphasized a corporate character, the emergence of status rivalry is seen in the conspicuous display of prestige objects, and it therefore appears likely that group leaders began to exert some degree of ownership over the engineered landscape.

The Classic Period

Some irrigation systems continued to be modified into the Classic period; for example, System 2 was extended somewhat to include 135 km of main canals with seven to nine head dams and nine major canals serving 6,800 ha of irrigated farmland (Howard 1993: table 5, figure 9). Howard (1993: 273) provides a succinct description of System 2 for this period:

Pueblo Grande, the largest site within the canal system and the location of one of the two largest platform mounds, is placed in the head gate area. This large administrative site was in direct control of water flow in the canal system. While the lengths of individual canals varied, the majority extended twelve to sixteen miles from their head. A minimum of fifteen village sites and numerous smaller sites (containing a minimum of nine platform mounds during the Classic period) were clustered in three occupation zones arrayed perpendicular to the canals and located at intervals of 5 km along them.

On the other side south of the Salt River were the Lehi and Los Muertos systems (System 1), much of which was constructed in this period. If the populations dependent on these were combined, System 1 would represent another community of similar scale to System 2. Suzanne Fish (1996) estimated the densely settled Classic period irrigation polities in the lower Salt River Valley at between 12 and 20 km^2 in area, with the political territories of less densely settled areas being spatially much larger. Fish and Fish (1994) suggest that the average community controlled about 1,000 ha of irrigated land and supported 2,300 to 5,800 people. It would appear, however, that the larger Classic period polities, such as Systems 1 and 2 in the Salt River Valley, would have exceeded this range substantially, organizing perhaps 6,000 to 10,000 people (Earle, Doyel, and Ravesloot n.d.).

In this period, an erratic stream flow regime apparently occurred, and streams cut down through the sediments to create deeply entrenched channels. Such down-cutting effectively limited canal diversion points to areas where exposed bedrock prevented entrenchment (Graybill 1989; Gregory 1991: 177; Waters and Ravesloot 2001). As a result, both the irrigation systems and their associated communities increased in size as fewer head dams on a complex required longer ditches to irrigate the same area. Decreasing water flow may have required that some downriver areas, such as Gila Bend, be totally depopulated (Doyel 2007b). Fewer locations for canal heads and fewer options for irrigated agriculture would have made the engineered landscape of the Sonoran Desert more concentrated and thus perhaps more controllable by Hohokam chiefs.

Howard (1993: 315) suggests that a "higher level of socio-political control" was established in the Salt River Valley in the Classic period. The trend toward larger polities is also documented by the distribution of the Classic period platform mound sites. For comparison, in the Preclassic period, the middle Gila River in the general vicinity of Snaketown contained seven ball court communities with 7,660 ha of irrigated land, an average of about 1,100 ha per community. In contrast, in the Classic period, these communities were consolidated into three communities that divided 6,700 ha of irrigated land, more than 2,200 ha for each (Ravesloot, Darling, and Waters 2004; Ravesloot and Rice 2004). Most platform mounds were built in the compact zone of greatest irrigation potential along the rivers; however, Fish and Fish (2000) emphasize that reliance on irrigation was not absolute. Although a canal was present, the Marana site along the Santa Cruz River, for example, was not associated with a major irrigation system, and its source of finance appears to have included specialized agave production. Variation in the financial base has been described for other classic staple finance systems, such as prehistoric Hawaii, where irrigation provided the most common basis for staple finance, but intensive dryland agriculture was also used (Kirch 1994).

The Classic period community of Casa Grande along the middle Gila River had five platform mound villages along a canal 34 km long feeding 6,250 ha of irrigated lands (Crown 1987; Craig 2000: 140). The Lehi irrigation network along the Salt River represents another major Classic period polity containing over 34 km of canals with several head dams and about 5,600 ha of irrigated land. Mesa Grande, the primary site on this system, covered 256 ha and included a large platform mound (over 20,000 m^2) enclosed by a massive compound; other features present include a smaller platform, an earlier ball court, and residential compounds. This site was located in close proximity to all the head gates for both the Lehi and System 1 canals, and likely controlled access to water for both of these systems. The thirty-six known compounds on this complex present at five other settlements with platforms represent only a fraction of the original residential architecture in the polity (Howard 1987: 214–16). The Mesa Grande and adjacent Los Muertos systems likely merged to create a polity comparable in size to, and perhaps in direct competition with, the Pueblo Grande polity of System 2. Through time these large complexes continued to expand and may have incorporated smaller communities.

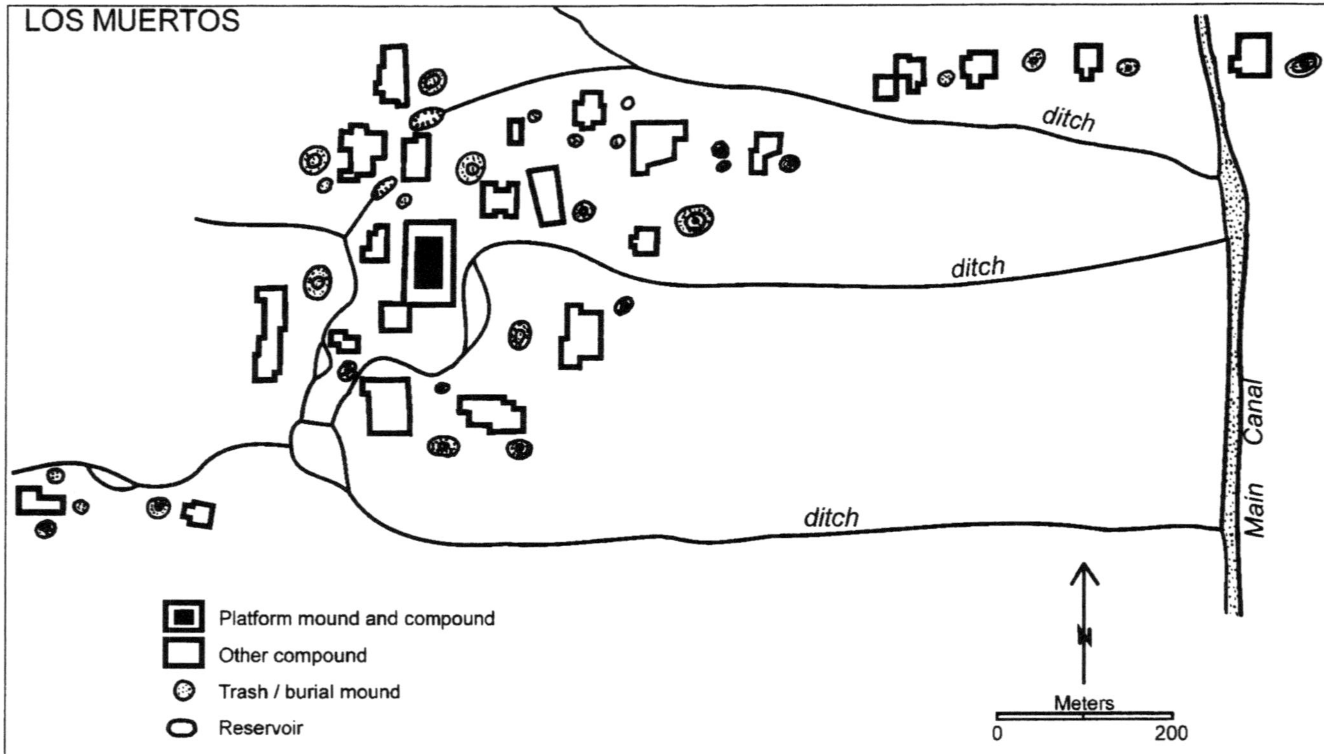

Figure 2.2 The large Classic period village of Los Muertos was situated at the end of Irrigation System 1 (see fig. 2.1). The site shows the pattern of situating residential and possibly other compounds around a larger central compound containing public architecture consisting of a platform and/or a great house. The site was destroyed by agricultural expansion in the historic period but not until after it was partially studied by the well-known archaeologist and ethnologist Frank Hamilton Cushing in the late 1800s (see Haury 1945).

Primary changes in the Classic period occurred in the built environment that structured social relations within new and more hierarchical institutions. Architectural patterns suggest a progressive shift from the open forms of earlier periods that included ball courts and large plazas to more restricted spaces enclosed by walls. By the middle Classic period, ball courts were no longer constructed and the horizontal social integration of the earlier periods had given way to more vertical and exclusionary social forces as suggested by walled-in residential compounds and residential structures constructed on top of elevated platforms. At Marana the thirty-five compounds in and near the platform precinct were quite large, averaging fifteen rooms each at the same time that other outlying settlements had no compounds (Fish and Fish 2004). The huge village of Los Muertos contained a large central compound containing a platform or possibly a great house, thirty other compounds, and other features including large mounds and reservoirs (Haury 1945).

Over one hundred large earthen architectural platforms and towers surrounded by walls were constructed within the region, most of them associated with riverine environments and irrigation agriculture (Doelle, Gregory, and Wallace 1995: 390). A new ideology became apparent (Doyel 1991a, 2000): it included new color patterns, symbols, and material forms; trade patterns emphasized mass production and extensive circulation of pottery wares, marine shell products, and other durable and perishable goods (Abbott 2000; Doyel 1991b).

Platforms and towers were used as residences and special facilities for powerful families (Doyel 1981, 1991a; Gregory 1991; Fish and Fish 2004). The culmination of platform architecture is exemplified by the Casa Grande site along the Gila River, which had a four-story structure with massive adobe walls situated on a platform mound surrounded by numerous other compounds; similar structures were likely present at other centers (Doelle, Gregory, and Wallace 1995; Wilcox 1991). The close association of highly patterned arrangements in platform mound precincts with their large structures and specialized facilities involving storage and processing suggests an identification with and control over ritual functions. Although there remain differences in the interpretation of the function of platforms and great houses (see Doyel 2004), Abbott (2003: 222) describes the leadership as "aggressive and self-aggrandizing individuals" who probably managed the irrigation system by controlling ritual that took place on the platforms. The leaders likely wore and displayed symbols including staffs of office and lived differently from the other people.

Hunt and others (2005) argue that central management among the Hohokam was unlikely, and they justify their conclusion by asserting that such management is found only in states. During the Classic period, the Hohokam appears not to have been a state organization, but the elements of scale, centrality, and stratification argue strongly for a complex chiefdom-like society. As illustrated by the Hawaiian case, chiefdoms must mobilize substantial surplus, and they can do that effectively by managing irrigation. We propose that the radical transformations of the Classic period involved instituting a new system of property rights, the primary objective of which was to extract surplus through control over irrigation, and that the systematic rebuilding of the ceremonial and residential landscape in the Classic period materialized the new social order. Based on a model of a house society (Gillespie 2000), the new Hohokam elite compounds may well have accommodated corporate units arranged hierarchically based on control over agricultural production. The actual form of ownership in land, water, or irrigation facilities is impossible to ascertain, but whatever its specific form, it would have provided the means to mobilize surplus. And how could this hierarchy of ownership have been maintained?

Although not generally accepted, warfare or at least a warrior ideology among the Hohokam may have been common. (For discussion and references, see Fish and Fish 1989; Rice and LeBlanc 2001; Wilcox 1989.) Among this paper's authors, Earle believes that a warrior segment may have been important throughout the Hohokam sequence. He refers to the ethnographic record wherein warfare is present in nonstate, irrigation-based societies due to the need to defend ownership in the landesque capital, and he thinks that the concentration of arrowheads in the mortuary complexes at major Preclassic centers suggests a warrior identity useful for an emergent ruling segment of the society. Doyel suspects, rather, that the concentration of arrowheads may simply represent a particular cult affiliation and ritual process. By the Classic period, however, towers and walled compounds seem to reflect an element of military power and elite protection over the regional polity, or at least the use of architecture to accrue social power in competitive display (what Doyel refers to as "power architecture"; see Doyel 1991c for an example). Doyel thinks that the amazing longevity of many irrigation systems, some measured in centuries, and the exceptional amount of trade documented for both the Preclassic and Classic periods suggest the importance of maintaining broad horizontal relationships that de-emphasized regional warfare. Because better evidence exists for warfare in adjacent areas (Fish and Fish 1989), the lack of evidence for warfare within the Hohokam core areas suggests that both the concentrated arrowheads of the Preclassic periods and the fortified towers of the Classic may have been more part of an ideology than of actual warfare. We recommend that researchers investigate in greater detail the possibility that a warrior ideology was linked to the social hierarchy of the Hohokam. Although warfare may have been relatively rare, a warrior ideology may have been shaped to create an atmosphere of intimidation that served internally to retain hierarchical property rights and surplus extraction.

For the Classic period, we conclude that the riverine Hohokam society was organized as chiefdomlike polities. A new institution of property was formalized by the construction in the engineered landscape of an architecture of power, elements of which emphasized exclusiveness and intimidation. Reasonably the new ownership extended to the irrigation systems that could have been managed to support the social stratification and finance the chiefly institutions. In simple terms, we can say that the development of Hohokam chiefdoms was facilitated by the high and sustainable productivity of irrigation, from which the ruling elites were able to mobilize surplus through the new property system.

The Postclassic Period

By AD 1450, Classic period Hohokam with its social complexity and high population densities came to an end. After more than a thousand years of sustained intensive production, the irrigation systems were abandoned. Evidently an unsettled environment that included erratic flow regimes in the main rivers and the occurrence of several large floods rendered large-scale irrigation impractical (Abbott ed. 2003; Gregory 1991; Graybill et al. 2006). The historic O'odham were an irrigation-based society but did not maintain the same political complexity or scale of integration. They did not build an engineered landscape with large irrigation systems, permanent monuments, and elite housing compounds. Predating Spanish conquest, the reduced complexity of the Hohokam to become the historic O'odham was probably linked to the abandonment of the extensive prehistoric irrigation systems. This simplification thus underscores the pivotal role that extensive irrigation and its associated landscape played in the development of Hohokam chiefdoms. Without the surplus derived from highly productive and controllable landscapes, the complex political superstructure of the Classic period could not be sustained, and the political organization was simplified to levels similar to the tribal organizations described for the Pioneer and Colonial periods.

Conclusion

The history of human economies and landscapes involves long-term intensification to support both higher population densities and more complex social institutions. Although the forms of intensification vary considerably, intensification invariably involves landesque capital that both increases and stabilizes food production. At the same time, landesque capital established a premium to form land tenure systems that set rights of use and transfer of improvements across generations. The engineered landscapes of irrigation are magnificent examples of the landesque capital that supported early complex societies. We have tried to address the question of why engineered landscapes involving irrigation were so critical to the evolution of social complexity, and argue that they provided the productive base for surplus extraction that financed new institutions of complexity.

The importance of highly engineered landscapes involving irrigation has long been recognized, but the actual reasons for that linkage are less clear. Based on the sustained work of ethnographers such as Robert Hunt, we know that managerial requirements of irrigation simply do not require central administration, because alternative forms of self-organizing irrigation communities function adequately. With the emergence of chiefdoms, however, the highly intensified landscapes of water management created an artificial world that could relatively easily be controlled by elites in order to generate surplus to fuel political ambitions. The landesque capital of these worlds helped structure patterns of everyday and long-term activities that made possible the imposition of new hierarchies of property ownership. Irrigation, whether large or small in scale, provided opportunities for control through property rights encoded in ritual practice and the built landscape and enforced by warriors. That a farming family held subsistence rights to a permanently marked plot effectively tethered that family and made it an easy target for emergent elites in search of reliable incomes.

To understand the role of irrigation in the emergence of complexity, we emphasize the importance of looking at prehistoric and historic cases of chiefdoms. The ethnographer's reliance on communities within states may represent conditions of power and property quite different from what had existed when social stratification and centralization emerged. The example of the Hohokam illustrates the diachronic processes by which irrigation systems could be built and maintained by self-organizing communities, but because of environmentally induced changes or internal power struggles, the engineered landscape of irrigation provided opportunities to control and mobilize surplus that financed new institutions of a chiefdomlike society. Over a fairly brief period, Hohokam elites apparently reorganized the built environments of their villages to institute a landscape of power materializing new property relationships to provide the basis for staple finance. Irrigation mattered for the emergence of the Hohokam chiefdoms, because their engineered landscapes provided the production needed for surplus and the opportunities to control the chiefdoms' mobilization.

Our chapter emphasizes the importance of the economy and landscape considered in terms of landesque capital and its embedded property relationships. We want to stress, however, that the engineered landscapes of complex societies were also studded with buildings and monuments that encoded social and ideological behavior and meaning to the landscape. These are themes for future work on the Hohokam and other societies both ancient and modern.

Notes

The collaboration for this chapter grew out of an Amerind Foundation Advanced Seminar, "Hohokam Trajectories in World Perspective," organized by Suzanne Fish and Paul Fish and held at the Amerind January 2004. We gained immensely from discussions at that seminar, as well as from the 2005 Annual Meeting of the Society of Economic Anthropology. We especially thank Bob Hunt for his comments on an earlier manuscript and his significant research on irrigation, and Jerry Howard for his thorough and well-documented studies of Hohokam irrigation.

1. Many chiefdoms and a few primary states relied on other intensive forms of production including horticulture and fishing. Mobilization of surplus can use alternatives, but the engineering of irrigation is very frequently used.

References

Abbott, David R. 2000. *Ceramics and Community Organization among the Hohokam.* Tucson: University of Arizona Press.

———. 2003. "The Politics of Decline in Canal System 2." In *Centuries of Decline during the Hohokam Classic Period at Pueblo Grande*, ed. D. Abbott, 201–28. Tuscon: University of Arizona Press.

———, ed. 2003. *Centuries of Decline during the Hohokam Classic Period at Pueblo Grande.* Tuscon: University of Arizona Press.

Ackerly, Neal W., and T. Kathleen Henderson, eds. 1989. *Prehistoric Agricultural Activities on the Lehi-Mesa Terrace: Perspectives on Hohokam Irrigation Cycles.* Tempe, AZ: Northland Research.

Adams, Robert McC. 1966. *The Evolution of Urban Society.* Chicago: Aldine.

Blaikie, P., and H. C. Brookfield. 1987. *Land Degradation and Society.* London: Methuen.

Boserup, Ester. 1965. *The Conditions of Agricultural Grown.* Chicago: Aldine.

Bray, Francesca. 1986. *The Rice Economies: Technology and Development in Asian Societies.* Oxford: Blackwell.

Brookfield, H. C. 1984. "Intensification Revised." *Pacific Viewpoint* 25:15–44.

Craig, Douglas. 2000. "Demographic Implications of Architectural Change at the Grewe Site (AZ AA: 2:2[ASM])." In Doyel, Fish, and Fish 2000, 139–66.

Crown, Patricia. 1987. "Classic Period Hohokam Settlement and Land Use in the Casa Grande Ruins Area, Arizona." *Journal of Field Archaeology* 14:147–62.

Crown, Patricia L., and W. James Judge, eds. 1991. *Chaco and Hohokam: Prehistoric Regional Systems in the American Southwest*. Santa Fe: School of American Research Press.

D'Altroy, Terence, and T. Earle. 1986. "Staple Finance, Wealth Finance and Storage in the Inka Political Economy." *Current Anthropology* 26:187–206.

Doelle, William H., David A. Gregory, and Henry D. Wallace. 1995. "Classic Period Platform Mound Systems in Southern Arizona." In *The Roosevelt Community Development Study: New Perspectives on Tonto Basin Prehistory*, ed. M. Elson, M. Stark, and D. Gregory, 385–440. Tucson: Anthropological Papers No. 15. Center for Desert Archaeology.

Doyel, David E. 1979. "The Prehistoric Hohokam of the Arizona Desert." *American Scientist* 67:544–54.

———. 1981. *Late Hohokam Prehistory in Southern Arizona*. Scottsdale, AZ: Gila Press Number 2.

———. 1991a. "Hohokam Cultural Evolution in the Phoenix Basin." In *Exploring the Hohokam: Prehistoric Desert Peoples of the American Southwest*, ed. G. Gumerman, 231–78. Albuquerque: University of New Mexico Press.

———. 1991b. "Hohokam Exchange and Interaction." In Crown and Judge 1991, 225–52.

———. 1991c. "The Hohokam: Ancient Dwellers of the Arizona Desert." In *The Hohokam: Ancient People of the Desert*, ed. David Noble, 3–14. Santa Fe: School of American Research Press.

———. 2000. "The Santan Phase in the Phoenix Basin." In Doyel, Fish, and Fish 2000, 221–44.

———. 2004. Review of *Centuries of Decline during the Hohokam Classic Period at Pueblo Grande. Journal of Archaeological Research* 60:314–16.

———. 2007a. "Irrigation, Production, and Power in Phoenix Basin Hohokam Society." In *The Hohokam at the Millennium*, ed. Suzanne Fish and Paul Fish. Santa Fe: School of American Research.

———. 2007b. "Edge Work: The Late Prehistory of the Gila Bend Frontier." In *Fragile Patterns: Archaeological Research in the Eastern Papagueria*, ed J. Altschul and A. Rankin. Tucson: Statistical Research Press.

Doyel, D., S. Fish, and P. Fish, eds. 2000. *The Hohokam Village Revisited*. Fort Collins, CO: SWARM Division, American Association for the Advancement of Science.

Earle, Timothy. 1978. "Economic and Social Organization of a Complex Chiefdom: The Halelea District, Kauai, Hawaii." In vol. 63 of *University of Michigan, Anthropological Papers*. Ann Arbor: University of Michigan Press.

———. 1980. "Prehistoric Irrigation in the Hawaiian Islands: An Evaluation of Evolutionary Significance." *Archaeology and Physical Anthropology in Oceania*, no. 15:1–28.

———. 1997. *How Chiefs Come to Power*. Stanford, CA: Stanford University Press.

———. 2000. "Archaeology, Property, and Prehistory." *Annual Review of Anthropology*, no. 29:39–60.

———. 2004. "Culture Matters: The Neolithic Transition and Emergence of Hierarchy in Thy, Denmark." *American Anthropologist*, no. 106:111–25.

Earle, Timothy, David Doyel, and John Ravesloot. n.d. "Political Economy of the Hohokam: A Consideration." Manuscript prepared for *Hohokam Trajectories in World Perspective*, ed. Suzanne Fish and Paul Fish. Tucson: University of Arizona Press. In preparation.

Feil, D. K. 1987. *The Evolution of Highland Papua New Guinean Societies*. Cambridge: Cambridge University Press.

Fernea, Robert. 1970. *Shaykh and Effendi: Changing Patterns of Authority among the El Shabana of Southern Iraq*. Cambridge, MA: Harvard University Press.

Fish, Paul R., and Suzanne K. Fish. 1989. "Hohokam Warfare from a Regional Perspective." In *Cultures in Conflict: Current Archaeological Perspectives*, ed. D. C. Tkaczuk and B. C. Vivian, 112–29. Proceedings of the 20th Annual Chacmool Conference. Calgary: Archaeological Association of the University of Calgary.

———. 2000. "The Marana Mound Site: Patterns of Social Differentiation in the Early Classic Period." In Doyel, Fish, and Fish 2000, 245–76.

Fish, Suzanne K. 1996. "Dynamics of Scale in the Southern Deserts." In *Interpreting Southwestern Diversity: Underlying Principles and Overarching Patterns*, ed. Paul Fish and J. Reid, 107–14. Tempe: Arizona State University Anthropological Research Papers No. 48.

Fish, Suzanne K., and Paul Fish. 1994. "Multisite Communities as Measures of Hohokam Aggregation." In *The Ancient Southwestern Community*, ed. W. Wills and R. Leonard, 119–30. Albuquerque: University of New Mexico Press.

———. 2004. "Reorganization and Realignment: The Classic Period in the Tucson Basin." Draft paper presented at the Amerind Foundation Symposium on Hohokam World Trajectories, organized by Suzanne K. Fish and Paul R. Fish.

Fisher, Christopher, and Gary Feinman, eds. 2005. "In Focus: Landscapes over Time: Resilience, Degradation, and Contemporary Lessons." *American Anthropologist*, no. 107:62–107.

Geertz, Clifford. 1963. *Agricultural Involutions*. Berkeley: University of California Press.

Gillespie, Susan. 2000. "Rethinking Ancient Maya Social Organization: Replacing 'Lineage' with 'House.'" *American Anthropologist*, no. 102:467–84.

Gilman, Antonio. 1981. "The Development of Social Stratification in Bronze Age Europe." *Current Anthropology*, no. 22:1–24.

Graybill, Donald A. 1989. "The Reconstruction of Prehistoric Salt River Streamflow." In *The 1982–1984 Excavations at Los Colinas: Environment and Subsistence*, ed. D. Graybill, D. Gregory, F. Nials, S. K. Fish, R. Gasser, C. Miksicek, and C. Szuter, 25–38. Archaeological Series No. 38 (5). Tucson: Arizona State Museum.

Graybill, Donald A., David A. Gregory, Gary Funkhauser, and Fred Nials. 2006. "Long-Term Stream Flow Reconstructions, River Channel Morphology, and Aboriginal Irrigation Systems along the Salt and Gila Rivers." In *Environmental Change and Human Adaptation in the Ancient American Southwest*, ed. David E. Doyel and Jeffrey S. Dean, 69–123. Salt Lake City: University of Utah Press.

Gregory, David A. 1991. "Form and Variation in Hohokam Settlement Patterns." In Crown and Judge 1991, 159–93.

Guillet, David. 1987. "Terracing and Irrigation in the Peruvian Highlands." *Current Anthropology*, no. 28:409–30.

Haury, Emil W. 1945 *The Excavation of Los Muertos and Neighboring Ruins in the Salt River Valley, Southern Arizona*. Papers of the Peabody Museum of American Archaeology and Ethnology, Vol. 24 (1). Cambridge, MA: Harvard University Press.

———. 1962. "The Greater American Southwest." In *Courses toward Urban Life*, ed. R. J. Braidwood and Gordon R. Wiley, 106–31. Chicago: Aldine.

———. 1976. *The Hohokam: Desert Farmers and Craftsmen*. Tucson: University of Arizona Press.

Howard, Jerry B. 1987. "The Lehi Canal System: Organization of a Classic Period Irrigation Community." In *The Hohokam Village: Site Structure and Organization*, ed. David E. Doyel, 211–21. Glenwood Springs, CO: SWARM Division, American Association for the Advancement of Science.

———. 1993. "A Paleohydraulic Approach to Examining Agricultural Intensification in Hohokam Irrigation Systems." In *Research in Economic Anthropology, Supplement* 7, ed. Vernon L. Scarborough and Barry L. Isaac, 263–324. Greenwich, CT: JAI Press.

Hunt, Robert. 1986. "Canal Irrigation in Egypt: Common Property Management." In *Proceedings of the Conference on Common Property Resource Management*, 199–214. Washington, DC: National Academy Press.

———. 1988. "Size and the Structure of Authority in Canal Irrigation Systems." *Journal of Anthropological Research* 44:335–55.

———. 2000. "Labor Productivity and Agricultural Development." *Human Ecology* 28:251–77.

Hunt, Robert, D. Guillet, D. Abbott, J. Bayman, P. Fish, S. Fish, K. Kintigh, and J. Neely. 2005. "Plausible Ethnographic Analogies for the Social Organization of Hohokam Canal Irrigation." *American Antiquity* 70:433–56.

Hunt, Robert, and E. Hunt. 1976. "Canal Irrigation and Local Social Organization." *Current Anthropology* 17:389–411.

I'i, John Papa. 1959. *Fragments of Hawaiian History*. Honolulu: B. P. Bishop Museum Press.

Kirch, Patrick. 1994. *The Wet and the Dry: Irrigation and Agricultural Intensification in Polynesia*. Chicago: University of Chicago Press.

Kolb, Michael. 1997. "Labor, Ethnohistory, and the Archaeology of Community in Hawaii." *Journal of Archaeological Method and Theory* 4:265–86.

Krech, Shepard. 2005. "Reflections on Conservation, Sustainability, and Environmentalism in Indigenous North America." *American Anthropologist* 107:78–86.

Lansing, Stephen. 1991. *Priests and Programmers: Technologies of Power in the Engineered Landscape*. Princeton, NJ: Princeton University Press.

Leach, Edmund. 1961. *Pul Eliya: A Village in Ceylon*. London: Cambridge University Press.

Lees, Susan. 1973. "Sociopolitical Aspects of Canal Irrigation in the Valley of Oaxaca." *Museum of Anthropology Memoir 6*. Ann Arbor: University of Michigan Press.

Malo, David. 1951. "Hawaiian Antiquities." *Bernice P. Bishop Museum Special Publications 2*. 2nd ed. Honolulu.

Mann, Michael. 1986. *The Sources of Social Power*. Cambridge: Cambridge University Press.

Marshall, J. T. 2001. "Hohokam Regional Ballcourt Data." In *The Grewe Archaeological Research Project*. Vol. 1, *Project Background and Feature Descriptions*, ed. D. B. Craig, app. J, 571–85. Anthropological Papers No. 99-1, Tempe, AZ: Northland Research.

Masse, W. Bruce. 1981. "Prehistoric Irrigation Systems in the Salt River Valley." *Science* 214 (23): 408–15.

———. 1991. "The Quest for Subsistence Sufficiency and Civilization in the Sonoran Desert." In Crown and Judge 1991, 195–225.

Mitchell, William. 1991. *Peasants on the Edge: Crop, Cult, and Crisis in the Andes*. Austin: University of Texas Press.

Mitchell, William, and David Guillet. 1993. *Irrigation at High Altitudes: The Social Organization of Water Control Systems in the Andes*. Arlington, VA: American Anthropological Association, Society for Latin American Anthropology Publication Series 12.

Morrison, Kathleen, and M. Lycett. 1994. "Centralized Power, Central Authority? Ideological Claims and Archaeological Patterns." *Asian Perspectives* 33:327–50.

Muro, Mark. 1998. "New Finds Explode Old Views of the American Southwest." *Science* 279:653–54.

Nelson, Richard S. 1981. "The Role of a Puchteca System in Hohokam Exchange." PhD diss., New York University.

Netting, Robert. 1993. *Smallholders, Householders: Farm Families and the Ecology of Intensive, Sustainable Agriculture*. Stanford, CA: Stanford University Press.

Nicholas, Linda M., and Gary M. Feinman. 1989. "A Regional Perspective on Hohokam Irrigation in the Lower Salt River Valley, Arizona." In *The Sociopolitical Structure of Prehistoric Southwestern Societies*, ed. Steadman Upham, Kent G. Lightfoot, and Roberta A. Jewett, 199–236. Boulder, CO: Westview Press.

Ravesloot, John C., J. A. Darling, and M. R. Waters. 2004. "The Prehistoric and Historic Landscapes of the Gila River: Lessons Learned from a Decade of Survey and Geoarchaeological Research." Paper presented at the 69th Annual Meeting of the Society for American Archaeology, Montreal.

Ravesloot, John C., and Glen Rice. 2004. "The Growth and Consolidation of Settlement Complexes and Irrigation Communities on the Middle Gila." Draft paper presented at the Amerind Foundation Symposium on Hohokam World Trajectories, organized by Suzanne K. Fish and Paul R. Fish.

Rice, Glen E., and Steven A. LeBlanc, eds. 2001. *Deadly Landscapes: Case Studies in Prehistoric Southwestern Warfare.* Salt Lake City: University of Utah Press.

Sahlins, Marshall. 1958. *Social Stratification in Polynesia.* Seattle: University of Washington Press.

———. 1962. *Moala.* Ann Arbor: University of Michigan Press.

Scarborough, Vernon. 2003. *The Flow of Power: Ancient Water Systems and Landscapes.* Santa Fe: School of American Research Press.

Scarborough, Vernon, and Barry Isaac, eds. 1993. "Economic Aspects of Water Management in the Prehispanic New World. *Research in Economic Anthropology Supplement* 7. Greenwich, CT: JAI Press.

Schoenfelder, John. 2003. "Negotiating Poise in a Multi-Hierarchical World: An Archaeological Exploration of Irrigated Rice Agriculture, Ideology, and Political Balances in the Coevolution of Intersecting Complex Networks in Bali." PhD diss., University of California, Los Angeles.

Spooner, Brian. 1974. "Irrigation and Society: the Iranian Plateau." In *Irrigation's Impact on Society*, ed. T. Downing and M. Gibson, 43–57. Tuscon: University of Arizona Press.

Steward, Julian. 1955. "Irrigation Civilizations: A Comparative Study." *Pan American Union Social Science Monograph 1.*

Waters, Mike, and John Ravesloot. 2001. "Landscape Change and the Cultural Evolution of the Hohokam along the Middle Gila River and Other River Valleys in South-Central Arizona." *American Antiquity* 66:285–99.

Widgren, Mats. n.d. "Pre-colonial Landesque Capital: A Global Perspective." Manuscript.

Wilcox, David R. 1987. "The Evolution of Hohokam Ceremonial Systems." In *Astronomy and Ceremony in the Prehistoric Southwest.* Papers of the Maxwell Museum of Anthropology 2, ed. J. Carlson and W. J. Judge, 149–68. Albuquerque.

———. 1989. "Hohokam Warfare." In *Cultures and Conflict: Current Anthropological Perspectives*, ed. D. Tkaczuk and B. Vivian, 163–72. Proceedings of the 20th Annual Chacmool Conference. Archaeological Association of the University of Calgary, Calgary.

———. 1991. "Hohokam Social Complexity." In Crown and Judge 1991, 253–75.

Wilcox, David R., and Charles Sternberg. 1983. *Hohokam Ball Courts and Their Interpretation.* Tucson: Arizona State Museum Archaeological Series No. 160.

Wittfogel, Karl. 1957. *Oriental Despotism.* New Haven, CT: Yale University Press.

Wolf, Eric. 1966. *Peasants.* Englewood Cliffs, NJ: Prentice Hall.

Woodbury, Richard. 1961. "Reappraisal of Hohokam Irrigation." *American Anthropologist* 63:550–60.

3

Reading History in an Irrigated Landscape
The Drama of the Commons in the Andes

PAUL TRAWICK

The Controlled Comparison of Local Landscapes

A surge of studies during the last two decades has shown that inhabited landscapes, once considered to be merely "anthropogenic" or human modified, are more accurately seen as highly domesticated cultural products that are inscribed with signs or traces of the human activities involved in their production. Those signs can be read and interpreted in various ways to reveal the outlines of environmental stories that need to be told; and anthropologists have lately devoted much effort to this kind of research. Such writing has been undertaken from various theoretical perspectives, with some analyses focusing on cultural memory and on landscapes as mnemonic devices, or monuments intentionally modified by local people in order to preserve a certain symbolic vision or version of the past (Hirsch and O'Hanlon 1995; Santos-Granero 1998; Harrison 2004). These works recognize the production of such monumental settings as an active process that, like human memory itself, requires that some signs be preserved and remembered while others be, just as deliberately, erased and forgotten.

Another perspective, the one to be adopted here, sees the remembering and forgetting involved in creating cultural landscapes as largely unintended consequences of human acts that, although quite deliberate, have another rationale, being concerned mainly with adaptation and with agriculture or some other kind of material production. Such landscapes are conceived of as having been shaped by ecological and economic transformations, ones driven by processes unfolding within the wider regional and national political economies of the colonial and postcolonial eras, ultimately driven, to some extent, by the emergence of global capitalism itself. Thus the creation of the landscapes as sign-inscribed spaces did not necessarily involve any intent by local people to make a statement or convey a message about anything, let alone about the past. According to this perspective, referred to as *historical ecology* (Balée 1998; Crumley 1994, 2003; Egan and Howell 2001), any narrative that emerges from a reading of the signs in such a landscape will do so only because the researcher adopts a theoretical stance that makes possible his or her interpretation. Such a "stance" is simply an interest on the investigator's part in revealing a certain dimension of environmental history, one that for theoretical reasons is considered to be important and, because some empirical traces of it seem to exist, is thought to have unfolded in a specific version in a particular place.

In the cases to be examined here, the "signs" are traces of several related narratives, various versions or strands of one general story line that can be told at different scales and levels of analysis: (1) the unfolding of diverse irrigation and cultivation practices that have shaped local landscapes, serving mainly as adaptations to an arid environment that has fluctuated dramatically through time; (2) the changing political economy of the province, the surrounding region, the nation, and the world, which, along with other exogenous factors, has been a primary driver of changes in practice, some of which have been maladaptive from both an ecological and a social point of view. In the present analysis, which focuses on a remote valley in the Peruvian Andes, the main "story" to be told through a comparative reading of landscapes is of general theoretical interest because it is one that has unfolded in numerous specific versions in most parts of the world: the "drama of the commons." Although it will be framed within the context of changes in the wider regional, national, and global political economies, like the analyses provided by Håkansson and Fratkin elsewhere in this volume, the main story line is that of a social drama that has unfolded dynamically, and somewhat unpredictably, in each specific place.

Following McCay and Acheson (1987), Ostrom et al. (2002), and others, I define this social drama as the dynamic tension or dialectical interplay, within a local society, between the short-term individual self-interest of people and a more long-term concern for their mutual welfare or the common good, specifically in their use of resources that are collectively owned. A vast literature (NRC. 1986; Bromley 1992; Ostrom 1990, 1992, 1998; IASC Digital Library of the Commons) has shown that this drama can lead to various outcomes—to "comedy" or the more familiar "tragedy" made famous by Hardin (1968)—with either of two basic human motivations (selfishness or cooperation) prevailing over the other as mediating conditions, practices, and institutions change. Such dramas are inevitably played out in the exploitation of resources held by a community as common property, often referred to as "common-pool" resources (Ostrom 1990). The now-vast literature on natural resource management has appropriately redefined the term *commons* to include those resources, such as irrigation water, which, unlike the ones discussed originally by Hardin, belong to communities whose members are able to restrict their use to some extent. Thus the "tragedy" spoken of here differs substantially from Hardin's, which was played out in those relatively rare situations (such as offshore ocean fisheries) where access to a resource is open and not restricted in any way. Such situations of open access may indeed by destined always to become tragic, but they are not typical of communal resources in general, making their breakdown a different process that is arguably less theoretically interesting and also less "tragic" than the breakdown of "commons" consisting of systems of common property. The main such resource involved in the places to be visited here is water, and the landscapes to be read and interpreted are irrigated ones that have been in continuous agricultural use for hundreds of years (Trawick 2003).

Another kind of information crucial to historical ecology, and to the kind of analysis being advocated here, is that of "environmental proxies" (Balée 1998; Crumley 2003), data that can serve as "proxies" for earlier environments. These can often be used to construct a relatively reliable account of past conditions, especially those pertaining to the commons around which local social dramas were played out within the landscape. Such proxies can take many forms (tree rings, ice cores, pollen counts, etc.), but among the most difficult to interpret are data on environmentally significant events that were caused by human activity. Several of these sources will be used here to, in effect, assemble a historical "lens" through which to examine contemporary irrigation practices in the Cotahuasi valley of Peru, which today are quite diverse. The analytical use of this "lens" will, by providing a kind of retrospective historical view, make it possible to construct the outline for a narrative of the origins of local practices and landscapes and an account of their gradual divergence in space and time. The most significant "proxy" will be a cataclysmic "event" of the human-induced type: the sustained population collapse that followed, as an unintended consequence, the conquest of the people of the New World by the people of the Old.

Even though it has only recently emerged as a well-defined field of study, historical ecology is known for research focused at different scales involving comparative work done at multiple sites. This is mainly due, however, to the substantial contribution made thus far by archaeology. Although ethnographers have done important historical environmental research, they have generally lagged behind in taking up this part of the challenge, tending to focus instead on single communities and landscapes. This slowness is due partly to the considerable difficulties involved, but it also reflects the fact that a well-defined procedure for the ethnographic study of multiple communities and landscapes has yet to be proposed (but see Mayer and Fonseca 1979; Mayer 1985; Netting 1968). Such a method for the controlled, comparative reading of local landscapes will be presented here, and its usefulness in studying the ecological, economic, and social history of a region will be demonstrated. Although the outlines of a story will be traced—the drama of the commons, in its various local outcomes—this story will serve primarily to illustrate the significance of a contribution intended mainly to be methodological. The goal is to show how a reading of contemporary village landscapes can, using the right "proxy" information, produce an outline of regional social and ecological history, an account of the divergence of communities, and their differentiation from one another in the past.

The Landscape Defined

A landscape is here defined as the irrigated terrain or territory belonging to a particular community and the productive activities that take place therein. Thus it is human, dynamic, and alive, including the land, soil, rock, and water in their present configurations as well as the agricultural practices commonly occurring today within such a technologically modified space. In Peru's Cotahuasi valley, as more generally along the arid western Andean slope, these dynamic spaces, or "production zones" (Mayer and Fonseca 1979), have generally been leveled and terraced, either entirely or in part, in order to facilitate irrigation and maximize the absorption of water by the terrain. Each local landscape differs somewhat in this regard, however, and its current practices are signs that signify and relate to other activities, attitudes, and even motivations of people, forming patterns that can be adaptively distinct from, and ethnically and historically different from, other patterns existing nearby in the same small region.

In a deep mountain valley characterized by remoteness and extreme topographic relief, outside influences originating in the regional, national, and global political economies have penetrated local communities at different rates and intensities, and have even had different degrees of influence on local practice, according to the relative ease of access to each village by outsiders. This is just as true today, when the relatively flat lower part of the valley and the provincial capital of Cotahuasi can be reached by road, as it was in the past when these places could not be reached. Such geographic and topographic variation has long been the most important factor determining the amount of freedom local people have had to maintain their own traditions, especially in the domain of water management, in the face of a weak, heavily indebted, and crisis-ridden Peruvian state.

By looking comparatively at several landscapes in a valley where such local differences now exist, among villages that in this case are known to have originally belonged to a single ethnic group (Trawick 2001b, 2003), one can trace the general outline of the process of the landscapes' divergence within a changing colonial and postcolonial regional economy. Again, this is possible because location and topography have, to different extents, limited people's exposure to dominating outside influences: that is, Spanish colonists, colonial officials, miners, traders, the market economy itself, development agencies, and the state. The key to a historical study of such a region is to compare and contrast local landscapes, examining the similarities and differences in practice within a valley environment that is broadly uniform in its general patterning today but which, even given all its typical Andean microenvironmental diversity, was clearly much more homogenous in the past.

For the sake of illustration, here the comparison will be limited mainly to five variables and/or general kinds of practice in each place: (1) how scarce the water available for irrigation is; (2) how that water is divided and shared between different user communities (if at all); (3) how individual shares are allocated and distributed to the fields and households within a given community; (4) how each share is dispersed and used by household members at the field level; and (5) how maintenance duties are apportioned among households with respect to their water rights. These variables seem to have a major impact on two dimensions that determine how well the irrigation systems function: the relative strength of people's motivation to cooperate and obey the rules rather than to "free ride," and the likelihood that any cheating or free riding will be detected. As we will see, in some cases the first variable, water scarcity, is much more a consequence than a cause of differences in the other techniques. In certain communities the scarcity is largely socially created—a situation that has tragic and self-reinforcing consequences—while in others it is not.

The Three Communities Studied

The three villages and landscapes chosen for study are all located in the department of Arequipa, in the southern part of the country, one of the more remote provinces on the western Andean slope. They were chosen for two reasons. They have in common the type of irrigation system found virtually everywhere throughout the sierra—small-scale canal systems fed by mountain springs—but they differ systematically and cover a wide range of the variation found among highland communities today. All three are unified, having some kind of a central irrigation authority (Hunt 1988)—although they show marked differences in this regard—and all are stratified. Composed of large and small landowners—*mayoristas* and *minoristas*—all three communities grow basically the same array of crops, including cultivated pasture for animals (alfalfa), but they vary in their ethnic composition and their degree of autonomy. They also differ according to altitude, proximity to the road and to adjacent provinces, and other factors, and form a kind of rural-urban continuum, though all within a very rural context. As peasant communities that in each case were once predominantly indigenous, perhaps the most important dimension along which they vary today is their degree of domination by outsiders, by an elite ethnic minority that (along with their ally, the Peruvian state) has generally ruled this part of the Andean countryside ever since the Spanish conquest.

The three landscapes have still another feature in common that is worthy of note. The irrigated territories of the communities today are bordered by vast areas covered with the traces of highly eroded terraces, stretching outward and especially upward to the altitudinal limit where cultivation becomes impossible, above 4,000 m. These large areas were evidently once devoted to high-altitude rainfall agriculture, but their near universality and their condition relative to other recently abandoned lands of this type seem to indicate that they have lain out of use ever since the Spanish conquest. They are such a prominent and extensive feature framing the village landscapes that they give the strong impression that the original community territories of Inka times were entirely terraced and cultivated from top to bottom. Although it is not possible to test this interpretation conclusively, the impression these landscapes give is relevant to the reading of local and regional history that follows.

Huaynacotas: A Stratified Indigenous Community

The first community is a peasant village (population roughly 1,100, elevation 3,400 m) inhabiting a vertically oriented landscape of approximately 400 ha that has been terraced meticulously from top to bottom. Ethnically indigenous, the village is widely considered by other valley residents to be distinctive, especially in the fact that its residents somehow managed to prevent colonization of the community by the Spanish landlords whose dominant presence is notable nearly everywhere else. Lying four hours' walk above the valley floor, it is stratified, like all Andean villages, but much less so than other local communities, with the biggest landowners (a minority of roughly 20 percent of households) having a maximum of 3 ha of irrigated land, compared to the average smallholder amount of approximately 1 ha. Huaynacotas is known for having the best organized and most efficiently run irrigation system in the province, but it also suffers from the most severe water scarcity, with irrigation cycles extending from two to three months long during the dry season.

The irrigation system is a communal one where water is de facto common property, a "common-pool" resource to which all landowners have equitable rights. The distribution system is a dual one, cooperatively run by the village members themselves according to customary rules that provide each parcel and its owner with a turn to irrigate in a fixed rotation (*turno*, or *mita*) that is repeated several times during the year. For the sake of brevity and simplicity, the working rules and operating principles, identified through periodic fieldwork extending over a total of more than four years, are tabulated below. Although not truly comprehensive, the list includes the five types of practice that are the focus of this reading and discussion of the landscape.

Interactive Effects of the Operating Principles

The working rules and principles are local institutions that interact in such a way as to ensure that water is distributed equitably and efficiently over the terraced landscape, with minimum waste because the total surface area of canals in use at any point in time (through which filtration and evaporation occur) is minimized. Infractions of the rules, such as theft and favoritism, are extremely rare because they are easily detected. Conflict among users is therefore infrequent, and the canal system is very well maintained. Although the importance of negative sanctions in achieving this outcome should not be underestimated, what is most remarkable about the tradition in Huaynacotas is the way that the other rules and practices together create a strong *positive* incentive to respect tradition and use water properly.

The simplicity and rigidity of the rules, together with the transparency thus created, provides individuals with a high degree of security regarding their water rights: de facto claimant rights in the terminology of Schlager and Ostrom (1992). The rights are clearly defined in terms of allotment frequency and the volume and duration of water flow for each field's share, and they are easily protected by the water users themselves. Note that control over water consumption per unit area is inherent in the *atu* pooling technique (see fig. 3.1), which is also used to water alfalfa, a cultivated pasture that is here treated just like any other crop.

Table 3.1. The Irrigated Landscape of Huaynacotas

Operating principle	Hydrological condition, working rule, or practice
Extreme water scarcity	The resource is chronically scarce, with dry season cycles extending from two to three months long.
Autonomy	The community has and controls its own flows of water (from alpine springs), distributing these over the landscape through a rotation procedure based on local customary law.
Contiguous distribution	The landscape consists of named sectors of land irrigated in a fixed sequence based on the planting order; within each sector water is distributed to fields in a fixed contiguous order based on their location along successive canals, starting at the bottom of each sector and moving upward plot by plot and canal by canal.
Uniformity	*In the watering frequency*: for each major water source, all fields receive allotments with the same frequency, which varies during the year. *In technique*: everyone irrigates in the same way, using water-pooling structures of uniform height (see fig. 3.2), even in watering alfalfa.
Proportionality (equity)	*Among water rights*: the pooling technique creates a uniform land-water ratio, ensuring that no party may use more water than the amount to which the extent of their land entitles—nor may they legally get it more often than everyone else. *Between rights and duties*: the contributions that households make to canal maintenance must be proportional to the amount of irrigated land that they have.
Regularity and boundary stability	Things are always done in the same way under conditions of scarcity; no exceptions are allowed, and any unauthorized expansion of irrigation is prohibited.
Transparency	Since the distribution order is fixed and contiguous and known to everyone, irrigation is a spatially concentrated and highly visible activity; all water users thus have the capacity to confirm, with their own eyes, that the rules are being obeyed and to detect any violations that might occur.
Graduated sanctions	Penalties for any rule violations are severe, involving some degree of loss of water rights, but vary according to the gravity of the offense.

Perhaps most crucial is the uniform watering frequency; this has the effect of creating a direct and obvious link to the individual farmer, between the efficiency and orderliness of water use, and for the duration of the irrigation cycle. The system is thus ruled by a simple and well-recognized logic: by obeying the rules and using water conservatively, people are maximizing the frequency and intensity of irrigation for themselves and everyone else, making the best of a bad situation. At the same time, because the system is highly transparent, the effects of any "free riding" are immediately obvious and ultimately negative for everyone, even the perpetrators. This configuration of practices creates a widely perceived correspondence between individual self-interest and the common good, as well as a general sense

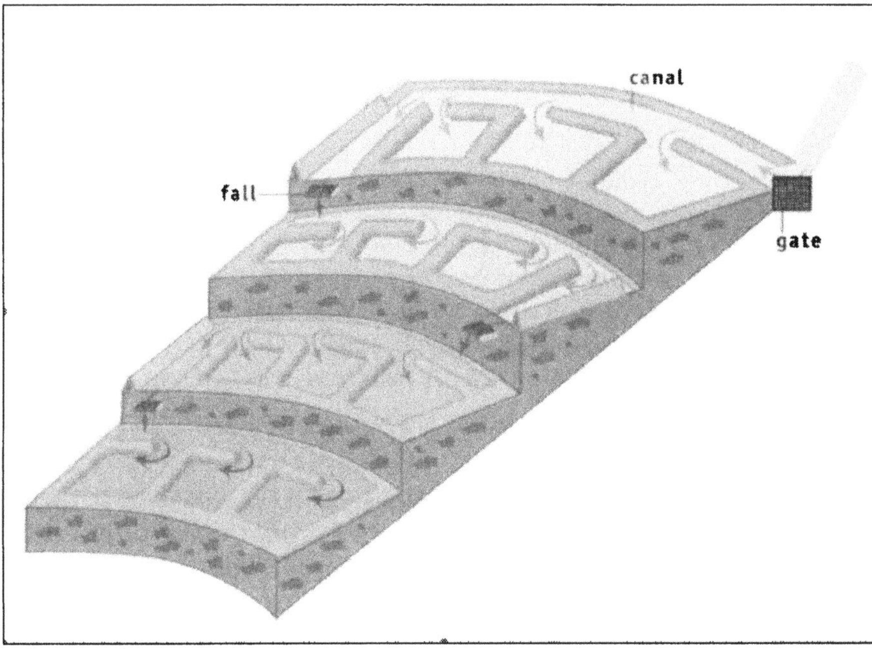

Figure 3.1 Typical terrace irrigation unit in Huaynacotas.

of equity or fairness in sharing a scarcity. An unsurprising result is a strong communal spirit or ethos among the village members, whose most visible expression is the very well-maintained condition of the canal system itself.

Perhaps the best characterization of this particular outcome of the commons drama is the following one, which contrasts starkly with Hardin's (1968) gloomy prediction of inevitable failure and tragedy. The term below is widely used in the literature today because we now know of innumerable cases throughout the world where success in managing water effectively and maintaining a sustainable irrigation society has been achieved by local people: "Comedy: the drama of humans as social rather than private beings . . . of social actions having a frankly corrective [and mutually beneficial] purpose" (Smith 1984).

The Question of Antiquity: Comedy as an Initial or "Foundational" Outcome

The people of Huaynacotas claim that their hydraulic tradition, like other important institutions, dates back to their ancestors, the Inkas. If true, this assertion would agree with the accounts of the chroniclers Guaman Poma (1978 [1613]: 356, 246, 848, 1040, 1237) and Garcilaso (see below); both these chroniclers claimed that the Inkas had a policy for local water management, at least in areas where the resource was scarce, and both spoke admiringly of it in very similar terms:

> In districts where the quantity of water for irrigation was small, they *divided it proportionately* (as they did with everything they shared out), so that there would be no dispute among the Indians about obtaining it. This was *only done in the years of scanty rainfall when the need was greatest.* The water was measured, and, as it was known from experience how long it took to irrigate a fanega of land, each Indian was accordingly granted the number of hours he needed for the amount of land he had. . . . Water was *taken by turns, according to the order of the plots of land, one after another. No preference was given* to the rich or nobles, or to favorites or relatives of the kuraca [chief], or to the kuraca himself, or to royal officials or governors. Anyone who neglected to irrigate his land at the proper time received an ignominious punishment. (Garcilaso de la Vega [1966] (1609): 248; italics mine)

The parallels between this brief account written so long ago and the more recent ethnographic observations are striking enough to lend strong support to the Huaynacoteños claim, even though Garcilaso is known to have at times exaggerated the wisdom of Inka governance. There is, however, other supporting evidence: for example, the presence of the same management tradition in two other local villages and in several others outside the province (Treacy 1994; Guillet 1994: 287), specifically in villages that were never directly colonized by landlords and are ethnically indigenous, but there and only there. It is also relevant to note that in Inka times the Cotahuasi valley is known to have been inhabited by a single very powerful ethnic group that may well have shared a single management tradition.

The full argument in support of this view has been presented elsewhere (Trawick 2001a, 2001b, 2002, 2003), but it suggests that the tradition of Huaynacotas was once found not just throughout most of this particular valley, but probably over a vast area of the highlands as well. This, of course, would mean that success, or "comedy" as defined above, and the institutions that sustain it in this particular case, can justifiably be used as a historical baseline or "initial" condition in order to trace the outline of the irrigation history, at least of this small region, if not of the highlands as a whole. Other "proxy" information adds support to this view; environmental data for Inka times (Thompson et al. 1985) show that the empire was founded toward the end of a long dry period lasting several hundred years, which would help to explain why irrigation development and expansion were a central concern for its rulers of the empire.

The vast engineered landscapes and "landesque capital" that had emerged during previous centuries in the Andes (the focus of the chapter by Earle and Doyel in this volume) were crucial to the imperial system, mainly because they provided for the subsistence and livelihood of local peasant communities. Both of the chroniclers referred to above claimed that the Inkas opened up new lands for the production of tribute—state lands that produced a storable surplus and provided "staple finance" to fund the empire. The goal is said to have been not to have to take away any land from the peasant communities and thus not to jeopardize their livelihood, a policy that presumably must also have involved tapping previously unused sources of water. Again, these assertions were given support by the research done in the Cotahuasi valley (Trawick 2001b; 2003: 42–46). The Inkas opened up for tribute production a vast area of previously uncultivated flatlands along the valley bottom, tapping the main flow of the river far upstream by building a long and very costly canal. Having gone to so much trouble and expense to build this new irrigated physical capital, surely the Inkas would have regarded a system for the successful local management of water, upon which the productivity of the new state lands would depend, to be highly useful. Perhaps they appropriated this hydraulic tradition, which may well have emerged and spread widely throughout the Andes long before them, especially for use in places where they subsequently established their imperial colonies, as the accounts of Garcilaso and Guaman Poma suggest.

Such a policy would have gone a long way toward overcoming the main challenges involved in achieving successful water management and maintaining success over a long period of time. These challenges have been analyzed by Ostrom (1990) in terms of three "nested" problems, the solutions to which are themselves public goods that have their own "free rider" problems and create their own social dilemmas: (1) the problem of initially inventing the rules for resource allocation and use; (2) the problem of achieving a credible and sustained commitment by people to those rules; and (3) the problem of providing effective monitoring to ensure cooperation and rule enforcement. In a successful system of local management such as that of Huaynacotas, people have solved all of these problems and escaped the three dilemmas. The most pivotal one, however, upon whose solution the solving of the other two problems depends, is mutual monitoring, as Olsen (1965), Ostrom (1990), and others have clearly shown. Without mutual monitoring, individual commitments to cooperate will tend, paradoxically, to weaken among some irrigators as time passes and circumstances change, in part due to the very effectiveness of the rules, which can easily come to be taken for granted.

The keys to achieving such success, and solving the nested dilemmas of communal irrigation, were revealed above: a prevailing "equity," or fairness among household water rights, and between those rights and accompanying maintenance duties—this equity has the effect of sharing the scarcity in a manner that people can agree on as just (a general value itself defined in terms of the principles of uniformity and proportionality); and, just as importantly, *transparency*, a characteristic created by the rigid and contiguous, or spatially determined, pattern of water distribution. A close reading of other local landscapes will now reveal how, and to some extent why, these key institutions changed and were gradually lost in neighboring communities, leading to a very different social outcome in each case.

Pampamarca: A Colonized Indigenous Community

The second community, Pampamarca (population 842, elevation 3,600 m), is more typical of the valley's "indigenous" settlements today, having long been dominated by a handful of elite Spanish families, who moved in sometime early in the nineteenth century. As these elite groups did wherever they settled, they assumed the leadership—political, economic, and religious—of the community, largely displacing the native chieftains who had governed it previously. The elites redefined the prerogatives that went with high status, expropriating land in order to found small *haciendas*, and laying claim to large amounts of the community's irrigation water for their own private use. They introduced alfalfa in order to feed the mules, horses, and cattle that were essential to their livelihood as merchants and long-distance traders, thereby promoting the same changes in land and water use that occurred in Cotahuasi, the provincial capital, though on a more limited scale.

The village is composed of four *ayllus*, or corporate kinship groups, each of which has its own water sources, canal network, and irrigated territory. The working rules and operating principles (listed below) are precisely the same within each area, however, and they form a single local tradition used to irrigate roughly 340 ha of land. The five Spanish families, who are not *ayllu* members, have between 6 and 15 ha under irrigation, while the *comuneros* (157 families in all) have an average of slightly more than 1 ha. Recently, however, eight of the peasant families, referred to as middle proprietors (*medianos propietarios*) have acquired additional land, now holding 2–5 ha each, and have become heavily involved in the cattle trade and in petty commerce. Although none have reached the level of the local elites, they are slowly occupying the commercial and political "niche" being given up by the landlords, who began withdrawing from the village after the regional wool trade declined in the 1970s and the agrarian reform (see below) broke up the estates in the lower part of the valley.

The working rules and operating principles of the local tradition have again been listed in summary form for the sake of brevity and in order to facilitate comparison of different landscapes. Two striking contrasts with Huaynacotas require discussion. The first are the hierarchical and somewhat flexible order of water allocation and the de facto private rights enjoyed by the landlords, both of which might, at first glance, seem to reflect the dominant presence of the Spanish families during almost two centuries of residence. However, a hierarchical pattern of distribution, like the more "egalitarian" regimen followed in Huaynacotas, is known to exist today in numerous communities in adjacent provinces and regions (Mayer and Fonseca 1979; Montoya, Silveira, and Lindoso 1979; Fonseca 1983; Mayer 1985; Gelles 1986), and it seems to represent yet another ancient tradition.

The available ethnohistorical and ethnographic data suggest that the Inka water policy described by Garcilaso may have been a dual one, with a second mode of operation for use during years of resource abundance. This was probably a hierarchical one in which, within each major sector of land, the watering order was determined by the age and prestige of the landowners within the social ranking of each ayllu (Trawick 2001b; 2003: 110–49). Although the watering frequency was probably the same for everyone, as it is in Pampamarca, the sequence may have been determined by the social and symbolic order rather than the lay of the agricultural land. This procedure was apparently originally used only where (or when) water was abundant, as in Pampamarca, but its use is not limited to that context today, also being common in situations of scarcity. Water abundance is extremely rare in the Andes, and it probably happened only rarely also during Inka times, which we know were generally arid (Thompson et al. 1985). As for the de facto private rights of the landlords, the Spaniards appear to have simply superimposed themselves on the ayllus' ranking system when they colonized the community, claiming as their own the first few days of water in the distribution cycle for every sector of land where they had property; they diverted and used the water without any supervision by the ayllus' water distributors.

The second feature worthy of note is the presence, in certain sectors of land, of a second watering technique generally used on sloped surfaces. Sloped fields, in contrast to what we saw in Huaynacotas, are common in certain sectors within some of the ayllu territories, particularly in areas that are relatively flat, though not in all of them. It is important to note that level terraces, or *andenes*, cover the majority of the village landscape

Table 3.2. The Irrigated Landscape of Pampamarca

Operating principle	Hydrological condition, working rule, or practice
Water abundance	The major spring flows come from fossil groundwater and remain abundant throughout the year regardless of rainfall and drought, with near-optimal watering cycles 15 to 20 days long.
Autonomy	Each ayllu has and controls its own flows of water on a rotation system (a turno, or mita) governed by local custom and operated by an ayllu official.
Hierarchical distribution	Sectors of land are irrigated in a fixed sequence based on the planting order; within each sector, however, landowners are given water according to the positions they hold in a prestige hierarchy based mainly on civil and religious service to the community (the cargo system); they are then free to irrigate their plots in any order they like.
Uniformity	*In irrigation frequency*: for each major source, all rights holders in each sector of land receive water with the same frequency on a single cycle.
Nonuniformity or variation	*In technique*: two watering methods are used: (1) the pooling (atu) method, by far the most widespread and generally used on terraces; and (2) a more wasteful inundation or flooding technique used on sloped pasture fields (i.e., on destroyed terraces; see fig. 3.2), and also on terraces in certain areas.
Nonproportionality or inequity	*Among water rights*: some people use much more water per unit of land than others because they use the flooding technique; some (i.e., the landlords) own entire days of water at the start of each cycle that are exclusively theirs and which, despite their use of the wasteful flooding technique, give them a surplus. *Between rights and duties*: ayllu members contribute the same amount of labor to yearly canal maintenance due to their uniformly small landholdings; in contrast, the elite families and largest landowners are not obligated to contribute any labor at all to the communal work.
Irregularity or flexibility	Within each land sector, the specific watering order among landowners and fields is hierarchical but flexible, often varying between cycles due to landowner preferences.
Limited transparency	Because the distribution order here is flexible rather than fixed, and irrigation a more dispersed and less public activity, water theft and other infractions are more difficult for the users themselves to detect than in Huaynacotas.
Graduated but weak sanctions	Sanctions are graduated but not frequently levied or very effective, because infractions (although increasingly common) are harder to "prove" and because the duty of monitoring falls entirely on the ayllus' water distributors.

and that the *atu* water-pooling technique is by far the most common method used on them today. The only noteworthy difference in what is otherwise an important basic commonality with Huaynacotas is that the atus are much shallower here, built to a height of only 15–20 cm, a practice that local people attribute to water abundance and the high frequency of irrigation.

The sloped fields where the other technique is mainly used are created through the destruction and consolidation of a series of level terraces, as shown in figure 3.2. This is evidently a Spanish practice: until recently it was done exclusively on hacienda land; its purpose is to maximize alfalfa production and make it possible to graze several cattle at once in the same plot. Because the resulting slope precludes use of the water-pooling method, another watering technique was developed when the landscape conversion started, one in which water is released continuously along the top of a field, allowing gravity to draw it over and flood the surface below for an extended, often indefinite period of time. This process typically leads to a large buildup of water at the lower end of the field, and much of the water escapes into the canal system as waste. Although acknowledged to be inherently wasteful, the top-down, or inundation, method has the advantage of requiring less labor; it can even be handled by a single person working alone, compared to the two or three family members needed for the pooling technique. This feature must have made the process attractive during an earlier era when labor, rather than water, was the scarce resource.

Today, the top-down method is the exclusive one used by the estate owners, even in the steeper areas where the terraces, now often devoted to alfalfa production, have been left intact. There the water is simply allowed to spill over from one terrace to the next. The sloped pasture fields or corral fields where the process is mainly used, called *potreros* or *canchones*, are a defining feature of hacienda or former hacienda lands, both here and elsewhere in the valley. But in both areas they are now slowly spreading throughout the landscape as ancient terraces are gradually being destroyed.

Interactive Effects of the Principles and Practices

The most general observation that can be made about the way the rules and principles interact in this case is that the pervasive inequity among both rights and duties has created a degree of resentment among the *comuneros*, or ayllu members, which in turn has weakened the communal tradition. Not surprisingly, this results in the canal and tank system's being notably less well maintained than in Huaynacotas. The arrangement is one that the

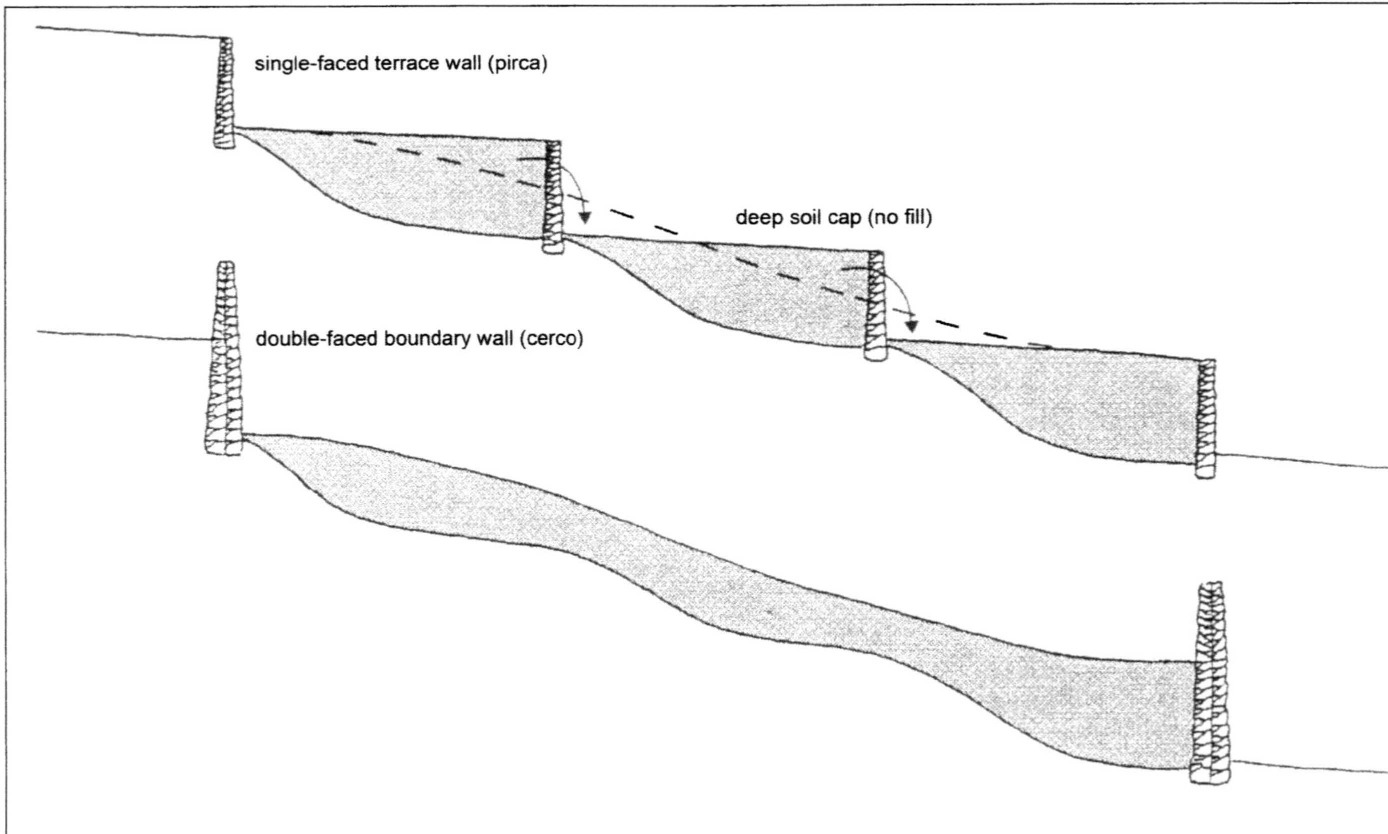

Figure 3.2 Drawing of how terraces are destroyed and consolidated into sloped fields.

comuneros are quite accustomed to, however, and, although the inequity in water use is slowly spreading among the ayllu members themselves, their negative reaction has not yet become strong or widespread. Given the marked variation in irrigation technique and resulting water consumption, household rights are both less equitable in practice and less clearly defined than in Huaynacotas. Furthermore, because the distribution order is flexible and changing, those rights are not as easily protected by the water users themselves. Theft is thus increasingly common and frequently spoken about today by ayllu members, as is a perceived gradual breakdown of order and "respect for tradition."

It is important to note, however, that due to the abundance of water and the high frequency of irrigation, people are not greatly upset about this slow increase in "free riding." And, despite the fact that the main culprits' identities are known (they are the emerging middle proprietors, who grow the most alfalfa), such complaints rarely result in overt conflict or in any formal action being taken. Thus the irrigation system can be described as undergoing stress or being challenged today by comuneros who have become heavily involved in alfalfa production and cattle raising for the market, and whose special water "needs" have led them to begin conducting themselves much like the landlords did in the past. Such actions do not really cause significant hardship for others, and have not yet become widespread enough to seriously disrupt the local tradition. But they are causing problems in the ayllus today that, according to most people, did not occur in earlier times.

Water Abundance: A Window into the Past

The most unusual feature of Pampamarca is one that is part of the history of all irrigation communities in the Andes, an awareness of which is crucial for any understanding of how things came to be as they are today in a given locale. The population collapse that followed the Spanish conquest of the New World was the first great holocaust in human history: a 60–80 percent collapse of village populations in the Andes that started with epidemics of European diseases that began before the conquerors actually arrived on the scene and, combined with heavy mortality and refugee flight caused by forced work in colonial mines, lasted for more than two hundred years (Cook 1981; Gootenberg 1991). Yet one of the population collapse's most significant impacts has been overlooked entirely in the ethnographic literature: water, like land, became abundant for the first time in centuries and remained so for a very long time, eliminating any need for conservation, while peasant labor became quite scarce. In order to illustrate these impacts, population figures for three communities in the Cotahuasi valley, gathered from all available colonial and modern census counts, are shown in figure 3.3. The graph illustrates dramatic changes in the availability of peasant labor, but the sustained depopulation and eventual rapid recovery shown can also, by simply inverting the graph, provide a "proxy" curve revealing changes in the general availability of water in the valley during this long period.

Pampamarca, being the only local village where water remains plentiful today, reflects hydrological conditions that must have prevailed throughout the highlands until the early part of the twentieth century, before indigenous populations had recovered fully from collapse (Gootenberg 1991). It was during this period, when pressure on the resource had remained relaxed for centuries, that the transformation of indigenous traditions began in the hacienda-dominated communities. Thus Pampamarca provides a unique glimpse of some of the dynamics that must have been at work. Basically, the negative impact of practices introduced by the Spanish—pasture cultivation, terrace destruction, slope irrigation, and permanent hierarchy and inequity in distribution—must not have been strongly felt until later, when water became scarce because of rapid population growth and other changes occurring at the same time. This, I think, must have been the context in which certain comuneros—only a handful of families in this case—began to depart from tradition and adopt the attitudes and behaviors typical of the Spanish elite. This is how the tragedy of the commons in irrigation began.

Cotahuasi: A Hacienda-Dominated District

The third case is a district composed of several communities: a town (Cotahuasi, population 1,073, elevation 2,700 m) and three outlying high-altitude villages (population 200–500 each, elevation approximately 3,200 m), which share a set of alpine springs that form three major flows and irrigate a landscape covering some 580 ha. Here, in the provincial capital, elite families of Spanish descent have made up a significant percentage of the population ever since early colonial times (Bingham 1922). Until recently these families were the owners of estates that together took up over half the irrigated land in the district, and they owned an even greater percentage of the total water. This pattern was the result of estate expansion beginning in the late nineteenth century and continuing through the middle of the twentieth—encroachment that, like the founding of the estates in Pampamarca, was spurred by the growing international trade in alpaca wool from the surrounding *altiplano* (Flores-Galindo 1977: 150–53; Appleby 1976; Orlove 1977). The landlords made their living as merchants

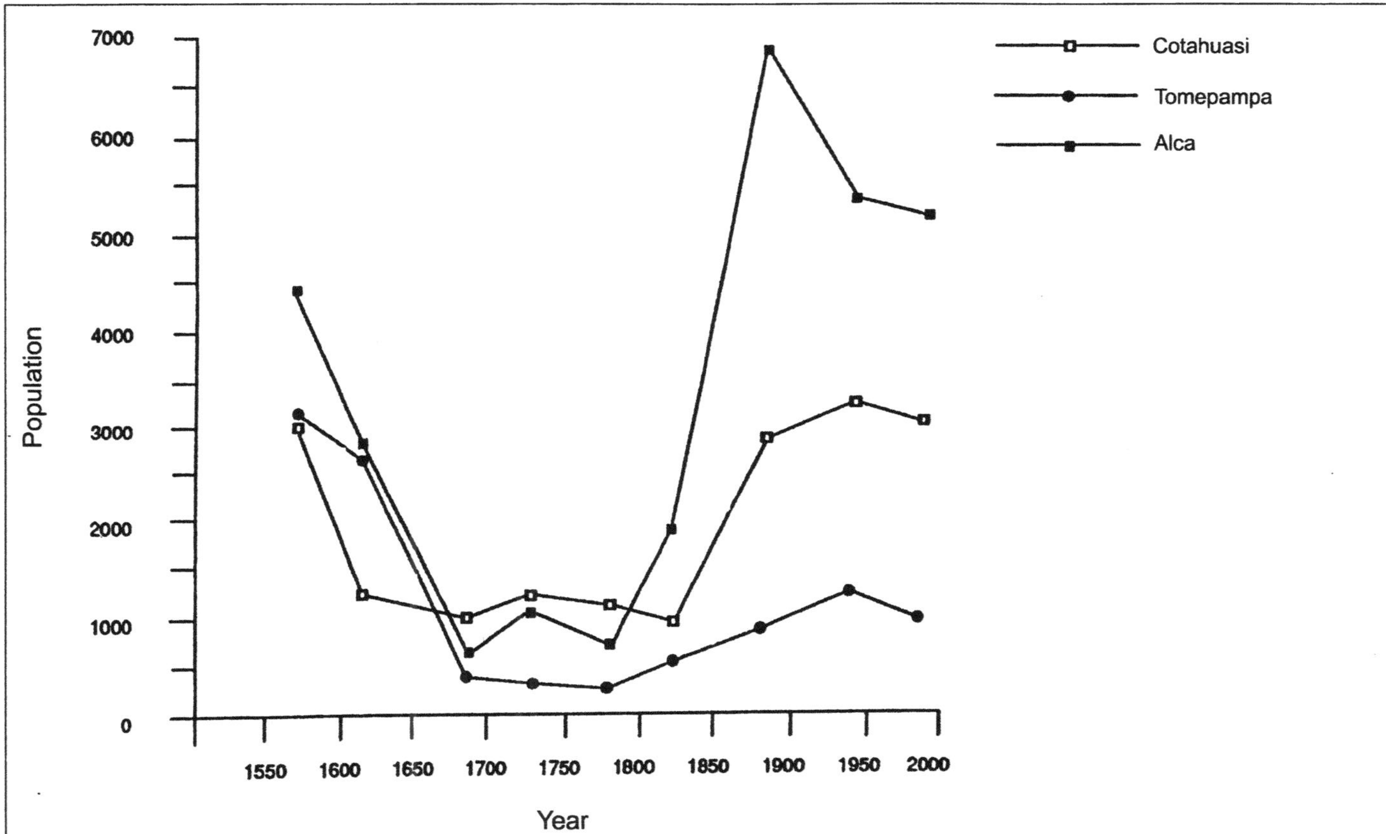

Figure 3.3 Graph of population collapse and recovery in three villages in the Cotahuasi valley.

and middlemen in the trade, collecting wool by bartering food crops, cane alcohol, and imported merchandise with native herders on the plateau (Montoya 1980: 142–44). This exchange system was based on muleteering and intensive alfalfa production, which remained dominant until the road finally reached the valley in 1960. At that time the wool trade went into decline and was soon replaced by the (also alfalfa-intensive) cattle trade.

From a hydraulic point of view, the result of this estate expansion was the loss through privatization by the landlords—both de jure and de facto—of more than half the water in the district, water that came to be known as the *agua de las haciendas* or *agua de alfalfa*. In 1902, when Peru's first water law was passed, water that had been in private estate use for twenty or more years was recognized as legitimate in formal property deeds, while the remaining communal water belonging to the indigenous communities—the *agua de las comunidades*—was designated as "public" water, to be used by existing Communities of Irrigators (Pasapera 1902). As the estates multiplied and continued to expand thereafter through purchases of land within the remaining community territories, a process that continued long after the water code was passed, the same hierarchical and inequitable system of water use emerged within each village territory (i.e., in each ayllu) that we see today in Pampamarca. The district's older and bigger estates each had titles to their own days of canal water (or parts thereof) in a separate flow that they used on a two-week cycle. Similarly, the newer and smaller estate properties within each community territory had de facto private use of the first day or two of the weekly communal water belonging to the ayllus, whose distribution cycles usually took several weeks to irrigate all the comunero lands.

Here, however, where the resource was relatively scarce to begin with and quite prone to drought, the consequences of estate expansion and community penetration were dramatic. In Cotahuasi we see the effects of the same new practices observed in Pampamarca—alfalfa production, terrace destruction and a new way of irrigating, water privatization, hierarchy and inequity among rights and duties, increasing water theft—but in a case where these began much earlier and were carried to an extreme. Here, due to the much greater intensity of the wool and cattle business, the Spanish practices associated with pasture production began spreading much earlier and did so more widely within the peasant population, producing a stratum of middle proprietors (the same segment who are causing problems today in Pampamarca) who worked as contracted muleteers in the wool trade. Another element entered the equation when the Peruvian government got directly involved in local water management: briefly at first in 1940–1942, then permanently in 1960 and, finally, in 1969, with the passage of a major water reform law. The overall effect of this intervention and centralization of power was to accelerate the conflict and the unfolding tragedy that had already long been under way: the actions allowed and encouraged the same kinds of changes that we saw happening in Pampamarca.

Before we examine these changing practices and their impacts, the role of the state and its existing water law must be assessed. Although the government's attempts to intervene in local water management have a long history, the most significant one was the passage, as part of the Agrarian Reform of 1969, of revolutionary legislation that sought to expropriate all privately owned water in the name of the state and, like hacienda land, redistribute it among rural communities and water users in a more equitable and efficient manner. The law, although well intentioned, is based on an inappropriate agronomic and technocratic model, probably imported from land-grant research institutions in the United States. Called the General Water Law, it requires volumetric measurement of all water flows by an official administrator or technician who, in consultation with local user groups, is supposed to allocate water according to the "needs" of specific crops in an order determined by the relative importance of each one to the community (CEPES 1984). Unfortunately, very few administrators in the sierra have either the instruments or the canal infrastructure needed for such a precise system of control, yet the legislation does not provide any well-defined backup procedure for use in these cases. Furthermore, the law is based on the assumption that enough water is available to meet those crop water "needs," when in fact scarcity and insufficiency are the normal state of affairs. The end result in practice is a system of rotating water use, supposedly governed with the help of the local user groups, whose rules of allocation are flexible and ill defined, so that the law has been poorly implemented and is not enforced.

Although the negative incentives created by such an inequitable, wasteful, and opaque system are perhaps obvious, even from a brief synchronic summary, some of the differences require discussion. The first is the pattern or distribution of the different watering techniques and associated landforms in space. Within each community territory one finds (1) level terraces in the steeper areas, where the *atu* pooling technique is generally used (a commonality with Pampamarca and Huaynacotas); (2) sloped fields in the flatter areas (formerly the sites of the biggest haciendas), where the flooding method is used exclusively; and (3) some terraces in relatively steep areas that are flooded from the top down, just like pasture fields, as we saw in certain sectors in Pampamarca. Here, however, the wasteful inundation

Table 3.3. The Irrigated Landscape of Cotahuasi District

Operating principle	Hydrological condition, working rule, or practice
Water scarcity	The resource is scarce, with dry season cycles extending up to two months long.
Water sharing and competition between user groups	Separate villages share use of the main water flows, in alternating communal allotments determined by a water administrator according to provisions of the 1969 General Water Law.
Dispersed and flexible distribution	Water distribution within each community territory should theoretically be as contiguous as possible, but special "emergency" allotments are allowed under the law and are typically given by the administrator, resulting in a flexible and somewhat dispersed pattern for each watering cycle.
Nonuniformity (inequity and/or corruption)	*In the watering frequency*: special allotments for certain fields are commonly given by the administrator, often in violation of the law; some big landowners also have de facto duplicate water rights (to both main canal water and to small local springs). *In technique*: both the pooling and the flooding techniques are used locally, but the latter is often used on terraces.
Nonproportionality (inequity)	*Among rights*: people using the top-down technique are allowed to irrigate until they are "finished", so that consumption per hectare varies widely and waste is rampant. *Between rights and duties*: large landowners are required by law to contribute only the same minimum amount of labor to canal maintenance as are smallholders.
Irregularity or flexibility	The order of allocation to fields within sectors of land commonly changes between cycles, often at the last minute and for reasons known only to the administrator.
Opaqueness	The reasons for changes in the distribution order are not explained to the affected landowners, nor is the justification for any special "emergency" allotments given; thus people do not necessarily know an infraction of the law when they see one.
Delayed ineffective sanctions	Water distributors do not have the authority under the law to deny water or to curtail irrigation in response to infractions; sanctions can be applied only by the administrator and always occur long after the fact.

technique—which individuals employ with no community control over either the volume or the duration of water flow—is the most common one because alfalfa dominates the district landscape, being produced on approximately 60 percent of registered properties, according to official figures gathered by the local office of the Ministry of Agriculture.

This, of course, means that water use within each village user group is highly disproportionate and inequitable, as are the legal claimant rights of the community members. The bigger landowners and middle proprietors in each village generally use the flooding technique, while the smaller peasant farmers continue to rely mainly, though not exclusively, on their more conservative traditional method. The inequity is further heightened by the aforementioned dual water rights, which tend to belong to the bigger landowners in each case (the former estate owners).

A final related feature is prominent in the district but not found within the two landscapes previously examined: a great amount of abandoned terraced land. One type is in fact found there: vast areas of highly eroded terracing that extend above all the local villages, lying outside the irrigated areas and reaching upward to the very limits of cultivation, above 4000 m, which have apparently been out of use ever since the conquest and the ensuing population collapse. These lands, which were once obviously rain-fed terraced fields, are found throughout the valley and are such a striking feature of the landscape that they give a strong impression that its inhabited areas were originally (i.e., in Inka times) terraced in their entirety. The other type of abandoned land is found only in Cotahuasi and lies within the irrigated areas belonging to each village: a total of 142 ha according to local ministry data. These lands, which were once irrigated, reflect the gradual privatization of water originally belonging to the ayllus by the estates as they expanded, with their pasture cultivation and their new landscaping and watering method. Thus the landscape itself contains tangible signs of the conquest and, more importantly, of the ensuing long struggle over water between local peasants and their landlords, visible traces of the drama of the commons.

The second crucial difference lies in the fact that here water flows are shared by separate communities and user groups, a kind of arrangement that dates back to the forced resettlement of native populations shortly after the conquest in the sixteenth century (Cook 1975). For each major alpine spring, all of which now have reservoirs for overnight water storage, a pair of communities alternates in using the outflow of the tank during a two- to three-week period—communal shares that were granted by the administrator during the water reform, supposedly based on the area historically irrigated by each village. This alternating interdependence, which contrasts so markedly with the autonomy enjoyed by Huaynacotas and the ayllus of Pampamarca, has several negative consequences. It nullifies the potential for intervillage cooperation and hampers all efforts (of which there have been many) to improve resource distribution and use, and to solve the district's water problem (Trawick 2003: 273–90). The arrangement is greatly complicated by a dispute between the groups that has been going on for decades; the dispute concerns the questionable legality of certain expansions of the area under irrigation in each community that occurred during the reform in the 1970s. The portion of the landscape that legitimately ought to be watered is strongly disputed by the groups involved in these dual sharing arrangements, and the amount of land actually under irrigation within each village territory is constantly questioned, as is the rightful number of days of water in each group's turn. The relationships are thus ones not of cooperation, but of intense competition and conflict, even open hostility between communities.

In this context the turn-taking itself, which was imposed by the administrator after the reservoirs were built with state financial help during the reform, results in a widespread perception among water users within each group that allocation is a "zero-sum" game in which one group's gain is the other's loss. Unless the administrator can ensure that any proposed improvements in water use will be fully implemented in both user communities, and the resulting benefits of conservation will be equally shared—something about which past experience causes strong doubt—people have no rational reason to comply and invest the small amount of extra labor that such improvements generally require. In their eyes, their own group's turn will likely be shortened by a few days and much of the benefit of their effort will be wasted, since it will be shared by the other group.

These sharing relationships are thus dysfunctional and antagonistic in a basic way, and have been for a long time. In a district where they are well separated from one another by rough terrain, the communities create a situation analogous to that which now exists within each user group—in which individuals who share water do not have the opportunity to observe each other irrigate on a regular basis—but on a bigger scale, between groups that in this case have a long history of water conflict. Perhaps the most unfortunate effect is that, within each group, the conflict of interest between large and small landowners over major inequities in water use—the resentment spoken of earlier—is deflected outward and turned into a conflict now perceived to be mainly between communities (Trawick 2003: 248–50). As a result, people tend to overlook the abuses and inequities by their neighbors within their own group—particularly the peasant smallholders, who potentially have a lot to gain by attending to the problems—because they do not really see these as depriving them of water. Instead, the peasant smallholders tend to focus the blame for the water shortage on the defects and problems within the other user group.

Interactive Effects of Local Practices

Water theft and corruption have continued and even proliferated in the district because the rules of distribution have not been clearly and firmly defined, and because the primary mechanism that should restrain such abuses—systematic monitoring by the irrigators themselves—has virtually ceased to function. The end result is that, even though everyone now participates to some extent in deciding on a yearly cultivation and irrigation plan, as required by the law, water allocation has become a largely private and covert affair—one dominated, much as it was before the reform, by the local elite. Of course, people are very much aware of this, of the inequities and abuses that commonly happen, but they have little power to do anything about it, a fact that causes widespread resentment, cynicism, and suspicion of others, and generally discourages cooperation. That "perverse" incentive (Ostrom 1990), which is the main cause of the ongoing tragedy of the commons, does not reflect any innate human selfishness. Rather, as this brief comparison of irrigated landscapes has shown, it is institutionally based and socially and historically derived. The landscape itself, along with the conflicting and counterproductive practices of people, basically nullifies the communal impulse, the tendency that people can have to work together in a mutually beneficial situation, because there is no sense of sharing the water scarcity. There is simply no equity or fairness in the system as it now stands, and it is thoroughly "murky," even opaque, from the water users' point of view.

Not surprisingly, the canal system is poorly looked after and periodic crises in maintenance occur, due to people's minimal and reluctant participation in communal labor. This, of course, is another manifestation of the free-rider problem, which becomes endemic, both within the communities and between them, under such an alternating water-sharing arrangement. In the Cotahuasi district, and no doubt in many other places like it, the institutions established by the state have created a social and political stalemate between communities whose main features, paradoxically enough, are constant rivalry and conflict. The situation is tragic indeed and has been for a long time. There are constant complaints and disputes over the resource, especially between communities, occasionally even physical confrontations between people, and periodic crises that result in assemblies at the district and community levels, where changes are recommended and approved by vote, year after year. Yet nothing has really changed, in a positive sense, in more than three decades.

Conclusion: Landscape Comparison and the Social Dynamics of the Drama of the Commons

None of the irrigation systems described in this brief overview are highly unusual or even difficult to understand, in terms of the general dynamics of their institutions or their current outcomes, given the advances recently made in the theories of the management of common-property resources and of "collective action" in general (McCay and Acheson 1987; NRC 1986; Bromley 1992; Ostrom 1990, 1992, 1998; Ostrom, et al. 2002; Dolšak and Ostrom 2003), both of which have grown out of a great amount of ethnographic research. We have known for some time now that the drama of the commons can just as easily lead to "comedy" as to "tragedy," particularly in small-scale irrigation systems run by relatively homogeneous populations, where people grow the same array of subsistence crops and therefore have rather uniform water needs (Ostrom 1986, 1987). Thus it is not entirely unexpected that a single solution to the challenge of sharing scarce water has been achieved in Huaynacotas and other places like it, a "Game 5 solution," or a self-imposed and self-financed binding-contract scheme (see Ostrom 1990: 15–18). Nor is it preposterous to think that this tradition could have spread widely throughout the Andes in pre-Inka times and ultimately been adopted as a policy by the rulers of an empire whose subjects were almost entirely peasants. The Inka system of governance was one for which irrigation water was the lifeblood; it sustained a political economy focused primarily on the production and widespread redistribution of storable staple crops among the peasantry in times of drought and famine—given in return for yearly tributary labor and surplus production—and the limited circulation of luxury and sumptuary goods to local hereditary chieftains or elites (Earle and D'Altroy 1989). For such an empire, an effective system for local self-governance of the water commons would have been highly advantageous to say the least.

Today the main challenge in theorizing about "the commons" lies in explaining the breakdown of successful systems of resource management once they have been established, in accounting for the outcome that Hardin (1968) and others thought to be inevitable and simply took for granted. Key traces of that history still lie quite visibly in the landscapes where such tragedies have taken place, in tangible signs—both landforms and the practices that create and maintain them—that also provide the outlines of a narrative of the changing political economies of the colonial and postcolonial periods. We can see in these traces the gradual decline of village autonomy in water management and of relative self-sufficiency of food production, as a new political economy of product extraction for export on the international market gained ascendancy: the collecting of alpaca wool through barter for surplus agricultural produce and manufactured goods, and the long-distance transport of these commodities by mule caravan. These two narratives, ecological and economic, are closely related and intertwined, essentially two versions of a story that can be told at different scales and levels of analysis, even told from the points of view of different social classes and ethnic groups: dominant and subordinate.

Visible signs of this history remain inscribed today in the rock and soil of the Cotahuasi valley as well as in its flows of water. Sloped pasture fields now predominate in many local landscapes—though not in all of them—as does the wasteful and inequitable way that slopes are irrigated. This new pattern emerged as terraces were destroyed and smoothed over, and land originally devoted to producing food for people was converted largely to growing food for animals instead, in a fundamental shift affecting the whole ecology of food production. What is widely imagined today to have been a kind of "golden era" for the indigenous population was followed by an abrupt but sustained depopulation resulting from more direct and extensive contact with the world outside the valley, an effect of an early form of "globalization." A close comparative and historically informed reading of local landscapes brings all of this to light, not only revealing the specific local versions of an overarching historical narrative but also showing how those local stories are intertwined. More importantly, such a reading goes a long way toward explaining what happened and why similar social dynamics ultimately led to such varying outcomes in different situations: to "comedy" as well as "tragedy."

How does a successful locally run system of irrigation and water management come unraveled and become dysfunctional long after it is first established, taking such disparate forms in different locales? Factors that undermine individual commitments to cooperate and obey the rules of equity, perhaps by creating special water needs and privileged water rights, are an obvious possibility, as are other factors that reduce transparency, perhaps by introducing seemingly harmless exceptions to the rules. In "developing" postcolonial countries like Peru, such changes seem to have originated most often from outside the local communities, in the larger regional, national, or global political economies, and to have begun in a very different, even highly artificial, demographic situation that effectively maintained a water abundance. These kinds of questions, however, are ultimately empirical ones that only a detailed ethnographic study can answer. Such a study must be as historical as possible and be concerned with explanation, rather than just with description and understanding, or with telling a story that is unique to one particular place. It must therefore be comparative, focusing on broadly similar landscapes where the drama of the commons is known to have taken place and yet led to significantly different outcomes.

A procedure for carrying out such a study has been presented here, along with an overview of the kind of results it can produce. There seems to be little doubt that this method for the controlled comparative reading of landscapes can be applied fruitfully to studies in other parts of the world, perhaps focusing on other kinds of "commons." Although that task has not yet been widely undertaken, hopefully it soon will be, so that our knowledge and understanding of perhaps the oldest of all human social dramas, and certainly one of the most significant, can be increased.

References

Appleby, Gordon. 1976. "Export Monoculture and Regional Social Structure in Puno, Peru." In *Regional Analysis*. Vol. 2, *Social Systems*, ed. Carol A. Smith, 291–308. New York: Academic Press.

Balée, William, ed. 1998. *Advances in Historical Ecology*. New York: Columbia University Press.

Bingham, Hiram. 1922. *Inca Land: Explorations in the Highlands of Peru*. New York: Houghton Mifflin.

Bromley, Daniel W., ed. 1992. *Making the Commons Work: Theory, Practice and Policy*. San Francisco: Institute for Contemporary Studies.

CEPES. 1984. "Ley de Aguas." *Informativo Legal Agrario, No. 18/19*. Lima: Centro Peruano de Estudios Sociales.

Cook, Noble David. 1975. *Tasa de la Visita General de Francisco de Toledo (1572)*. Lima: Universidad Mayor Nacional de San Marcos.

———. 1981. *Demographic Collapse: Indian Peru, 1520–1620*. New York: Cambridge University Press.

Crumley, Carole, ed. 1994. *Historical Ecology: Cultural Knowledge and Changing Landscapes*. Santa Fe: School of American Research Press.

Crumley, Carole. 2003. "Historical Ecology: New Paths toward Collaboration." Paper presented at the Conference on Urban Landscape Dynamics and Resource Use, Uppsala, Sweden.

Dolšak, Nives, and Elinor Ostrom, eds. 2003. *The Commons in the New Millennium: Challenges and Adaptations*. Cambridge, MA: MIT Press.

Earle, Timothy, and Terrence D'Altroy. 1989. "Political Economy of the Inka Empire: The Archaeology of Power and Finance." In *Archaeological Thought in America,* ed. C. C. Lamberg-Karlovsiky, 183–204. Cambridge: Cambridge University Press.

Egan, Dave, and Evelyn A. Howell, eds. 2001. *The Historical Ecology Handbook: A Restorationist's Guide to Reference Ecosystems*. Washington, DC: Island Press.

Flores-Galindo, Alberto. 1977. *Arequipa y el Sur Andino: Siglo XVIII*. Lima: Editorial Horizonte.

Fonseca, Cesar. 1983. "El Control Comunal del Agua en la Cuenca del Río Cañete." *Allpanchis* 19 (22.8): 61–74.

Garcilaso de la Vega, Inca. 1966 [1609, 1617]. *Comentarios Reales de los Incas*. Vols. 1 and 2, ed. H.V. Livermore. Austin: University of Texas Press.

Gelles, Paul. 1986. "Sociedades Hidraúlicas en los Andes: Algunas Perspectivas desde Huarochirí." *Allpanchis* 18 (27) 99–148. Cusco: Instituto de Pastoral Andina.

Gootenberg, Paul. 1991. "Population and Ethnicity in Early Republican Peru: Some Revisions." *Latin American Research Review* 26 (3): 109–57.

Guaman Poma de Ayala, Felipe. 1978 [1613]. *Letter to a King: A Peruvian Chief's Account of Life under the Incas and under Spanish Rule*. New York: Dutton.

Guillet, David. 1994. "Canal Irrigation and the State: The 1969 Water Law and Irrigation Systems in the Colca Valley of Southern Peru." In *Irrigation at High Altitudes: The Social Organization of Water Control Systems in the Andes*, ed. W. P. Mitchell and D. Guillet, 167–88. SLAA Publication Series, Vol. 12. Washington, DC: American Anthropological Association.

Hardin, G. 1968. "The Tragedy of the Commons." *Science* 162:1243–48.

Harrison, Simon. 2004. "Forgetful and Memorious Landscapes." *Social Anthropology* 12 (2): 135–51.

Hirsch, Eric, and Michael O'Hanlon, eds. 1995. *The Anthropology of Landscapes: Perspectives on Place and Space*. Oxford: Clarendon.

Hunt, Robert C. 1988. "Size and Structure of Authority in Canal Irrigation Systems." *Journal of Anthropological Research* 44 (4):335–55.

IASC. n.d. Digital Library of the Commons. International Association for the Study of the Commons. At www.iascp.org.

Mayer, Enrique. 1985. "Production Zones." In *Andean Ecology and Civilization*, ed. S. Masuda, I. Shimada, and C. Morris, 45–84. Tokyo: University of Tokyo Press.

Mayer, Enrique, and Cesar Fonseca. 1979. *Sistemas Agrarios en la Cuenca del Río Cañete*. Lima: Oficina Nacional para Evaluación de Recursos Naturales (ONERN).

McCay, Bonnie, and James Acheson, eds. 1987. *The Culture and Ecology of Communal Resources*. Tucson: University of Arizona Press.

Montoya, Rodrigo. 1980. *Capitalismo y No-Capitalismo en el Perú: Un Estudio de su Articulación en un Eje Regional*. Lima: Mosca Azul Editores.

Montoya, Rodrigo, María Silveira, and Felipe Lindoso. 1979. *Producción Parcelaria y Universo Ideológico: El Caso de Puquio*. Lima: Mosca Azul Editores.

National Research Council (NRC). 1986. *Proceedings of the Conference on Common Property Management*. Washington, DC: National Academy Press.

Netting, Robert. 1968. *Hill Farmers of Nigeria: Cultural Ecology of the Kofyar of the Jos Plateau*. Seattle: University of Washington Press.

Olsen, Mancur. 1965. *The Logic of Collective Action: Public Goods and the Theory of Groups*. Cambridge, MA: Harvard University Press.

Orlove, Benjamin S. 1977. *Alpacas, Sheep and Men: The Wool Export Economy and Regional Society in Southern Peru*. New York: Academic Press.

Ostrom, Elinor. 1986. "Issues of Definition and Theory: Some Conclusions and Hypotheses." In *Proceedings of the Conference on Common Property Management*, 599–616. Washington, DC: National Academy Press.

———. 1987. "Institutional Arrangements for Resolving the Commons Dilemma." In *The Culture and Ecology of Communal Resources*, ed. B. McCay and J. Acheson, 250–65. Tucson: University of Arizona Press.
———. 1990. *Governing the Commons: The Evolution of Institutions for Collective Action*. New York: Cambridge University Press.
———. 1992. *Crafting Institutions for Self-Governing Irrigation Systems*. San Francisco: Institute for Contemporary Studies Press.
———. 1998. "Reformulating the Commons." In *The Commons Revisited: An Americas Perspective*, ed. J. Burger, R. Norgaard, E. Ostrom, D. Policansky, and B. Goldstein, 279–86. Washington DC: Island Press
Ostrom, Elinor, T. Dietz, N. Dolsak, P. C. Stern, S. Stonich, and E. U. Weber, eds. 2002. *The Drama of the Commons. Committee on Human Dimensions of Global Change*. Washington, DC: National Academy Press.
Pasapera, Manuel S. 1902. *La Ley de Aguas con sus Antecedentes*. Lima: Imprenta y Libreria de San Pedro.
Santos-Granero, F. 1998. "Writing History in the Landscape: Space, Myth, and Ritual in Contemporary Amazonia." *American Anthropologist* 25:128–48.
Schlager, Edella, and Elinor Ostrom. 1992. "Property-Rights Regimes and Natural Resources: A Conceptual Analysis." *Land Economics* 68 (3): 249–62.
Smith, M. E. 1984. "The Triage of the Commons." Paper presented at the annual meeting of the Society for Applied Anthropology, Toronto.
Thompson, I. G., M. E. Mosely, J. F. Bolzan, and B. R. Koci. 1985. "A 1,500 Year Record of Tropical Precipitation from the Quelccaya Ice Cap." *Science* 229:971–73.
Trawick, Paul. 2001a. "Successfully Governing the Commons: Principles of Social Organization in an Andean Irrigation System." *Human Ecology* 29 (1): 1–25.
———. 2001b. "The Moral Economy of Water: Equity and Antiquity in the Andean Commons." *American Anthropologist* 103 (2): 361–79.
———. 2002. "Comedy and Tragedy in the Andean Commons." *Journal of Political Ecology* 9:5–68.
———. 2003. *The Struggle for Water in Peru: Comedy and Tragedy in the Andean Commons*. Palo Alto, CA: Stanford University Press.
Treacy, John. 1994. "Teaching Water: Hydraulic Management and Terracing in Corporaque, the Colca Valley, Peru." In *Irrigation at High Altitudes: The Social Organization of Water Control Systems in the Andes*, ed. W. P. Mitchell and D. Guillet, 99–114. SLAA Publication Series, Vol. 12. Washington, DC: American Anthropological Association.

4

Household Labor and Landscape Transformation in Ancient Mixteca Alta, Oaxaca, Mexico

VERÓNICA PÉREZ RODRÍGUEZ

ALL SOCIETIES MAKE AN IMPACT ON THE ENVIRONMENT either through planned action or unintended consequence. Much of this impact has been made in the name of food production, a task that has profound social, economic, political, and environmental implications. Human activity linked to food production can be studied archaeologically by looking at agricultural landscapes and their change through time. The mode and degree of landscape transformation, the purpose behind it, and how this transformation was achieved vary. The study of this variability provides invaluable information about ancient societies and their economies, sociopolitical organization, and environmental sophistication.

In this volume we explore the relationships between landscapes and human economies. Although the concept of landscape is a topic of ongoing discussion, I favor the definition that conceptualizes it as "the material representation of the relation between humans and the environment" (Crumley 1994: 6). I would add that landscapes also reflect human organization and the relationships among different groups of people. As this and other chapters in this volume illustrate, the landscape is not just the environment in which we live, but also the environment as it is perceived, used, understood, modified, and experienced through time (Anschuetz, Wilshusen, and Scheick 2001; Deetz 1990; Wilkinson 2003). Landscapes encompass the meanings, decisions, and actions of those who build, live in, and inherit them. They are palimpsests that reflect economic infrastructure, and long- and short-term changes in social, political, and religious views and practices. Landscapes reflect humanity and our history.

Through the study of landscapes, we can learn about the symbolic and ritual beliefs that have shaped the use and our understanding of a place, the sociopolitical systems involved in landscape creation, and the economies that have operated, modified, and at the same time depended on these landscapes. In this volume we focus on the economic dimensions of landscapes, but this is not disassociated from labor and social organization, political consequence, and ritual and personal uses and perceptions (see Pool and Cliggett in this volume). In this chapter I turn my attention to the terraced landscape of the Mixteca Alta region, in Oaxaca, Mexico. My work integrates regional archaeological data, excavation, and ethnography to learn about this landscape-transforming agricultural technique, the dramatic modification of the Mixtec landscape, and the social organization behind terrace use and construction.

I present an analysis of the spatial association of lama-bordo terraces and pre-Hispanic settlements that suggests that their initial construction predates the emergence of states. This would indicate that terracing might have originated in community-level initiatives, not requiring state intervention. New ethnographic and archaeological data on modern and Postclassic lama-bordos will be presented to provide a model for terrace building. The model illustrates how household-level actions and decisions can create complex agricultural landscapes.

On the Organization behind Landscapes

It has long been recognized that landscape transformation aimed at intensive agricultural production seemingly co-occurred in place and time with the emergence of states. In his hydraulic hypothesis, Wittfogel (1957) argued that the labor and organizational requirements of irrigation works acted as catalysts for the emergence of sociopolitical complexity. This hypothesis was favored by Armillas (1951, 1964), Millon (1957), Palerm and Wolf (1957), and Sanders, Parsons, and Santley (1979) for the valley of Mexico. In the valley of Oaxaca, research found that the Monte Albán state arose despite the lack of irrigation or other agricultural earthworks large enough to merit state organization, however (O'Brien et al. 1982: 210–11). Still, intensification features that create patterned landscapes automatically evoke the idea of a centralized state that organized the landscapes' construction.

Not all intensification features are equal. The anatomy of an irrigation system works to centralize control over the central resource, water, into the hands of a few people or nodes in the system. The flow of water cannot only be controlled, but must also be managed to avoid salinization and flooding (Scarborough 2003). Experimental projects to revitalize raised-field agriculture in the Titicaca basin have shown that management is perhaps the single most important factor that can determine agricultural success (Kolata et al. 1996). On the other hand, nonirrigated agricultural features, terraces, have always been harder to characterize in terms of their labor requirements. Nonirrigated terraces are heterarchical in morphology. As long as terraces are maintained and located in places where rain falls, production may continue. And although maintaining the stability of terrace walls located downslope helps protect those higher up, terraces can be independently constructed and maintained if sufficient labor is available.

Anthropological research on ancient and modern anthropogenic landscapes is beginning to explore the different forms of social and economic organization that can and could have created complex landscapes previously attributed to the state (e.g., Dunning and Beach 1994; Netting 1993; Scarborough 2003). Agricultural landscapes in Bali and Ifugao provide interesting examples where both kinds of agricultural landscapes, irrigated and terraced, come together to create some of the most awe-inspiring places in the world (Conklin 1980; Lansing 1991). Study of these landscapes and the way they function has shown that they can be built and effectively managed through highly patterned but self-organized ritual and economic communal and household behavior. Recent evidence coming from the Hohokam and Maya regions suggests that irrigation systems may operate through communal or heterarchical forms of organization (Dunning and Beach 1994; Hunt et al. 2005; Scarborough 2003; Scarborough, Valdez Jr., and Dunning 2003). In the Classic Maya case, this happened within state-level polities. In South America, Inka terraces, often attributed to the state, were constructed as part of a macroregional program that dramatically changed entire regions. But, after careful study it has been found that this transformation was actually enacted by local and collective socioeconomic groups, *allyus* (Brundage 1967; Davies 1995; Moseley 1992; Wittfogel 1957). In these cases we see an intricate interaction, not always hierarchical, between communities, households, and states. In all mentioned cases the results are impressive engineered agricultural landscapes.

Taking a top-down or bottom-up approach limits our understanding of how the economies and politics of intensive agriculture and landscape transformation functioned (Janusek and Kolata 2004). The reality is a complex interplay of local initiatives and organization, state-level demands, household capabilities and strategies, and environmental opportunities and limitations, along with climate, crops, and genetic variation, and finally, engineering, hydraulic, architectural, and agricultural knowledge. Teasing out the particulars of just one archaeological case study can take a lifetime of work, but as researchers we must at least attempt to do it.

This chapter is about terracing. Terracing transforms the face of the land, dramatically. The amount of labor required for terrace construction can easily compare to other ancient achievements of construction that have received more attention, such as pyramids. Although not all feats of ancient construction are appreciated equally, we are becoming increasingly conscious of the amount of labor and planning that goes into agricultural landscapes (Erickson 2003; Kowalewski et al., forthcoming). In the Mixteca Alta region we find an impressive terraced landscape that is currently in danger of disappearing due to erosion and the abandonment of ancient ways of life. How did the Mixtec landscape change over time to become what it is today? How and when did slopes become terraces? And what relationship did terrace construction and expansion have with the rise of states in the Mixteca Alta? This chapter explores these questions.

The Mixtec Landscape

In the Mixteca Alta the main landscape signature is terracing, which can be either contour or lama-bordo (fig. 4.1). Contour terraces follow the shape and contour of the hill on which they are built and can perform a residential or agricultural function. Lama-bordos are series of exclusively agricultural terraces built in drainages where eroding soils from adjacent hills continuously fill the terraces with new sediments, creating some of the most fertile lands in Oaxaca (Spores 1969; M. Kirkby 1972). Given the clear economic and agricultural importance of lama-bordo terraces, this study will focus on them.

By the sixteenth century the Mixteca Alta was described as a rich agricultural region that has since been transformed by rampant erosion. The richness of the pre-Hispanic Mixtec landscape was not only natural but was also built and maintained. Its maintenance virtually stopped as a result of post-European-contact population loss and modern-day out-migration. Lama-bordo terracing was an effective and long-lasting technological innovation that mitigated erosion and supported dense populations in ancient times. Their construction had previously been attributed to the rise of urban centers and states in the Terminal Formative. In later periods these agricultural resources were central to state economic power. Given its central importance to civilization, it is critical that this agricultural method be examined and recorded.

I present the results of an analysis that looked at the proximity of lama-bordo terraces and human settlement throughout the pre-Hispanic sequence. The results show interesting patterns and periods of expansion in lama-bordo use and construction, mainly that lama-bordos first appear in

Figure 4.1 Aerial view of lama-bordo terracing, which is located in the drainages surrounding a Ramos and Las Flores phase terraced hilltop site in San Vicente Nuñu.

association with preurban Late Formative settlements. This early development suggests that lama-bordos might have been initially constructed by communities or households, not states. I summarize recent ethnographic and excavation data from a Postclassic lama-bordo terrace and provide a model of lama-bordo terrace construction.

Methodology

The data presented are from a regional survey of the Mixteca Alta whose primary purpose was to record pre-Hispanic settlements (Balkansky et al. 2000). The survey also located other culturally relevant features, including lama-bordos. The features were recorded on topographic maps that were later digitized. We also obtained orthophotos and a digital elevation model (DEM) to build a GIS data set that contained all the settlement and terrace data. I reclassified the DEM to create aspect and slope surfaces of the natural terrain. From aerial photos I digitized all the visible lama-bordo terracing and checked the location and extension of field-recorded lama-bordos. Last, we digitized the geological map of the region.

I integrated the field-recorded, digitized, and digitally obtained cultural and geographical data to create maps that show the spatial distribution of lama-bordos and settlements, as well as information on geological areas, aspect, slope, and overall characteristics of the terrain. The analysis I present consisted of examining the location and distribution of lama-bordos in relation to different natural and cultural parameters:

1. I examined the distribution of lama-bordos in relation to human settlement through the pre-Hispanic sequence. I identified the number of settlements spatially associated with lama-bordo terraces (0, 250, 500, 750, and 1,000 m) and determined the various time periods with which lama-bordos are associated.
2. I examined lama-bordo distributions in relation to the aspect and slope characteristics of the terrain. Aspect pertains to the direction in which a slope is facing: north, northeast, east, southeast, south, southwest, west, northwest, and flat terrain. I reclassified the terrain coverage according to the degree of slope of the terrain from 0° to 90°.
3. I examined the distribution of lama-bordos with respect to the geology of the region.

By overlaying the lama-bordo coverage onto the aspect, slope, and geological maps I obtained information about the physical characteristics of the terrain on which lama-bordos were built. The distribution of settlements and lama-bordos through various time periods suggests interesting patterns of periods of growth and lama-bordo construction that correspond to different stages of sociopolitical transformation and development in the Mixteca.

More on Lama-Bordos

Oaxaca has been an important region for the study of sociopolitical complexity and the adoption of agriculture. In the Mixteca Alta the main method of agricultural intensification was terracing, specifically, lama-bordos (fig. 4.1). Lama-bordos were first described by Spores (1969) and were later studied by M. Kirkby (1972), who found that lama-bordos can produce up to two tons of maize per hectare. Although this is a ton less than what a hectare of *chinampa* can produce (Brannan 1971), it is half a ton more than what irrigated piedmont agriculture can produce in the valley of Oaxaca (A. Kirkby 1973). If we consider that two tons of maize could feed a family of five for an entire year (Brannan 1971), we can understand what a hectare of lama-bordo land is worth to any household.

While conducting a regional settlement survey of the Mixteca Alta, we recorded and mapped hundreds of settlements and lama-bordo terraces. Some were still in use and most were still preventing erosion even five hundred to two thousand years after their construction and abandonment (Balkansky et al. 2000). This longevity, despite the lack of maintenance, demonstrates that this agricultural technique was effective in mitigating erosion and creating flat land for a long time. Even though the Mixteca was a rich agricultural land in the sixteenth century, today it is an eroded region. As in other places in the Americas (Fisher et al. 2003; Erickson 2003), population loss after Spanish contact and the abandonment of agricultural landscapes that heavily depended on human labor and maintenance led to substantial erosion and soil loss.

By using GIS tools and obtaining descriptive statistics on the main physical characteristics of areas covered by lama-bordo terracing, I found that lama-bordos are effective in creating flat land. Most lama-bordos fall in terrain where slopes are no greater than 25°–30°. In fact, 62 percent of lama-bordos fall in areas where the terrain does not exceed a 10° slope, even though areas around them are steep slopes that span from the high peaks to the low valleys (table 4.1).

Lama-bordos may be found facing all cardinal directions (table 4.2). While the most common directions for slopes to face were northeast, north, northwest, west, and southwest, aspect direction could vary according to

Table 4.1. Percentage of Lama-bordo (LB) Terrace Areas Found on 0° to >30° Slope

LB location slope	
Slope degrees	**% LB coverage**
0°–10°	62
10°–15°	25
15°–20°	10
20°–30°	2
>30°	0.17

subregion or valley. This suggests that lama-bordo placement may be more a function of local topography, microclimate, and other environmental conditions than a conscious decision to face a particular direction for ideological reasons. Other local conditions that may have determined lama-bordo placement could have been water availability in a particular drainage and location of favorable soils or constant sunlight, not to mention rain shadow effects that change from valley to valley.

The overlay of lama-bordo data on a geological raster coverage showed that lama-bordos are located mostly within five geological zones, out of seventeen present in the region (table 4.3). These are Lower Tertiary sandstone-conglomerate, Oligocene-Miocene andesite, Lower Tertiary siltstone-sandstone, Lower Cretaceous limestone, and Lower Cretaceous limestone-shale. Two of these geological zones, Lower Tertiary sandstone-conglomerate and Lower Tertiary siltstone-sandstone, are also soil and rock types favored for agriculture and pre-Hispanic occupation. About 50 percent of pre-Hispanic settlements are located in these geological areas (Ren 2005, personal communication). These soils correspond with the Yanhuitlan bed formation, which M. Kirkby (1972) argued was the most favorable for agriculture. Ancient farmers not only sought these soils, but also created a way to access them on high slopes through terracing.

Dating Lama-Bordo Terraces

Dating terraces has been problematic not only in Mesoamerica but in other famously terraced regions such as the Andes (Erickson 1994). Thus far only one lama-bordo terrace has been archaeologically excavated in Oaxaca, at the Postclassic site of Nicayuju in the municipality of San Juan Teposcolula (Pérez Rodríguez 2003). Beyond this excavation, dating has relied mostly on spatial association with archaeological sites that were in turn dated by surface artifacts. When a particular lama-bordo terrace is associated with archaeological sites dating to several time periods, the feature can most conservatively be dated to the latest time period; however, dating the feature to earlier phases is more dubious. Dating these features based on their spatial

Table 4.2. Percentage of Lama-bordo (LB) Areas According to Aspect Location

LB location aspect	
Aspect	**% LB coverage**
Northeast	13.25
North	14.39
Northwest	15.77
East	9.21
Southeast	8.84
South	8.35
Southwest	12.78
West	14.89
Flat	2.50

Table 4.3. Geological Zones That Showed the Greatest Number of Lama-bordo (LB) Terraces

Top ranks	All LB	#
Geology	**Type**	**LB**
I	Lower Tertiary sandstone-conglomerate	194
II	Oligocene-Miocene andesite	118
III	Lower Tertiary siltstone-sandstone	116
IV	Lower Cretaceous limestone	85

association with habitation sites is not ideal, but it is the best method that can be used until a systematic study of lama-bordo terraces is undertaken.

Using the site and lama-bordo spatial distribution data, I identified the lama-bordos that are directly adjacent to settlements and sorted them by time period. Table 4.4 shows that all lama-bordos associated with Early/Middle Cruz period sites are also associated with other time periods, mostly Natividad. In contrast, almost a third of the lama-bordos associated with Late Cruz settlements could date solely to this time period. The number of lama-bordos directly adjacent to Las Flores settlements is double the number of those in Ramos, but it was in Natividad times that the pattern of lama-bordo and site association became most widespread.

Site and Lama-Bordo Associations through Time

The analysis I present consisted of quantifying the number of sites that were spatially associated with lama-bordos and sorting them by time period. I counted direct association, when sites were directly adjacent to lama-bordos, and more distant associations within 500 and 1,000 m. Table 4.5 and figure 4.2 compare the total number of sites, by time period, that were associated with lama-bordos (Pérez Rodríguez 2004).

Table 4.4. Lama-bordo (LB) Terraces Directly Adjacent to Settlements According to Phase

Associated phase	Total # LB	1 phase association	E/M Cruz	L Cruz	Ramos	Las Flores	Natividad
E/M Cruz (1200–800 BC)	7	0	---	4	0	2	6
Late Cruz (800–300 BC)	30	8	4	---	1	4	22
Ramos (300 BC–AD 300)	35	15	0	1	---	15	12
Las Flores (AD 300–800)	61	17	2	4	15	---	36
Natividad (AD 800–1521)	151	90	6	22	12	36	---

Table 4.5. Number and Percentage of Sites, by Phase, Found in Proximity to Lama-bordos

Phase	Total #	0 m		500 m		1,000 m	
	of sites	# sites	% sites	# sites	% sites	# sites	% sites
E/M Cruz	51	7	14	29	57	42	82
Late Cruz	213	21	10	120	56	151	71
Ramos	154	20	13	84	55	114	74
Las Flores	344	40	12	157	46	236	69
Natividad	848	88	10	399	47	580	68

For the Early/Middle Cruz phase (1200–800 BC)[1] we recorded fifty-one sites. Seven of these, or 14 percent, had lama-bordos directly adjacent to them; however, in every case the lama-bordo in question was also associated with settlement of another time period. Early/Middle Cruz sites were hard to identify because of their antiquity and superimposed later occupations. Fifty-seven percent and 82 percent of Early/Middle Cruz sites have lama-bordos at 500 and 1,000 m distance respectively. I argue that these associations could be the result of Postclassic occupation.

Out of 213 Late Cruz sites (800–300 BC), twenty-one, or 10 percent, have adjacent lama-bordos and up to 55 percent are located within 500 m of a lama-bordo (fig. 4.3). For Late Cruz we find that 26 percent of adjacent lama-bordos are associated solely with this time period. The number of settlements found in association with lama-bordo systems clearly increased from the previous time period. Although many of these lama-bordos possibly date to the Classic and Postclassic periods as well, there is evidence

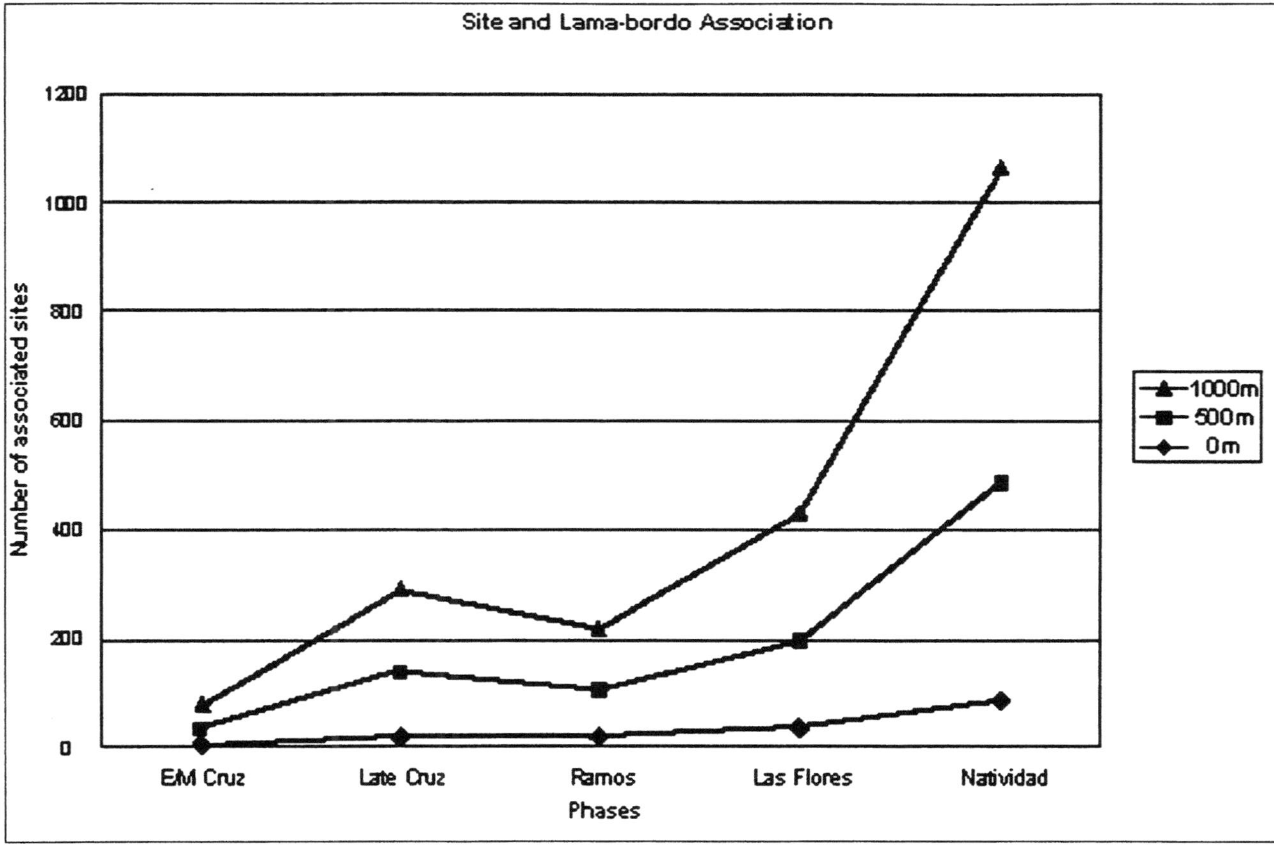

Figure 4.2 Graph showing the percentage of sites associated with lama-bordo terraces by phase.

to suggest that at least 26 percent of Late Cruz–associated lama-bordos may date exclusively to this time period, marking the beginning of their construction.

For the Ramos phase (300 BC–AD 300) we recorded 154 sites (fig. 4.3). Twenty of these, or 13 percent, have lama-bordos directly adjacent to or within them. The pattern of about 55 percent of sites located within 500 m of lama-bordos remained constant from the previous time period, although in actual numbers there is a clear increase from the previous time period (fig. 4.2). Considering the overall reduction in number, not extent, of Ramos sites, these numbers suggest a more clustered pattern of association between sites and lama-bordos. It would also seem that larger, more densely packed urban Ramos settlements built more and new lama-bordos nearby. Perhaps Ramos inhabitants may have had to walk a shorter distance to their lama-bordos than earlier Late Cruz inhabitants. This pattern is in keeping with the regional move upslope, to fortified hill towns, during the Ramos phase. Only one of the Ramos-associated lama-bordos is also associated with Late Cruz settlement, suggesting that Ramos-phase lama-bordos and settlements were a true departure from previous residential patterns. These transformations evident for the Ramos phase go along with the emergence of the first states and urban centers in this region.

For the Las Flores phase (AD 300–800) we recorded 344 sites; about 10 percent of them had lama-bordos directly adjacent to or within them (fig. 4.4). Of the total number of lama-bordos directly associated with Las Flores sites, 28 percent of them are associated solely with this time period. Forty-six percent of Las Flores sites have lama-bordos within 500 m, and 69 percent within 1 km. Although this pattern marks a decrease in the total percentage of associated lama-bordos from the previous time period, in actuality it was also an increase in the total number of lama-bordos and associated sites. On the other hand, this decrease in the Classic period indicates a shift in the intensity of lama-bordo use and construction, which may be related to the periods of abandonment and settlement reorganization that marked the transition in and out of the Las Flores phase (Balkansky et al. 2000). This issue must be looked at more closely in the future. For now, the analysis shows that during the Classic period there is a change in settlement location and intensity of terrace construction.

We recorded 848 Natividad sites (AD 800–1521; fig. 4.4). During this phase there was a transformation in the number and percentage of sites associated with lama-bordos. Sixty percent of Natividad-associated lama-bordos are exclusively found in that time period alone (fig. 4.5). Ten percent of Natividad sites, or eighty-eight, have lama-bordos within or directly

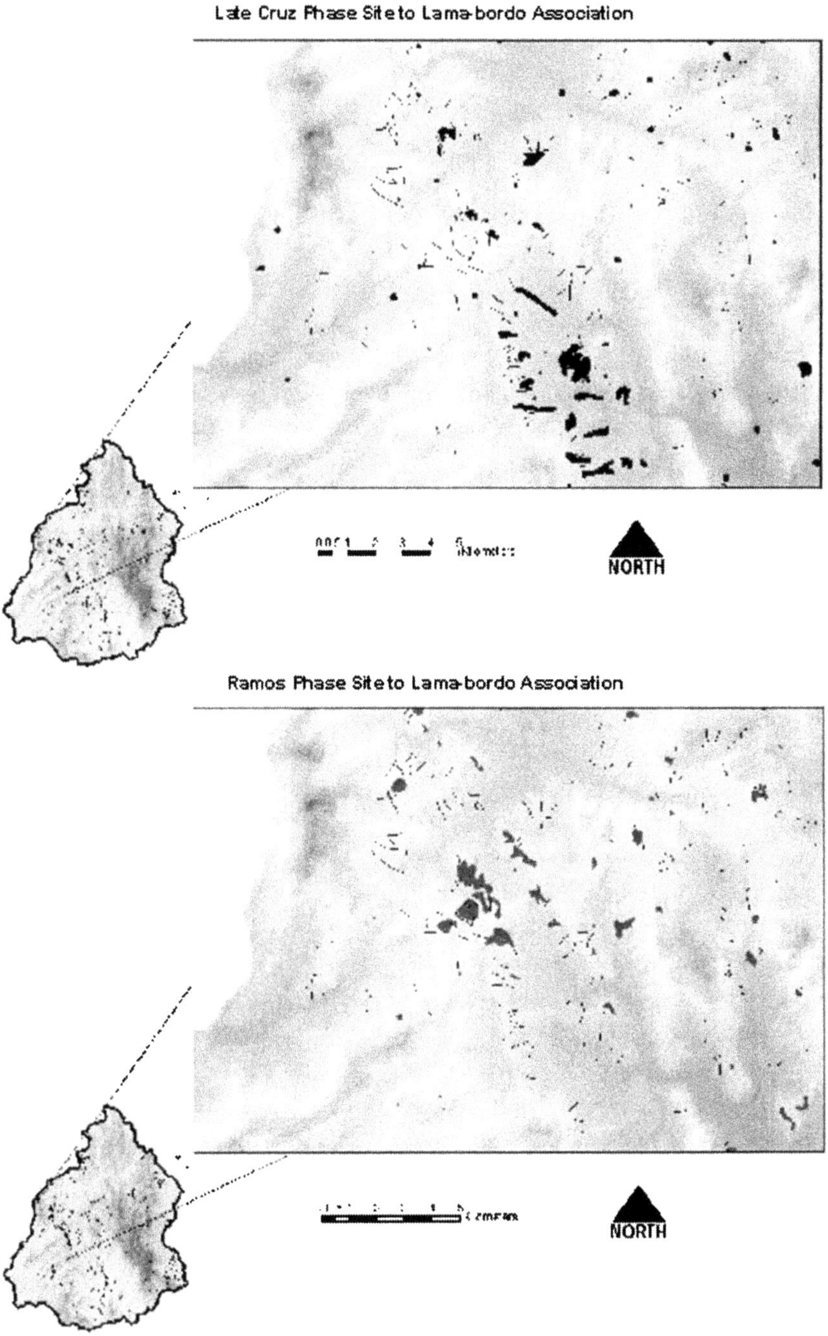

Figure 4.3 Map showing the regional distribution of settlement and lama-bordo terraces for the Late Cruz and Ramos phases.

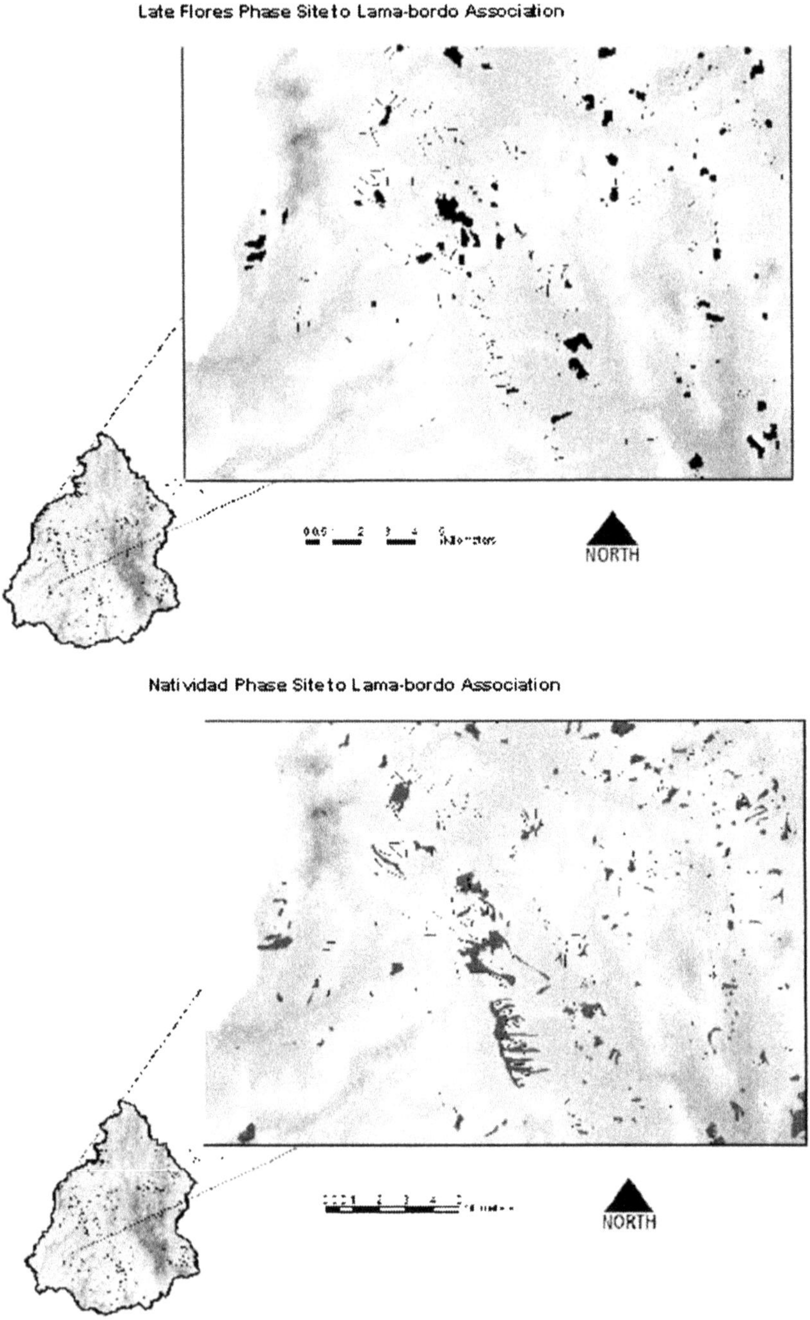

Figure 4.4 Map showing the regional distribution of settlement and lama-bordo terraces for the Las Flores and Natividad phases.

adjacent to them; 47 percent are within 500 m; and 68 percent are within a kilometer of lama-bordos. Although the total percentages are similar to those dating from the Las Flores phase, the total number of lama-bordos and settlements increased dramatically. In addition, the most plausible date for these sites and features is the Postclassic, rather than the Classic period.

Another important point to consider is that Postclassic settlements, unlike earlier ones, sometimes extended for kilometers on continuous hills and drainages. A single settlement that spanned several hills, surrounding several lama-bordo terraces, counted only as one in this analysis. If I were to use a different set of parameters to define the limits of sites, the numbers and percentages of lama-bordo-associated settlements would increase dramatically. A visual inspection of settlement and lama-bordo distribution maps shows how extensive Postclassic settlement was and how lama-bordos are found in the majority of cases in nearby drainages. Clearly this is a time when the lama-bordo pattern was at its fullest.

The Postclassic was also the time of the *cacicazgos*; these were pre-Hispanic kingdoms, or city-states, that ruled the Mixteca up to colonial times. During this time the arts, agricultural production, population, and market systems boomed. In a previous study on the distribution of lama-bordos in relation to Postclassic settlements I found that Postclassic settlement clustered around agricultural lands, valley-bottom lands, and lama-bordos (Pérez Rodríguez 2001). In that study I also defined, through ethnohistorical documentation, the territories of Postclassic cacicazgos and compared the densities of lama-bordos within and outside these areas. I found that cacicazgo territories have two to four times more lama-bordos than other areas, suggesting that these terraces and their production were crucial to these polities and their economies.

Ethnographic Lama-Bordo Construction

Lama-bordo terraces were crucial to pre-Hispanic societies and their economies, but how were lama-bordos constructed? I interviewed modern San Juan Teposcolula farmers and elders about lama-bordo terraces; these are people who have had firsthand experience in terrace or house construction. They had much to say about how these terraces were built. They called lama-bordo terraces *retenes*, and according to the interviewees, lama-bordos or *retenes* are easy to build. Their construction starts by getting a family work group together. Within the work group there must be at least four men and two women; the women's job is to go to the work site to cook, feed the family, and help carry the brush and stone for construction. During the rainy season the family goes to the drainage where the terrace

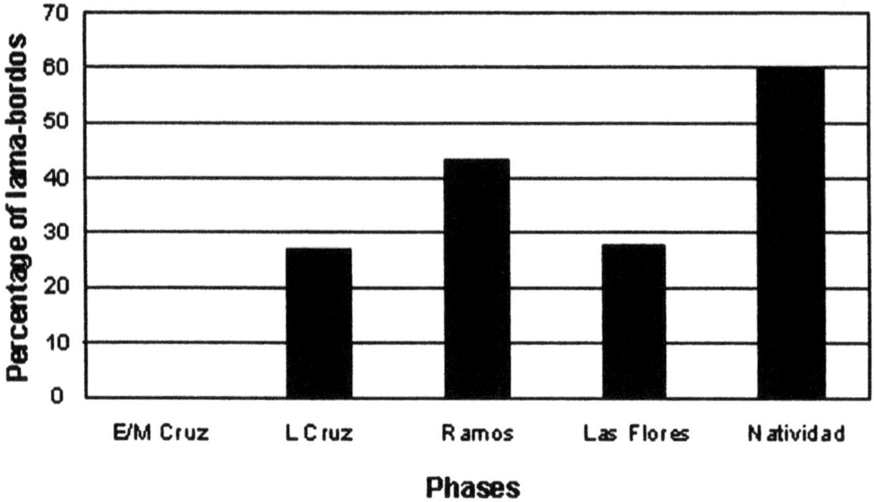

Figure 4.5 Graph showing the percentage of lama-bordos associated with settlement that dates to a single phase only.

will be built. They pile rocks a meter high and wide and then cut brush and place it right behind the rock pile so that the incoming water does not knock down the rock pile wall. The family can do this work in a day—a hard day's work. Then, they wait for a torrential downpour—these usually occur during the summer season. The runoff after the rain rapidly fills the terrace with new sediment. According to modern farmers, they can build a 2-m-deep terrace within a couple of rainy seasons.

Lama-Bordo Terrace Excavation

I excavated a lama-bordo terrace associated with a Postclassic rural settlement that was part of the cacicazgo of Teposcolula (fig. 4.6). The objective was to learn about lama-bordo construction and test the accuracy of using surface remains and site association for dating these features. Detailed descriptions of the excavation are in my dissertation (Pérez Rodríguez 2003). The excavated lama-bordo was in the site of Nicayuju (SJT 4), a site that was originally recorded by Stiver (2001), who described it as a 53-ha site with dozens of residential terraces and four lama-bordo terrace systems. She argued that the residential settlement of Nicayuju along with that of the adjacent hill of Diquinó was the largest population center in the Teposcolula polity.

Nicayuju's setting is enviable for agriculture. It is near flat land, a resource that is a true commodity in the highlands, and there are many

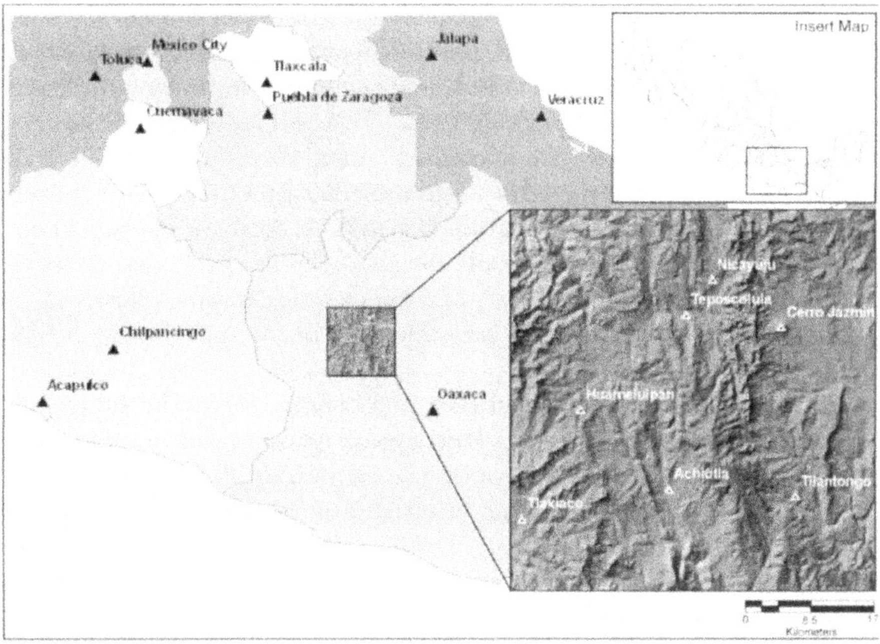

Figure 4.6 Map showing the location of the Postclassic cacicazgo of Teposcolula, the polity where the site of Nicayuju was located, and the regional distribution of pre-Hispanic settlement within the area that was surveyed.

springs nearby. Today this area is a source of drinking water and is used for agriculture. The site shows little evidence of public architecture. Only one to possibly three 1–1.5-m high mounds survive on the hilltops of Nicayuju and the surrounding hills. These mounds are not conclusively civic-ceremonial and may have served as high-status domestic structures. As such, Nicayuju is considered a rural settlement with little prominence in the political hierarchy. Given the site's setting and sociopolitical context I argue that the results of this study are representative of common rural towns in Postclassic cacicazgos.

I mapped the entire extent of pre-Hispanic occupation at Nicayuju and adjacent hills and drainages, and took surface collections. Then I excavated two houses and one lama-bordo terrace, and sampled over twenty-one terraces throughout the various sectors of the site. The lama-bordo terrace chosen for excavation was located in a fairly intact, broad drainage directly south of the main hill of Nicayuju. The drainage, Nduatijubacu, was not in use, but despite its abandonment the terraces were well preserved. Spores (1969) has noted that lama-bordo terrace systems grow from the top down. Earlier terraces are found near the hilltops, and new ones are farther down, near the valley floor. For learning about the "birth" of a terrace system, terraces found higher up are more informative because they have a longer history. The excavated terrace at Nduatijubacu was near the hilltop. Its terrace wall was entirely complete.

The lama-bordo excavation consisted of a 16-m-long-by-1-m-wide trench. It dissected half the terrace and provided a profile view of the terrace and retaining-wall construction (fig. 4.7). In total we opened 11 m^2, containing 21.12 m^3 of terrace fill, in five different excavation units. We excavated every other unit to keep the trench stable and this allowed us to dig up to 3.15 m, until we hit sterile deposits in the unit directly behind the terrace wall.

In the lama-bordo we found only 103 ceramic sherds, no lithics, and no modern or colonial materials. Postclassic diagnostics were found only in the top two layers. Of those, seventy-five came from the top layer, which most likely represents the eroding materials from the Postclassic residential terraces adjacent to the drainage. Lower sediment layers revealed small, undiagnostic rough Tan body sherds and bowl rims that were undoubtedly pre-Hispanic. Given the low density of ceramic materials in the terrace fill we can say that the ancient people did not live on these terraces and that artifacts most likely were washed down from adjacent residential areas.

The stratigraphy showed that the terrace was filled by multiple erosion events in which sediments washed down from the adjoining hills. The terrace fill was not brought in by people, packed, or leveled behind the terrace wall. Instead, the excavation profile still preserves the natural slope that the sediment layers took as they were deposited. Strata were thicker toward the center of the terrace where more material was deposited and tapered at the sides.

The terrace wall construction consisted of informal rock piling with a more formal wall facade on its downhill side. The wall facade stood 1 m high above the surface level. As we reached lower levels behind the terrace wall, 2.4 m below, we saw that the terrace wall began as a wide rock pile of small- (5–10 cm) to medium-sized (10–30 cm) rocks. Later, the builders added to the rock pile, making the terrace wall grow as the terrace gradually filled up with each rain. The rock pile wall was wider at the base, tapered at the top, and finished with a formal rock facade on the front. The rocks used to build the facade were larger, 40–50 cm, and made of locally available stone that was uncut and unfitted. Rocks were simply piled up without mortar.

The lama-bordo excavation tested the ethnographic model of "retén building" and the results so far correspond with the model. The lama-bordo

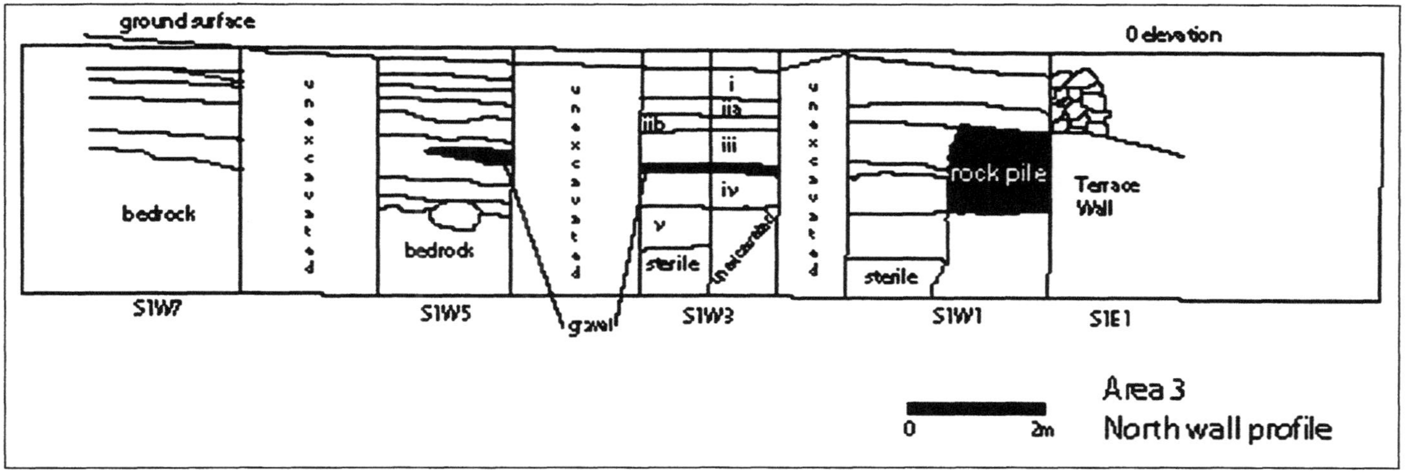

Figure 4.7 Lama-bordo trench excavation, north wall profile. Nduatijubacu drainage sector of the site of Nicayuju in San Juan Teposcolula, Oaxaca.

terraces at Nicayuju could have been built through gradual accretion with household labor, as suggested by the ethnographic model. However, additional lama-bordo data must become available to test this proposition.

Discussion

From the study of the regional distribution of sites and lama-bordos, several patterns emerged. First, this analysis proved to be very useful in revealing a possible initial date for lama-bordo terrace construction. A small number of lama-bordos are directly adjacent to Early/Middle Cruz sites; however, all these features are also associated with other time periods, notably the Postclassic, thus making this early date unlikely for the construction of the lama-bordos. But, it was the Late Cruz period (800–300 BC) to which I first attributed a pattern where about 10 percent of all sites were adjacent to or within a short distance of lama-bordos, and for the first time up to a third of these lama-bordos could be attributed (through spatial association) solely to the Late Cruz period.

Although it has been argued that lama-bordo construction was the product of the urban transformation that swept the Mixteca Alta in the Ramos period (Spores 1969), it appears that the pattern of lama-bordo construction may have predated the establishment of the first states and urban centers in the region. This would suggest that initial lama-bordo construction may not have been a function of state-level sociopolitical organization, but perhaps of household and community decision making and innovation in the face of increasing population and resource scarcity, and, after the rise of states, of growing social complexity and tribute demands.

As a departure from previous work on the subject, I argue that site and lama-bordo association in Ramos times may have been simply a continuation of a preestablished pattern of terrace construction and not a consequence of state involvement. Early states and urban centers may simply have tapped into an already established working system of agricultural production that had its roots in household and community "self-organizing," if I may use Lansing's (1991) terms. Ramos states, however, did intensify and expand the use and construction of a known agricultural method, lama-bordo terracing, and took it to a new level.

This assertion is significant because in the tradition of Wittfogel (1957), it has been argued that lama-bordos played a key role in the emergence of sociopolitical complexity in the Mixteca (Spores 1969). They have been considered to be either catalysts of social change or the direct product of state-level initiatives in the face of increasing population. It has also been argued that lama-bordo terracing was an innovative response to a need to secure food production within the defensive walls of the newly founded urban cores.

If regional lama-bordo distributions suggest that they may predate states by as much as five hundred years, and if excavation and ethnographic data illustrate how these terraces may be constructed without state-level involvement, then lama-bordos may not have been solely responsible for the emergence of social complexity. Instead, they may have been instrumental in supporting emergent urban populations and state-level institutions that simply adopted an already existing strategy for food production in the highlands. Further research will be required to test this statement. For now, however, I wish to open the door to the possibility that Mixtec social complexity developed as the result of other factors that had little to do with the planning, organizational, or labor requirements of lama-bordo terracing.

Ramos settlements did, however, mark a dramatic shift from previous occupations in terms of location and in the full adoption of lama-bordo terracing as an integral part of the urban pattern and the agricultural economy. Ramos-period societies built more and larger lama-bordos, many originating within the monumental sectors of each settlement. Clearly this expansion in terrace use and construction was linked to a need to support emergent state-level societies and a growing population that was living in a more clustered and urban pattern. Some of the most impressive lama-bordo systems I have seen have been associated with Ramos settlements; the main lama-bordo system found in Monte Negro stands out in my mind.

While a few urban centers outlasted periods of regional transformation, most settlements did not make a continuous transition into the Classic period (Balkansky et al. 2000). It is perhaps due to this difficult transition into smaller, more local Classic polities that we see a decrease in the percentage of lama-bordo–associated sites for this time period. Although the proven method of lama-bordo agriculture was known, sociopolitical uncertainty, which was evident in the settlement record, would have made the expansion of lama-bordo terracing, especially that located away from defensible locations, difficult. Still, although there was a slight decrease in the percentage of sites found within 500 m of terraces between the Ramos and the Las Flores and Natividad phases, the total number of lama-bordos continuously increased, as did the number of sites and people.

Last, in the Postclassic phase we see a marked increase in lama-bordo construction. For the first time up to 60 percent of Natividad-associated terraces are linked to this time period alone. Additional analyses of the density of lama-bordo terracing in and outside ethnohistorically defined cacicazgo territories further attest to the importance of this agricultural technology in cacicazgo society and economy. This boom in lama-bordo use and construction comes at a time of population increase and the implementation of a political system, the cacicazgo, which, at least according to ethnohistorical records, made tribute demands on the population. I suggest that the shift to a more intense use of lama-bordo terrace agriculture stemmed from a rise in population that was accompanied by an increase in resource scarcity and, later on, tribute demands coming from the state. The state involvement in lama-bordo use and construction may have been indirect given that ethnographic and excavation data suggest that Postclassic terraces could have been built through the accretion of household and community labor and planning. Postclassic polities simply tapped into an already established, self-running system, the same way Ramos-period states did. However, state demands undoubtedly fomented an even greater use and construction of this ingenious form of agricultural production.

Conclusion

As reflections of humanity, landscapes reveal clues about the technological abilities, labor capabilities, economic demands, social organization, and cultural perceptions of those who built and lived in them. This chapter, like others in this volume, focuses on landscapes of production in order to learn about ancient societies and economies. The study I present illustrates how complex and seemingly patterned engineered landscapes of production can be locally and communally constructed and run in a manner that can be successful. Other contributions in this volume, such as those by Trawick and Earle and Doyel, reach similar conclusions by looking at the highly patterned irrigated landscapes of the Andes and Hawaii. While no one questions Wittfogel's assertion that irrigation involves a set of unique organizational demands having to do with canal maintenance and water allocation, ethnographic and historical data from around the world provide models for how households and communities effectively built and managed engineered landscapes previously attributed to states.

The integration of regional survey, excavation, and ethnographic data on lama-bordos provides information on this landscape-transforming agricultural technique that was central to Mixtec civilization. New ethnographic data from modern farmers provides a model for lama-bordo construction, and excavation data from a Postclassic lama-bordo coincides with the ethnographic model for terrace building. Still, the data available so far comes from a single terrace. More work is needed to confirm this initial statement and I am currently working toward that goal. For now, the conjunction of these lines of research provides an initial, testable framework that can be used to conceptualize how preurban communities may have originally created the agricultural terracing technology that would later support states.

In this chapter I suggest that community and household labor and decision making transformed the Mixtec landscape through the construction of terraces, and that the Mixtec case is perhaps not as unusual as previously thought. Ethnographic and historical research in regions such as Ifugao, Bali, the Andes, and Hawaii has shown how households and cooperating work groups can create and continuously successfully manage complex agricultural and hydraulic landscapes (Conklin 1980; Lansing 1991; Trawick and Earle and Doyel, this volume). In the Southeast Asian examples individual households work either alone or as cooperating groups that are directed through communal and, in the case of Bali, temple institutions. The results are terracing and hydraulic agroecosystems that are far more complex than those of the Mixteca Alta. On the other hand, research on the Mesopotamian landscape, often associated with Wittfogel's hydraulic hypothesis, has suggested that the complex systems of channels and footpaths associated with early urban centers may be the result of hundreds of years of individual action and decision making (Ur 2004; Wilkinson 2003). The fact that these small actions can create a patterned landscape may be due to shared traditional practices and environmental constraints that allow only a limited number of possible responses.

Agricultural production and landscape transformation in peasant farming communities are directed and informed by traditional environmental knowledge that has been tested and passed down through generations. Peasant farmers are highly committed to their lands; the lands are the farmers' livelihood and patrimony and as such the farmers are more likely to consider the future consequences of any decision or action taken (Conklin 1980; Lansing 1991; Netting 1993). The combination of these factors results in very sophisticated and effective agricultural practices and landscapes. Although this volume focuses on the study of ancient landscapes to learn about the past, the study of them may also have important implications for present and future farming communities. Today and in the future we should investigate not only agricultural landscapes, but also the environmental knowledge required for their creation and effective management, because it is perhaps this knowledge that is most at risk of disappearing.

Note

1. All dates are in uncalibrated radiocarbon years.

References

Anschuetz, Kurt F., Richard H. Wilshusen, and Cherie L. Scheick. 2001. "An Archaeology of Landscapes: Perspectives and Directions." *Journal of Archaeological Research* 9:157–211.

Armillas, Pedro. 1951. "Tecnología, formaciones socio-económicas y religión en Mesoamérica." In *The Civilizations of Ancient America, XXIXth International Congress of Americanists*. Chicago: University of Chicago Press.

———. 1964. "Hydraulic Civilizations." *UNESCO Courier* 17 (7–8): 60–62.

Balkansky, Andrew K., Stephen A. Kowalewski, Verónica Pérez Rodríguez, Thomas J. Pluckhahn, Charlotte A. Smith, Laura R. Stiver, Dmitri Beliaev, John F. Chamblee, Verenice Y. Heredia Espinoza, and Roberto Santos Pérez. 2000. "Archaeological Survey in the Mixteca Alta of Oaxaca, Mexico." *Journal of Field Archaeology* 27 (4): 365–89.

Brannan, Curtiss. 1971. "Modern Oaxacan Agriculture and Prehispanic Mesoamerican Subsistence Systems." Manuscript on file, Department of Anthropology, University of Texas, Austin.

Brundage, Burr Cartwright. 1967. *Lords of Cuzco: A History and Description of the Inca People in the Final Days*. Norman: University of Oklahoma Press.

Conklin, Harold C. 1980. *Ethnographic Atlas of Ifugao: A Study of Environment, Culture, and Society in Northern Luzon*. New Haven, CT: Yale University Press.

Crumley, Carole L. 1994. "Historical Ecology: A Multidimensional Ecological Orientation." In *Historical Ecology: Cultural Knowledge and Changing Landscapes*, ed. C. Crumley, 1–16. Santa Fe: School of American Research Press.

Davies, Nigel. 1995. *The Incas*. Boulder: University Press of Colorado.

Deetz, James. 1990. "Landscapes as Cultural Statements." In *Earth Patterns: Essays in Landscape Archaeology*. ed. William M. Kelso and Rachel Most, 1–4. Charlottesville: University of Virginia Press.

Dunning, Nicholas, and Timothy Beach. 1994. "Soil Erosion, Slope Management and Ancient Terracing in the Maya Lowlands." *Latin American Antiquity* 5 (1): 51–69.

Erickson, Clark L. 1994. "Methodological Considerations in the Study of Ancient Andean Field Systems." In *The Archaeology of Garden and Field*, ed. Naomi F. Miller and Kathryn L. Gleason, 111–52. Philadelphia: University of Pennsylvania Press.

———. 2003. "Agricultural Landscapes as World Heritage: Raised Field Agriculture in Bolivia and Peru." In *Managing Change: Sustainable Approaches to the Conservation of the Built Environment*, ed. Jeanne-Marie Teutonico and Frank Matero, 181–204. Los Angeles: Getty Conservation Institute.

Fisher, Christopher T., Helen P. Pollard, Isabel Israde-Alcántara, Victor H. Garduño-Monroy, and Subir K. Benerjee. 2003. "A Reexamination of Human-Induced Environmental Change within the Lake Pátzcuaro Basin, Michoacán, Mexico." *PNAS* 100 (8): 4957–62.

Hunt, Robert C., David Guillet, David R. Abbott, James Bayman, Paul Fish, Suzanne Fish, Keith Kintigh, and James A. Neely. 2005. "Plausible Ethnographic Analogies for the Social Organization of Hohokam Canal Irrigation." *American Antiquity* 70 (3): 433–57.

Janusek, John Wayne, and Alan L. Kolata. 2004. "Top-Down or Bottom-Up: Rural Settlement and Raised Field Agriculture in the Lake Titicaca Basin, Bolivia." *Journal of Anthropological Archaeology* 23:404–30.

Kirkby, Anne V. T. 1973. "The Use of Land and Water Resources in the Past and Present Valley of Oaxaca, Mexico." In *Memoirs of the Museum of Anthropology and Human Ecology of the Valley of Oaxaca*, ed. Kent V. Flannery, 53–70. Ann Arbor: University of Michigan Press.

Kirkby, Michael. 1972. "The Physical Environment of the Nochixtlán Valley, Oaxaca." *Vanderbilt University Publications in Anthropology, 2*. Nashville: Vanderbilt University Press.

Kolata, Alan L., Oswaldo Rivera, Juan Carlos Ramirez, and Evelyn Gemio. 1996. "Rehabilitating Raised-Field Agriculture in the Southern Lake Titicaca Basin of Bolivia." In *Tiwanaku and Its Hinterland: Archaeology and Paleoecology of an Andean Civilization*. Vol. 1, ed. Alan L. Kolata, 203–30. Washington, DC: Smithsonian Institution Press.

Kowalewski, Stephen A., Gary M. Feinman, Linda M. Nicholas, and Verenice Y. Heredia. Forthcoming. "Hilltowns and Valley Fields: Great Transformations, Labor, and Long-Term History in Ancient Oaxaca." In *Labor in Cross-Cultural Perspective*, ed. E. Paul Durrenberger and Judith E. Marti. Walnut Creek, CA: AltaMira.

Lansing, J. Stephen. 1991. *Priests and Programmers: Technologies of Power in the Engineered Landscape of Bali*. Princeton, NJ: Princeton University Press.

Moseley, Michael E. 1992. *The Incas and Their Ancestors: The Archaeology of Peru*. London: Thames and Hudson.

Millon, René. 1957. "Irrigation Systems in the Valley of Teotihuacán." *American Antiquity* 23:160–66.

Netting, Robert. 1993. *Smallholders, Householders: Farm Families and the Ecology of Intensive, Sustainable Agriculture*. Stanford, CA: Stanford University Press.

O'Brien, Michael J., Roger D. Mason, Dennis E. Lewarch, and James A. Neely. 1982. *A Late Formative Irrigation Settlement below Monte Albán: Survey and Excavation on the Xoxocotlán Piedmont Oaxaca, México*. Institute of Latin American Studies. Austin: University of Texas Press.

Palerm, Angel, and Eric Wolf. 1957. "Ecological Potential and Cultural Development in Mesomaerica." In *Studies in Human Ecology*. Washington, DC: Pan American Union.

Pérez Rodríguez, Verónica. 2001. "Achiutla and Yanhuitlán: History and Configuration of two Cacicazgos." Paper presented at the Society for American Archaeology, New Orleans.

———. 2003. "Household Intensification and Agrarian States: Excavation of Houses and Terraced Fields in a Mixtec Cacicazgo." PhD diss., University of Georgia.

———. 2004. "Terrace Construction and Household Labor in the Mixtec Cacicazgo." Paper presented at the Society for American Archaeology 69th Annual Meeting, Montreal.

Sanders, William T., Jeffrey R. Parsons, and Robert S. Santley. 1979. *The Basin of Mexico: Ecological Processes in the Evolution of a Civilization*. New York: Academic Press.

Scarborough, Vernon. 2003. *The Flow of Power: Ancient Water Systems and Landscapes*. Santa Fe: School of American Research Press.

Scarborough, Vernon, Fred Valdez Jr., and Nicholas Dunning. 2003. *Heterarchy, Political Economy, and the Ancient Maya: The Three River Region of the East-Central Yucatán Peninsula*. Tucson: University of Arizona Press.

Spores, Ronald. 1969. "Settlement, Farming Technology, and Environment in the Nochixtlán Valley." *Science* 166 (3905): 557–69.

Stiver, Laura 2001. "Prehispanic Mixtec Settlements and the State in the Teposcolula Valley of Oaxaca, Mexico." PhD diss., Vanderbilt University.

Ur, Jason. 2004. "Urbanism and Society in the Third Millennium Upper Khabur Basin." PhD diss., University of Chicago.

Wilkinson, Tony J. 2003. *Archaeological Landscapes of the Near East*. Tucson: University of Arizona Press.

Wittfogel, Karl. 1957. *Oriental Despotism*. New Haven, CT: Yale University Press.

5

Mining and Ranching on the Landscape of Southwestern New Mexico, 1850–2005

CAROL MACLENNAN AND CHRISTA WALCK

Two powerful industries—mining and ranching—have rapidly altered the high desert and forested landscape of southwestern New Mexico near Silver City since 1850. In barely a century, the plant and animal communities that survived for millennia with light human use have disappeared or been transformed into objectified natural resources to support a built landscape of large mines, towns, and expansive ranches. As a consequence, land health[1] has been seriously degraded: intensive grazing has removed productive perennial grasses, logging for fuel and mining has eroded forest cover and watersheds, extensive use of limited surface and underground water sources for mining and urban use has challenged the hydrology of the region, and open-pit mining and copper refining have polluted soils and surface waters with toxic chemicals.

Based on archival and ethnographic research in the Silver City region, we trace the rise of mining and ranching as first interdependent and then increasingly independent economies in the region surrounding Silver City, New Mexico. A central focus of our inquiry is the political economy/ecology of the region that depends on the interrelationships between industrial development (including technology and access to resources), the ecology of the region, and especially the role of the state[2] in both accelerating and ameliorating industry impacts on the landscape.

Our investigation parallels those of Fratkin and Rivera in this volume. Questions of land degradation (Fratkin) in Kenya due to changes in grazing regimes, and of issues of shifting rights to land resources (Rivera) in nineteenth-century Brazil with changes in coffee production speak to the intimate connection between land, economic institutions, and human communities. We also explore these themes in the North American high desert setting.

The Landscape of Southwestern New Mexico[3]

The Silver City region occupies 50 mi^2 of Grant County, New Mexico, and encompasses an ecotone between two major mountain and desert systems of the Southwest: Rocky Mountains to the north, Sierra Madres to the south, Sonoran Desert to the southwest, and Chihuahua Desert to the southeast. Spanning nearly 5,000 ft. in elevation change are six ecological zones that receive differing amounts of rainfall. Overlapping these ecological zones, this landscape rises from lower desert of mesquite, cacti, and agave, through the pinyon-juniper grasslands and high desert in the southern end of Grant County to ponderosa pines, spruce, and fir in the north. Two major rivers cut through this region along the Gila and Mimbres rivers, each on opposite sides of the Continental Divide.

The dominating feature of the landscape is its aridity. Water is available from surface water in rivers and streams, and groundwater in porous sand or gravel beds. Both are replenished exclusively from local precipitation, principally from snowmelt in the high mountains to the north, and also from monsoon season rains (July–September). Precipitation is erratic with intervals of drought that can last for several years.

These lands have been inhabited by humans for over ten thousand years, but only since the arrival of Anglo-Americans have the land-intensive economies of mining, ranching, and farming seriously compromised the health of the land. Woody shrubs encroach on high desert grasslands as a result of grazing. Forests of small trees populate the mountains after intensive logging to support the mines. Significant erosion of soils along arroyos[4] is the result of flash floods from logging and decades of fire suppression. Human population has increased in Silver City and surrounding mine districts twenty- to thirtyfold and is now spreading across the region in new developments.

One hundred and fifty years of land degradation in southwestern New Mexico has brought the return of federal and state power to this landscape, this time for protection and restoration of land health. By 1900, ranching had so altered the grasslands that federal rangeland management was needed. By midcentury, open-pit mining technologies carved out visible industrialized regions with pits, tailings pond, and processing facilities that distributed polluting chemicals and heavy metals into the air, nearby soils and streambeds, and underground reservoirs, creating the need for federal controls on mine technology and pollution.

The Political Economy of Ecology

A discussion of power in the mining/ranching landscape directs us to the subject of political ecology. In an article in a recent special issue of *Human*

Organization, the authors stressed the need to "locate the political in political ecology" (Paulson, Gezon, and Watts 2003), correctly pointing out that insights from political economy play a weak role in current political ecology research. Paulson and Gezon (2005) continue to add to the discussion the multidimensional role of politics in ecologies and human communities. However, the historical role of the state as an institution of sovereign authority remains to be examined. Geographers such as McCarthy (2002) and Walker (2003) ask us to move beyond exclusive attention to "marginality" and the third world, expanding our scope to conflict and power in industrialized settings. Resource conflicts in the American West are not new items of study,[5] but bringing political power into the discussion of industrialized landscapes is—especially a discussion of institutionalized state power.

We hope to demonstrate how the politics of a sovereign power (the state) in a rural, yet industrial, economy dominated by mining and ranching have shaped the landscape of southwestern New Mexico. In the historical narrative that follows, we emphasize three themes.

First, as we investigate changes in the landscape from 1850 until today, we stress the power of the state to shape human communities, land use, and industries. This is the first and primary theme. Government institutions are clearly instrumental in creating, defining, and managing the landscape of this region. The federal government and, to a lesser extent, the territorial and state governments, have implemented policies enabling mining and ranching interests to establish themselves and occupy the entire region. The goal of federal policy was productive use of the land and natural resources and establishment of new Anglo-American economies on the landscape.

The second theme is the power of industries and their associated technologies and management practices to mold the landscape. Although the mining and ranching industries were intertwined during the nineteenth century, they moved in separate directions after 1900. Mining companies have wielded sizable economic power in the region and political power in government, while occupying relatively small portions of the landscape. But their twentieth-century open-pit and chemical technologies have scarred and polluted the nearby lands. Ranches have grazed cattle for over a century on private and public grasslands and forests. The application of federal management strategies to grazing lands has done little to remedy depleted and eroded landscapes. Yet, as ranching becomes a more marginal industry, ranching families hold regional political power and ranching remains a strong source of local identity.

The third theme is the entry of new stakeholders into the political process with the purpose of requiring the state (in the form of environmental law) to protect public health, prevent pollution, and conserve public land. New urban migrants and environmentally oriented residents have challenged the once unquestioned power of mines and ranches to occupy, use, and shape the landscape. Rangelands and forests have multiple uses and grazing is limited by recreation and environmental values. Mining waste is no longer private property, but subject to public control.

We explore these three themes through an environmental history of the landscape that illustrates the complex political ecology of mining and ranching economies. We divide our story of New Mexico's southwestern corner into four historical phases: (1) clearing the landscape (1850–1880); (2) promoting productive use (1870–1900); (3) rangeland management and industrial mining (1900–1960); and (4) political limits to production (1960–2005). This periodization is based on shifts in state power and policies and in ranching and mining economies that have significantly changed the landscape. The next several sections explore these themes through an environmental history of the landscape that illustrates the complex political ecology of mining and ranching economies.

Clearing the Landscape: Violence in the Land of the Chìhène[6]

What is now southwestern New Mexico has been inhabited for millennia by waves of small indigenous populations. Paleo-Indians and Mogollon (Mimbres) populations successively resided in the region from 10,000 BP until the dispersal of Mogollon settlements northward to the Rio Grande pueblos around AD 1450 (Cordell 1997). When the Spaniards arrived in southwestern New Mexico in the late 1700s,[7] they encountered bands of Apaches, an Athabaskan-speaking people that had migrated from the north into the larger southwest.[8] Use of the land and resources by Apache bands was limited to the hunting and gathering of specific animal and plant species,[9] and the use of fire to aid in collecting game, but incorporated no to very little agriculture.[10] The Apache introduced horses to the region, but mobility and low population density of Apache bands did not significantly tax the gamma grass production. In this arid region with few annual water sources, bands moved over vast areas—as far north as northern Texas in search of buffalo and as far south as several hundred miles into the Mexican state of Chihuahua in search of more plentiful game and agave.

Apache mobility and hunting practices, however, put the tribe in direct conflict with the Spaniards who entered the Mimbres watershed in the late 1700s to mine native copper at Santa Rita del Cobre. The Spanish presidio near the mines suffered repeated attacks from Apache who claimed rights to animals and land (including Spanish horses and mules). Between 1800 and 1850 (when the United States assumed possession of the region), the presidio and nearby farms on the Mimbres had been occupied sporadically, as settlers fled for years at a time to avoid Apache raids. The 1837 massacre at Santa Rita del Cobre, ordered by the Mexican governors of Sonora and Chihuahua, dispersed the Mimbres bands into the mountains, and initiated the first wave of the well-known Apache wars. The Mexican policy of "extermination" and payment to bounty hunters for Apache scalps increased the violence, threatening the passage of all travelers to the region (Schroeder 1974).

Intensive use of the southwestern New Mexico landscape began in earnest after the Gadsden Purchase in 1853, when the United States acquired southern New Mexico in the aftermath of the 1848 war with Mexico. A steady stream of Anglo-American settlers arrived with very little understanding of the ecological dynamics of this arid environment, but with a strong belief that nature's purpose was to serve human needs for production. The new settlers claimed homesteads and mine properties and set in motion dramatic changes in grasslands, forests, and hydrology of the region.[11]

The federal government was the most important force behind the rapid Anglo-American colonization of the landscape. The first task was the removal of resistant Apache bands that had occupied this area for nearly three hundred years. The use of military violence to open the land to settlement was the beginning of a dynamic of continuous state involvement in development and management of the landscape for the next 150 years.

Early relations between the U.S. Cavalry and Apache bands were uneasy but peaceful. Assuming that Americans were interested only in passage to the West, Apache chiefs did not organize raids on their horses and cattle as they had done with Spanish and Mexican settlers. The truce ended, however, with the discovery of gold in the late 1850s, the arrival of permanent settlers, and the murder of Mangas Colorado (chief of the Warm Springs Apache) by miners and U.S. troops. A violent Apache resistance to Anglo-American occupation of the landscape ensued. Competition for game increased as trappers, miners, and homesteaders moved into the region. The policy of the Indian Agency in Santa Fe was to entice Apache to settle and take up farming, but it failed to interest the resident bands in the Pinos Altos and Santa Rita area, where early pressure to set up mines was most intense.[12] Regularly routed by the violence of Apache raids, settlers implored the president to permanently remove all nearby Apache families. The federal government established Fort Bayard, near Santa Rita, in 1866, but it took nearly twenty years to end conflict over the land and its resources.

Throughout the 1860s and 1870s mines continued to spring up—gold in Pinos Altos, silver near Silver City, and continued copper mining at Santa Rita—from claims by both Mexicans and Anglo-Americans. Primitive technology for the era—*arristas* utilizing horsepower to grind rock—limited production. Receding forests, which had already been quickly depleted for mine timbers, charcoal, and buildings, curtailed the use of steam power. By 1873, Silver City had a population of 1,000 and five small mills that ground rock from three outlying silver districts (*American Journal of Mining* 1873: July 15). Mines spawned farms along the Mimbres and Gila rivers, which supplied food to the settlements, further restricting Apache access to important resources.

The soldiers from Fort Bayard eventually succeeded in discouraging Apache raids, but were unable to end them completely. Apache bands would move south to Mexico for months at a time and then return when food supplies forced them north again to raid mining camps and ranch settlements for horses, mules, and cattle. Declining game species fueled more raids on the domestic animals that had become essential to the Apache food supply during the 1870s and 1880s (Schroeder 1974). Worn down by starvation and reduced in population, the last band (under the leadership of Geronimo) surrendered in 1886 and was transported to prison in Florida. This ended a fifty-year campaign, beginning with Mexican policies, to completely remove Apache people from southwestern New Mexico.

Until the early 1880s, the Apache wars had served as a check on mining and grazing. A few small communities claimed by miners and small ranchers clustered around Silver City and Santa Rita,[13] and a few homesteads were claimed in the Gila and Mimbres river valleys. Most of the acreage in this region remained in the public domain. The U.S. policy of Apache removal through either relocation or extermination sparked a boom of silver mining in Silver City at the same time that metal prices spiked in the national markets. Arrival of rail transportation, investment of Eastern capital, and use of contemporary steam technology in Silver City brought families who started the ranches and built the towns that harbored the new economy of the region. Without intervention and use of violence by the state, the mining and ranching economy of the past 125 years would not have created the landscape we know today.

Promoting Productive Use: The Boom in Silver and Cattle

With the Apache gone, federal land agencies actively promoted the disposal of public lands to private owners. The mines, farms, homesteads, and ranches were the result of a series of earlier federal acts that began with the Preemption Acts of 1830–1841 for unsurveyed land and the Homestead Act of 1862 for surveyed land, both of which allowed settlers to claim 160 acres (1/4 section) of public land in order to make it productive. Later, the Mining Act of 1872 promoted mine claims on public lands with rights to cut timber in nearby forests and draw water from nearby streams for mining development. After the capture of Geronimo, settlers arrived from all over—from as close as Texas and as far away as Europe.

The gold mines of Pinos Altos (1860s) and the silver mines of Silver City and surrounding areas (1870s) brought the first wave of permanent Anglo-American settlers to the region. Gold mining proved limited by lack of water except during monsoon season (July–October) when moisture from the southern Pacific crossed the land. The discovery of silver, however, near Silver City at Chloride Flats, Burro Mountains, Georgetown (near the Mimbres River), and Pinos Altos beginning in 1871, created a flood of mining claims by the late 1870s, "ushering in the most romantic, the most exciting, the most lawless, and certainly the wildest period in the history of mining in New Mexico" (Christiansen 1974: 56). A period of railroad building in New Mexico, beginning in 1880, eventually linked Silver City and Santa Rita/Hanover to Deming (to the south) by 1883. The laborious wagon and oxen transport of machinery into and copper and silver out of the district ended, making possible the importation of larger mills and a smelter powered by modern steam-powered engines. All of this attracted capitalists from the Eastern United States to invest in silver mining.

The town of Silver City nearly doubled in population from 4,539 in 1880 to 9,657 in 1890 (Huggard 1994a: 293). Located on an important water source, the San Vicente arroyo, the town became the site of the largest mills and a smelter (which superseded the rudimentary adobe furnaces) that serviced all of the surrounding mine districts. Processing ore requires volumes of water for washing ores and separating metal from rock. Diversion streams were built to supply reservoirs used during drier months. Pumps were constructed to tap underground waters. Larger mills drew on even larger sources of wood for fuel. The forested Pinos Altos Mountains to the north of Silver City were quickly denuded of trees; this then triggered regular floods down *arroyos* and through the center of town[14] (Huggard 1994a).

The boom in silver mines was a product of national government policy between 1876 and 1890 that limited silver coinage in order to protect a national monetary policy based on gold and kept silver mining throughout the West profitable. In 1890, the Silver Purchase Act forced prices up even higher. But when Congress repealed the act in 1893, silver prices plummeted. The impact on silver mining in Silver City, and throughout the West, was disastrous and ended large-scale silver mining (Christiansen 1974).

While mining expanded, it also encouraged farming along the Mimbres and Gila rivers[15] and sparked a cattle-ranching boom. The federal government's land policy at this time was to put public land into private hands in order to make it productive, primarily for agriculture. The General Land Office (Department of the Interior) disposed of land by preemption and homesteading, which allowed claims of 160 acres (1/4 section) to encourage settlement by the small farmer and homesteader. However, a viable homestead in semiarid lands required, according to John Wesley Powell, 2,560 acres fronting a stream for grazing (Graf 1990). Public lands not claimed under federal legislation constituted "open range," where stockmen grazed livestock free of charge, without enclosures. Despite dreams of a western landscape of productive farms, the laws were used to acquire access to grazing lands. General Land Office officials, knowing the aridity of the land, looked the other way as ranchers used homesteads as a base to graze cattle on large acreages of open range lands (Westphall 1965). Many homesteads were short lived, however, since the land was not suitable for agriculture. This provided opportunities for large ranches with capital to buy up lands. Several of the biggest ranches were started by men in the mining industry looking for a place to invest their wealth.

The Silver City region includes two ecologically different ranching areas (Cockerill, Hunter, and Pingrey 1939). North of Silver City the rangeland is higher in elevation (4,000–10,000 ft.), and therefore wetter (12–30 in. annually) and forested; south of Silver City the drier, semiarid grasslands and pinyon-juniper woodlands receive only 10–16 in. On the drier lands in the south, ranches such as the large LC Ranch devised sophisticated pumping and transport systems to water cattle on the range. Both regions provided huge expanses of unclaimed public lands for semiferal cattle to graze. Calves were branded in the spring and rounded up for market in the fall.

By 1881, ranching was already a significant part of the economy; the ranch was the organization created to take advantage of the opportunity for free grass. Merchants and banks serviced and loaned capital to ranchers to buy stock and land and ship their cattle to market. By 1885 the range was considered "fully stocked" and cattle shipments began the following year. An 1887 assessment listed 94,620 head of cattle exclusive of the calf crop in Grant County at a value of $2.8 million. By 1895, the number of cattle in Grant County doubled to 200,000 (Twitchell 1917: 225). This overstocking of the range was the result of available capital for investment

(Sayre 1999) and the arrival of the railroad to haul large volumes of cattle to market; it was also the result of ignorance of the ecological dynamics of this semiarid landscape.

By 1900 these free-ranging cattle had depleted native grasses and contributed (along with mining and logging) to serious erosion in Grant County. Years of good rains that encouraged investment were followed by a period of drought. Drought in 1884–1887 led to poor herds and the inability of ranchers to pay debts; New Mexico ranchers were in a "deplorable condition" by 1886 (French 1928: 196). As range conditions worsened, borrowing increased, leading to bank failures.

Within a short twenty years, the boom-bust cycle of silver mining and cattle ranching between 1880 and 1900 created devastated communities and depleted and eroded landscapes. The central force behind the alteration of the grasslands and forests was the federal government with its power to allocate land and the resources of ore, grasses, and trees without constraint on their use and abuse. The federal philosophy of public land disposal for "productive" use set in motion a series of ecological impacts that continued throughout the next century.

Rangeland Management and Industrial Mining

Mining and ranching economies each changed significantly in the decades between 1900 and 1960. Ranching declined in economic importance as the federal government restricted grazing on degraded public lands in order to restore land health. Mining, on the other hand, became an economic powerhouse in the region and in New Mexico's state economy, often diminishing the power of government. As the federal government became more prominent in the ranching economy and receded in the mining economy, it developed policies and organizations that continued to alter the regional landscape. Federal land and water policies guided by continuation of the "productive use" philosophy evolved to include strategies for restoring productivity of the landscape through federal research and application of science to the range and the water supply. Regarding the public rangelands, the federal government shifted its strategy from land disposal to land management, with objectives of maintaining both watersheds and a ranching economy. Regulation and management based on scientific research was intended to improve grazing productivity; although fewer cattle were permitted to graze, the prohibition of grazing on public land was never the goal. Ranching probably survived *because* of this shift in policy.

From 1900 to 1960, the federal government shaped the range landscape in two significant ways: it closed the range and it funded range research. In

1899 the federal government established the Gila River Forest Reserves on 3.3 million acres north of Silver City. This became the Gila National Forest in 1907, closing the range north of Silver City. Then, the Taylor Grazing Act of 1936 closed the range to the south. Land that had been free for grazing was now divided into allotments and leased for a fee to ranchers who already owned deeded ("base") properties nearby. Two different federal agencies, with differing policies and funding levels, managed these lands: the U.S. Forest Service in the Department of Agriculture managed the Gila National Forest, while the Department of the Interior managed the rest through the Grazing Service, until the Bureau of Land Management (BLM) was established in 1946.

The second and equally important way in which government shaped the landscape in this period was by funding research on the rangelands in order to increase forage and livestock productivity. This fostered the development of the new discipline of range science, which studied the degradation of rangelands and methods of restoration to productive use. Research undertaken by the Forest Service and Bureaus of Plant Industry and Animal Industry (Department of Agriculture) as well as state experimental research stations such as New Mexico's Jornada Experimental Range (established in 1912) provided substantial information for ranchers.

Closing the range regulated use and improved management of degraded rangelands. The intent was not to close forest and arid grasslands to cattle ranches, but rather to implement an "objective of sustained productive range" for the purpose of building "a sound grazing enterprise and to provide economic family units" (Chapline 1944: 131). The Gila National Forest covered over half of the Gila-Mimbres watershed in Grant County, already the more productive land, and benefited ranching by setting up a management system of allotments to ranchers based on the capacity of the land to sustain grazing. This system quickly forced reductions in the number of livestock grazing on the forest, which led to better forage than on the unregulated open range. Baker, Maxwell, Treat, and Dethloff consider this grazing control system, which was in place by 1905, a "remarkably advanced administrative and land management system, given the time and state of technical knowledge" (1988: 87).

The Taylor Grazing Act established the Grazing Service and set up grazing districts to implement a system of allotments, and it assessed usage fees (Stout 1970). However, it lacked the administrative funding and research capabilities of the Forest Service. Grazing districts and boards were run by local stockmen who gave preference in assigning permits, and hardened "past use of the public ranges into permanent property rights" (Stout 1970: 328).

Even though ranchers resisted curtailment of open and free access to the range, contemporary and modern observers have credited the Forest Service with revitalizing and even prolonging the cattle industry in the Southwest by regulating grazing (Cockerill, Hunter, and Pingrey 1939; Baker, Maxwell, Treat, and Dethloff 1988). Fluctuating stocking rates from 1900 to 1960 can be attributed to weather, war, prices, and government policies. Large ranches continued to operate into the 1920s and 1930s, albeit at a reduced capacity, after which many began to be subdivided and sold for nonranch use.[16] Stocking rates were reported at less than half of the boom days. By the 1930s, conditions deteriorated significantly. Beginning with the fall of livestock prices in 1920–1921, along with the collapse of banks in 1926, the crash of 1929, and a long drought in 1934, the Depression years hit Grant County ranchers hard (Bryan 1940). Still producing for the national markets, ranches held on to their land, but maintained smaller herds for cow-calf production and often borrowed from banks to buy stock. Ranchers who could not support families on ranching income alone worked in town and at the mines to maintain family incomes. Owning and using a mix of private, New Mexico state trust, U.S. Forest Service, and BLM lands (all of which provided collateral for borrowing from the banks), ranchers tried to survive with smaller numbers of cattle on their lands. As ranching became economically marginal and land prices rose, some began to sell or subdivide their lands.

By 1960, ranching was no longer a significant income producer for Grant County. However, ranching remained an important identity for the region and ranchers continued to be active in local Grant County and Silver City politics, and participated in the New Mexico Cattle Growers Association, Soil Conservation District, Farm Home Administration, and other government boards that determined local land policies.

As ranching income declined between 1900 and 1960, mining became the backbone of Grant County income and employment. The "productive use" philosophy of the federal and state governments enhanced mine profits, but unlike cattle ranching, the mines did not depend on federal power to manage the landscape for their economic benefit. In fact, the New Mexico state economy became increasingly dependent on Grant County's copper mines. This shift in power from government to mining company was noted as early as 1921 in an appraisal of all New Mexico mines. By that time only nine companies conducted profitable metal mining, of which copper mining by the Chino Copper Company (at Santa Rita) and the Burro Mountain branch (at Tyrone) of Phelps Dodge Corporation accounted for 90 percent of the value in New Mexico (Coan 1925: 514).

Large-scale industrial copper mining started in the Silver City region after 1910 with the transition to extraction of low-grade porphyry coppers[17] from the Santa Rita area. Steam shovels, first used in Ely, Nevada, shortly before their appearance at Santa Rita, could move 5,000 tons of rock per day at an open-pit operation. With the requisite rail transportation to a rock-crushing plant (mill), "flotation" and "precipitation" facilities, and piping of slurries (with the copper removed) to the tailings ponds, Santa Rita's copper facility produced 50,000 tons of copper by 1929 and employed 12,000 workers (Huggard 1994b: 128). In 1909 New York investors established the Chino Copper Company, which was purchased in 1932 by Kennecott, who then built a smelter and worker housing near the mill in Hurley.

Santa Rita coppers had been mined nearly continuously since 1850 by various interests, including at times small contractors, as an underground operation. The Chino Copper Company, however, introduced to the region an *industrialized* landscape that encompassed 50,000 acres from the two open pits in the north, the mills and smelter in Hurley, and the tailings ponds stretching several miles to the south (Huggard 1994b: 55). A second copper district was opened in the early 1900s by Phelps Dodge to the southwest of Silver City in the Burro Mountains. The underground mine at Tyrone operated a mere decade, closing in 1922 during a difficult period for copper prices. But Phelps Dodge held on to the property, and reopened the mine as an open-pit operation in the 1960s; this will be discussed later.

Between 1900 and 1960, the role of the federal government in promoting productive use of ore bodies and surrounding lands and their available waters remained much the same as it was in the nineteenth century. Originally, mining companies benefited from access to public lands for their claims. After that, however, mining companies in Grant County owned all of their own resources—minerals, water rights, and necessary lands for mine waste, grazing of working animals, and transportation and milling facilities. Thus, in the era of corporate mining after 1910, companies answered to no one when planning and building their open-pit extraction and milling-leaching-smelting facilities. As employers of thousands and income generators for the local economy, Kennecott and Phelps Dodge towered over the region, and indeed the state government.

There were two ways, however, in which mining companies relied on the state and federal governments for services. First, the granting of water rights from New Mexico taken from noncompany lands was especially critical to the continued expansion of mine production. The second, of lesser importance, was the research support from the federal Bureau of Mines and the educational and research benefits from the New Mexico School of Mines.

Water is the most critical variable in industrial mining in the Southwest. It is necessary for the extraction of copper from the ore through flotation (with oil and water), and precipitation (leaching with chemicals and water). Water is also used in large quantities to transport waste rock and chemicals in the form of slurry to tailings ponds. And, it must be managed carefully because it is either present at the wrong time (flash flooding, filling of open pits when below groundwater level) or not present in enough quantities during a large portion of the year or during successive years of drought. Access to surface and especially underground water rights was necessary for the continued development of the Chino Copper Company and, later, for reopening the Phelps Dodge mine as an open pit at Tyrone in the 1960s. In New Mexico, these rights could be had by purchase of lands over underground sources or alongside streams from which water could be diverted.

New Mexico water law, much of it established during the Spanish era, privileges appropriation rights over riparian rights. Thus, the prior appropriator acquired the right (often to diversion of water) against subsequent applicants as long as that quantity of water was put to "beneficial use." New Mexico declared in 1931 that underground waters were "public waters" and therefore subject to appropriation for beneficial use (Clark 1987). The beneficial-use clause was critical for the continuance of industrial mining in Grant County. During the 1910s the Chino Copper Company had gained access to more than 300,000 acres of drainage in the Santa Rita basin through purchases of new lands with water rights when it could not obtain water rights assigned by the State of New Mexico (Huggard 1994b: 180). The company built heavy-duty pumping facilities to deliver water to the Hurley mill. Water *management* was also important, since underground waters were not adequate to supply the 600 million gal. necessary each month. Chino constructed elaborate pipelines and concrete-lined reservoirs to store new and reused water as early as the 1910s, recovering about 83 percent of waters used each month (Huggard 1994b: 188). In the 1930s, the company established a massive diversion system to collect the annual floodwaters from the Santa Rita pit and rail facilities, thus adding to the water supply. The heavy pumping of waters from underground basins, however, still took their toll. In 1929, the U.S. Geological Survey (USGS) determined that the water table had fallen between 2 and 15 ft. throughout the region. In response, the company spearheaded an education program in Grant County for water conservation.

Phelps Dodge also found it necessary to acquire extensive water rights in order to open its open-pit facility at Tyrone along the Mangas Creek watershed (which emptied into the Gila River). Learning from its experience at its Morenci copper mine in eastern Arizona, Phelps Dodge knew it had to build and control a water empire in order to open Tyrone to pit mining. Beginning in the 1940s and continuing over a twenty-year period, Phelps Dodge planned for water diversion from the Gila River. It purchased 15 miles of land (19,000 acres) along the Mangas Creek as well as water rights along the Gila River through its subsidiary, the Pacific Western Land Company. This gave the company access not only to the irrigation canals on the upper Gila, but also to large reserves of underground waters. By 1966, Phelps Dodge had acquired extensive water rights along the upper Gila watershed with the approval of the New Mexico State Engineer's Office. This accounted for all but 4,000 acre feet of water awarded to New Mexico along the upper Gila in a 1968 agreement with Arizona (Huggard 1994b: 383). With water rights secured, the company built an elaborate water-diversion project that included Bill Evans Lake and Dam to supply the mine and mills to open in 1966.

Relatively easy access to water rights by a policy of "public waters for beneficial use" was the most significant contribution of the state government to mining in the first half of the twentieth century. Of lesser significance, but still important, was government-funded research on mining (especially the search for new ore deposits) by the U.S. and New Mexico Bureaus of Mines, and the detailed hydrological investigations by the USGS. For instance, research on ore deposits in the Central Mining District (which included Santa Rita) was conducted by the USGS and the New Mexico Bureau of Mines at critical points in the development of the district's mines—in the 1910s and again in the 1930s—to locate additional ore deposits, estimate their productivity, and determine the location and availability of underground water to support new mining (Lasky 1936).

Political Limits to Production: Pollution and Conservation

The 1960s brought important changes to federal land policies that impacted both mining and ranching in new ways. In response to demands from citizen groups and new residents of rural communities in the West, the federal agencies shifted their policies to include the interests of multiple users of the landscape. New urban migrants to southwestern New Mexico introduced new constituencies to the community with interests in environmental and public health protection. Conservation and recreation values of the new migrants competed with the single focus on the landscape for grazing. Similarly, federal clean air and water laws of the 1970s and citizen demands for mine-waste cleanup and protection against toxic mine pollutants throughout the West signaled a change in the federal hands-off policies toward mining. A growing national awareness of the health effects of mine pollutants galvanized Grant County citizens behind new mining laws and a program to clean up mine wastes. With public demands on the federal government, the relationship between ranchers, mines, and government changed from one of cooperation to one of conflict.

As the economic position of ranching declined in the region, it also became apparent that decades of attempts by the Forest Service and BLM to "improve" the condition of range lands through scientific management and research seemed to have little effect on the steady invasion of woody shrubs—pinyon and juniper—across the grazing landscape. The shift from grass to trees can be attributed as much to decades of fire suppression and drought as to continued grazing, as well as to dropping groundwater levels from mining. Concerns about land conservation led to new federal programs for land management.

Beginning with the 1960 Multiple Use–Sustained Yield (MUSY) Act, which established the "multiple-use" policy for National Forests, federal land policy began to change to allow for land management based on "amenity values" of recreation, wildlife, and watershed protection, as well as commodity production such as grazing, timber, and mining. The MUSY Act of 1960 and the Wilderness Act of 1964 reduced grazing on the Gila National Forest as management emphasis was directed toward "protecting and restoring natural conditions." Wilderness areas were now to be maintained in "near natural condition, untrammeled by man and his influences." This protection had priority when establishing allotment-stocking levels (USFS 1974: 2–23). BLM lands were also subject to new federal policies promoting conservation.

Through a sequence of federal laws that included the 1969 National Environmental Policy Act, 1973 Endangered Species Act, and 1978 Rangelands Improvement Act,[18] the single-focus productive-use philosophy evolved to include the interests of competing groups new to southwestern New Mexico such as recent urban migrants and environmentalists interested in "consumption" of the landscape. This new constituency was interested in wilderness land protection, retirement- and second-home construction, wildlife, and biodiversity.

Ranchers perceived this shift in federal land management policies as increasing their risk, and shifted cattle to BLM and New Mexico state trust lands. Agricultural economists implicated these policies in the rapid decline in the 1980s of market values of ranches with significant public land dependence, exacerbating an already difficult ranch economy (Torell and Kincaid 1996). In the 1990s the BLM and the Forest Service began to fence off access to rivers due to growing concern for riparian areas. Cattle had to be watered with earth dams and wells, and the BLM spent significant resources on range improvements for watering cattle. These changes antagonized ranchers and created increased conflict between the industry and federal land agencies.

Ranching remained the primary extensive use of the grasslands and forestlands over these decades, but it continued to decline in economic importance. Land prices, rising steadily from the 1940s to the 1980s, encouraged ranchers to subdivide and sell their lands. The crash of land values in the 1980s reduced the collateral value of ranches that depended on debt financing, forcing more sales. By the 1990s, Grant County had an estimated 55,000 head of cattle on 850,000 acres of federal and private lands and 204 ranches. The average ranch was 43 percent public range, so the impact of federal land policy for multiple use was significant. Ranch population accounted for only 2.5 percent of the population and only four ranches were believed to support full-time ranchers in the county (Thall et al. 1992: 28, 34). The average cow-calf ranch supported only 154 cows, yet it was not economical to ranch with fewer than than 300 head. As a result the smaller ranches had at least one family member working off-ranch in town or at the mines to supplement family income (Torell and Drummond 1997). In spite of its economic decline, however, ranching culture remained a part of Silver City and Grant County identity as well as a mainstay in local politics.

Changes in federal land policy and new environmental laws also had a major impact on Grant County's mining economy. For the first time in the nearly one hundred-year history of mining, powerful mining corporations such as Kennecott and Phelps Dodge found the federal and state agencies and citizens actively impinging on corporate decisions by imposing regulations, which were dictated by environmental health standards, to curb air pollution and manage mine waste. Mining historian Christopher Huggard (2003) notes that the new ecological consciousness of the post-1960s era called for an end to "the modernist belief in industrial progress" and that in the American West, environmentalists found mining to be a logical villain. The first challenge to the economic and political power of mining was the Clean Air Act of 1970, which called for curtailment of smelter emissions from aging facilities such as Kennecott's Hurley smelter, which had been built in 1938. The organization New Mexico Citizens for Clean Air and Water (NMCCAW) targeted the sulfur dioxide emissions from the Hurley smelter (which, with no filters, pumped three hundred tons of sulfur into the air each day) as a major source of overall air quality decline in the Southwest[19] (Huggard 1994b: 432). Compliance with air-quality standards came about slowly. With help from New Mexico senator Pete Domenici, mining companies successfully lobbied Congress to postpone smelter compliance with the 1977 Clean Air Act amendments for five years, until 1983.

Beginning in the 1980s, toxic runoff from mine waste was a second target for federal and state regulations. In October 1980 the dam on tailings pond no. 3 breached, sending 200 million m^3 of acidic sludge downstream 8 km on Mangas Creek, inundating 300 acres of farmland (Huggard 1994b: 495). Continual spills of sulfuric solutions from tailings ponds at Chino and Tyrone mines in the 1980s and 1990s encouraged state regulators to tighten discharge permitting and led to passage of New Mexico's mining law in 1993. Between 1990 and 2000, the Chino facilities alone had twelve significant spills of acid waste into Whitewater and other nearby creeks (Kourous 2001: 18). Of concern are the idle tailing ponds—six of the seven at Chino mines plus all of those at Tyrone (2,200 acres) since its closure in 1992. Part of New Mexico's 1992 mining law requires that mining companies submit and have approved closure and closeout plans for all operating mines that account for monitoring of tailings ponds, remediation if necessary, and bonding by the company to pay the costs. It took over ten years for New Mexico to approve a closeout plan for Chino (in 2003) and Tyrone (in 2004) after delays, extensions, and in the case of Tyrone a fine for not meeting the last of several deadlines. Phelps Dodge continues to operate leaching facilities at Chino Mine, but will begin reclamation at Tyrone.

Phelps Dodge, owner of both mining facilities after purchasing Chino from Kennecott in the early 1980s, is still a major landowner and employer in Grant County. In 2002, it was still the largest employer, with 1,385 employees in the county (6 percent of the county population)—down from 2,655 in 1990. It also owned 180,090 acres of mine and grazing lands in the county[20] (Kourous 2001: 9–13).

Regional and local organizations in Silver City, such as Gila Resources Information Project (GRIP), have been successful in making state agencies responsive to citizen concerns about pollution and environmental health. The closeout plan for Phelp Dodge's Tyrone mine was close to the requirements GRIP had lobbied for. Mining laws, permitting for discharge of pollutants, and requirements for air and water quality have turned mine waste from a private (and invisible) property right into a public good regulated by governments. Mining interests faced new challenges to their once unbridled authority to shape the local landscape. The state, in the form of state and federal government agencies, became the mediator between environmental activists and industries.

Conclusion

By 2005, grazing and mining landscapes of southwestern New Mexico had become a contested terrain. In the Gila National Forest and on the BLM rangelands, grazing competed with recreation and riparian recovery. Mining companies, too, had to share their power over the lands they polluted with local residents concerned about public health and a state government that expected cleanup of historic mine waste. In the new political ecology of the landscape, state institutions are again central actors shaping land-use futures. Only today, instead of opening the land to private mining and ranching interests, government is busy rectifying the chemical, soil, and vegetative alterations that have degraded the land over the last 150 years.

Notes

1. Land health, as Leopold (1949: 258) succinctly defines it, is the capacity of land for self-renewal.

2. When we speak of "the state" we refer to the general concept of a sovereign authority that acts, in the case of this study, to actively shape activity on the land, property rights, and land-use policies. In this sense, the state *is* an important actor. When we discuss specific state actions in historical time we will refer to federal and state governments and agencies.

3. We define *landscape* here as the biophysical, or natural, features of the Silver City region in New Mexico. This includes forests, underground ore bodies, soils, grasses, and water. This is distinct from the cultural (or built) landscape. However, it will become apparent throughout this chapter that industry creates new landscapes that are the *product* of cultural forces.

4. *Arroyo* is usually translated into English as "small stream" but is now used to describe a gully characterized by steeply sloping or vertical walls in cohesive, fine sediments, and a flat and generally sandy floor. There is a significant debate about the role of human action versus natural action in the formation of arroyos (Cooke and Reeves 1976).

5. See Sayre (2002) on ranching and Ward (2003) on water in the U.S. Southwest.

6. According to Opler (1941), the Chiricahua Apache called themselves *Chìhène*, "Red Paint People," and included the Apache bands of southwestern New Mexico (Eastern Chiricahua, Warm Springs Apache, Ojo Caliente Apache, Coppermine Apache, Mimbreños Apache, and Mogollones Apache).

7. Spanish settlement in New Mexico began much earlier, in the 1500s, along the Rio Grande and north to Santa Fe. Apache resistance to the Spanish incursion kept the Spaniards' presidios and farms confined primarily along the Rio Grande corridor for nearly two hundred years. Once the Spaniards discovered the copper deposits at Santa Rita in the 1790s, however, they quickly claimed the land and established a mine and small farms long the Mimbres River, and began grazing mules and horses nearby.

8. Now Arizona, western Texas, and New Mexico. Apaches are closely related to the Navajo and Kiowa, who also migrated to the northern range of this region.

9. Certain foods in the environment were culturally unacceptable for the Apache: fish and especially bear. Protein came primarily from horses (a favorite), deer, elk, buffalo (to the northwest), and small game. The primary plant food was mescal, made from the native agave.

10. Apache bands to the east in central Arizona in the wetter San Carlos region were more practiced agriculturalists, supplementing their hunting with cultivated maize. The land of the Chiricahua was just too arid for maize production.

11. Some scholars even argue that this short period of rapid ecological change was as dramatic as that of the late Pleistocene in the Southwest (Hirt 1989).

12. The bands to the west were settled on the San Carlos reservation in 1871 and to the east on the Mescalero reservation in 1873. Some effort to settle Mimbres Apaches to the northeast in Ojo Caliente (Warm Springs) was made in the 1860s–1870s by the Indian Agency. But the effort failed due largely to the lack of adequate food (game and plant) in a limited region of arid land. While residing at Ojo Caliente, the resident band regularly roamed southward to Mexico and raided settlements for horse meat (to be eaten for protein). It was difficult for the Indian Agency in Santa Fe to grasp that agriculture was not feasible.

13. Gold mines in Pinos Altos lasted only through the 1860s.

14. By the end of the century, the annual floods had created a "big ditch" down the main street that still exists today.

15. The Mimbres was quickly settled in the 1870s, possibly by Hispanic farmers, to support silver mining camps; homesteading on the Gila and its tributaries followed in the later 1870s and 1880s, for farming in the valleys and access to grazing in the mountains.

16. Information is sketchy for 1900–1960 on ranch operations. Most useful sources include ranch family histories (Campbell and Hill 2002; French 1928; McCauley and Shelley 1982) and a study of ranching in the Gila National Forest (Drummond 1993).

17. Porphyry coppers are low-grade ore deposits where the metal is found dispersed throughout the rock at levels from 0.075 percent to about 3 percent. This requires complete crushing of the rock to small particles (tailings) in order to extract the copper through a process called "flotation" for sulfide ores and "precipitation" for oxide ores, both of which were done at Santa Rita (Parsons 1933).

18. There were, in fact, multiple federal laws through the 1990s that altered land policy on multiple levels and affected both the ranching and mining economies: the 1964 Wilderness Act, 1972 Federal Water Pollution Act, 1974 Forest Rangeland Renewable Resource Planning Act, 1976 Amended National Forest Management Act, 1970 and 1977 Clean Air Act and amendments, 1972 and 1977 Clean Water Act and amendments, and 1994 "Rangeland Reform."

19. The Tyrone ores were smelted at a new facility (with up-to-date emissions technologies) near the Mexican border to the south.

20. The Tyrone mine site alone comprises 7,400 acres of disturbed land, including 2,300 acres of open pits and processing facilities, 2,800 acres of stockpiles, and 2,300 acres of tailings impoundments (NMENRD 2004).

References

American Journal of Mining. Vol. 2 (1866)–31 (1881).

Baker, R. D., R. S. Maxwell, V. H. Treat, and H. C. Dethloff. 1988. *Timeless Heritage: A History of the Forest Service in the Southwest*. Report FS FS-409. U.S. Forest Service.

Bryan, K. 1940. "Erosion in the Valleys of the Southwest." *New Mexico Quarterly* 10:227–32.

Campbell, Ida Foster, and Alice Foster Hill. 2002. *Triumph and Tragedy: A History of Thomas Lyons and the LCs*. Silver City, NM: High Lonesome Books.

Chapline, W. R. 1944. "The History of Western Range Research." *Agricultural History* 18:127–43.

Christiansen, Paige W. 1974. "The Story of Mining in New Mexico." *Scenic Trips to the Geologic Past*. No. 12. Socorro, NM: New Mexico Bureau of Mines and Mineral Resources.

Clark, Ira G. 1987. *Water in New Mexico: A History of Its Management and Use*. Albequerque: University of New Mexico Press.

Coan, Charles F. 1925. *A History of New Mexico*. Chicago: American Historical Society.

Cockerill, P. W., B. Hunter, and B. H. Pingrey. 1939. *Type of Farming and Ranching Areas in New Mexico*. Part II. State College: Agricultural Experiment Station of the New Mexico College of Agriculture and Mechanic Arts.

Cooke, Ronald U., and Richard W. Reeves. 1976. *Arroyos and Environmental Change in the American Southwest*. Oxford: Clarendon.

Cordell, Linda. 1997. *Archeology of the Southwest*. 2nd ed. San Diego: Academic Press.

Drummond, Tracy W. 1993. "The Economic Impacts of Increased Grazing Fees on Gila National Forest Ranchers." MS thesis, New Mexico State University.

French, William. 1928. *Recollections of a Western Ranchman*. New York: Frederick A. Stokes, Repr., High Lonesome Books, 1990.

Graf, William L. 1990. *Wilderness Preservation and the Sagebrush Rebellions*. Savage, MD: Rowman & Littlefield.

Hirt, Paul. 1989. "The Transformation of a Landscape: Culture and Ecology in Southeastern Arizona." *Environmental Review* 13 (4): 67–189.

Huggard, Christopher J. 1994a. "Copper Mining in Grant County, 1900–1945." In *Essays in Twentieth-Century New Mexico*, ed. Judith B. DeMark, 43–61. Albuquerque: University of New Mexico Press.

———. 1994b. "Environmental and Economic Change in the Twentieth-Century West: The History of the Copper Industry in New Mexico." PhD diss., University of New Mexico.

———. 2003. "Squeezing Out the Profits: Mining and the Environment in the U.S. West, 1945–2000." In *The American West in 2000: Essays in Honor of Gerald D. Nash*, ed. R. W. Etulain and F. Szasz, 105–26. Albuquerque: University of New Mexico Press.

Kourous, George. 2001. *Copper, Phelps Dodge, and the Future of Grant County's Mining District: An IRC Community Report*. Silver City, NM: Interhemispheric Resource Center.

Lasky, Samuel G. 1936. *Geology and Ore Deposits of the Bayard Area, Central Mining District, New Mexico. Bulletin 870. Geological Survey, US Dept. of the Interior.* Washington, DC: U.S. Government Printing Office.

Leopold, Aldo. 1949. *A Sand County Almanac, and Sketches Here and There*. New York: Oxford University Press.

McCarthy, James. 2002. "First World Political Ecology: Lessons from the Wise Use Movement." *Environment and Planning A* 34:1281–1302.

McCauley, LaVerne, and Terrell Shelley. 1982. *Pioneer Families of Grant Co., NM. History of Hooker and Shelley Families and the 916 Ranch*. Baltimore: Gateway Press.

New Mexico. Energy, Minerals, and Natural Resources Department (NMERD). 2004. "Mining and Minerals Division Issues Tyrone Reclamation Plan." Press release. At www.emnrd.state.nm.us/Mining/Press/2004-04-13%20Tyrone%20Approval.pdf (accessed April 2005).

Opler, Morris E. 1941. *An Apache Life-Way: The Economic, Social, and Religions Institutions of the Chiricahua Indians*. Chicago: University of Chicago Press.

Parsons, Arthur B. 1933. *The Porphyry Coppers*. New York: A. B. Parsons.

Paulson, Susan, and Lisa Gezon, eds. 2005. *Political Ecology across Spaces, Scales, and Social Groups*. New Brunswick, NJ: Rutgers University Press.

Paulson, Susan, Lisa Gezon, and Michael Watts. 2003. "Locating the Political in Political Ecology: An Introduction." Theme issue, *Human Organization* 62 (3): 205–17.

Sayre, Nathan. 1999. "The Cattle Boom in Southern Arizona: Towards a Critical Political Ecology." *Journal of the Southwest* 41 (2): 239–71.

———. 2002 *Ranching, Endangered Species, and Urbanization in the Southwest: Species of Capital*. Tucson: University of Arizona Press.

Schroeder, Albert H. 1974. *A Study of the Apache Indians*. Part IV, *The Mogollon, Copper Mine, Mimbres, Warm Spring, and Chiricahua Apaches*. New York: Garland Publishing.

Stout, Joe A. 1970. "Cattlemen, Conservationists, and the Taylor Grazing Act." *New Mexico Historical Review* 45 (4): 311–32.

Thall, A., A. Polley, R. Mendenhall, M. Romo, and P. Nelson. 1992. *Economic and Social Importance of Cattle Ranching in Southwest New Mexico*. Southwest Center for Resource Analysis, Department of Applied Technology. Western New Mexico University.

Torell, L. A., and M. E. Kincaid. 1996. "Public Land Policy and the Market Value of New Mexico Ranches, 1979–94." *Journal of Range Management* 49 (3): 270–76.

Torell, L. Allen, and Tracy R. Drummond. 1997. "The Economic Impacts of Increased Grazing Fees on Gila National Forest Grazing Permittees." *Journal of Range Management* 50 (1): 94–105.

Twitchell, Ralph Emerson, ed. 1917. *The Leading Facts of New Mexico History*. Vol. 5. Cedar Rapids, IA: Torch Press.

United States Forest Service (USFS). 1974. *Forest Service Handbook, Gila: Forest Multiple Use Guide for the Gila National Forest*. November 1994.

Walker, Peter. 2003. "Reconsidering 'Regional' Political Ecologies: Toward a Political Ecology of the Rural American West." *Progress in Human Geography* 27 (1): 7–24.

Ward, Evan R. 2003. *Border Oasis: Water and the Political Ecology of the Colorado River Delta, 1940–1975*. Tucson: University of Arizona Press.

Westphall, Victor. 1965. *The Public Domain in New Mexico, 1854–1891*. Albuquerque: University of New Mexico Press.

II

TRANSFORMATIONS, POLITICAL STRATEGIES, AND DECISION MAKING

6

From Foraging to Farming
The Emergence of Exclusive Property Rights in Kentucky Prehistory

GEORGE M. CROTHERS

IN ECONOMIC HISTORY, THERE HAS BEEN NO GREATER TRANSFORMATION of landscapes worldwide than the shift in human labor from hunting and gathering to agriculture. On a global scale, there is not a single human group that is not affected by agricultural economies, even if only by marginalization (see, e.g., Wilmsen 1989). This transformation is both obviously physical in the material sense of landscape—the landforms of a region in the aggregate—and sensory in the cognitive sense of landscape—how humans perceive the external world: psychologically, historically, and socially (Green 1995: 31).

Identifying the plants and animals involved in domestication, locating centers of domestication, and understanding why humans were compelled to adopt this new form of food production have been an important focus of anthropological archaeology. In this chapter, I examine from an institutional economic perspective the origins of agriculture and its transformative power on landscape. Fundamental to this perspective are the differing forms of institutional property rights between foragers and farmers. My archaeological perspective is from the middle Green River region of west-central Kentucky where there are significant sites from preagricultural hunting and gathering populations and information on a substantial shift to domesticated plant production during the subsequent period.

Archaeologically, while we can recover remains of the earliest domesticated plants, physical transformation of the landscape is difficult to ascertain in low-level food-production economies (Smith 2001). Intentional modification of a landscape—opening the forest canopy, protecting select trees, burning fields and forest understory, cultivating soil, sowing seeds, or encouraging select plants—has a major effect on forest ecology, but may leave only subtle archaeological signatures. The transformation, however, is fundamentally an institutional change in the way humans perceive resources, negotiate rights of access or ownership, and organize the social relations of production (Hann 1998). The challenge for archaeology is to build the inferential cases of landscape transformation that are inextricably linked to mind and matter. The prehistory of the Green River region provides us one of those cases.

In 1977, Douglass North and Robert Thomas (1977; a revised version is published in North 1981) published an essay on the origins of agriculture among hunting and gathering peoples, or what archaeologists once termed the Neolithic Revolution (Childe 1929). North and Thomas termed this watershed event in prehistory "the first economic revolution," apropos of Childe, because they believed that the transition to agriculture required a fundamental change in property rights before humans would shift their labor from hunting and gathering to agriculture.

> It was a revolution because the transition created for mankind an incentive change of fundamental proportions. The incentive change stems from the different property rights under the two systems. When common property rights over resources exist, there is little incentive for the acquisition of superior technology and learning. In contrast, exclusive property rights which reward the owners provide a direct incentive to improve efficiency and productivity, or, in more fundamental terms to acquire more knowledge and new techniques. It is this change in incentive that explains the rapid progress made by mankind in the last 10,000 years in contrast to his slow development during the long era of primitive hunting/gathering. (North 1981: 89)

North and Thomas make a very important point: the shift from foraging to agricultural production requires the emergence of a fundamentally new form of property rights among hunting and gathering groups. It is the incentive structure between differing forms of property rights that explains the long-term advantage of farming over foraging in economic history. An increase in the productivity in farming rewards the farmer with increased yields, while increased productivity in foraging over time will dissipate the stock of natural resources. If for no other reason, North and Thomas should be credited with changing the discussion on the origins of agriculture from a technological/ecological process to a social/institutional process.

To my knowledge, little specific comment has been forthcoming from archaeologists or anthropologists with regard to North's property rights argument (but see Mayhew's [1982] acerbic critique of North and

Thomas, and North's [1982] response). Without citing North as a source of ideas, however, Bowles and Choi (2002) use group selection models and agent-based simulation to examine what they call the "first property rights revolution." With a more sophisticated use of archaeological and ethnographic information than that employed by North, they suggest from their simulations that the persistence of common property institutions among hunters and gatherers could have been sustained by frequent intergroup conflict, significant levels of conformist cultural transmission, and second-order punishment of those who did not punish first-order transgressors. They conclude that exclusive communal property rights provided a better system of coordination among members of the group only after ownership was more clearly delineated with the domestication of plants and animals. In other words, "agriculture did not predate the emergence of individual property rights, for successful agriculture required these rights. . . . Thus, the eventual superior productivity of agriculture required the introduction of individual property rights and cannot account for the initial success of these rights" (Bowles and Choi 2002: 7). These findings would seem to be fully in agreement with North's property rights argument.

In an independent but related argument, James Woodburn (1980) distinguishes two mutually exclusive types of economic systems among extant hunters and gatherers and agricultural societies, which he terms "immediate-return economic systems" and "delayed-return economic systems." Delayed return simply means that there is some period of time (usually weeks to months) between the time labor is invested in a product and when a yield is obtained from that labor. Woodburn (1980: 97) notes that among the majority of human societies (including hunters and gatherers), return on labor is delayed. Among agriculturalists, delay is intrinsic to the system of production.

Immediate-return systems encompass those hunters and gatherers who, in general, obtain their food and other requirements on a daily basis and consume them daily or within a short period of time. Members of such societies avoid long-term commitments in using their labor and rarely develop food storage or other elaborate possessions. Tools and other technical items used in obtaining food and other requirements do not involve substantial time investment. Both economic systems (immediate and delayed) are common among hunting and gathering groups; however, only delayed-return systems characterize agricultural societies (Woodburn 1980: 98).

Woodburn's purpose in distinguishing these two types of economic systems was to point out that delayed return on labor is the fundamental basis for structural inequalities among members of the same group. Those vested with mobilizing and deploying labor also control yields on that labor. In contrast, immediate-return hunters and gatherers largely retain an egalitarian social order. While not explicit in Woodburn's argument, the nature of property rights is an essential distinguishing element between the two systems (however, see Barnard and Woodburn [1988] for discussion in this regard).

These two seminal ideas—the property rights revolution and delayed-return economies—are my impetus for examining the nature of property rights among hunters and gatherers and how the transition to agricultural production occurred in prehistory in my area of research: the Green River valley of west-central Kentucky. I will begin by describing the evidence we have for property rights institutions among Archaic period (ca. 10,000 to 3,000 years ago) hunters and gatherers and for a significant change in property rights during the subsequent Early Woodland period (ca. 3,000 to 2,200 years ago), contemporaneous with the first evidence of horticultural economies in eastern North America. The first archaeological evidence comes from a region of the middle to lower Green River known to contain a large number of freshwater shell midden sites, and the second set of evidence comes from the Mammoth Cave region of the middle Green River valley (see fig. 6.1). I will follow this description with a discussion of a general model of hunter-gatherer property institutions and end with a transaction cost hypothesis to explain the fundamental change in property rights that transformed the incentive structure to invest labor in horticultural pursuits beginning some 3,000 years ago in eastern North America.

Archaeology of the Green River Region

The Green River is a tributary of the middle Ohio River. It contained numerous stable river shoals that were prime habitat for freshwater mussels and provided rich fishing areas (Morey and Crothers 1998; Morey et al. 2002). The shell midden sites of the Green River valley have been the focus of several large archaeological projects beginning with Clarence B. Moore (1916) and William S. Webb (Webb 1946, 1950a, 1950b; Webb and Haag 1939, 1940, 1947), and continuing today (Marquardt and Watson 2005).

Although humans first occupied the Green River valley more than 10,000 years ago, the intensive use of these shoal areas dates primarily from 6,500 to 3,000 years ago (based on calibrated radiocarbon ages; see Crothers 1999). Intensive collecting of mussels and fish by prehistoric hunters and gatherers created dense, deep shell middens along the riverbank. Riverine resources, however, were only part of the diet of the hunters and gatherers who used these locations. The midden deposits also contain abundant

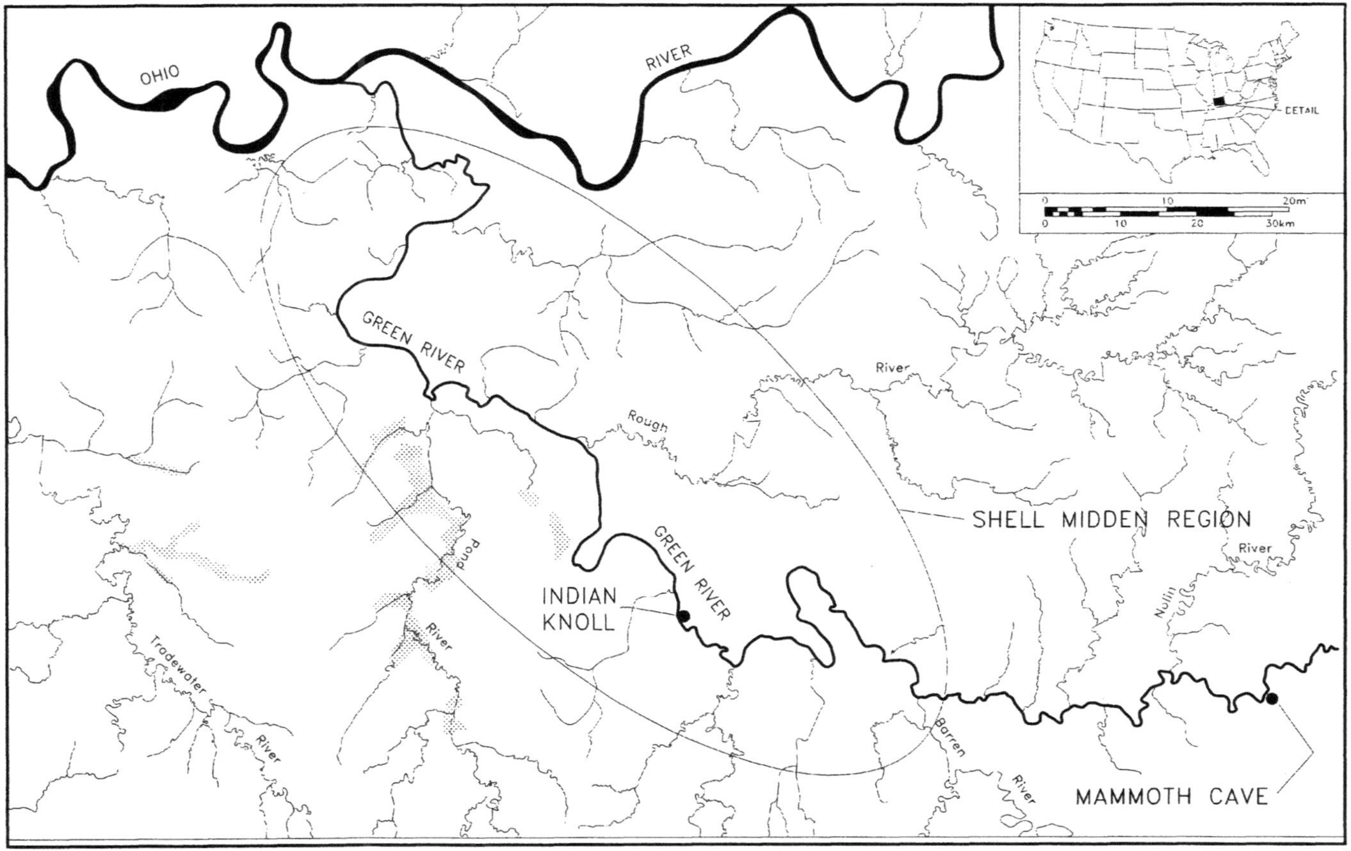

Figure 6.1 The lower and middle Green River area and location of sites discussed in the text. (Drawing by George Crothers.)

animal bone (deer, squirrel, rabbit, and turkey, as well as bones of fish and turtles; Crothers 1999, 2005; Glore 2005), copious amounts of nutshell (hickory, black walnut, and acorn), and less commonly, seeds of fleshy fruit (e.g., grape, persimmon, blackberry, and honey locust) and grains (e.g., knotweed types and grasses; Crawford 2005; Crothers 1999; Wagner 2005). Archaeological features include clusters of fire-cracked rock and large hearths or cooking surfaces, but no evidence of permanent structures or facilities that indicate long-term occupation. However, human interments are an important component of these sites. For example, more than 1,100 burials were excavated just from the Indian Knoll site, the most famous of the Green River shell middens (Moore 1916; Webb 1946).

Historically, the archaeology of these sites is integral to conceptions of Archaic period society (e.g., Haag 1942) and research on the origins of agriculture (e.g., Watson 1985). In particular, Bruce Smith (e.g., 1989, 1992) identifies the deep midden sites of eastern North America as the settings where prehistoric hunters and gatherers began a coevolutionary relationship with several native plant species that ultimately led to their domestication. Smith believes that the initial domestication of eastern North American seed-bearing plants (i.e., sunflower—*Helianthus annuus*, sumpweed—*Iva annua*, goosefoot—*Chenopodium* sp., and squash—*Cucurbita* sp.) occurred in these "continually disturbed anthropogenic habitats" where seeds had been introduced as weedy camp followers or as commensal floodplain weeds.

> Introduced from wild floodplain stands into midden mound and shell mound settlements each year either by floodwaters or human collectors, the seeds of *Cucurbita*, sumpweed and goosefoot would have quickly colonized these disturbed habitat patches where they would have thrived as weedy invaders. While the sunflower (*Helianthus annuus*) also initially colonized these "domestilocalities" . . . as a weedy invader, it was apparently adventive to the Eastern Woodlands during the Middle Holocene, rather than being indigenous to the region. (Smith 1992: 283)

Smith (1986) and others (e.g., Brown 1985; Winters 1974) see in the archaeological record of mid-Holocene shell midden sites evidence for the beginning of sedentary behavior and gradual intensification of low-level food production economies (see also Smith 2001). I will return to Smith's ideas in the context of hunter-gatherer property rights institutions below.

There are several problems with the evolutionary model of increasing sedentary behavior and food production as it relates to the archaeology of the Green River shell middens (see Crothers and Bernbeck 2004 for additional discussion). First, the quantity of shell in the deposits and other evidence suggest that the sites were formed by rapidly paced, intensive depositional events (e.g., large-scale feasting associated with burial ritual). Second, the sites lack evidence of structures or other facilities typically associated with sedentary or semisedentary occupations. Third, despite major efforts to recover carbonized remains of the plants that are part of the eastern North America horticultural complex from these shell midden sites, very little evidence has been forthcoming to indicate the use of these seeds either as wild, ruderal forms or as early stage domesticates (Crawford 2005; Wagner 2005).

The archaeological record of the subsequent Early Woodland period in the Green River valley is of a very different nature than that of the Archaic period shell middens. Although we do not have comparable midden sites from the Early Woodland period, the remains found in the Mammoth Cave system and rockshelter sites like Peter Cave (Crawford 2005) suggest that the transition to horticultural production was under way by 3000 BP and reflects many of the attributes of a delayed-return economic system as suggested by Woodburn (1980). The archaeology of Mammoth and Salts caves has been well documented by Patty Jo Watson (1969, 1974) and several specialized analyses conducted on remains preserved within the cave environment (e.g., Gremillion and Sobolik 1996; Sobolik et al. 1996; Watson and Yarnell 1966, 1986).

To briefly summarize, Mammoth and Salts caves are two extensive cave systems that were explored prehistorically for several kilometers beginning ca. 5,500 years ago, and then extensively mined for at least two cave minerals beginning ca. 3,000 years ago and lasting until 2,200 years ago. The two minerals are gypsum (hydrous calcium sulfate, $CaSO_4{\cdot}2H_2O$) and mirabilite (hydrous sodium sulfate, $Na_2SO_4{\cdot}10H_2O$). Prehistorically, gypsum may have been used to make white paint, or possibly the exotically shaped crystals were prized. Mirabilite, however, is a medicinal salt with cathartic effects if ingested in sufficient quantity. The prehistoric use of mirabilite as a cathartic seems self-evident because the dry environment in the cave has preserved thousands of desiccated human paleofeces. It is the analysis of the paleofeces that provides us with incontrovertible evidence that the Early Woodland people who explored and mined Mammoth and Salts caves were engaged in growing several domesticated plants (i.e., sunflower, sumpweed, chenopodium, maygrass, and squash) and consuming the seeds as important dietary items (Gremillion and Sobolik 1996; Watson 1969).

I have argued elsewhere that the archaeology of Mammoth and Salts caves represents something more than the prehistoric mining of exotic minerals for trade (Crothers 2001; Crothers 2004). First, among cultures worldwide, caves and cavelike structures are often used when secrecy or intimidation is important to conducting a ritual or ceremony. Rites of passage are one common use of caves (see Crothers 2004 for examples). Second, a study of the relative amounts of two of the steroids, testosterone and estradiol, measured in twelve paleofecal samples from Mammoth and Salts caves, indicates that all twelve samples were deposited by males. (Sobolik et al. 1996). In addition, historically, two prehistoric bodies have been found in the cave. One is of an adult male, approximately forty-five years old, who had been crushed by a large rock while mining gypsum in Mammoth Cave (Neumann 1938; Pond 1937), and the second was of a young boy, approximately nine years of age, who presumably died after becoming lost or hurt in Salts Cave (Robbins 1971). Third, ingestion of cathartic salts in the cave appears to have been for its more or less immediate effect, which suggests that purging was also important to events taking place in the cave setting. Based on the totality of archaeological evidence, I have suggested that Early Woodland peoples used Mammoth and Salts caves to conduct male initiation rites that included use of the deep cave environment for secrecy and possibly as a means of sensory deprivation, ritual purging by ingesting cathartic salts, and collection of gypsum for white body paint or other symbolic use as a marker of the initiate's new position in society.

An important part of my interpretation of cave use as a setting for male initiation rites is also to explain its timing during the Early Woodland period. Caves in the Early Woodlands were routinely explored to impressive depths (using torch light to penetrate several kilometers beyond any known entrances) for nearly 2,500 years before any mining of cave minerals is evident (Crothers et al. 2002). It is precisely (archaeologically speaking) with the rise of horticultural economies in eastern North America that we see a change in the use of caves and intense interest in cave minerals. This is where Woodburn's concept of delayed-return economic systems is important. Socially, the differences between immediate- and delayed-return systems are related to the development of corporate households and other extradomestic forms of social groupings. That is, delayed-return economies are associated with a range of committed, binding social relationships of kinship or of contract in which the participants have formal, dependent obligations to one another. One broad theme among delayed-return systems is the intensification of control by men over women and young men (Woodburn 1980: 111). The process involves increasing incorporation of women and young men into committed kinship and affinal relationships in which ideological control is vested predominantly in older men. "Ideologies of domination are developed, especially in ritual contexts, in which the substantial real control which, in immediate-return systems, women enjoy over their own sexual and reproductive capacities and their own labour is increasingly denied" (Barnard and Woodburn 1988: 29).

In the prehistory of the Green River valley, we see two distinct forms of economy and social organization. In the earlier Archaic period, represented by the large shell midden sites, we see a forager model based on an immediate-return economic system. In the subsequent Early Woodland period, represented by Mammoth and Salts caves, we see the development of extradomestic social groupings in ritual contexts as predicted by Woodburn for the transition to delayed-return economic systems. What we still lack is an understanding of property rights institutions among immediate-return hunting and gathering populations and the mechanisms that would cause hunters and gatherers to delineate new forms of property rights, which North predicts are necessary before labor will be invested in delayed-return agricultural pursuits.

Property Rights Institutions among Hunters and Gatherers

Reinhard Bernbeck and I (2004) attempted to derive a model of hunting and gathering behavior based on an institutional structure of open access to resources and sharing of resources and information that enables mobility and autonomy at the individual level. We believe that this institutional structure results in hunting and gathering populations with fluid group composition, highly flexible social relations, and a system of dynamic interaction with other foragers and the environment. In other contexts, these forms of forager agency have been described as the "original affluent society" by Marshall Sahlins (1998), the "giving environment" by Nurit Bird-David (1990), "limited wants, unlimited means" by John Gowdy (1998), and, as already discussed, "immediate-return economic systems."

Mobility is the fundamental feature of immediate-return hunters and gatherers and the means through which foragers cope with variability in the environment and maintain interaction among a dispersed population. Mobility enables foragers to take advantage of open resources in an environment and to collect information on resources and other people in that environment. We argue that there are potentially two kinds of crises that hunters and gatherers may experience: overpopulation and accompanying depletion of local resources, and maximal population dispersal resulting in a negative reproduction rate. Mobility is essential to minimizing risk in both economic production and biological reproduction of the forager group (Crothers and Bernbeck 2004: 407–9).

In an environment with low population density, repeated interaction, and free information, there is no incentive to establish exclusive property rights as long as comparable resources remain ungarnered. In fact, there may be an incentive to maintain open access to resources where biological reproduction risks falling below replacement.[1] Institutions of common property and sharing are incentives that increase forager interaction, enabling hunters and gatherers to operate with low population density in highly variable or novel environments. These same institutions, however, constrain individuals from investing in delayed-return endeavors, which is the point of North's (1981) concept of the first economic revolution.

Rada Dyson-Hudson and Eric Alden Smith (1978) propose an economic defendability model to predict when groups might assert exclusive use to a resource or territory. According to this model, territoriality is expected to occur when critical resources are sufficiently abundant and predictable in space and time, so that the cost of exclusive use and defense of an area or resource are outweighed by the benefits gained from resource control. North (1981: 86) essentially proposes this same idea driven by population pressure to explain the agricultural transition. He believes the process, historically, "consisted of first excluding outsiders from harvesting [a rich] resource and then devising rules to limit the intensity of exploitation of the resource by insiders." This is also Bruce Smith's (1992) argument with regard to the creation of domestilocalities represented by floodplain shell midden sites (albeit, not in explicit economic terms). Hunters and gatherers, first attracted to rich riverine resources, created anthropogenically disturbed habitats where they introduced seed-bearing plants that ultimately entered into a domesticatory process. In Smith's explanation, defendability results from the rich riverine resources and only secondarily (and unconsciously) do domesticated plants enter into the equation. Smith assumes that these sites, or domestilocalities, are occupied, and presumably defended, at least on a seasonal basis. However, as described earlier, I do not believe the archaeological record of shell midden sites supports this scenario, nor do we have evidence to infer exclusive property rights that we should expect for sedentary populations, such as permanent facilities, structures, or monumental architecture.

Elizabeth Cashdan (1983) describes an alternative model of property rights that she believes is more representative of hunting and gathering groups. She calls this the "social boundary defense" (as opposed to "perimeter defense" or the economic defendability model). In the case of overt competition for resources, groups typically mark the perimeter of their territory boundary and control access to the space itself (i.e., perimeter defense; Cashdan 1983: 49). However, where territories are large and resources are variable, hunters and gatherers control access to resources by limiting access to the social group inhabiting the area (i.e., social boundary defense). Rather than defending a perimeter, the institutional structure requires groups or individuals wishing to access resources in an area to ask permission for acceptance into the local land-using group. Citing the work of Peterson (1975; see also Peterson 1993) in Australia, Cashdan indicates that rites of entry into a social group take the form of elaborate greeting ceremonies. Failure to observe these ceremonies increases the likelihood of aggression from the offended group. Once a party has been through a rite of entry, however, it has equal access to resources of the territory (Cashdan 1983: 49).

Rites of entry also have the ability to form important social networks. Information exchange is an important function of these use rights. Where habitual territories are large and resources vary both spatially and annually, outsiders can minimize their foraging costs if they obtain information from residents concerning the location of resources. There is an incentive to seek access to the social group because it is through the social interactions of these rituals that information on resources is obtained.

The historically dominant model of increasing sedentary behavior or the economic defendability model has limited our understanding of the institutional structure of prehistoric hunters and gatherers. I suggest that immediate-return hunters and gatherers held a form of common property institutions best captured by Cashdan's concept of the social boundary defense. That is, resources remained common property as long as protocol was followed to request access from the local group. Presumably, this form of property rights evolved as a stable strategy devised by hunters and gatherers to manage environmental variability and maintain interaction among dispersed populations.

Rich shellfishing and fishing locations in the Green River initially may have attracted groups of hunters and gatherers to repeatedly exploit these resources, engage in rites of entry, and exchange information. These locations were probably central to the local resource-using group for numerous social engagements. Clearly, burial ceremony was important at these sites. However, these sites do not conform to the notion of discrete burial mounds or cemetery locations, which become common in later time periods, because a whole range of other activities are represented among the material remains—food preparation, tool production, and manufacture of beads, pendants, and other nonutilitarian objects (see also Milner and Jefferies 1998). It is also evident that among the burial sample a portion of the population experienced perimortem violent injuries. Mensforth (2001) indicates that between 5 and 11.3 percent of the individuals interred at three Green River Archaic sites (including Indian Knoll) show evidence of perimortem violence—penetrating wounds, blunt force trauma—and trophy-taking behavior such as scalping, decapitation, and dismemberment. Adult males were the primary victims of these conflicts (approximately 77 percent of the individuals with violent injuries that could be reliably identified by sex). All of the sites examined by Mensforth contain graves with multiple individuals, and in all cases one or more of the individuals in these multiple burials show evidence of perimortem violent injury (Mensforth 2001: 117–18).

It would seem that policing, sanctioning, and punishment were also important activities carried out collectively among the local resource-using group, as suggested by Bowles and Choi (2002) in their simulation of hunter-gatherer social order. Presumably, death and violence were not the only contexts for social engagement at these sites, however. Birth, naming ceremonies, marriage, visiting, entertaining, alliance formation, or simply celebration of plentiful resources could have been occasions to participate in feasting and communal activity. Hunter-gatherer life was a complex dynamic that is not adequately captured by a scenario of increasing sedentary behavior or the economic defendability model. In the elegant words of Eric Wolf (1984: 397), "Human life depends on how humans engage the reality of nature. I do not think, however, that it is all a matter of protein capture and the whelping of human litters. We do not attack reality only with tools and teeth, we also grasp it with the forceps of the mind—and we do so socially, in social interaction and cultural communication with our fellows and enemies."

Although an institutional ethic of sharing may have precluded anyone from being denied access if he or she made the proper request, herein lies the problem. As long as population density remained low and resources remained ungarnered, there was an incentive to participate in this decorous form of common property defined by social boundaries and negotiated through rites of entry. Social networks were intimate, interaction was iterative, and information was freely obtained and given. Hunters and gatherers were able to move with fluidity and relative autonomy in a dynamic environment.

In North's (1981: 77) comparative static economic model, three changes could account for the transition from hunting and gathering to agriculture: "Individually or acting in concert, (1) a decline in the productivity of labor in hunting, (2) a rise in the productivity of labor in agriculture, or (3) a sustained expansion of the size of the labor force." (See Weisdorf 2003 for additional discussion.) Conditions one (decline in the productivity of labor in hunting) and three (expansion of the size of the labor force) are related. An increase in local population that creates more demand on resources, or a change in environmental conditions that reduces productivity of resources would cause a decline in the productivity of labor in hunting and gathering. Condition two (rise in the productivity of labor in agriculture) depends on the technology of agriculture already in place. As North suggests, and Bowles and Choi (2002) reaffirm, the transition to agriculture first requires an incentive change brought about by a change in property rights institutions. What conditions, then, would cause the collective action of a social boundary group to deny more entrants, and, conversely, to forgo one's own entry into other extralocal groups?

The economic concept of *transaction costs* is useful here. Transaction costs are the costs associated with making an economic exchange (as opposed to production costs—i.e., transforming a resource into a usable product). Transaction costs include acquiring knowledge, bargaining, and policing and enforcement of agreements between transacting parties (Acheson 2002: 29; Eggertsson 1990: 14; North 1990: 27). In the case of social boundary defense, the group requesting entrance to a region incurs relatively small and fixed transaction costs to perform greeting ceremonies to gain the right of entry. The receiving group, likewise, does not incur significant transaction costs as long as local resources remain plentiful. Both groups benefit by exchanging information: information that is immediately useful to the requesting group and information that can be banked by the receiving group for future consideration in its own mobility decisions. Engaging in greeting ceremonies for rights of entry and permitting new groups access to resources of an area will be mutually beneficial as long as resources are abundant and populations remain dispersed over large areas.

At some threshold of available resources vis-à-vis population, however, the cost of policing and enforcement of agreements among transacting groups in a social boundary model begins to have a real cost. Population increase (an expansion in the size of the labor force, in economic terms) and/or a decline in the productivity in labor of hunting and gathering (e.g., by climatic change or by overhunting and overgathering) increases the cost of negotiating rites of entry and policing and enforcement of social boundary contracts. Efforts to hide resources (e.g., by giving false information) may be a means to exclude entrants, but, if caught, could lead to retribution. While ultimately this is a population pressure/resource imbalance argument, the result does not necessarily result in measurable physiological stress to the population (i.e., indicators of starvation or chronic malnutrition). Stress, however, is occurring at an organizational structural level: the ability to monitor multiple social boundaries and competing interests. For example, Dunbar (1992) shows that among primates, group size is a function of relative neocortical volume. He suggests that the number of neocortical neurons limits an organism's information-processing capacity and that this limits the number of relationships an individual can monitor simultaneously. When group size exceeds this limit, the group becomes unstable and begins to fragment. Ethnographically, groups of about twenty-five people are common among foragers. Of these groups, on average about seven or eight individuals will be full-time foragers (the others being adolescents or infirm). Kelly (1995: 213) states: "In most environments, a group containing this number of foragers probably minimizes daily variance in return rates while also minimizing the rate of local resource depletion."

Immediate-return hunters and gatherers maintain mobility in order to react fluidly to conditions of resource depletion and local overcrowding. However, a model of hunter-gatherer mobility is stable only where a frontier remains open to absorb surplus population. This condition seems to have remained from the first entrance of humans into the continent (conservatively put at 11,500 to 12,000 years ago) until approximately 3,000 years ago in eastern North America. During the Late Archaic period, represented by shell midden sites in the Green River valley, hunters and gatherers would have attempted to maintain the institutional structure of an immediate-return economy even under increasing transaction costs. The levels of interpersonal violence and acts of trophy taking identified by Mensforth (2001) may be a reflection of these increased costs.

There are two ways that a group might have broken with the immediate-return hunter-gatherer economic system and delineated exclusive rights to property. In the first case, as already discussed in terms of Dyson-Hudson and Smith's economic defendability model and Smith's concept of domestilocalities, a group might establish exclusive communal property rights by refusing new entrants access to a resource area and having sufficient force to defend the newly claimed exclusive property. In this case, it would seem that the cost of policing and enforcing this new property regime would be even greater than the already overtaxed social boundary model. As I have already discussed, the archaeological evidence, at least in the Green River valley, does not support this alternative. Sites in these resource-rich zones lack evidence of permanent structures and facilities, the principal plants involved in the domestication process are lacking, and these sites appear to be largely abandoned after 3000 BP when domesticates begin showing up in other contexts (Crothers and Bernbeck 2004; Crothers 1999).

In the second case, the strongest groups could continue to compete for the richest resource zones, but the cost of policing access among using groups and negotiating with new entrants would continue to increase. A group attempting to reduce transaction costs, however, might forgo access to the richest resource zones and be satisfied with resources in less productive portions of the environment, which were less likely to be contested. Whether one wants to characterize this as a defiant break with the dominant social boundary model and the imposition of a new property rights regime, or a case of weaker groups being excluded from richer resource zones and forced to get by with secondary resources, the result is the same. The group that no longer competes for access to the richest resource zones has reduced its transaction costs, as long as the dominant groups allow it to claim exclusive access to "undesirable" resources. Excluded from the social boundary model, the new land-using group would have to develop new strategies of storage and increased labor inputs to ensure productivity of key resources—strategies to reduce risk that were formerly mitigated by being mobile, engaging in reciprocal alliances, and having a wide knowledge of surrounding regions. Once removed from the immediate-return economic system, the "incentive" to invest in marginal resources may have been necessitated by limited options. In turn, investment in delayed-return labor pursuits would have further limited mobility options. It was only with morphological change in the plants that were brought into the domesticatory process that a rise in the productivity of labor in agriculture would encourage incipient farmers to shift even more labor inputs from hunting and gathering to farming.

The argument that I have presented here relies on an element of population pressure, in the tradition of Binford's (1968) demographic argument and Flannery's (1969, 1973) "marginal zone" hypothesis on the origins of agriculture. The demographic element in a transaction cost model requires that population be of sufficient density so that the addition of new groups into a region puts stress on the overall system. As population density increases, the acquisition of knowledge to continually redistribute groups or individuals relative to available resources becomes increasingly complex and costly. Pressure occurs not at the level of physiological and nutritional well-being, but rather at the social and economic level of transacting with competing groups for access and sharing information.

The concept of marginal zones is highly subjective depending on the technology employed to produce food and on a concept of what constitutes food. We can speak of marginal zones only in reference to what is considered desirable, whether we rank that desire based on maximum caloric intake, minimal time investment, or some other attribute. What is critical for the transaction cost argument is that portions of the landscape and resources within that environment did not rank sufficiently as an important food resource to be contested in the dominant social boundary model. My purpose is not to characterize specific environments as marginal, but rather to emphasize the underlying institutional structure that might bring about this change in economic systems.

I have tried to draw a plausible explanatory sketch to account for the archaeological evidence in the Green River valley as it relates to the transition from foraging to the first farming societies in eastern North America. While I have put emphasis on the institutional structure as the underlying social and economic reason for this fundamental transition, I have not tried to account for the pace and spread of this transition. On the one hand, I can imagine that agriculture came to be the dominant mode of production, once the institutional structure of exclusive communal property was established, by gradually outcompeting hunters and gatherers. On the other hand, the transition appears to be so rapid and widespread that I can also imagine that the creation of a new form of property rights had a cascade affect across the region. In this case, the immediate-return economic system must have reached a point of catharsis in which an entirely new social and economic order had to emerge on a panregional basis. At present, we lack the theoretical sophistication and adequate resolution in the archaeological record to address this aspect of the phenomenon.

The first economic revolution, as North termed it, transformed the landscape in fundamental ways. This transformation included both perception of what constitutes property and the incentive structure to invest in delayed-return labor. Exclusive communal property rights were necessary to ensure ownership of the fruits of that labor. A transaction cost analysis suggests that the origins of agriculture, rather then being the product of increasing social complexity, at its core may have been an attempt to decrease the complexity of social interactions resulting from a social boundary model of common property. This transformation, of course, created new problems requiring new forms of social organization and new forms of property relations that we define as complex society.

It is in the archaeology of Mammoth and Salts caves that this transformation is most clearly expressed. Caves were casually entered and explored by hunters and gatherers as subterranean extensions of the landscape for some 2,500 years. With the first horticultural economies in eastern North America, caves took on a new meaning in the cognitive landscape. The deep interiors of caves became ritual space, and cave resources were imbued with symbolic importance. During the Early Woodland period, caves became places to solidify social relations that involved the ritualized incorporation of young men into committed relations controlled by older men (Woodburn 1980). In essence, the social landscape was transformed from a hunter-gatherer model of immediacy, autonomy, and sharing into a societal model of segmentation and exclusion that we live with today.

Notes

Lisa Cliggett and Chris Pool provided instructive comments throughout the editorial and review process. Patty Jo Watson read and commented on an early draft of this paper. Tony Eff provided comments and, in particular, provided several references that help clarify my argument.

1. By *property rights* I mean the "rights of individuals to use resources" (Eggertsson 1990: 33). Exclusive property rights can be held by individuals (i.e., private ownership) or by a group (i.e., communal ownership), whereby a community controls access to a resource by excluding outsiders and regulating its use by insiders (Eggertsson 1990: 36). Institutional economists do not typically distinguish between *common property* and *open access*. Most economic anthropologists, however, define *open access* as situations in which no one holds any rights, and *common property* as situations in which only members of the agnatic group have rights of use (e.g., Bell 1998: 32). For my purposes here, I use common property broadly to include open access resources (cf. McCay and Acheson 1987).

References

Acheson, James M. 2002. "Transaction Cost Economics: Accomplishments, Problems, and Possibilities." In *Theory in Economic Anthropology*, ed. J. Ensminger, 27–58. Walnut Creek, CA: AltaMira.

Barnard, Alan, and James Woodburn. 1988. "Property, Power, and Ideology in Hunter-Gatherer Societies: An Introduction." In *Hunters and Gatherers 2: Property, Power, and Ideology*, ed. T. Ingold, D. Riches, and J. Woodburn, 4–32. Oxford: Berg.

Bell, Duran. 1998. "The Social Relations of Property and Efficiency." In *Property in Economic Context*, ed. R. C. Hunt and A. Gilman, 29–45. Lanham, MD: University Press of America.

Binford, Lewis R. 1968. "Post-Pleistocene Adaptation." In *New Perspectives in Archaeology*, ed. S. R. Binford and L. R. Binford, 313–41. Chicago: Aldine.

Bird-David, Nurit. 1990. "The Giving Environment: Another Perspective on the Economic System of Gatherer-Hunters." *Current Anthropology* 31:189–96.

Bowles, Samuel, and Jung-Kyoo Choi. 2002. "The First Property Rights Revolution." Santa Fe Institute working paper presented at the Workshop on Coevolution of Behaviors and Institutions, Santa Fe Institute, January 10–12, 2003.

Brown, James A. 1985. "Long-Term Trends to Sedentism and the Emergence of Complexity in the American Midwest." In *Prehistoric Hunter-Gatherers: The Emergence of Cultural Complexity*, ed. T. D. Price and J. A. Brown, 201–31. Orlando: Academic Press.

Cashdan, Elizabeth. 1983. "Territoriality among Human Foragers: Ecological Models and an Application to Four Bushman Groups." *Current Anthropology* 24:47–66.

Childe, V. Gordon. 1929. *The Most Ancient East: The Oriental Prelude to European Prehistory*. New York: Knopf.

Crawford, Gary W. 2005. "Plant Remains from Carlston Annis (1972, 1974), Bowles, and Peter Cave." In Marquardt and Watson 2005, 181–212.

Crothers, George M. 1999. "Prehistoric Hunters and Gatherers, and the Archaic Period Green River Shell Middens of Western Kentucky." PhD diss., Washington University.

———. 2001. "Mineral Mining and Perishable Remains in Mammoth Cave: Examining Social Process in the Early Woodland Period." In *Fleeting Identities: Perishable Material Culture in Archaeological Research*, ed. P. B. Drooker, 314–34. Occasional Paper No. 28, Center for Archaeological Investigations. Carbondale: Southern Illinois University Press.

———. 2004. "Ritual Use of Caves in Eastern North America during the Early Woodland Period." Paper presented at the 69th Annual Meeting of the Society for American Archaeology, Montreal.

———. 2005. "Vertebrate Fauna from the Carlston Annis Site." In Marquardt and Watson 2005, 295-314.

Crothers, George M., and Reinhard Bernbeck. 2004. "The Foraging Mode of Production: The Case of the Green River Archaic Shell Middens." In *Hunters and Gatherers in Theory and Archaeology*, ed. G. M. Crothers, 401–22. Occasional Paper No. 31, Center for Archaeological Investigations. Carbondale: Southern Illinois University Press.

Crothers, George M., Charles H. Faulkner, Jan F. Simek, Patty Jo Watson, and Patrick S. Willey. 2002. "Woodland Cave Archaeology in Eastern North America." In *The Woodland Southeast*, ed. D. G. Anderson and R. C. Mainfort Jr., 502–24. Tuscaloosa: University of Alabama Press.

Dunbar, R. I. M. 1992. "Neocortex Size as a Constraint on Group Size in Primates." *Journal of Human Evolution* 20:469–93.

Dyson-Hudson, Rada, and Eric Alden Smith. 1978. "Human Territoriality: An Ecological Reassessment." *American Anthropologist* 80:21–41.

Eggertsson, Thráinn. 1990. *Economic Behavior and Institutions*. Cambridge: Cambridge University Press.

Flannery, Kent V. 1969. "Origins and Ecological Effects of Early Domestication in Iran and the Near East." In *The Domestication and Exploitation of Plants and Animals*, ed. P. J. Ucko and G. W. Dimbleby, 73–100. London: Duchworth.

———. 1973. "The Origins of Agriculture." *Annual Review of Anthropology* 2:271–310.

Glore, Michael T. 2005. "Vertebrate Faunal Remains from the Carlston Annis Site (15Bt5): An Evaluation of Cultural Stratigraphy." In Marquardt and Watson 2005, 315–37.

Gowdy, John. 1998. "Introduction: Back to the Future and Forward to the Past." In *Limited Wants, Unlimited Means: A Reader on Hunter-Gatherer Economics and the Environment*, ed. J. Gowdy, xv–xxxi. Washington, DC: Island Press.

Green, Nicholas. 1995. "Looking at the Landscape: Class Formation and the Visual." In *The Anthropology of Landscape: Perspectives on Place and Space*, ed. E. Hirsch and M. O'Hanlon, 31–42. Oxford: Oxford University Press.

Gremillion, Kristen J., and Kristin D. Sobolik. 1996. "Dietary Variability among Prehistoric Forager-Farmers of Eastern North America." *Current Anthropology* 37:529–39.

Haag, William G. 1942. "Early Horizons in the Southeast." *American Antiquity* 7:209–22.

Hann, C. M. 1998. "Introduction: The Embeddedness of Property." In *Property Relations: Renewing the Anthropological Tradition*. Cambridge: Cambridge University Press.

Kelly, Robert L. 1995. *The Foraging Spectrum: Diversity in Hunter-Gatherer Lifeways*. Washington, DC: Smithsonian Institution Press.

Marquardt, William H., and Patty Jo Watson, eds. 2005. *Archaeology of the Middle Green River Region*. Institute of Archaeology and Paleoenvironmental Studies Monograph No. 5. Gainesville: Florida Museum of Natural History.

Mayhew, Anne. 1982. "'The First Economic Revolution' As Fiction." *Economic History Review* 35:568–71.

McCay, Bonnie J., and James M. Acheson. 1987. "Human Ecology of the Commons." In *The Question of the Commons: The Culture and Ecology of Communal Resources*, ed. B. J. McCay and J. M. Acheson, 1–34. Tucson: University of Arizona Press.

Mensforth, Robert P. 2001. "Warfare and Trophy Taking in the Archaic Period." In *Archaic Transitions in Ohio and Kentucky Prehistory*, ed. O. H. Prufer, S. E. Pedde, and R. S. Meindl, 110–38. Kent, OH: Kent State University Press.

Milner, George R., and Richard W. Jefferies. 1998. "The Read Archaic Shell Midden in Kentucky." *Southeastern Archaeology* 17:119–32.

Moore, Clarence B. 1916. "Some Aboriginal Sites on Green River, Kentucky." *Journal of the Academy of Natural Sciences of Philadelphia* (Second Series) 16:431–87.

Morey, Darcy F., and George M. Crothers. 1998. "Clearing Up Clouded Waters: Paleoenvironmental Analysis of Freshwater Mussel Assemblages from the Green River Shell Middens, Western Kentucky." *Journal of Archaeological Science* 25:907–26.

Morey, Darcy F., George M. Crothers, Julie K. Stein, James P. Fenton, and Nicholas P. Herrmann. 2002. "The Fluvial and Geomorphic Context of Indian Knoll, an Archaic Shell Midden in West-Central Kentucky." *Geoarchaeology: An International Journal* 17:521–53.

Neumann, G. K. 1938. "The Human Remains from Mammoth Cave, Kentucky." *American Antiquity* 3:339–53.

North, Douglass C. 1981. *Structure and Change in Economic History*. New York: W. W. Norton.

———. 1982. "Reply to 'The First Economic Revolution' as Fiction." *Economic History Review* 35:572.

———. 1990. *Institutions, Institutional Change and Economic Performance*. Cambridge: Cambridge University Press.

North, Douglass C., and Robert P. Thomas. 1977. "The First Economic Revolution." *Economic History Review* 30:229–41.

Peterson, Nicolas. 1975. "Hunter-Gatherer Territoriality: The Perspective from Australia." *American Anthropologist* 77:53–68.

———. 1993. "Demand Sharing: Reciprocity and the Pressure for Generosity among Foragers." *American Anthropologist* 95:860–74.

Pond, Alonzo. 1937. "Lost John of Mummy Ledge." *Natural History* 39:176–84.

Robbins, Louise M. 1971. "A Woodland 'Mummy' from Salts Cave, Kentucky." *American Antiquity* 36:200–206.

Sahlins, Marshall. 1998. "The Original Affluent Society." In *Limited Wants, Unlimited Means: A Reader on Hunter-Gatherer Economics and the Environment*, ed. J. Gowdy, 5–41. Washington, DC: Island Press.

Smith, Bruce D. 1986. "The Archaeology of the Southeastern United States: From Dalton to de Soto, 10,500–500 B.P." In *Advances in World Archaeology*. Vol. 5, ed. F. Wendorf and A. E. Close, 1–92. Orlando: Academic Press.

———. 1989. "Origins of Agriculture in Eastern North America." *Science* 246:1566–71.

———. 1992. *Rivers of Change: Essays on Early Agriculture in Eastern North America*. Washington, DC: Smithsonian Institution Press.

———. 2001. "Low-Level Food Production." *Journal of Archaeological Research* 9:1–43.

Sobolik, Kristin D., Kristen J. Gremillion, Patricia L. Whitten, and Patty Jo Watson. 1996. "Technical Note: Sex Determination of Prehistoric Human Paleofeces." *American Journal of Physical Anthropology* 101:283–90.

Wagner, Gail E. 2005. "Anthropogenic Changes in the Carlston Annis Site." In Marquardt and Watson 2005, 213–42.

Watson, Patty Jo. 1969. *The Prehistory of Salts Cave, Kentucky. Report of Investigation No. 16*. Springfield: Illinois State Museum.

———. 1985. "The Impact of Early Horticulture in the Upland Drainages of the Midwest and Midsouth." In *Prehistoric Food Production in North America*, ed. R. I. Ford, 73–98. Anthropological Papers No. 75, Museum of Anthropology. Ann Arbor: University of Michigan Press.

———, ed. 1974. *Archeology of the Mammoth Cave Area*. New York: Academic Press.

Watson, Patty Jo, and Richard A. Yarnell. 1966. "Archaeological and Paleobotanical Investigations in Salts Cave, Mammoth Cave National Park, Kentucky." *American Antiquity* 31:842–49.

———. 1986. "Lost John's Last Meal." *Missouri Archaeologist* 47:241–55.

Webb, William S. 1946. "Indian Knoll, Site Oh 2, Ohio County, Kentucky." *Reports in Anthropology*. Vol. 4, no. 3, part I. Lexington: University of Kentucky Press.

———. 1950a. "The Carlson [*sic*] Annis Mound, Site 5, Butler County, Kentucky." *Reports in Anthropology*. Vol. 7, no. 4. Lexington: University of Kentucky Press.

———. 1950b. "The Read Shell Midden, Site 10, Butler County, Kentucky." *Reports in Anthropology*. Vol. 7, no. 5. Lexington: University of Kentucky Press.

Webb, William S., and William G. Haag. 1939. "The Chiggerville Site, Site 1, Ohio County, Kentucky." *Reports in Anthropology*. Vol. 4, no. 2. Lexington: University of Kentucky Press.

———. 1940. "Cypress Creek Villages, Sites 11 and 12, McLean County, Kentucky." *Reports in Anthropology*. Vol. 4, no. 2. Lexington: University of Kentucky Press.

———. 1947. "Archaic Sites in McLean County, Kentucky." *Reports in Anthropology*. Vol. 7, no. 1. Lexington: University of Kentucky Press.

Weisdorf, Jacob L. 2003. "From Foraging to Farming: Explaining the Neolithic Revolution." Discussion Paper No. 03-41, Institute of Economics, University of Copenhagen.

Wilmsen, Edwin N. 1989. *Land Filled with Flies: A Political Economy of the Kalahari*. Chicago: University of Chicago Press.

Winters, Howard D. 1974. "Introduction." In *Indian Knoll*, ed. William S. Webb, v–xxvii. Knoxville: University of Tennessee Press.

Wolf, Eric R. 1984. "Culture: Panacea or Problem?" *American Antiquity* 49:393–400.

Woodburn, James. 1980. "Hunters and Gatherers Today and Reconstruction of the Past." In *Soviet and Western Anthropology*, ed. E. Gellner, 95–117. New York: Columbia University Press.

7

Pastures Lost
The Decline of Mobile Pastoralism among Maasai and Rendille in Kenya, East Africa

ELLIOT FRATKIN

KENYAN PASTORALISTS, PEOPLE WHO SUBSIST OFF DOMESTIC livestock including cattle, camels, goats, and sheep, have faced a steady loss of their grazing resources over the last century. Maasai people, who herd cattle in the grassland savannas of southern Kenya and northern Tanzania, were excluded from nearly half of their former lands by European settlers during colonial rule, and saw the areas they were confined to further divided to make room for large national game parks. In the more arid and sparsely populated north of Kenya, pastoral groups including Rendille were constricted by "tribal grazing boundaries" imposed by British administrators to separate and reduce conflict between tribes; these boundaries significantly reduced grazing territories. Following independence in 1963, Kenyan pastoralists saw further declines in their herding environments as populations grew and towns and farms spread in the lowland areas. In the 1970s and 1980s, drought, famine, and ethnic violence sharply reduced herding ranges, particularly in Kenya's north where automatic weapons poured into pastoral areas from surrounding war-torn Sudan, Ethiopia, Somalia, and Uganda. Today, about one-half of Kenya's pastoral populations are able to keep enough livestock—cattle, camels, goats, and sheep—to maintain household viability, and many former pastoralists have drifted into towns and farmlands seeking alternative, and generally poorer, livelihoods.

In many ways, the situation in Kenya shares features with those described for New Mexico (MacLennan and Walck) and Brazil (Rivera) in this volume. All three countries or regions have seen large-scale transformations in landscape and land use in the past two centuries, brought about by a particular constellation of state or settler domination, the extraction of new forms of wealth from the land, the transfer or influx of immigrant populations, and the development of a class-based society built on ethnic or racial differences. These changes have been vast and over-reaching, and for the most part, have led to seemingly irreversible transformations in the social, economic, and physical landscapes.

This chapter describes transformations in the economy and changes in the way of life for pastoralists in Kenya, looking in particular at the Maasai in southern Kenya and the Rendille in northern Kenya. While the situations of these two groups are unique and distinct—the Maasai live in the immediate vicinity of Nairobi (population 3–4 million) and close to the crowded agricultural highlands of central Kenya while the Rendille live in the large and underpopulated Marsabit District near Ethiopia—both societies have undergone dramatic changes due to land loss and declines in livestock ownership. Until recently, the majority of these people were able to live off nomadic pastoralism, subsisting on the milk, meat, and trade of their livestock herds. As their grazing lands have been reduced, many Maasai and Rendille have been forced out of the pastoral economy, to take up farming or seek wage-paying jobs at low levels of the economic ladder.

There have been several significant developments in Kenya's recent history that have contributed to the loss of pastoral resources. These factors have affected all populations in Kenya—urban, agricultural, and pastoral—but they have had particular impact on pastoral peoples. The most important developments are rapid population growth, increased occurrences of drought and famine, the loss of common property resources and privatization of the rangelands, and increased violence, ethnic conflict, and political insecurity.

Population Growth

Kenya has one of the highest population growth rates in the world (2.5 percent in 2005, down from 3.75 percent in 1980). Kenya's population grew from about one million people in 1900 to six million in 1950 to its current figure of thirty-five million (Population Statistics 2006). As throughout Africa, this rapid growth is due to declining infant and child mortality rates with improved health care and vaccinations coupled with persistently high fertility rates. The HIV/AIDS epidemic has led to high mortality among young adults and declining life expectancies (forty-eight years for males, forty-seven for females in Kenya), but has not yet significantly affected population growth (UNFPA 2006). Rapid population growth has led to pressures on land use in both rural and urban areas. Farmers increasingly move onto less productive lands, including dry lands previously occupied by livestock pastoralists. Furthermore, pastoralists themselves have turned to farm cultivation, leading to a loss of pasture and water resources for other Maasai. In the more arid north where agriculture is possible only in isolated highland areas, population growth in both herds and humans has led to increasing competition between pastoral groups for pasture and water. Increased conflict over resources has been a main factor in interethnic violence, particularly in Marsabit District, Kenya (Galaty 2005).

Drought and Famine

Drought is not a recent phenomenon but a periodic condition that pastoralists have coped with in the past through continuing physical mobility, maintaining large herds to absorb loss, and keeping mixed species of animals to endure species-specific losses. But the frequency and intensity of droughts have increased since 1968, and famine—widespread dislocation and starvation—occurred in the 1970s, 1980s (the Ethiopian famine of 1982–1984), and 1990s as political disruption and civil war increased in the region (Ethiopia, Sudan, and Somalia). During these periods, northern Kenyan herders lost up to 80 percent of their small stock and half of their cattle to starvation, infectious diseases, and stock theft (Fratkin 2001).

Loss of Common Property Resources

Where livestock among most East African pastoralists constitutes individual or family property, access to land (for pasture, water, minerals, and security) historically was shared as a communal resource by territorial or kinship groups. Kenya, like other countries in Africa, has seen a rapid privatization of formerly communal lands, following policies encouraged by international donor organizations, specifically the World Bank and the United States Agency for International Development (USAID). The Maasai areas in southern Kenya in particular have seen a "land rush" resembling the one in the United States in the late nineteenth century, as small farmers and large commercial estates and ranches gained title to former Maasai pasture lands (Galaty 1992, 1999). In addition, the major game parks of Amboseli, Masai Mara, and Samburu, which are lucrative foreign-revenue earners for Kenya, have been located in pastoralist regions. These parks have highly restricted access to the pastoral herders who formerly depended on the land for grazing and water (Igoe 2003). The loss of common property rights is most severe in the populated regions of southern Kenya, and has not affected northern Kenyan pastoral groups to the same extent. However, the trend of privatizing and individualizing land rights continues to grow (Lesorogol 2005).

Violence, Ethnic Conflict, and Political Insecurity

Competition for grazing lands is not new among pastoralists. In the 1930s, the British set up tribal grazing areas in northern Kenya to keep competing groups separated. But ethnic conflict increased in the 1980s and 1990s under former president Daniel Arap Moi's *majimboism* (federalism). Maasai warriors served Moi in driving out Kikuyu voters from Rift Valley Province during the 1992 national elections. Armed cattle raiding has increased in northern Kenya between varying groups due to the large influx of automatic weapons from Sudan, Ethiopia, and Somalia (Galaty 2005). The violence and general political insecurity have led pastoralists to move closer to police posts and towns, putting pressure on existing grazing resources and leading to further loss of pasture and impoverishment of pastoral populations.

It is the interaction of these factors—demographic, political, economic, and social—that has contributed to the large-scale transformation in land use among pastoralists in Kenya, mainly the loss of open pastures and the ability of households to maintain viability. These factors do not happen equally. In some situations, as among the Maasai, it is the loss of common property rights that has had the most profound effect. Among the Rendille, common property rights are not a major issue; rather, it is the question of physical security in the face of drought and raids. By comparing the two cases, we may reach some general conclusions about the decline of pastoral viability in Kenya today, and of threats to mobile livestock pastoralism in general.

Traditional Pastoral Production

Until the mid-twentieth century, livestock-keeping pastoralists occupied over 70 percent of Kenya's land, although they never made up more than a small fraction of the country's total population. Today pastoralists number less than two million of Kenya's thirty-five million people, the overwhelming majority of whom are farmers, fishermen, or town dwellers. Kenya is an arid country, where annual rainfall above 1,000 mm is concentrated along the Indian Ocean coast, the western highlands near Lake Victoria, and the central highlands around Mount Kenya and Nairobi. The majority of the country is made up of savanna grassland or semidesert, areas generally too dry to support widespread agriculture. Savanna grasslands receive 500–1,000 mm of rain per year, and lie mainly in the south and east of the country; the north of Kenya is semidesert receiving less than 500 mm of rain annually and supporting almost no agriculture. Rather, it is home to nomadic pastoral groups relying on camels, cattle, and small stock.

Kenya's dramatic topography of large volcanic mountains separated by broad plains relates to the presence of the Great Rift Valley, a vast depression lying along the juncture of two tectonic plates from Mozambique to the Red Sea. Livestock-keeping pastoralists historically inhabited the Rift Valley lowlands, while farming groups settled in the highlands around Mount

Kenya and Mount Kilimanjaro. Cattle-keeping groups including Maasai, Samburu, and Boran live in higher elevations, while camel and small stock (goats and sheep) pastoralists occupy the drier deserts, including Turkana, Rendille, Gabra, and Somalis in the north (see fig. 7.1).

African pastoralists adapt to arid lands by their dependence on domestic animals that thrive in dry grazing conditions, including humped zebu cattle,

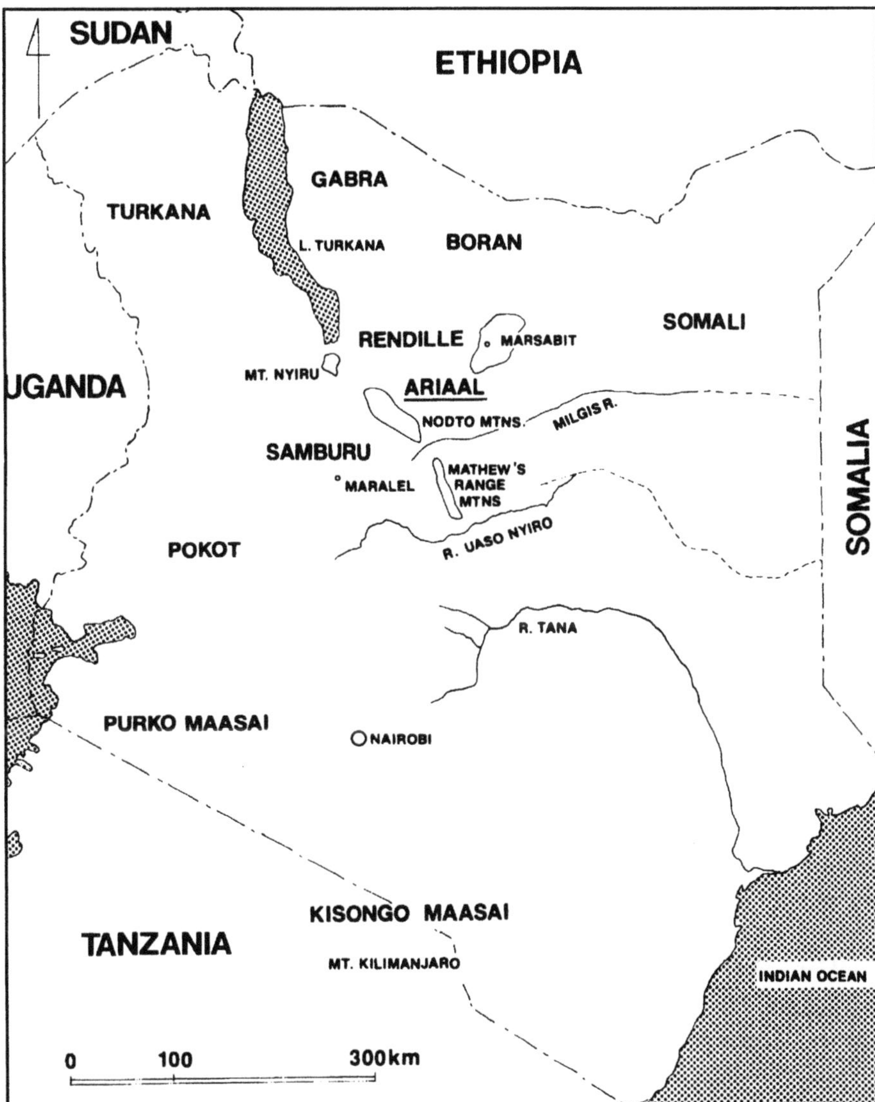

Figure 7.1 Pastoral peoples of Kenya.

camels, and short-haired sheep and goats. These animals convert patchy and varying vegetative resources into a daily supply of food for their herders, mainly milk but also meat, blood, and livestock products (milk, meat, hides, livestock) that are exchanged for grains, tea, and sugar. In functioning pastoral economies, large animals are kept principally for milk and as wealth, and small stock are consumed or traded for store-bought commodities. All livestock are important for rituals and social obligations, including bride wealth marriage payments and for sacrifice at age-set ceremonies. In the recent past, herd sizes were typically large, where individual Maasai herders owned two hundred cattle per stock owner, while northern pastoralists had fifty camels or cattle and large herds of sheep and goats per herd owner (Fratkin 2004).

Living in arid lands with periodic water resources and patchy vegetation, pastoral populations relied on mobility to graze their herds over wide areas. Because of the seasonality in rainfall and the high evaporation rate, vegetation resources deteriorate quickly, and herds were taken to short-lived pastures following periodic rainfall. Herding movements were consequently seasonal, with cattle alternating between highland and lowland resources and camels between home settlements and wide grazing areas away from the settlements. Mobility was the most prominent risk-aversion strategy available to pastoralists, allowing "full exploitation of forage resources that are unequally distributed in space and time" (Schwartz 2005: 69).

Restrictions in grazing range directly affected the size and condition of household herds, particularly in the more arid north. The Maasai, living in better-watered regions of the south, moved less frequently and were able to build large and permanent villages, including the large manyattas, or warrior villages, a feature that gave the Maasai considerable military strength in the nineteenth century (Spear and Waller 1993).

Pastoralists reduce risk of livestock loss by several strategies. One way is to maximize the number of animals they own. Although some ecologists and development economists argue that this method leads to overgrazing and environmental degradation (Lamprey 1983), others show that livestock numbers in pastoralist societies are held in check by disease, drought loss, limited household labor force, and market sales (Fratkin and Roth 1990; McCabe 2004). Another strategy is to diversify the types of animals in their herds, and East African pastoralists typically keep mixed herds of cattle, camels, goats, and sheep, so that if one type declines (e.g., cattle when infected with East Coast fever), other animals survive and even thrive (e.g., goats, who also reproduce quickly after droughts). A third risk-aversion strategy is herd dispersion, where stock owners separate their herds and have them herded in areas up to several hundred kilometers apart, as do the Ariaal Rendille in Kenya (Fratkin 2004).

None of these mechanisms of risk aversion can work if there is not enough territory to move one's herds (Behnke, Scoones, and Kerven 1993). When pastoralists find their herding range restricted, they risk deterioration in the condition of their animals due to lack of adequate forage, greater risk of herd loss to infectious disease or drought, and greater risk of theft from other pastoralists. The examples from Maasai and Rendille illustrate the declining productivity and risk to herd viability brought about by reduced herding environments.

The Maasai of Southern Kenya

In the nineteenth century, Maasai land stretched in an hourglass shape from Lake Turkana in northern Kenya down the broad plains of the Rift Valley to the Maasai Steppe of northern Tanzania. Never a single political entity, the Maasai are composed of a dozen independent groups including the Kisongo of Tanzania, and the Purko, Loita, Matapato, Kaputei, Sikiari, Loitokitok, Damat, Keekonyukie, ilKankeri, and Lo'odokilani Maasai of Kenya. In 1885, colonial conquest cut Maasai land in half with an international boundary between British Kenya and German Tanganyika. Treaties in 1904 and 1911 in Kenya allowed the British to push the Maasai south of the Mombassa-Uganda railroad (which passes through Nairobi) on to a single reserve in southern Kenya, later administered as Kajiado and Narok districts. Just as European settlers took the most fertile agricultural lands around Mount Kenya from the Kikuyu, the Maasai lost their prime grazing lands and water sources to make way for European ranches and farms, particularly near Nairobi around the Ngong Hills and along Lakes Naivasha and Nakuru (Spear and Waller 1993).

Confined to 35,000 km^2 in Kenya and 60,000 km^2 in Tanzania (60 percent of their precolonial range), the Maasai were further restricted from grazing their cattle in the large game reserves created by the British: the Serengeti Park and Ngorongoro Crater in Tanzania in 1954, and the Nairobi, Amboseli, Tsavo, Masai Mara, and Samburu National Parks in Kenya (1948–1964) (Homewood and Rodgers 1987). Following Kenya's independence in 1963, the Maasai faced competition for land by poor farmers moving off the highlands, spurred by population growth and overcrowding. Kajiado District's population grew from 22,000 (1948) to 86,000 (1969) to 149,000 (1979) to 250,000 (1989), an average annual growth of 3.5 percent. While some of this growth reflects natural increase among Maasai, most is due to immigration by Kikuyu farmers onto Maasai lands. In 1962 the Maasai constituted 78 percent of Kajiado District's population, but today they make up less than 50 percent. Much of this land has been leased, rented, or sold outright by Maasai owners, who can no longer graze their animals on their former lands (Campbell 1999).

In addition to losing land to ranchers and farmers, pastoralists have seen their mobility drastically reduced by the expansion of national game parks. Tourist revenues now contribute 45 percent of the Kenyan gross domestic product, and the influence of international conservation groups rivals that of major corporations and international donors in government decisions. National governments and their international consultants from environmental groups blamed domestic cattle for competing with wildlife populations, and Maasai and other herders were banned or restricted from most game parks. In 1959 in Tanzania (then British-ruled Tanganyika), Maasai agreed to abandon the rich plains of Serengeti National Park (14,760 km^2) in exchange for grazing privileges on the external slopes of the Ngorongoro Conservation Area (8,292 km^2), but were prohibited from practicing any cultivation in the area (Igoe 2003). Today, the Maasai pastoral economy is on the verge of collapse in the Ngorongoro area (McCabe 2003).

Because the savanna of the Maasai areas is suitable for grain agriculture, pastoral lands in southern Kenya were targeted for large-scale commercial ranch and farm enterprises. In Narok District, Kenya, hundreds of thousands of hectares of land were sold to land speculators and farmers in the 1980s, where the rich and arable land of the Mau Escarpment is now producing commercial wheat and barley. More recently, Maasai in Kajiado District have seen water from Mount Kilimanjaro diverted to commercial greenhouses growing flowers for the European market.

The Maasai ability to transfer land individually is a recent phenomenon. In traditional Maasai society, no individual "owned" grazing or water resources; rather, all members of the *oloshon* (territorial section) shared land and water in a given area. Following independence, the Kenyan government began to allocate individual sections of land (usually that with the best pasture and permanent water) to wealthy and influential members of the community. It was believed by international development agencies that individual ranches would better contribute to the national livestock market than would communal pastoralism, and would set an example for other Maasai. This was based on the view that commercial ranches as practiced in the United States and Australia provided the best model for commercial beef production (Sanford 1983). But few Maasai benefited from the early privatization, nor did they keep their animals from grazing on the private ranches if drought forced them to move their herds. In 1968, with support from USAID and the World Bank, Kenya proposed "group ranches," which conferred formal and legal land tenure to a community of coresidents. The Maasai in general accepted the group ranch concept as a way to prevent continuing agricultural encroachment on their land and to acquire legal tenure enabling them to qualify for loans and the development of bore holes and cattle dips. Conflicts emerged, however, during periods of drought when Maasai herders needed to cross group ranch boundaries to find pasture (Galaty 1992).

In the 1980s, again with encouragement from the World Bank and its structural adjustment programs, Kenya began to allocate individual titles to farming households, usually 5–10 ha plots for smallholders growing maize and other market crops. There has been a virtual stampede for land claims, especially in the Maasai areas of Kajiado and Narok districts, as farmers as well as Maasai themselves rush to claim title to some land, lest they lose it all. Maasai living in group ranches have increasingly agreed to break up their holdings into individual titles. According to one recent study, thirty-two of Kajiado's fifty-two group ranches had subdivided by 2006, and another fifteen were in the process of doing the same (BurnSilver and Mwangi 2006).

Several authors have argued that although the transition to private ownership of the range has brought about hardship, it has nevertheless increased the participation of Maasai in the commercial livestock economy. The sale of livestock is not new to pastoralists. Tanzanian Maasai were trading livestock for grain with neighboring Arusha in the mid-nineteenth century (Spear 1997), but were restricted from trading livestock in European-controlled markets during the colonial era, ostensibly to prevent disease but also to reserve a market monopoly for the settlers. Following independence, demands and opportunities for market sales of livestock grew, particularly for beef to feed growing urban populations, and today Maasai typically sell about 10 percent of their animals each year. Today one steer exchanged on the market can bring in four to six times the caloric worth of maize in drought years, and eight to seventeen times the amount in wet years. Milk sold enjoys a similar six to ten advantage to maize in caloric terms of trade (Zaal and Dietz 1999).

However, as Zaal and Dietz point out, increased commoditization of the livestock economy has led to a growing polarization of pastoralists into haves and have-nots, particularly in Maasai areas that are close to urban markets. In the Ol Karkar group ranch in Kajiado District, Kenya, the top third of households owned over 35 TLUs per person, mostly in cattle, while the bottom third had less than 7 TLUs, mostly in small stock (Zaal and Dietz 1999). (One TLU, or total livestock unit, equals one cow or eleven goats or sheep.) Market integration in general has led to a greater polarization within pastoral societies, and the emergence of a wealthy commercial elite among herd owners (Little 1985).

The loss of previously shared rangelands is having a profound effect on the ability of pastoral Maasai households to remain viable. The trend toward subdivision in Maasai land has led to a large transformation in land use—from a system predicated on extensive seasonal movement of short-duration grazing of successive areas of the pastoral landscape, toward intensive grazing on private parcels, a situation that can work only for those households with sufficient capital or credit to intensively ranch their livestock: that is, growing or buying forage, providing veterinary medicines, and transporting livestock to market.

The nutritional status of local Maasai is declining: there are measures of increased rates of malnutrition, particularly among children, and Maasai are increasingly compelled to grow maize to supplement their food supply (McCabe, Schofield, and Pedersen 1997). Maasai now find themselves in perhaps the most precarious situation in their existence. Local indigenous rights organizations are attempting to regain lost lands and prevent further losses to their communal pastures (Hodgson 2004; Ole Simel 2004)

The Rendille of Marsabit District

The Rendille, former camel pastoralists of northern Kenya, illustrate a different set of problems affecting loss of grazing lands—drought, famine, and ethnic violence—which has led to the rapid settling of poor pastoralists in towns and highland farms. The Rendille are a population of 25,000 made up of lowland-dwelling camel and small stockkeepers, and highland cattle keepers called Ariaal who are mixed groups of Rendille and Samburu. Marsabit District is Kenya's driest (250–800 mm rainfall) and least populated area (with 138,500 people occupying 75,078 km^2 in 1993), and the majority of the district's residents are nomadic livestock-keeping Rendille, Boran, Gabra, and Dasenetch. During colonial rule (1900–1963), Britain enforced a "Pax Britannica" maintaining peace among these competing and warring pastoralist groups. The 1930s saw the creation of society-specific "tribal grazing areas," which separated and restricted pastoral movement by local groups and fixed administrative boundaries to maintain the groups' separation. Thus Rendille were confined to the Kaisut Desert, protected from Turkana and Boran but severely restricted in their former herding range. Previously, the Rendille had herded their animals from Lake Turkana to the Ethiopian border down to the Uaso Nyiru River. Now they found their herding range reduced from 57,600 km^2 to 8,000 km^2 (Sobania 1988).

Following independence in 1963, a secessionist war broke out in northern Kenya between Muslim Somali and Boran populations, who wanted to join the new Republic of Somalia, and the Kenyan government. Rendille, Gabra, and non-Muslim Boran remained loyal to the Kenyan government, and were targeted for attacks. Precipitating the secession was a British-sponsored plebiscite vote in 1962, whereby the majority of Somalis voted for union with Somalia. However, the British reneged and merged the Northern Frontier District as a seventh province into Kenya, in part to maintain a military buffer against Ethiopia and Somalia. Local Somalis, Muslim Boran and Sakuye known as *shifta* (bandits), began a five-year-long armed struggle with the Kenyan government in the country's northeast, and engaged in mining roads, attacking police and army convoys, and raiding the livestock herds of loyalist Rendille and Gabra. Kenya, with support from the British air force, retaliated brutally, bombing Somali towns and confining Boran living along the Uaso Nyiru River into "strategic hamlets" (Hogg 1980).

During this period, nomadic Rendille moved their encampments close to police posts at Korr, Kargi, and Laisamis, while their warriors fought Somali shiftas in several large encounters (one leading to sixty Somali deaths). As the shifta conflict died down in the late 1960s, a new period of hardship set in with the advent of prolonged drought, first in 1968–1973 and again in 1982–1984. Many Rendille lost over half their livestock; some were wiped out completely. Small settled communities became larger, as Rendille (as well as impoverished Gabra, Boran, and Samburu) settled near Laisamis, Archer's Post, and Marsabit town (Fratkin 2005). (See fig. 7.2.)

In the early 1970s, a coalition of religious missions including the African Inland Church (AIC), Catholic Diocese, and National Christian Council of Kenya encouraged impoverished Rendille and Boran pastoralists to settle on separate agricultural schemes on Marsabit Mountain and take up maize and vegetable agriculture as an alternative to pastoralism. Large numbers of destitute Rendille and Boran, possibly one-quarter of their populations, moved to Marsabit Mountain to adopt farming on the agricultural schemes. Today two thousand Rendille are settled near the dryland scheme at Nasikakwe, and another two thousand live in irrigated farms in Marsabit forest at Songa. Marsabit Mountain's population had grown from three hundred in 1936 to four thousand in 1974 to over thirty thousand people today, almost a quarter of the district's population (Adano and Witsenburg 2005).

In addition to the highland settlements, Catholic and Protestant missions established famine distribution centers near their churches in the lowlands towns of Laisamis and Logologo, and at the permanent water holes at Kargi and Korr. These small towns grew into larger and permanent settlements, attracting destitute pastoralists or families who had to herd the animals at great distances away from the settlements. Nearly one-half of the Rendille now live near these settlements, without daily access to their animal herds. Extensive studies in the 1990s showed that Rendille children

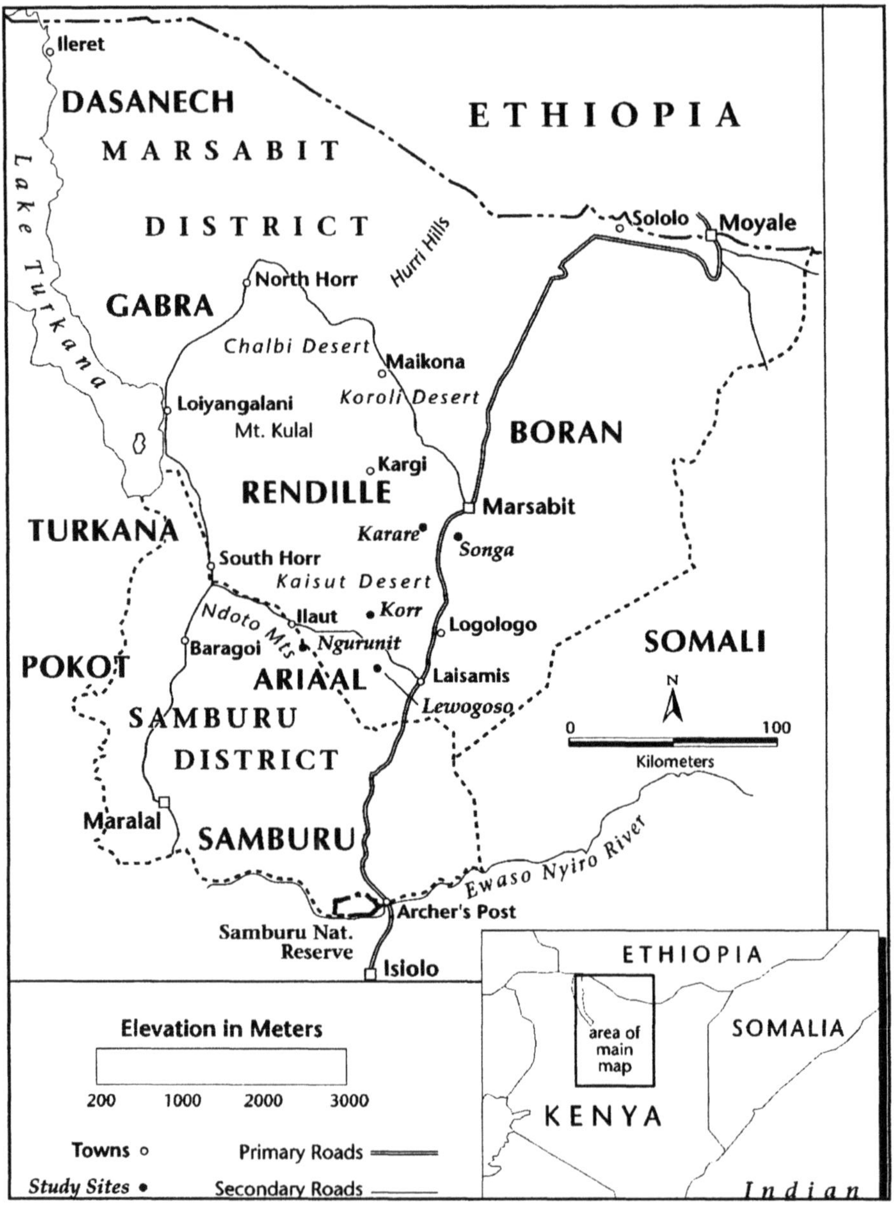

Figure 7.2 Pastoralists of Marsabit District, Kenya.

living in the settled towns and farms were three times more likely to suffer severe malnutrition than those living in the nomadic communities, a fact that was attributed to the lack of milk in the settled communities (Nathan, Fratkin, and Roth 1996; Nathan et al. 2005).

The settling of formerly nomadic peoples in the towns and farms of the district has led to a profound transformation in the landscape. Ecologists point to a steady degradation of pastoral rangeland in northern Kenya, particularly in the vicinity of the lowland towns that have become denuded of vegetation (O'Leary 1990; Schwartz 2005). A "sedentary pastoralism" has emerged in the vicinity of the small towns, where animals need to be taken farther away in mobile camps. Veterinary biologist H. Jürgen Schwartz, who worked with German development projects in northern Kenya, writes,

> The emerging trends toward short-range herding systems have definitely deleterious effects on range vegetation and soils. Severest impacts are found around permanent wells and boreholes and in the immediate vicinity of permanent settlements. . . . Grazing pressure on the residual open range is becoming exhaustive, migrations have to be rerouted, some migration routes may be closed permanently, thus increasing pressure on others, and since areas with higher potential are usually enclosed first, the residual open range areas possess lower support capacities and are prone to faster degradation. (Schwartz 2005: 82)

As a result, both total numbers of livestock and the numbers of households able to subsist on livestock production has declined dramatically. Figure 7.3 shows these declines in total number of livestock and the per capita ownership of livestock in Marsabit District between 1975 and 2000, as obtained by Dutch geographer Ton Dietz (Dietz, Adano, and Witsenburg 2005).

Most of the households forced out of the pastoral economy are poor to begin with, and life in settled communities is not necessarily easier. Settled life brings a host of changes to formerly nomadic populations, including increased exposure to respiratory problems, diarrhea, and sexually transmitted diseases, and greater risk of malnutrition (Nathan, Fratkin, and Roth 1996; Nathan et al. 2005). But settled life also provides a range of new opportunities for former pastoralists including income from increased livestock and dairy sales and opportunities for wage labor. McPeak and Little (2005) found that the opportunity of educating one child provides significant risk reduction to a pastoral family, as it increases their success in gaining employment. The ability of the rangeland to support pastoral households, however, has greatly diminished due to drought and political insecurity that have driven livestock-keeping families closer to towns and away from their pastures.

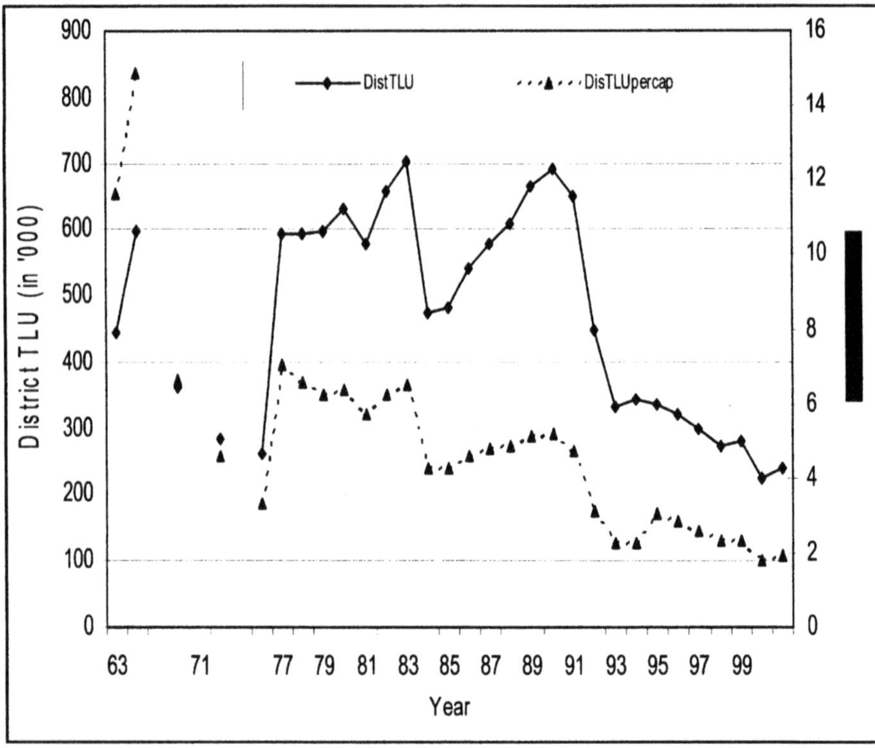

Figure 7.3 Total livestock units in Marsabit District, 1975–2000. (After Dietz, Adano, and Witsenburg 2005.)

Discussion

Kenyan pastoralists have seen their herding range greatly reduced in the past forty years due to growing populations (of farmers, herders, and domestic livestock), the expansion of commercial ranches, wheat estates, and game parks, and increased political insecurity and ethnic conflict. Among Maasai in southern Kenya, land loss has increased most rapidly due to loss of common property rights and the division of formerly shared grazing resources into individuated and privately titled parcels. In the more arid north, pastoral populations such as the Rendille face increased ethnic conflict and competition for pasture, water, and farmlands, made more violent with the introduction of automatic weapons. While the loss of common property rights there has not been as dramatic as in southern Kenya, there are currently efforts to privatize farming plots in the agricultural communities on Marsabit Mountain.

The loss of access to formerly wide pastures has decreased pastoral mobility and directly threatened the ability of pastoral households to survive off their livestock herds. Without mobility, the range deteriorates, conditions of the animals decline, and the households reduce the number of animals they can support. A difficult cycle has set in—land degradation increases, livestock productivity decreases, and economic impoverishment and vulnerability to food insecurity increases. Many former pastoralists have left the pastoral system altogether and face limited options—to wrest a living from farming, to migrate to urban areas and seek low-paying jobs, frequently as night watchmen, or to move into famine-relief centers as dependents on food aid. The chances of any of these individuals returning to their former self-sufficiency in the pastoral economy are slim.

The sloughing off of poor pastoralists has often been a response of East African pastoralists to drought and livestock loss. Destitute herders have attached themselves to farmers in the highlands, and others have entered the forests to become hunter-gatherers—in fact, the Maasai word for forager is *il-dorrobo* (the poor ones). Those with sufficient livestock remain pastoralists. Today, the night watchmen and men searching for jobs are the new *il-dorrobo*, although many dream of returning home with enough money to buy animals and recover their pastoral lives.

A major factor in Maasai impoverishment as been the decline in customary institutions that formerly regulated resource use, particularly rights to communally shared pasture. Livestock-development projects between the 1960s and the 1980s called for sweeping privatization of land and commercialization of livestock production. Development planners and agronomists agreed that a major problem in Africa was one of increasing livestock productivity to feed Africa's growing population. They saw Western ranching models of limited numbers of animals on privatized land as the logical direction livestock production should proceed, and saw traditional livestock keeping on commonly shared rangeland as an impediment to development (Sanford 1983; Simpson and Evangelou 1984).

In the 1980s and 1990s there emerged a strong counterargument by anthropologists, political scientists, geographers, and economists that contended that pastoral lands are highly unstable and herders need a large range to successfully manage their herds (Behnke, Scoones, and Kerven 1993; Scoones 1995; Swift 1996). Others have demonstrated that overexploitation is the result of an *absence* of effectively enforced rules for the management of common property, not of the presence of such arrangements, and that customary tenure systems are often quite specific about who may or may not use grazing and water resources, how, and at what times (Bromley and Cernea 1989; Swift 1991).

The new approach to pastoral development rests on a major reconsideration of dryland ecology and of what it means to derive livelihoods from environments that are intrinsically at disequilibrium, and aims wherever possible to build on customary institutions (Behnke, Scoones, and Kerven 1993; Fratkin and Mearns 2003; Scoones 1995). At the heart of the new approach is the recognition that sustainability in pastoral production systems demands livestock mobility, and that land tenure policy, rural infrastructure, and social service provision, among other policies, all need to support this basic requirement. Yet national governments including Kenya continue directly to curtail mobility through the alienation of land for agriculture or environmental conservation. Moreover, the Kenyan government has displaced local authority over range and water use, undermined the effectiveness of customary sanctions, and facilitated manipulation of development outcomes by the wealthy and influential (Little and Brokensha 1988; Little 1987).

For pastoral populations to continue to live off their herds, however, several changes in development policy must occur. First and foremost herders must have rights to pasture and water, rights that may include communal, village-based, or cooperative tenure guaranteed by law. National policies should guarantee shared grazing resources, access to markets, and access to veterinary care. The greatest impediment to Maasai pastoralism in Africa is the enclosure, privatization, and fencing of grazing lands that exclude former owners from their traditional lands. Second, the international development community needs to recognize that pastoral livestock management in arid lands is productive, rational, and an essential way of utilizing scarce and patchy resources. Pastoral strategies of herd diversity, pastoral mobility, and residential flexibility offer a means to convert patchy, seasonal, and scarce vegetation into water, calories, and protein for human consumption in arid or marginal lands. Policies to support such strategies are more important now than ever. Most important among them, for example, may be appropriate forms of conflict mediation and resolution, as in northern Kenya (Galaty 2005). Third, pastoral risk management ought to be supported through strategies and interventions to increase preparedness of herders and local authorities for drought and other climatic risks. Efforts currently under way in Kenya, including the Arid Lands Resource Management Project, have identified promising approaches to drought preparedness, including community-based early-warning systems, rapid destocking of livestock to protect pastoralists' purchasing power during droughts, community-based water development (e.g., wells, rainwater harvesting using microcatchment dams), and the use of special or restricted areas (e.g., wildlife reserves, military training areas) for emergency grazing

(Little et al. 2001). Other measures to support pastoral risk management deserve closer attention in the future, including the use of microfinance services (savings and loans, insurance) to widen the range of options herders may pursue before, during, and after risk events, so as to reduce their dependence on external agencies.

Without fully implementing these programmatic solutions, the fate of Kenya's herders will be similar to that of other marginalized populations described in this volume in Brazil and New Mexico. Maasai and Rendille may increasingly find themselves with pastures lost and livestock production unsustainable.

References

Adano, Wario R., and Karen Witsenburg. 2005. "Once Nomads Settle: Assessing the Process, Motives and Welfare Changes of Settlements on Mount Marsabit." In Fratkin and Roth 2005, 105–36.

Behnke R. H., and I. Scoones. 1993. "Rethinking Range Ecology: Implications for Rangeland Management in Africa." In *Range Ecology at Disequilibrium: New Models of Natural Variability and Pastoral Adaptation in African Savannas*, ed. R. H. Behnke, I. Scoones, and C. Kervin, 153–72. London: Overseas Development Institute.

Behnke, R. H., I. Scoones, and C. Kerven, eds. 1993. *Range Ecology at Disequilibrium: New Models of Natural Variability and Pastoral Adaptation in African Savannas*. London: Overseas Development Institute.

Bromley, D.W., and M. M. Cernea. 1989. "The Management of Common Property Natural Resources: Some Conceptual and Operational Fallacies." *World Bank Discussion Papers* 57. Washington, DC: World Bank.

BurnSilver, S., and E. Mwangi. 2006. "Beyond Group Ranch Subdivision: Collective Action for Livestock Mobility, Ecological Viability and Livelihoods." CAPRI Working Paper, 2006. CGIAR Systemwide Program on Collective Action and Property Rights (CAPRI). At www.capri.cgiar.org.

Campbell, D. J. 1999. "Response to Drought among Farmers and Herders in Southern Kajiado District, Kenya: A Comparison of 1972–1976 and 1994–1995." *Human Ecology* 27 (3): 377–416.

Dietz, Ton, W. Adano, and K. Witsenburg. 2005. "Natural Resources and Conflicts: Theoretical Flaws and Empirical Evidence from Northern Kenya." Paper presented to African Studies Association meetings, Washington, DC.

Fratkin, E., and R. Mearns. 2003. "Sustainability and Pastoral Livelihoods: Lessons from East African Maasai and Mongolia." *Human Organization* 62 (2): 12–122.

Fratkin, E., and E. A. Roth. 1990. "Drought and Economic Differentiation among Ariaal Pastoralists of Kenya." *Human Ecology* 18 (4): 385–402.

Fratkin, E. M. 2001. "East African Pastoralism in Transition: Maasai, Boran, and Rendille Cases." *African Studies Review* 44 (3): 1–25.

———. 2004. *Ariaal Pastoralists of Northern Kenya: Studying Pastoralism, Drought, and Development in Africa's Arid Lands.* 2nd ed. Needham Heights, MA: Allyn and Bacon.

———. 2005. "The Setting: Pastoral Sedentarization in Marsabit District, Northern Kenya." In Fratkin and Roth 2005, 29–52.

Fratkin, E. M., and E. A. Roth, eds. 2005. *As Pastoralists Settle: Social, Health, and Economic Consequences of Pastoral Sedentarization in Marsabit District, Kenya.* New York: Kluwer Academic/Plenum Press.

Galaty, J. G. 1992. "'This Land Is Yours': Social and Economic Factors in the Privatization, Subdivision and Sale of Maasai Ranches." *Nomadic Peoples* 30:26–40.

———. 1999. "Grounding Pastoralists: Law, Politics and Dispossession in East Africa Nomadic Peoples." *NS* 3, no. 2 (1999): 56–73.

———. 2005. "States of Violence: Ethnicity, Politics, and Pastoral Conflict in East Africa." *Geography Research Forum* 25:104–27.

Hodgson, D. 2004. "Precarious Alliances: The Cultural Politics and Structural Predicaments of the Indigenous Rights Movement in Tanzania." *American Anthropologist* 104 (4): 1086–97.

Hogg, R. 1980. "Pastoralism and Impoverishment: The Case of the Isiolo Boran." *Disasters* 4 (3): 299–310.

Homewood, K., and W. A. Rodgers. 1987. "Pastoralism, Conservation and the Overgrazing Controversy." In *Conservation in Africa: People, Policies and Practice*, ed. D. Anderson and R. Grove, 111–28. Cambridge: Cambridge University Press.

Igoe, J. 2003. *Conservation and Globalization: A Study of National Parks and Indigenous Communities from East Africa to South Dakota.* Belmont, CA: Wadsworth.

Lamprey, Hugh F. 1983. "Pastoralism Yesterday and Today: The Overgrazing Problem." In *Tropical Savannas*, ed. F. Bourliere, 643–66. Vol. 13 of *Ecosystems of the World*. Amsterdam: Elsevier Scientific Publishing.

Lesorogol, C. K. 2005. "Privatizing Pastoral Lands: Economic and Normative Outcomes in Kenya." *World Development* 33 (11): 1959–78.

Little, P. D. 1985. "Absentee Herd Owners and Part-Time Pastoralists: The Political Economy of Resource Use in Northern Kenya." *Human Ecology* 13 (2): 136–51.

———. 1987. "Land Use Conflicts in the Agricultural/Pastoral Borderlands: The Case of Kenya." In *Lands at Risk in the Third World: Local Level Perspectives*, ed. P. D. Little and M. M. Horowitz, 195–211. Boulder, CO: Westview Press.

Little, P. D., and D. W. Brokensha. 1988. "Introduction: Anthropology, Development and Change in East Africa." In *Anthropology, Development and Change in East Africa*, ed. D. W. Brokensha and P. D. Little, 1–12. Boulder, CO: Westview Press.

Little, P. D., K. Smith, B. A. Cellarius, D. L. Coppock, and C. B. Barrett. 2001. "Avoiding Disaster: Diversification and Risk Management among East African Herders." *Development and Change* 32:401–33.

McCabe, J. T. 2003. "Sustainability and Livelihood Diversification among the Maasai of Northern Tanzania." *Human Organization* 62 (2): 100–111.

———. 2004. *"Cattle Bring Us to Our Enemies": Turkana Ecology, Politics, and Raiding in a Disequilibrium System.* Ann Arbor: University of Michigan Press.

McCabe, J. T., E. C. Schofield, and G. N. Pedersen. 1997. "Food Security and Nutritional Status." In *Multiple Land-Use: The Experience of the Ngorongoro Conservation Area, Tanzania*, ed. D. M. Thompson, 285–301. Gland, Switzerland: IUCN.

McPeak, J., and P. D. Little. 2005. "Cursed If You Do, Cursed If You Don't: The Contradictory Processes of Pastoral Sedentarization in Northern Kenya." In Fratkin and Roth 2005, 87–104.

O'Leary, M. F. 1990. "Drought and Change amongst Northern Kenya Nomadic Pastoralists: The Case of Rendille and Gabra." In *From Water to World-Making: African Models in Arid Lands*, ed. G. Palsson, 151–74. Uppsala, Sweden: Scandinavian Institute of African Studies.

Nathan, M. A., E. Fratkin, and E. A. Roth. 1996. "Sedentism and Child Health among Rendille Pastoralists of Northern Kenya." *Social Science and Medicine* 43 (4): 503–15.

Nathan, M. A., E. A. Roth, E. Fratkin, D. Wiseman, and J. Harris. 2005. "Health and Morbidity among Rendille Pastoralist Children: Effects of Sedentarization." In Fratkin and Roth 2005, 193–208.

Ole Simel, J. 2004. "The Century-Long Displacement and Dispossession of the Maasai in Kenya." *Indigenous Affairs* 4/2004. International Working Group of Indigenous Affairs. At iwgia@iwgia.org.

Population Statistics. 2006. Central Library of the Utrecht University, the Netherlands. At www.library.uu.nl/wesp/populstat/populhome.html.

Sanford, S. 1983. *Management of Pastoral Development in the Third World*. Chichester: Wiley.

Scoones, I., ed. 1995. *Living with Uncertainty: New Directions for Pastoral Development in Africa*. London: ITS Publications.

Schwartz, H. J. 2005. "Ecological and Economic Consequences of Reduced Mobility in Pastoral Livestock Production Systems." In Fratkin and Roth 2005, 69–86.

Simpson, J. R., and P. Evangelou, eds. 1984. *Livestock Development in Sub-Saharan Africa: Constraints, Prospects, Policy*. Boulder, CO: Westview Press.

Sobania, N. 1988. "Pastoralist Migration and Colonial Policy: A Case Study from Northern Kenya." In *The Ecology of Survival: Case Studies from Northeastern African History*, ed. D. Johnson and D. Anderson, 219–39. London: Crook Greene (and Westview).

Spear, T. 1997. *Mountain Farmers: Moral Economies of Land and Agricultural Development in Arusha and Meru*. London: James Currey.

Spear, T., and R. Waller, eds. 1993. *Being Maasai: Ethnicity and Identity in East Africa*. London: James Currey.

Swift, J. 1991. "Local Customary Institutions as the Basis for Natural Resource Management among Boran Pastoralists in Northern Kenya." *IDS Bulletin* 22 (4): 34–37.

———. 1996. "Desertification: Narratives, Winners & Losers." In *The Lie of the Land: Challenging Received Wisdom on the African Environment*, ed. Melissa Leach and Robin Mearns, 73–90. Oxford: James Currey.

UNFPA. 2006. State of the World's Population, 2006. United Nations Population Fund. At www.unfpa.org/swp.

Zaal, Fred, and Ton Dietz. 1999. "Of Markets, Maize, and Milk: Pastoral Commoditization in Kenya." In *The Poor are Not Us: Poverty and Pastoralism in Eastern Africa*, ed. D.M. Anderson and V. Broch-Due, 163–98. Oxford: James Currey.

8

Landscape Acts and Property Regimes in the Ecuadorean Amazon

JULIET S. ERAZO

STARTING IN THE MID-1960S, INDIGENOUS PEOPLE in the Upper Napo region of the Ecuadorean Amazon were forced to change their understanding of how land could be legitimately claimed. Prior to that time, the region remained largely beyond state development schemes due to its inaccessibility, and indigenous residents of the region enjoyed a high level of autonomy relative to their Andean counterparts. However, in the 1960s, the government faced pressures to provide land to highland peasants; rather than breaking up Andean haciendas, state officials looked to the Amazon as a frontier zone where agricultural production could be intensified and modernized through resettlement projects. Once viable oil reserves were discovered in the region in the early 1970s, the Amazon became even more central to state development plans. Thus, if indigenous Amazonians hoped to maintain claim to any land at all, they needed to learn about and pursue official channels of land titling. If they hoped to maintain claims to amounts of land that surpassed the 50 ha per household being offered to colonists, they also needed to show their commitment to state-led modernization projects. The rapidity of these changes makes the Upper Napo an ideal setting to think about the intersection of changing economies and transformation of landscapes.

One of the state's main strategies for facilitating its titling of lands was pushing both long-term residents and colonists to form peasant organizations, which could apply for large, collectively owned titles. Some indigenous people were able to form relatively large organizations (with over two hundred adult male members and their families) and were granted relatively large pieces of land (more than 200 ha per adult male, compared to 50 ha for households that applied separately). However, once the members of these organizations obtained title to their land, members needed to build consensus on how to distribute and utilize the collectively owned property; this necessity led to heated debates. In at least some cases, these disputes still have not been resolved, despite the fact that more than three decades have passed.

In the cooperative that will be discussed in this chapter, some members see collective land holdings and collective economic pursuits as key components of building a stronger indigenous movement that can confront the state and elite groups in Ecuador. Other members are skeptical about the earning potential of collective endeavors and prefer to engage in household-centered economic activities. Within the latter group, some members feel that the highly inequitable claims to land that existed prior to the formation of the cooperative should be respected, and that the descendants of founding members should be given access to the land that belonged to their fathers. Others feel that their participation in founding the cooperative and in early collectivist projects entitles them to an equal parcel of land, regardless of the size of their de facto claim prior to legalization of the collective title. As I will show in this chapter, the proponents of these three clashing perspectives have constructed entire landscapes to publicly promote their particular perspective in these debates. These landscapes affect the daily activities and viewscapes of all the cooperative's residents, inducing them to weigh the perspective of those who constructed them against other possibilities.

I will refer to these members' activities as *landscape acts*, building on the concept of *speech acts*, introduced by J. L. Austin during a series of lectures at Harvard University in the early 1960s. Austin used the term to highlight that some statements are not simply descriptive. Rather, they are best thought to be engaged in the performance of acts. One of the most commonly cited of Austin's examples is the act of saying "I do" at the altar, which transports the actor into a new social category and relationship with the state. Other examples of speech acts, or "performative statements," include "I bet you a dollar that it will rain tomorrow," "I promise to do so," or "I hereby name this ship *Queen Elizabeth*." These statements, uttered in the correct circumstances, do not merely describe an action or frame of mind, but *are* actions in and of themselves (Austin 1962).

Similarly, I use the term *landscape acts* to emphasize that at times, we construct landscapes for what they do. This is not earth shattering; a simple example would be the construction of a large fence, which could be intended to block access or obstruct views. But not all landscape acts are simple demonstrations of territoriality; some express more complex desires and attempt to influence broader economic and political processes. They are ideological, aiming to radiate a particular point of view outward and persuade others. As such, they differ from the place-making acts described by Doreen Massey, which intend to "fix the meaning of particular spaces, to enclose them, endow them with fixed identities and to claim them for one's own" (Massey 1994: 4). If landscapes are ongoing processes that relate the "foreground" of everyday life (how things are experienced) to the "background" of "potential social existence" (shared conceptions of what might be or should be) (Hirsch 1995: 22), ideologically inspired landscape acts reverse this positioning, foregrounding imagined futures and effacing the complexities of everyday life in an attempt to change that life.

As is the case with speech acts, landscape acts conducted by the state and by the elite garner most of the scholarly attention, implying a state/civil society split that has become too rigid. In particular, there has been significant attention to how modern forms of state surveillance and control of populations as well as of capitalist organization and work discipline have depended on the homogenizing, rationalizing, and partitioning of space (Harvey 1989: 213; Lefebvre 1991; Scott 1998). For some, the particular ideology of the state is unimportant. Lefebvre argues that the state "plans and organizes society 'rationally,' with the help of knowledge and technology, imposing analogous, if not homologous, measures irrespective of political ideology, historical background, or the class origins of those in power" (1991: 23; see also Scott 1998). Conversely, Richard Walker (1997) argues that attention to ideology is key to understanding the production of landcapes by the elite and ruling classes (see also Smith 2003: chap. 6).

Discussions of landscapes produced by marginalized peoples rarely receive the same attention to ideology, unless it is posited as "resistance" to state development plans. Landscapes are most often understood as reaffirming identities, strengthening ties between the living and their ancestors or conveying moral lessons (see, for example, Basso 1996; Feld and Basso 1997; Leonard 1997; Stewart and Strathern 2003). As with speech, landscapes are often interpreted as infused with meaning, both cultural and historical, but not as having been created *largely* to influence others. Fourth world peoples in particular are more likely to be seen as having strong "senses of place" (Feld and Basso 1997), forged through generations of dwelling in particular sites, than engaged in ideological struggles over landscapes with their neighbors. At most, marginalized peoples are seen as engaged in "permanent transgression" (Lefebvre 1991) against state plans, or in complex, illegible, and locally specific social practices (Scott 1998). However, to describe marginalized people's production of landscapes as constituted solely through "dwelling," rather than recognizing their long-term engagement with the state, or to view this engagement as simply conveying resistance to state power, is to deny people on the margins the ability to creatively embrace, rework, or simply ignore state projects within local disputes (Warren 1998: 70–74). As MacClennan and Walck's chapter in this volume argues, our understanding of how the economies and politics of landscape transformation occur is severely limited when we focus solely on the activities of states or, conversely, solely on processes at the local level; rather, it is critical to recognize the intricate interactions, not always hierarchical, between them (see also Janusek and Kolata 2004).

Although it is relatively easy to imagine examples of ideologically inspired landscape acts conducted by the powerful, including such things as awe-inspiring public plazas or downtown revitalization campaigns, we must ask what the ideologically inspired landscape acts of the marginalized might look like. How might models that are created to describe state-directed production of space, occurring primarily in urban environments, illuminate a rainforest environment of trees, multistoried gardens, and unassuming buildings? How do indigenous Amazonians construct landscapes to influence others in questions of economic ideology and practice? As Gow has pointed out, "It is hard to see Amazonia as a landscape, in the sense this term has for people from temperate climes. The land does not recede away from a point of observation to the distant horizon, for everywhere vegetation occludes the view" (1995: 43). This chapter is not meant to be an exhaustive discussion of all of the ways in which Amazonians use landscapes to promote their perspectives, but rather is intended to describe some of the ways in which they do, and to highlight that these acts are often directed toward one another, rather than toward the state, tourists, developers, or other adversarial groups.

While the acts that I will describe are part of local disputes, their effects do not necessarily remain local, potentially extending toward the center and beyond. The children who grew up in the landscapes constructed by opposing camps in the property regime debate in the 1970s in the Upper Napo region of the Ecuadorean Amazon have gone on to fill important posts in the regional- and national-level indigenous rights movement in Ecuador, labeled "the most well-organized indigenous movement in the Americas" (Collins 2000: 14). These indigenous leaders' understandings of property and space have had important implications for the newest version of the Ecuadorean constitution as well as governance regimes in indigenous territories across the Ecuadorean Amazon. After a brief introduction to the Upper Napo region and its Kichwa inhabitants, I outline the ways in which three factions within one collectively held, indigenous territory engaged in landscape acts to advance their own political views over appropriate property regimes and forms of land use.

The Upper Napo Region

The Rukullakta Cooperative is located near the mission town of Archidona, in what is sometimes referred to as the "Upper Napo" region of the Ecuadorean Amazon.[1] The history of the Upper Napo and its relationship to colonial and state power has been remarkably nonlinear; various boom periods for the region's natural resources—particularly gold, cinchona bark, rubber, and most recently, oil—have occurred ever since Spanish explorers and colonists made their first forays and established their first haciendas there in the sixteenth century. During these boom periods, the political center's interest in controlling the region spiked. Between these periods, the region returned to marginality, and the residents who had managed to survive the often brutal penetration by outsiders were allowed a certain level of autonomy (Taylor 1994). Starting in the mid-seventeenth century, missions played a much more important governing role in most Amazonians' everyday lives than either the colonial government or the state, but even that form of domination was contested and intermittent (Muratorio 1991).

In confrontations with missionaries, patrons, and public administrators, the Amazonian Kichwa repeatedly asserted their rights to spend periods of time in the forest, despite the other groups' attempts to settle them in towns in order to more effectively exploit their labor (Muratorio 1991). Most would move between two or more homes, one located near a mission town or trading center, where they would work on haciendas, construct public works, or carry individuals and mail on their backs on the eight-day trip between the Upper Napo region and Quito. These brief periods of work gave them access to trade goods, particularly matches, machetes, salt, and cloth. A second and even third home would be located deep in the forest, where they would engage for months at a time in hunting, fishing, and horticulture. Engaging at least part-time in subsistence horticulture, hunting, and fishing in the forest was considered a central component of Kichwa identity, and most moved between their "town life" and "forest life" periodically during the year (Macdonald 1979, 1981).

As of the mid-twentieth century, the Kichwa had well-established ways of demonstrating to one another claims to the garden plots and hunting grounds, although these claims were occasionally contested (Macdonald 1979: 43–45). Initial claim to an area began when an individual cleared land for a *chakra*, or garden, giving the site a degree of permanence and providing occupants with de facto claim to the land. Stealing products from other people's gardens was rare, even though the owner might be absent for several months. The planting of domesticated peach palms (*Bactris gasipaes*) would signify property claims far beyond the limits of the home garden, ensuring the availability of sufficient space to accommodate the shifting cultivation, hunting, and fishing that the Kichwa practiced. Any member of the household, which typically included multiple generations of patrilineal kin, could utilize the forest resources within the household's territory. By the same token, hunting was permitted only on one's own land or in areas of the forest that had not already been claimed by another family group (Macdonald 1979: 35, 53).[2] Udo Oberem, an anthropologist who spent time in the Upper Napo region between 1954 and 1956, commented that "if someone hunts in someone else's property [without permission], he sets himself up for a good beating" (1980: 30; see also Wray 1996: 68). Borders for hunting and fishing territories were often vague, and until some dispute occurred, there was usually intermediary "buffer space" available to all. When disputes did arise, boundaries were set through a process of mutual agreement and negotiation between family groups through consultation with powerful shamans (Macdonald 1979: 44–47).

Thus, prior to the need to legally fix property titles created by the increasing presence of homesteaders from the highlands in the late 1960s and 1970s, property claims were marked through relatively subtle landscape acts that were territorial in intent. Specifically, the planting of the domesticated peach palm in the forest was done primarily to lay claim to an area (even though the fruit and other parts of the tree might also be consumed). Each tree exerted a presence like a candle, encompassing the area around it, although the precise distance from each that was included within the land claim was open to dispute.[3] Sometimes, clearer markers such as rivers or footpaths created a greater level of certainty as to what was "inside" and what was "outside," but the presence of these relatively precise boundaries was by no means the rule.

Throughout the 1960s and early 1970s, the national government increasingly encouraged settlement of the Amazon by people from other regions through the funding of resettlement schemes. It also constructed several access roads, connecting the frontier zone to the national transportation network and greatly facilitating the colonization of the region. Given the enormity of the task of carving up the region into thousands of small family plots and initiating agricultural extension and public services, the state colonization agency was particularly interested in titling land collectively to organized peasant groups rather than to individual farmers. The state agency IERAC (Ecuadorean Institute of the Amazon Region and Colonization) hoped that farmers' organizations would extend the state's reach and modernizing projects into areas distant from roads and the local offices of state agencies.

The promotion of cooperatives was part of a broader trend in Latin America at the time, where states attempted to restructure society into class-based federations that would mediate between peasants (or workers) and the state. However, within less than a decade, the Ecuadorean government's interest in the Amazon waned, and the reduced level of control that it exercised in the Amazon region undermined its earlier centralizing goals. While many of the peasant federations and cooperatives that had been formed to facilitate land titling and agricultural extension remained intact, the state's attempts to manage these organizations diminished (Yashar 1999). This allowed indigenous residents more autonomy in deciding how to distribute and use collectively owned lands. It also invited more heated debates as to what those designs should entail.

The Rukullakta Cooperative

When migrants from the highlands began to look for lands in the Upper Napo region in the late 1960s, some Kichwa saw it as an opportunity, selling their cultivated lands near the new roads in exchange for cattle, which they then took to less accessible parts of the region to raise and breed. Other Kichwa became increasingly nervous about land availability, particularly those who had spent some time on banana plantations on the Ecuadorean coast and thus had been exposed to rhetoric contesting foreign ownership of the most desirable land. They saw a need to form collective organizations to educate their people about the dangers of giving up so much land to outsiders, and began attending courses sponsored by the class-based organization CEDOC.[4] There, they learned how to form and lead an organization, and how to manage cooperative work projects, accounting, and other related skills.[5]

At the 1970 and 1971 organizational meetings for what later became the Cooperativa Agropecuaria San Pedro de Rukullakta, Ltda. (Saint Peter of Rukullakta Agricultural Cooperative), some of the Kichwa men who had attended the courses put forth a vision for a new social movement and for a different future for their people. They talked not only about applying for collective land title to defend the land from colonists, but also about a situation in which some families had more land than others. They pushed for a dramatic type of land reform with more equitable distribution of land compared to what existed at the time.

Additionally, they envisioned large areas of land set aside for collective, commercial endeavors such as cattle ranching. While those members who contributed their labor to collectivist agricultural projects would be paid a wage for each day they worked, the profits from the endeavor would go to the organization for social programs, particularly educational programs.

Those pushing for the formation of the cooperative justified their vision of land reform by emphasizing that they would be eligible for state programs, such as land titling and agricultural credit, only by working collectively. While it was true that the state was interested in the formation of collective organizations that would mediate the distribution of land, agricultural loans, and social services, it was not pushing for collective labor in agricultural projects per se (Salazar 1989: 125–26).[6] Rather, the state model was one in which the cooperative would act as an intermediary between each individual farmer's productive activities and the state loan and extension programs, and in which land would be divided up among the organization's members (Wray 1996: 71).

Because of their interest in collective agricultural projects, early leaders hoped that members would be willing to change where they resided and worked within the collective title, based in part on models of zoning presented to them in cooperative-formation training courses. They wanted all members to live closer to one another in what they referred to alternately as a "populated center" (*centro poblado*) or a "commune" (*comuna*). This center would include a few public and administrative buildings and small lots where each of the members would build a house. Because of protests from members that everyone's living in one populated center would make access to gardens unduly difficult, this plan was later revised to include five smaller populated centers, which came to be known as "subcenters" (*subcentros*).

The five subcenters were all located west of the Hollín River, which roughly divided the land members claimed in half. The western half of the cooperative was already fairly densely populated and would include space for family-owned subsistence-oriented gardens (*minifundios*). Additionally, leaders hoped to turn the eastern half of the cooperative's lands into collectively owned and managed land, calling it *latifundio* (large property). Dormitories would be constructed in this zone, and members would reside there periodically, when it was their turn to take care of the collectively owned cattle. Earnings from ranching activities would be used to fund social programs and infrastructure development within the cooperative.

This plan was not exactly what had been presented to those who attended the cooperative training courses. In some ways, the state's model was modified to more closely resemble many Kichwa families' practice of maintaining two distinct areas of work and residence, one near the mission town (the western half) and another in a distant forest area (the eastern half). In other ways, it goes much further than the state model by placing half of the land within a collective management category.

Those who led the meetings needed to convince a significant number of people who held contiguous parcels of land to join their organization for the plan to work. However, those who held claim to large parcels of land were suspicious about the leaders' plans to redistribute some land and centrally manage the rest. As the meetings wore on, the leaders became increasingly vague as to how land would be divided once the title was secured in order to achieve this consensus. While they promised that each of the members would have enough land to "fill their needs" and repeatedly spoke of the many benefits that could result from working together, the leaders also eventually conceded that the cooperative would remain an organization of "traditional land-holdings," suggesting that the previous, unequally sized land claims would remain intact. In the end, 202 men and a few widowed women had signed up to become founding members of the organization. The delineation of 41,888.5 ha claimed by members was completed in 1973, the state recognized the cooperative as a legal entity in 1974, and the collective land title was finalized in 1977.

The debates over property regimes in the cooperative were simultaneously about what sorts of economic activities members would pursue (collective cattle ranching versus household-oriented endeavors) and therefore also about the role that the cooperative organization and its elected leaders would play in members' lives. As the state became less of a force in the organization's governance and as loans for cooperative economic activities dwindled in the late 1970s, cooperative members began dedicating themselves full-time to household-oriented economic endeavors (even as the organization continued to be called a "cooperative"). Even so, those who argued for collective labor projects and land tenure saw a strong, centralized organization as critical to improving all members' quality of life and continued to seek ways to promote and fund collectivist projects. Both those who refused to rescind claim to the lands they controlled prior to the cooperative's formation and those who sought the equal division of cooperative lands into privately managed, family-managed plots distrusted the fledgling organization from the beginning, and this distrust turned to disgust as state subsidies subsided.

Landscape Acts and the Property Regimes They Promoted

Both members and leaders varied on their level of acceptance of this proposed division of space. While most people did not squarely fit into particular camps, holding ambivalent and sometimes contradictory values associated with property and collective labor, a few individuals had very strong opinions and began to engage in the construction of landscapes intended to draw others to their point of view. In the following sections, I will describe the three most prominent of these landscape acts: collectivist, conservative, and neoliberal.

Collectivist Landscape Acts

The first leaders elected to the cooperative offices such as president, vice president, and treasurer were the most in favor of centrally managed agricultural projects and collective management of land. For example, Carlos Alvarado, the first president of the cooperative, has argued consistently that only a minimal portion of the land should be divided into privately owned areas while the vast majority should remain under collective management, firmly stating that "dividing up the land will be the beginning of the end of the cooperative," (personal communication, March 26, 2000). Collectivists looked to a strong, centralized cooperative organization to seek funding for welfare programs, agricultural credit, and construction materials for infrastructural projects for its members; to manage the organization's finances, including substantial agricultural loans that had been afforded to it by the state development bank; and to organize members' labor schedules for both ranching and public works. The landscapes that collectivists began to construct thus celebrated both members' collective accomplishments and the importance of the organization in their lives.

Like the peach palm trees and other signs of domestication that were used by Kichwa prior to the formation of the cooperative to designate land claims, designers of these collectivist landscapes intended to radiate their ideological influence far beyond their boundaries. Unlike the periodic peach palms that stood among naturally occurring trees in a dense forest landscape, the landscapes constructed by collectivists constituted a dramatic change in what and whom people viewed as they went about their everyday activities.

One of first landscape acts, which began in 1972, was the clearing of hundreds of hectares of rainforest and the planting of pasture grasses for the collective cattle ranch east of the Hollín River. This collective ranch is easily seen in both aerial photographs and satellite images of the region dating back to at least 1977 (Erazo 2003). When members went to the cattle ranch to contribute two weeks of their labor to the collective endeavor, the relatively open expanses of the cattle ranches were a potent reminder of how much could be accomplished in a relatively short amount of time when working together. When hundreds of cattle (on loan from the state development bank) were added to the landscape, cooperative formation and collective labor became associated with wealth, progress, and a new era in which indigenous people could run their own haciendas.

Simultaneously, leaders sought funds and organized collective labor days for the "urbanization" of the *centros poblados*. These centers included, at the very least, common open spaces for athletic activities, a school, and a few homes. Prior to the 1960s, patrilineal descent groups, or *muntuns*, shared large houses, invisible from other families' houses, and the relatively small proportion of children who attended school did so in the mission town of Archidona.[7] Having people's homes concentrated into hamlets that included rural schools allowed for greater access to formal education and better organization of ranching responsibilities. People also came into more regular contact with one another as they went about their daily activities.

Since all land within the cooperative's boundaries was claimed previously by one *muntun* or another, some individuals came forward and offered some of their lands to the collectivist enterprise of constructing populated centers. Everyone in today's subcenters knows who made this sacrifice on behalf of the collectivist project, and the person is heralded as a "founding father" of the subcenter. Figure 8.1 gives a bird's-eye view of one of these subcenters, constructed in the early years following the cooperative's formation.

Obtaining funds for infrastructure projects that improved the quality of life in these populated centers, such as assembly halls, bridges, and access roads, provided a substantial boost to early leaders' efforts to concentrate the population into fewer areas. If people lived close to one another, local leaders could more easily travel from house to house to announce a subcenter meeting or cooperative-level assembly, to request assistance in ranching or other collective activities, and to "educate" about the value of collectivist living and labor. As Marx notes in *The Eighteenth Brumaire of Louis Bonaparte*, the dispersed nature of smallholder production "isolates them from one another instead of bringing them into mutual intercourse . . . and the identity of their interests begets no unity, no national union and no political organization" (Tucker 1978: 608). Thus, collectivist leaders attempted to create landscapes and living patterns that would increase mutual intercourse among members, thereby (they hoped) increasing unity and political organization.

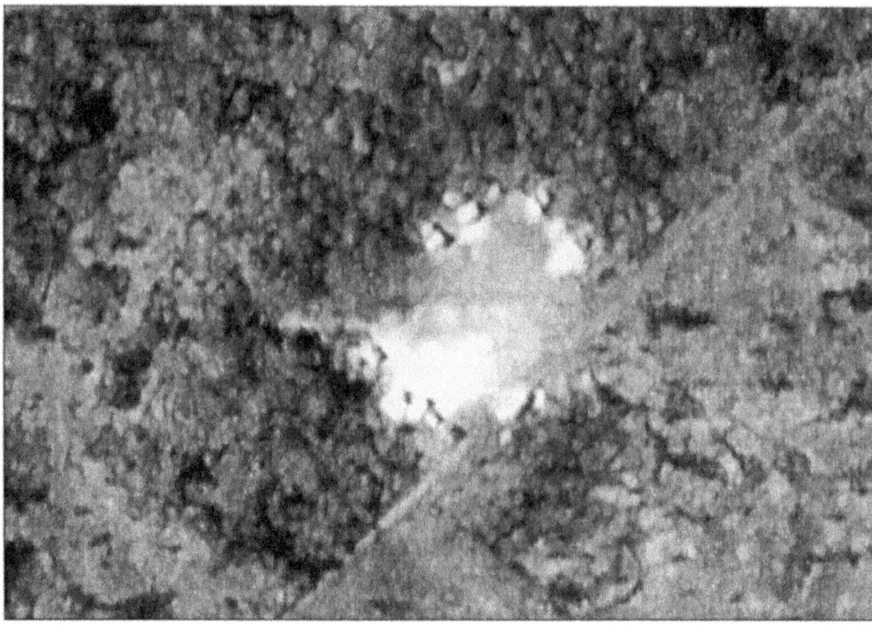

Figure 8.1 Purutuyaku Subcenter, 1973. Several homes were built around the school (located on the lower left side of the diamond) and a central recreational area during the early years of cooperative formation, facilitating organization of meetings, management of collective work projects, and community building. (Black and white photo, Instituto Geográfico Militar, Quito, Ecuador.)

The administrative center of the cooperative, called Rukullakta Subcenter, became a showcase for the leaders' vision of a collectivist modernity. Individually owned gardens and homesites were relatively small, while public buildings and spaces occupied a relatively large portion of the space. Rukullakta Subcenter also included multiple roads that connected its growing population and pilot, collectivist projects such as artificial ponds for the raising of fish (see fig. 8.2).

Admittedly, the landscape acts described thus far could be interpreted as demonstrating how much the cooperative leaders had conceded to the state's logic of modernization, rather than as evidence of a concerted effort to promote collectivism among the organization's membership. However, the rationalizations for increased collectivism that the cooperative's elected leaders used in speeches (as documented in the cooperative's archives), their tireless work in convincing others to go along with their ideas, and their own retrospective analyses indicate that they truly *believed* in the power of getting organized socially, economically, and spatially. Additionally, collectivist landscape acts continue to occur as new subcenters are formed

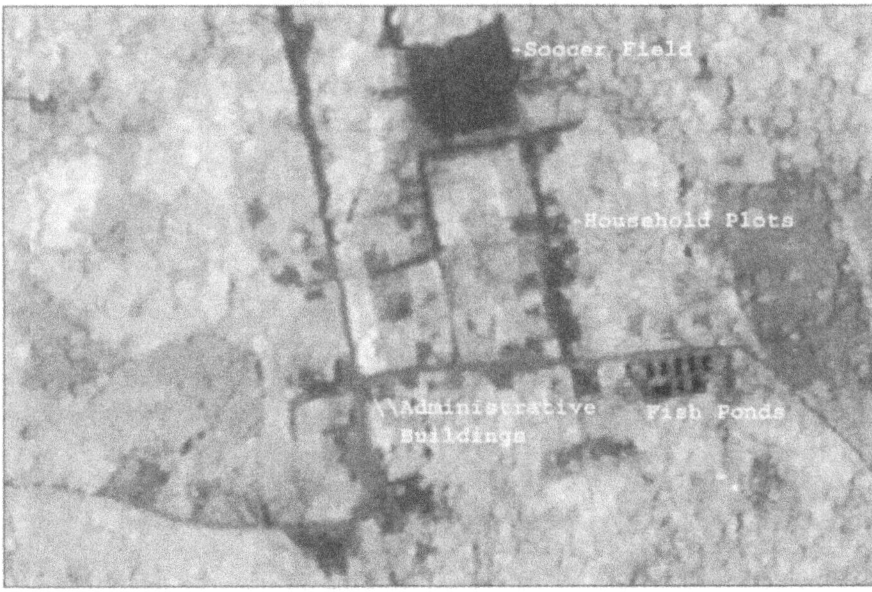

Figure 8.2 Rukullakta Subcenter (administrative center of the cooperative), 1982. (Infrared aerial photo, Instituto Geográfico Militar, Quito, Ecuador.)

(although the amount of time spent in these landscapes is less than it was during the early 1970s, as will be described in the section on neoliberal landscape acts). When people speak of the history of their subcenter or of the cooperative as a whole, collectively built bridges, assembly halls, and schools are referred to as "accomplishments of the [subcenter or cooperative] organization" (*logros de la organización*), and both subcenter and cooperative presidents are remembered by which infrastructural projects they were able to complete. These projects entailed obtaining funds for building materials from the state or a private organization, but what is equally if not more important in the minds of the cooperative residents is the leaders' ability to convince residents to donate several hours or days of their time to construction. Thus, the ideal of indigenous people working together toward common ends under indigenous leadership is now closely associated with a particular kind of landscape—one that includes a school, an assembly hall, and common open space for playing soccer and other sports.

The collectivist cattle ranch has grown over and returned to forest in the years since its creation and the termination of cattle loans to the cooperative, but collectively planted gardens (which supplement school lunches provided by the state) and other collectivist agricultural projects are contemporary reminders that collective projects can bring benefits, if at a more modest scale. These landscape acts announce to other cooperative members that the people involved were able to get past whatever tensions existed within the group and place their hope in a collectively managed project. While it is true that these landscape acts are simultaneously premised on a form of exclusion (Gupta and Ferguson 1997: 13) (since not everyone is part of the project or a resident of the subcenter that boasts a new assembly hall), they also advertise that collective endeavors are worthwhile, inviting (or challenging)other cooperative members to engage in similar activities.

Conservative Landscape Acts

Other members of the cooperative never accepted early leaders' calls to think of its space as collectively owned and centrally managed. They participated in the formation of the cooperative not because they were attracted to the ideal of collectivist agriculture, but because state representatives made it clear that it was the surest way to gain title to a large piece of land, and they wanted to maintain control over all of the land to which they had previously held de facto claim. Some of these conservatives actively worked to prevent redistribution of land, often by running for elected office themselves. For example, Jorge Aguinda, who was elected twice as president of the cooperative, regularly inserted his own interpretations of agreements that the governing council had made in previous meetings. The following passage is recorded in the cooperative's archival documentation of administrative board meetings:

> Solution to the land problem. To which the president of the cooperative [Jorge Aguinda] referred to the accord we had in the other session to receive individual lots. In that sense, those who have 30–40 hectares in their first lot would also receive 50 hectares in a second lot. Various *compañeros* and members did not approve the previous accord. Rather, we want 50 hectares for each member in equality. Those who have 30–40 hectares in their first lot, will receive 20–10 hectares to complete the 50 hectares. (*Actas*, December 14, 1976)

Despite the implication that Aguinda was confounded in his attempts, and despite the fact that conservatives represent a minority of cooperative members, he and others have managed to prevent their relatively large landholdings within the cooperative's collective title from being divided among other members. As recently as 1999, when one subcenter gained permission from the central cooperative leadership to delimit 25-ha parcels for its members, it did so for all of its members, including those who already held de facto ownership of large parcels in other parts of the cooperative.

Without the same level of state funding enjoyed by the collectivists, conservatives did not engage in bold landscape acts at first, but rather attempted to dampen the effects that collectivist landscape acts were having on the membership through their efforts to prevent collectivization or redistribution of lands they considered to be theirs. Their undivided landholdings exerted their own type of radiance, dampening the effects of collectivist landscape acts and ridiculing the attempts of those elected leaders who sought to change previous property regimes. In a more recent statement, Jorge Aguinda explained to me:

> In my case, I have about 200 hectares of land in the cooperative. I'm the owner—that land is from before the cooperative formed. It's from before the making of the cooperative. So, I've got my kids. If we start dividing the land among the members, all that land that is under my power, I wouldn't like to cede it to another member. I'm always jealous that nothing happens; rather it should stay with me, with my kids. Therefore, my kids affiliate [with the cooperative] and we'll situate them. So, I remain calm that all that land, which I struggled and fought for so much, isn't for nothing, rather that it stays with the kids. . . . So, everyone thinks like that—no one wants to let go. . . . So you can't enter in a fair legalization, as cooperativism dictates, that everyone is the same, every member has the same rights, the same obligations. You can't apply that because we are an organization of traditional land-holdings. That is the most problematic point that exists in the cooperative. . . . Always in our culture, one respects others, whether they have more or have less, each person's natural [land] boundaries are respected, and if one wants something, he has to speak to the *compañero* to ask him to cede a few hectares. Always with dialogue. And if not, they enter into fights, hatred, and vengeance. So, we have respected that. Well, until now we've respected it even though we have replicated like crazy (personal communication, March 1, 2000).

Aguinda speaks of "natural boundaries," referring to the way in which trees, hills, rivers, and other natural features were used to demarcate land claims. He also argues that while people were willing to allow others to hunt or fish on their claims, it was always with prior permission and with the understanding that ownership remained with the original claimant. He justifies his claim through reference to the work he invested in modifying the land thirty years before. Finally, he prioritizes previously existing social bonds, specifically patrilineal kinship groups, rather than the bonds formed by shared membership in the cooperative.

The landscapes that conservatives have been able to defend, particularly those that remained forested, gained their status as landscape acts over time and in contradiction to landscapes that included collectivist projects or household-managed gardens. As Gastón Gordillo (2004) has argued, landscapes often gain their meaning through tensions with other geographies, through a negative dialectic. Specifically, he describes how the Toba of the Argentinean Chaco came to view "the bush" where they live as a place of poverty, hardship, and unrewarding efforts in contrast to sugar plantations where they migrated temporarily, earning wages and gaining access to commodities. The sugar plantations came to be viewed as places of sexual excess, free of missionary discipline, after the foundation of an Anglican station in Toba lands. Interpreting Adorno (1973), Gordillo writes that "these contradictions are not resolved and hence do not reach closure in a synthesis. This is one of the major arenas in which a negative dialectic departs from Hegelianism and positivist Marxism, for such a synthesis could only be conceivable if the dialectic is removed from history and locked into the realm of abstract thought" (2004: 258).

Similarly, the conflict between those who want to maintain the unequal, precooperative claims to land and those who want to impose new land tenure regimes has not reached closure, even though more than thirty years have passed since the organization was formed. Even today, people frequently grumble about how larger tracts of land are not being used by the people who claim them, and how they should be redistributed among those who do not have any land. But this redistribution has not occurred, except in instances where the original claimant has allowed it. As people walk by the larger tracts of forest or see them standing tall beyond more intensively used landscapes, they are reminded of the power that some of their neighbors have continued to enjoy in resisting calls for a more collectivist commitment. In Aguinda's case, most of his children have reached adulthood and have dedicated themselves to careers other than cash crop agriculture. This has contributed even further to the "landscape act" status of his holdings.

Henri Lefebvre argues that social contradictions create spatial contradictions (1991: 365), but focuses on tensions between the state and its subjects rather than among groups of "ordinary people." In the cooperative, one of the greatest social tensions is created when the cooperative leadership asks its members to put their obligations to the larger group ahead of obligations to specific kin, to act in ways that will benefit the organization and the broader group that it ideally represents, rather than in ways that reinforce reciprocal ties with the select group of family and friends with whom one has worked to create ties of interdependence. The collectivist and conservative landscapes mirror the social contradictions created by the conflicting allegiances of cooperative and kin group. Viewing conservative landscapes reminds cooperative members that some people have chosen to retain power to determine who can use their parcels of land and when, rather than giving up this right to an elected body that represents the larger, more anonymous group (currently about six thousand people). In this way, tracts controlled by conservatives have become landscape acts equal in power to the collectivist landscape acts described above.

Neoliberal Landscape Acts

A third model existed for how tenure should be divided in the cooperative, under which most of the cooperative would be divided into equally sized, household-managed plots. While present from the early days of cooperative formation, this model became increasingly popular in the 1980s, when the state greatly reduced financial support to class-based federations. A generalized debt crisis in Latin America, spurred partially by monetary policies in the United States and England, abruptly ended a period of high governmental borrowing and greatly reduced the funds available for public spending (Sheahan 1987: 120–24). It was also during this time that the cooperative was expected to pay off loans it had taken out in cattle during the 1970s, and it experienced great difficulties in doing so for a variety of reasons (Erazo 2003). Many members lost faith in the cooperative as an organization that could obtain development moneys for their benefit, stopped attending meetings, and refused to take money out of their own pockets to help pay the organization's debt.

Deborah Yashar (1999) has utilized the term *neoliberal citizenship regimes* to describe this most recent era in many Latin American countries, during which states reassessed their ability to fund social services, credit programs, and support peasant organizations in favor of structural adjustment policies and privatization. I therefore use the term *neoliberal landscape acts* for the particular landscapes created by families asserting their need to privately own land for the production of cash crops in the wake of the state's liberalizing of agricultural prices, elimination of agricultural subsidies, and diminishment of credit programs. After a brief description of how neoliberal policies played out in the cooperative, I will describe these neoliberal landscape acts.

As of the late 1980s, most families still had not been assigned a parcel of land by the cooperative administration, due both to the reluctance of conservative members to rescind control over their lands and to declining legitimacy of central leaders as it became clear that they would not be able to obtain the same levels of development project funding that they had obtained in the past. Furthermore, due to the maturing of large families, the number of men living in the cooperative old enough to qualify as members had more than doubled since the cooperative formed, adding to nervousness surrounding access to land. Prompted in part by plans to cut a military road into the northeast edge of the cooperative's lands (the area that was previously labeled the "forest reserve"), some members made a bold move. They entered the zone east of the Hollín River and demarcated a line of 25-ha parcels for themselves. Cooperative leaders were very opposed to this, and protested frequently during Administrative Council and Assembly meetings (*Actas* January 2, 1990; May 19, 1990; May 24, 1990; January 30, 1991). The earliest land claimers essentially ignored the leaders and engaged in cash crop agriculture without worrying about upsetting central leaders.

Unlike the older subcenters, where the school, meeting hall, and public plaza were seen as the center point around which subcenter members would construct their houses and garden plots (see figs. 8.1 and 8.2), the new zones of development organized themselves around roads or paths for transporting products to market. They did create new public centers with a school, soccer field, and assembly hall, using roughly the same spatial design developed in the early days of the cooperative, demonstrating the power of this model. However, rather than selecting farmlands that radiated from these centers, these new homesteaders selected them in long lines along the road and extending beyond it. The new public centers were constructed intermittently along the road, and children had to walk up to three hours each way to attend school (see fig. 8.3).

While the initial land claimers were likely motivated to place their parcels along the planned military road in hopes of having easier access to markets, the linear pattern has continued in other areas of the cooperative, even when no road is present (also as demonstrated by the parcels that extend to Lupinu). As in the case of the conservative landscape acts described above, these acts gained their "landscape act" status partially through their contradictions with the landscape ideals promoted by collectivism. In many cases, homesteaders could have selected parcels in more of a grid pattern without lengthening the amount of time to get products to market, but shortening the amount of time to get to the populated centers. But they have not done this, as demonstrated in figure 8.3. Even though the road ends in the middle of the map, homesteads extend farther southward from the main road (mistakenly labeled as the "Carretera Interoceanica" on the map), although they do branch out somewhat into a Y rather than simply extending along one line.

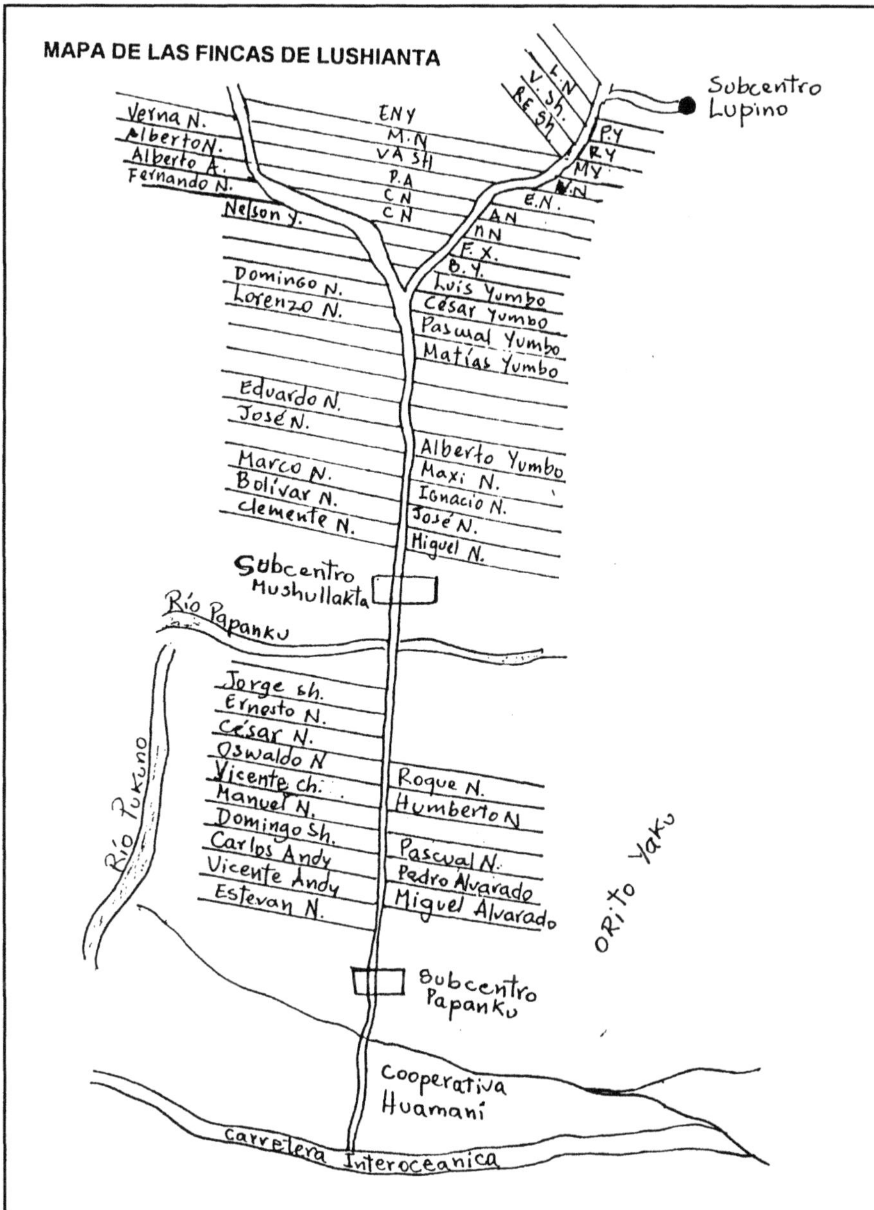

Figure 8.3 Community-drawn map of properties along the military road (which ends near the words "Subcentro Mushullakta" in the middle of the map), and those that extend beyond it (south = "up" on the map). There are three public centers denoted on the map—Papanku and Mushullakta are accessible by a dirt road. Lupinu, located in the upper right corner of the map, is accessible only by a muddy path and can take several hours to reach, depending on the path's condition. (Coordinated by Desarollo y Autogestión.)

Aside from the students and their teacher, the newer public centers are often devoid of population, except during periodic community gatherings (ironically, they are still referred to as "populated centers"). The distantly spaced houses are set back off the road behind gardens, so as members walk along the road, all they see are the weedy species of fallowed gardens or, at best, perennial garden plants. This produces a "used" but "desolate" impression, since one rarely sees other people. These decisions—to establish sites in a linear rather than grid or radial fashion and to set homes back far from the road—are in some ways reminiscent of the period prior to the cooperative's formation, when people chose to live far enough from one another so that they would not come into contact on a regular basis. In other ways, the central position of roads and paths used to take cash crops to market are a bold rejection of the promise that collective cattle ranching held in the 1970s.

Conclusion

As Raffles (1999, 2002) has so eloquently demonstrated, Amazonian landscapes have long been shaped by people and not just natural processes. In this chapter, I have sought to show that in addition to shaping the landscape to facilitate their own lives and engagement with markets, Amazonians shape their landscape to assert their positions in land tenure debates and to convince others to agree with them. Just as property relations are fundamentally social relations (Rose 1994; Verdery 1994, 1996), the viewpoints that cooperative members have taken on how the division of land within the cooperative should occur are indicative of their perspectives on what appropriate relationships among people should be, including those between people and their elected leaders. While it is common to think of the state's efforts to discipline human activities through landscape making, this chapter has illustrated the varied ways in which even the most marginalized people seek to influence or control through the shaping of landscapes (both symbolic and material). Through landscape acts, cooperative members have alternately embraced, reworked, or rejected state projects with lasting local implications.

It is one thing to assert that certain statements or landscapes are actually actions and not merely reflections, and quite another to quantify the consequences of those actions. It would be impossible to determine the level of influence of particular landscape acts on the populace's notions of property, collective labor, or proper relationships among people. However, trends within the indigenous movement today echo many of the values that drove the collectivist landscape acts of the 1960s and 1970s. Leaders in the Ecuadorean Amazon, many of whom grew up in the 1960s and

1970s, have continued to push for titling land to indigenous organizations rather than to individual families. They also continue to see engagement in collective labor projects as key to the strengthening of indigenous organizations, which, in turn, they see as key to indigenous people's abilities to push for policy changes at the national and international levels. While community-based ecotourism has replaced cattle ranching in many leaders' imagined economies, the emphasis the leaders place on having consensus-based organizations to mediate indigenous people's engagement with the state, markets, and outside organizations has remained constant. Concurrently, the landscape acts of resistance posed by more conservatively minded *compañeros* and of desperation by those driven to cash-crop production subsequent to neoliberal policy shifts at the national level have undoubtedly had their own influence on the new generation of leaders; at the very least, these landscape acts and the associated messages rejecting the value of the cooperative movement have forced the younger leaders to realize that implementing collectivist economies is an ongoing struggle (*lucha*) rather than a simple task to be completed, requiring constant negotiation and flexibility.

Notes

1. Some argue that this region is not part of the Amazon cultural region, and therefore is better thought of as the foothills of the Andes. Muratorio (1991) has argued convincingly, however, that the Upper Napo is more Amazonian than Andean in archeological record and contemporary culture.

2. Theodore Macdonald Jr. conducted dissertation research in the Upper Napo region between 1974 and 1975 and questioned several people about what he refers to as "pre-1960s settlement patterns, territorial rights, and subsistence practices." While his assumption of unchanging practices prior to the 1960s is problematic, his description is useful for understanding practices in the mid-twentieth century.

3. The analogy of a candle was inspired by Thongchai Winichakul's usage in *Siam Mapped: A History of the Geo-Body of a Nation*. In his use of the metaphor, power fields radiated from individuals (specifically, supreme overlords) rather than from places.

4. CEDOC has maintained the same acronym despite various changes in name. In 1938, they were the Ecuadorean Confederation of Catholic Workers (Confederación Ecuatoriana de Obreros Católicos); in 1957, the Ecuadorean Confederation of Catholic Workers, Employees, and Artisans (Confederación Ecuatoriana de Obreros, Empleados y Artesanos Católicos); and in 1965, the Ecuadorean Confederation of Christian Workers' Organizations (Confederación Ecuatoriana de Organizaciones Sindicales Cristianas), indicating a broadening to include Prot-

estant workers. In 1972, a few years after the courses mentioned in the text, they changed once again to the Ecuadorean Central for Class-Based Organizations (Central Ecuatoriana de Organizaciones Clasistas), indicating a growing separation from any particular religious institution or group of institutions.

5. I compiled this history of the Rukullakta through eleven months of ethnographic fieldwork in 2000 and 2001, including oral history interviews with founding members of the cooperative and through consultation with the cooperative's *Actas* (handwritten meeting notes totaling over two thousand pages and covering the period 1970–2001).

6.In fact, at least one state-financed colonization project in the Amazon, that of the Centro de Reconversión Económica del Azuay, Cañar y Morona Santiago (Center for the Economic Conversion of Azuay, Cañar and Morona Santiago [provinces] or CREA), specifically rejected any form of collective agriculture, including United States Peace Corps Volunteers' hopes of instituting an Israeli kibbutz-style, collective labor system (Salazar 1989).

7. The construction of rural schools within what later became the cooperative's boundary actually started in the early 1960s, when a priest from the Archidona mission convinced some families to build one-room school houses closer to people's homes and to send their children there. However, people did not begin to build new homes within view of the school or to create collective plazas until the formation of the cooperative.

References

Actas. 1990–1991. Unpublished meeting minutes and acts of the San Pedro de Rukullakta Agricultural Cooperative. Rukullakta, Ecuador.

Adorno, Theodor. 1973 [1966]. *Negative Dialectics*. Trans. by E. Ashton. New York: Continuum.

Austin, J. L. 1962. *How to Do Things with Words*. Cambridge, MA: Harvard University Press.

Basso, Keith H. 1996. *Wisdom Sits in Places: Language and Landscape among the Western Apache*. Albuquerque: University of New Mexico Press.

Collins, Jennifer N. 2000. "A Sense of Possibilities: Ecuador's Indigenous Movement Takes Center Stage." *NACLA Report on the Americas* 33 (5): 40–47.

Erazo, Juliet S. 2003. "Constructing Autonomy: Indigenous Organizations, Governance, and Land Use in the Ecuadorian Amazon, 1964–2001." PhD diss., University of Michigan.

Feld, Steven, and Keith H. Basso. 1997. *Senses of Place*. Santa Fe: School of American Research Press.

Gordillo, Gastón. 2004. *Landscapes of Devils: Tensions of Place and Memory*. Durham, NC: Duke University Press.

Gow, Peter. 1995. "Land, People, and Paper in Western Amazonia." In *The Anthropology of Landscape: Perspectives on Place and Space*, ed. E. Hirsch and M. O'Hanlon, 43–62. Oxford: Clarendon.

Gupta, Akhil, and James Ferguson. 1997. "Culture, Power, Place: Ethnography at the End of an Era." In *Culture, Power, Place: Explorations in Critical Anthropology*, ed. A. Gupta and J. Ferguson, 1–29. Durham, NC: Duke University Press.

Harvey, David. 1989. *The Condition of Postmodernity*. London: Blackwell.

Hirsch, Eric. 1995. Introd. to *The Anthropology of Landscape: Perspectives on Place and Space*, ed. E. Hirsch and M. O'Hanlon, 1–30. Oxford: Clarendon.

Janusek, John Wayne, and Alan L. Kolata. 2004. "Top-down or Bottom-up: Rural Settlement and Raised Field Agriculture in the Lake Titicaca Basin, Bolivia." *Journal of Anthropological Archeology* 23:404–30.

Lefebvre, Henri. 1991. *The Production of Space*. Trans. D. Nicholson-Smith. Cambridge, MA: Blackwell.

Leonard, Karen. 1997. "Finding One's Own Place: Asian Landscapes Re-Visioned in Rural California." In *Culture, Power, Place: Explorations in Critical Anthropology*, ed. A. Gupta and J. Ferguson, 118–36. Durham, NC: Duke University Press.

Macdonald, Theodore Jr. 1979. "Processes of Change in Amazonian Ecuador: Quijos Quichua Indians Become Cattlemen." PhD diss., University of Illinois.

———. 1981. "Indigenous Response to an Expanding Frontier: Jungle Quichua Economic Conversion to Cattle Ranching." In *Cultural Transformations and Ethnicity in Modern Ecuador*, ed. N. E. J. Whitten, 356–83. Urbana-Champaign: University of Illinois Press.

Massey, Doreen. 1994. *Space, Place and Gender*. Minneapolis: University of Minnesota Press.

Muratorio, Blanca. 1991. *The Life and Times of Grandfather Alonso: Culture and History in the Upper Amazon*. New Brunswick, NJ: Rutgers University Press.

Oberem, Udo. 1980. *Los Quijos. Historia de la Transculturación de un Grupo Indígena en el Oriente Ecuatoriano*. Otavalo, Ecuador: Instituto Otavaleño de Antropología.

Raffles, Hugh. 1999. "'Local Theory': Nature and the Making of an Amazonian Place." *Cultural Anthropology* 14 (3): 323–60.

———. 2002. *In Amazonia: A Natural History*. Princeton, NJ: Princeton University Press.

Rose, Carol M. 1994. *Property and Persuasion: Essays on the History, Theory, and Rhetoric of Ownership*. Boulder, CO: Westview Press.

Salazar, Ernesto. 1989. *Pioneros de la Selva*. Quito: Museos del Banco Central.

Scott, James C. 1998. *Seeing like a State: How Certain Schemes to Improve the Human Condition Have Failed*. New Haven, CT: Yale University Press.

Sheahan, John. 1987. *Patterns of Development in Latin America: Poverty, Repression, and Economic Strategy*. Princeton, NJ: Princeton University Press.

Smith, Adam T. 2003. *The Political Landscape: Constellations of Authority in Early Complex Polities*. Berkeley: University of California Press.

Stewart, Pamela J., and Andrew Strathern. 2003. *Landscape, Memory, and History: Anthropological Perspectives*. London: Pluto.

Taylor, Anne Christine. 1994. "El Oriente Ecuatoriano en el Siglo XIX: 'El Otro Litoral.'" In *Historia y Región en el Ecuador: 1830–1930*, ed. J. Maiguashca. Quito: Corporación Editora Nacional/FLACSO-Sede Ecuador/CERLAC.

Tucker, Robert. 1978. *The Marx-Engels Reader*. New York: W. W. Norton.

Verdery, Katherine. 1994. "The Elasticity of Land: Problems of Property Restitution in Transylvania." *Slavic Review* 53 (4): 1071–1109.

———. 1996. "Fuzzy Property: Rights, Power, and Identity in Transylvania's Decollectivization." In *Uncertain Transition*, ed. M. Burawoy and K. Verdery, 53–81. Boulder, CO: Rowman & Littlefield.

Walker, Richard. 1997. "Unseen and Disbelieved: A Political Economist among Cultural Geographers." In *Understanding Ordinary Landscapes*, ed. P. Groth and T. W. Bressi, 162–73. New Haven, CT: Yale University Press.

Warren, Kay B. 1998. *Indigenous Movements and Their Critics: Pan-Maya Activism in Guatamala*. Princeton, NJ: Princeton University Press.

Winichakul, Thongchai. 1994. *Siam Mapped*. Honolulu: University of Hawaii Press.

Wray, Natalia. 1996. "Economía Indígena e Integración al Mercado: El Caso de los Quichua del Alto Napo Ecuador." In *Amazonía: Economía Indígena y Mercado*, ed. R. C. Smith and N. Wray, 61–82. Quito: COICA and Oxfam America.

Yashar, Deborah J. 1999. "Democracy, Indigenous Movements, and the Postliberal Challege in Latin America." *World Politics* 52 (1): 76–104.

9

Coffee, Abolition, and Immigration
Driving Forces in Nineteenth-Century Brazilian Landscape Transformation

PAUL A. RIVERA

IN MAY 1994, WHILE CAMPAIGNING FOR THE PRESIDENCY OF BRAZIL, Fernando Henrique Cardoso was asked whether he claimed African heritage. His answer that he, like many, had "one foot in the kitchen" ("*um pé na cozinha*") inspired heated criticism from Afro-Brazilian groups both for its deliberate vagueness and somewhat pejorative language (Folha 1994). However, the statement resonated well with many Brazilians whose cultural identity reflects a rich blend of European, African, and indigenous ancestry. Further, the complex system of racial identity and classification in Brazil points to the intricacy of larger social and economic relationships, as well as a historical legacy defined by logical contradictions, competing interests, and power struggles. In this context, this chapter postulates the growth of coffee and the abolition of slavery as driving forces—primary and causal factors—that have shaped the social, political, cultural, and economic landscape of Brazil over the last sesquicentenary.

Given the geographic and temporal scale of this work, the concept of landscape and its transformation requires a macrolevel approach. Viewed as a physical mosaic of heterogeneous interacting systems (Forman and Godron 1986), the vastness of the Brazilian territory stretches the notion of landscape by necessitating the aggregation of much analytical richness. However, the emergence of coffee and the adjustment away from a slave economy generated robust and fundamental changes in nineteenth-century Brazilian land use patterns, both urban and rural, as the value of land increased and the traditional, ill-defined boundaries of enormous *fazendas* gradually gave way to secure property rights and smaller immigrant-owned farms. The growth of coffee also promoted urbanization and substantial economic linkages, spurring the growth of an urban middle class as well as a shift in the locus of economic power from the northeast to the south of Brazil. Perhaps most significantly, the breadth of these transformations highlights the depth of their impact on the cultural landscape: the interactions of groups, distinct in social status and phenotypic traits but similarly rooted to physical places, faced with shifting economic incentives and external pressures.

While the scale and depth of the transformations initiated by the emergence of coffee and the demise of slavery are individually well known, explicit recognition of the interconnected motivations and effects of these events in shaping the trajectory of Brazilian history has been lacking. Traditional economic analyses view the market, in the broadest sense, as the ultimate driving force, effecting change as the organic and natural response to economic incentives. Certainly, such approaches minimize the human dimensions of transformation, but perhaps more importantly, also conceptually limit the analytical scope of transformation by failing to acknowledge the intimate linkages between culture, economy, demography, and politics.

Differing from traditional analyses, this work offers a complementary approach. In a broad sense, the impacts of the coffee industry and the abolition of slavery are easily related to elements of present-day Brazil. Less understood, however, are the intermediate mechanisms through which coffee and abolition manifested their effects on Brazilian society. The focus here is thus a story about the middle. Facing a booming coffee industry and the potential demise of slavery, Brazil in 1850 embarked on a series of programs both to establish property rights in land and gradually to replace slave labor with an abundant pool of European immigrant labor. Deeply rooted in both racism and economic logic, these policies ensured the continued accumulation of wealth by the elite and the persistence of a largely black and mulatto underclass.

Driving force analysis provides a relevant conceptual and methodological counterpoint to traditional approaches. By assuming a wide array of influences and motivations for change, driving force analysis incorporates both simultaneity and intertemporal effects within a hierarchical structure. End results—for example, present socioeconomic conditions—are postulated as the culmination of primary, causal factors and a series of intermediate mechanisms. This analytical perspective thus proves ideal for the present goal of highlighting the intermediate effects induced by coffee and abolition in an interdisciplinary and multifaceted context.

Students of Brazilian history will quickly note that the emergence of the Brazilian coffee industry and the abolition of slavery are separated by approximately fifty years. By the mid-1840s, coffee had already surfaced as the source of economic power in Brazil, and slavery was not formally abolished until 1888. However, 1845 marks the passage of Britain's Aberdeen Act and the subsequent imposition of the slave trade blockade (a geopolitical change in the driving force analysis presented below), providing a credible signal of the ultimate demise of slavery in Brazil. It is thus essential to specify that, for the present analysis, the *threat* of abolition was the relevant driving force. Indeed, in many respects, the actual abolition of slavery in 1888 had a relatively limited impact since most social and economic structures had already begun to accommodate the expected "shock" of abolition. The *fazenda* (plantation) system and the growth of the coffee industry, however, depended on slaves as both a source of low-cost labor and economic collateral. Any indication of the demise of slavery thus signaled a substantial threat to coffee, the nascent source of economic, social, and political power.

To mitigate the perceived risk associated with the potential abolition of slavery, the economic and political elite of Brazil initiated in the 1840s two programs that would prove revolutionary to economic and social structures in Brazil: immigrant attraction programs and the development of property rights in land. In the driving force analysis, these are considered intermediate effects, subsequent to the primary factors of coffee and abolition, but their role is pivotal to specifying the linkage between primary factors and their direct, continuing effects on Brazilian society. Otherwise stated, immigrant programs and the development of secure property rights in land were the vehicles through which the primary forces of coffee and abolition transformed key elements of the Brazilian landscape. It is worth noting that the argument for the development of property rights presented here differs from the neoclassical economic explanation in its explicit linkage to immigration and the need to replace slave labor. Also, in a very different setting, the chapter by Fratkin in this volume addresses the effects on the economy and landscape resulting from changes in property rights over land.

The term *landscape* in this chapter is not necessarily taken to indicate a somewhat self-contained, human-altered expanse of physical space. Instead, it is utilized as a conceptual guideline, much like driving force analysis, meant to highlight the influences and processes generated by diverse interactions. Through this lens, the economic reorganization in Brazil during the nineteenth century and its large-scale impact on the physical landscape are certainly evident; however, the same economic changes also affected the path of social development, generating as well a Brazilian cultural landscape that has persisted for over a century. This chapter shares common ground with work by MacLennan and Walck (this volume) on the mining and ranching industries in New Mexico, both in its temporal scale and emphasis on the role of the state in ameliorating (or causing) the effects or transformation.

Overall, the goals of this chapter are twofold. The first is to posit driving force analysis as a methodological tool to analyze influences and directions of change from a broad and interdisciplinary perspective. Second, I seek to employ the concept of landscape to highlight the intimate connections between culture and economy in the development of social structures, and to bring a degree of cohesion to the analysis of Brazilian history.

The remainder of this chapter proceeds as follows. A discussion of the basic elements of Driving Force Analysis is presented with the specific modifications appropriate to its application to the Brazilian case. Subsequently, the relevant aspects of Brazilian social, cultural, and economic history are traced in the context of the driving force model. A brief section concludes and offers avenues for further study.

Driving Force Analysis

In its original application to the analysis of physical landscape transformation, driving force analysis provides a useful tool to link, for example, the ultimate sources of environmental degradation to the formulation of mitigation policies and the expected outcomes of those policies (Klijn 2002). Relative to more linear approaches, driving force analysis is defined by the explicit recognition that simple cause-and-effect models necessarily minimize the complexity of human decisions and their effects and, in so doing, are often naive and prescriptive in their conclusions. Instead, driving force models assume a broad array of potential sources of change and provide a forum for the interaction of seemingly disparate influences. In a sense, driving force analysis represents a genre of qualitative simultaneous "equation" modeling. For the present purposes, however, the concept of landscape extends beyond the strictly physical into its less tangible human dimensions, and the original analytical tool thus requires commensurate modification.

Figure 9.1 shows the basic structure of driving force analysis in its present application to the Brazilian case.[1] The diagram specifies three stages of influence: primary, intermediate, and direct. The concentric form of the diagram highlights the interconnectedness of influences because the totality of primary influences is assumed to affect subsequent levels. The labels attached to each level are meant to be general and serve to organize the researcher's thought process around a particular problem. Also, the driving force approach specifies a dynamic model that identifies sources of change, but the very notion of change implies the necessity to specify preexisting or initial conditions. Indeed, figure 9.1 lacks the historical background that establishes the context for subsequent changes (elaborated in the next section).

The concentric form of the driving force diagram is most conducive to broad-based "macro" analyses. Driving force models might also be characterized as a kind of tree diagram where the trunk (primary) extends to branches (intermediate) that culminate in leaves (direct). However, while leaves are clearly part of the whole, they are also separated from one another such that it is difficult to maintain the sense of interconnectedness. The tree diagram thus proves applicable to in-depth case studies while the concentric form lends itself to a larger analytical scope.

The primary (outer) level captures the broadest level of instigators of change, and the time dimension associated with driving force analysis suggests that primary factors should generally be first in the chronology of events. For the Brazilian case, these are loosely categorized as economic, natural, geopolitical, demographic, and political. The development of the coffee industry in Brazil is taken as an economic change, while the abolition of slavery might be thought of as a combination of both global and national political forces.

The intermediate level represents the mechanisms through which primary factors manifest their direct effects. Indeed, intermediate effects are often ignored in linear "black box" analyses where they are modeled as pass-through mechanisms that have no effect on the final outcomes.[2] However, ignoring such effects, particularly in the analysis of human society, amplifies the risk of oversimplifying explanations and missing significant elements of analytical richness. Such would certainly appear to be the case in the Brazilian example. The attraction of immigrant labor to Brazil and the development of secure property rights in land were direct consequences of the combination of primary factors, and further, immigration and property rights in Brazil were intimately linked phenomena. However, traditional analyses, especially in economics, have studied these processes individually and have focused only on the influences of market forces in explaining both their causes and effects.

The innermost circle in figure 9.1 represents the direct effects, or outcomes, of the driving force process. As a historical tool, outcomes in a driving force model are both known and, to some extent, specified *ex ante*. The value of the model is thus its ability to elucidate the processes by which a broad array of motivations and decisions converge to a general result.

One potential drawback of driving force analysis stems from its initial use as an environmental policy analysis tool aimed at the measurement of tangible effects: culture as a shared set of values and beliefs are somewhat awkwardly represented in the diagram, and the problem would seem to be

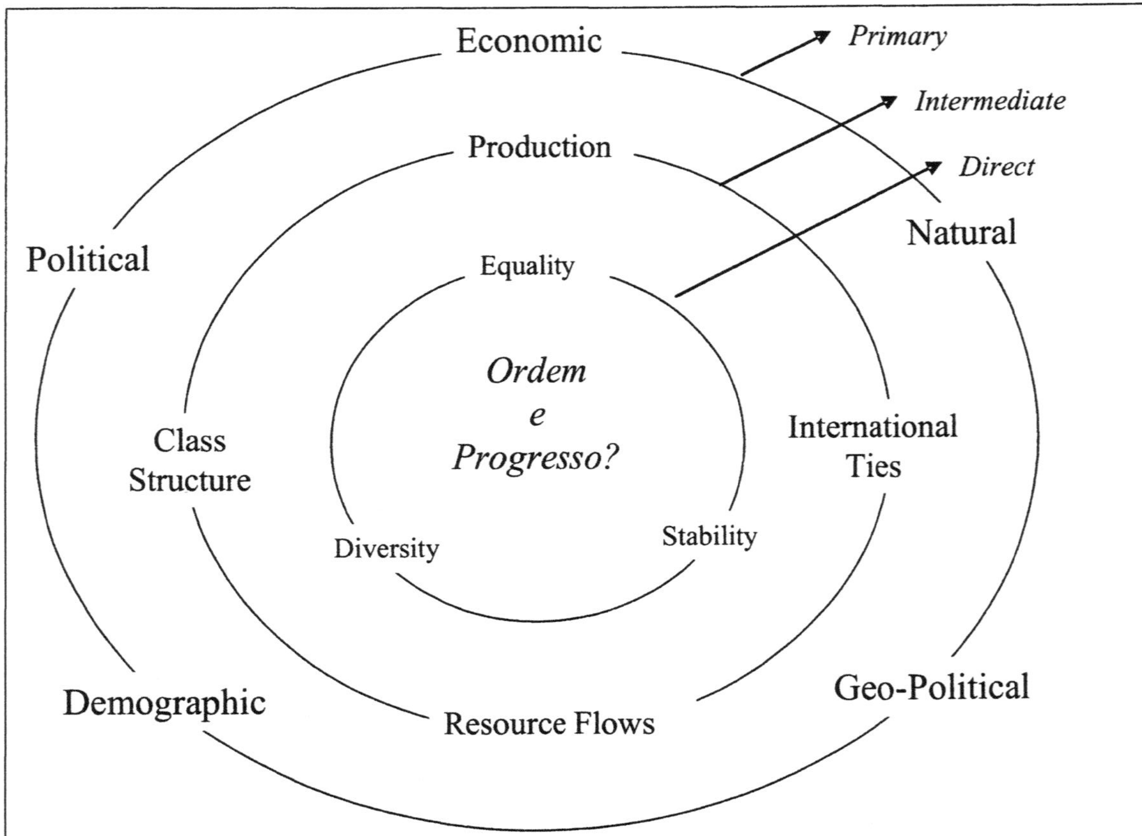

Figure 9.1 Basic structure of driving force analysis. (Adapted from Klijn 2002.)

amplified in broad spectrum analyses. Certainly, the elements within the driving force model reflect the culture that initiated them, but, for example, the level of specificity associated with quantitative modeling is difficult to achieve. Instead, culture is here envisioned as both a cause and effect that permeates each level such that its inclusion at any particular point would tend to limit its scope of influence. However, the omnipresent culture approach is also risky: being everywhere may be the same as being nowhere, and it is easy to disregard entirely the impact of culture.

The Brazilian Case

The Setting at Independence

Brazil's declaration of independence from Portugal in 1822 was a somewhat inauspicious event.[3] Most of the actual battles in the fight for independence are best described as skirmishes, and, in the end, Pedro, the son of the Portuguese king, became the emperor of Brazil. Further, the social, economic, and even political structures established during the colonial era were not substantially modified after independence; indeed, the preservation of the existing social order appears to have been a primary concern for the Brazilian revolutionaries. The fact that the average Brazilian remained largely unaffected as a result of independence comes as no surprise since, by any genre of statistical definition, the "average" Brazilian was a black or mulatto slave. The elite constituted less than 2 percent of the free population, and there was no significant middle-class population. The mercantilist legacy of the colonial era, focused on the extraction of primary goods, had left Brazil without a manufacturing base, lagging in the technologies of the Industrial Revolution, and reliant on exports for income and trade for final goods.

At independence, Brazil was a major exporter of cotton, sugarcane and raw materials, but rapid economic expansion made clear that there remained a vast untapped potential; however, the character of the expansion is also of interest. The colonial land grants had allocated enormous tracts of land to a relatively small number of individuals, establishing from the beginning a concentration of power and wealth focused on the *fazenda* system of production. It is also significant that, once harvested, both cotton and sugarcane are relatively sturdy crops that do not demand immediate, extensive, or complex processing. This permitted agriculture and transportation to be the foci of economic activity with less emphasis on the development of associated industries typically associated with more perishable goods.

It was clear from even the earliest discussions of Brazilian independence that the revolution would not be for "the people." Efforts to co-opt the masses to the national cause were extremely limited, and the emancipation of the slaves was not part of the revolutionary platform. Indeed, this encapsulates the Brazilian cultural landscape at independence: a legacy of deep social divide that not only established, but also justified, the dominance of a comparatively small group over the massive slave population.

However, in stark contrast to the profound social divide, the genetic composition of the typical Brazilian suggested a relatively large degree of intermixing, especially as compared to the experiences of other colonial powers in the Americas. From the beginning, Portuguese explorers and, later, representatives of the Portuguese monarchy were faced with a seemingly endless expanse of land and thus a persistent shortage of labor to exploit adequately the productive potential of the territory. In relation to other parts of the Americas, the indigenous population was insufficient in number to undertake the scale of production intended by the colonizers, and the widespread use of slave labor was almost immediate. Isolated from European society and vastly outnumbered by the slave population, it is not surprising that Europeans in Brazil sought liaisons with slaves and that, even early in colonial history, mulattoes constituted a rapidly growing minority.

The ubiquity and pervasiveness of a mulatto population profoundly impacted the development of race relations and the perceptions of race in Brazil. In contrast to the "one drop" tradition in the United States, mulattoes were, in effect, only as black as they looked. The social status of mulattoes, however, was by no means obvious. Often born of slave mothers, they were originally part of the Brazilian slave population, but their phenotypic traits often made clear their mixed ancestry. Further, as mulattoes increased as a proportion of the nonslave population, some were quite successful, both socially and economically, even penetrating on occasion the upper echelons of Portuguese society; however, their potential for success was directly correlated to their degree of phenotypic "blanching." Implicitly, then, Brazilian racial categorizations became somewhat disconnected from actual parentage and relied on physical characteristics and the elimination of traits of blackness.[4]

From the point of view of the Portuguese, the vast cultural separation from the mass of the population and secure domination over them was an economic necessity. The expanse of the Brazilian territory meant that the labor power of slaves was required for the extraction of value—whether from the gold and diamond mines, or from cotton and sugar production—but slaves were also the de facto basis for wealth in the colony. The tremendous supply of land gave rural land almost no value as a form of collateral;[5] however, credit was an important aspect of trade in agricultural commodities given that the growing cycle typically necessitated a significant temporal lag between sowing and harvesting. As the use of productive capital was relatively minimal, slaves were clearly the scarce, and therefore valuable, input in the production process. Property rights over slaves were thus clear, well established, and strictly enforced, giving slave owners a tool to participate in the agricultural credit market (Hanley 1997).

The slave system in Brazil was therefore essential to the development of the *latifundia* (plantation) as the dominant economic organization. The most fertile arable land had been acquired by land grant from the crown, and slave labor allowed the *fazendeiro* to take advantage of the scale economies supposedly available on the relatively large parcels of land.[6] Further, the role of slaves as economic collateral—often ignored in empirical studies—meant that successful landowners, by investing in additional slaves, could increase not only their agricultural output, but also their capacity for future expansion.

Finally, it goes almost without saying that economic power was a direct avenue to political influence. The wealthiest *fazendeiros* formed a sort of vertically integrated cartel that controlled the transportation and shipping industry, the commercial banking industry, and the local administration of the Catholic Church to ensure that government policies, their enforcement, and the development of local infrastructure favored their economic interests.

North-South Differences and the Physical Landscape

The *fazendeiro* generally had great certainty of his dominion over his land, and the lack of a developed rural land market suggested that the *fazendeiro* had no incentive to sell or substantially subdivide his property. This meant that, at the time of the revolution, the rural Brazilian landscape reflected over three centuries of development but also a genre of physical openness. Property rights in land were not yet an important concept, fences were poorly maintained, and property boundaries often relied on tradition and estimation. A notable exception comes from the mining areas, where the commodity produced was both very valuable and highly portable, and in these areas, space was tightly controlled and boundaries clearly demarcated.

The north-south differences in Brazil also influenced the trajectory of development. The northeastern regions are relatively flat areas that experience both torrential rains and severe periodic droughts. This landscape is demarcated by dense jungle, particularly along the Amazon and some parts of the coast. The northeast thus proved conducive to the vast plantings of cotton and, later, sugarcane. As these were the signature exports from Brazil, the northeast represents the traditional locus of economic power from the colonial era.

The southern regions of Brazil instead exhibit a more mountainous topography and benefit from rich volcanic soils. Throughout the colonial era, these regions provided wood and raw materials, as well as a relatively limited amount of "exotic" agricultural exports, including coffee. However, with the availability of large and deep ports in Rio de Janeiro and São Paulo, southern Brazil represented the nexus of urbanization and commerce.

The landscape created by the north-south interaction in Brazil reflects both tension and interdependence. As the most convenient access point for overseas trade, the south was the administrative center of Brazil, the entry point for most of the slave trade, and the export channel for most goods. Although always less cosmopolitan than the south, the north collectively commanded the core of Brazil's economic power, and development in the south was motivated largely by a growth in international demand for output from the north. However, the economic symbiosis stood in contrast to the social character of the two regions. While the south's relatively close ties to Europe made that area the focal point for intellectual and artistic influences from abroad, the north reflected a somewhat dichotomous blend of a relatively traditional colonial society with a uniquely Brazilian cultural identity that persists to the present.

Coffee and Abolition[7]

Although the volume of production of cotton and sugarcane made Brazil a significant contributor to the world markets for those commodities during the colonial era, competition was intense, particularly from (former) British colonies. By the 1820s, coffee had been a consistent but relatively minor export commodity for nearly half a century. Its status as a luxury item gave it a high price but also limited its potential as a growth industry. However, in total and since its inception as a colony, it was clear that Brazil's productive competitiveness as a commodity exporter was a direct consequence of the relatively low marginal cost and high average productivity of slave labor in the mines and on the plantations. In this context, the historically unprecedented rates of global economic expansion during the nineteenth century proved enormously beneficial, and commodities like coffee, previously limited in distributional scale, experienced both growing demand and diminishing price elasticity, creating the opportunity for the expansion of the Brazilian coffee industry in the nineteenth century.

Beginning in the 1820s, the price signals in the coffee market motivated a considerable transformation of Brazil's economic structure, and the role of coffee as a primary driving force became increasingly evident. The speed and scale of the coffee expansion induced producers to alter their perceptions of the value and importance of their land, and a movement toward enclosure and more careful delineation of boundaries occurred. Perhaps the most obvious physical transformation resulting from the expansion of coffee, however, was the shift in growth and economic activity from the northern to the southern regions of Brazil. Not well suited for the relatively arid lowland regions of the northeast, coffee production began to move south as efficiency considerations associated with coffee cultivation favored the relatively rainy climate and volcanic soils in the south over the more arid north. Primary crop production in the south was shifted to more marginal areas, and the production of traditional cash crops was substantially downsized to make way for coffee. Further, the accessibility of major ports in the São Paulo and Rio de Janeiro areas and the associated infrastructural amenities (transportation, packaging, shipping, etc.) meant that the transaction costs of coffee cultivation were also lower in the south.

Over time, the acceleration of southern development as a result of the expansion of coffee cultivation permanently shifted the locus of economic power away from the northeast to the south. Showing the greatest growth potential, São Paulo and Rio de Janeiro invested most heavily in infrastructure, as well as in the development of formal banking institutions, leaving the northeast lagging. Further, the intensified use of productive resources in the south drove up the average price of slaves, the key input in the productive process. Many *fazendeiros* in the northeast indeed found it advantageous to liquidate portions of their slave assets in the face of rising slave prices, engendering a marked north-south internal migration of the slave population. The northeast thus fell into a kind of recession with revenues falling and production costs rising.

Economists describe this genre of shift in the economic landscape as Dutch disease. A booming sector, such as coffee, draws resources toward itself and, more importantly, away from traditional sectors. In the case of coffee, the effect is amplified as the more capital-intensive nature of coffee cultivation and processing relative to cotton or sugarcane creates the opportunity for growth in new industries peripheral to coffee. The end result reflects unbalanced growth: an overall boom with a significant lagging sector. The Brazilian case represents a particularly stark example as the shock of transformation—typically absorbed in the long run—persists in a still-lagging northeastern Brazil.

The growth of coffee transformed Brazilian society. Compared to sugarcane or cotton, the coffee industry required more developed economic "linkages" between the agricultural, manufacturing, service, and public sectors of the economy. Coffee thus promoted urbanization and the development of a nonagricultural, nonslave population to service the needs of a growing, wealthy, and predominantly European elite. Cultural developments in the 1820s and 1830s reflected the schizophrenic side of postcolonial development as aspects of European art, literature, and thought gained prevalence amid a nascent nationalistic movement.

While the coffee boom thus provided opportunities for a genre of middle class to emerge, inequality is likely to have deepened. Traditionally entrenched families exploited their enhanced economic status to consolidate and expand their influence, and while a budding middle class existed, the ballooning slave population provided little opportunity to close the traditional social divide. There is some speculation that the conditions and overall treatment of slaves may have improved during this period as landowners began to perceive of slaves as valuable capital rather than as expendable tools, but the fact remains that slaves were nonetheless private property with few rights or privileges.

The Brazilian economic juggernaut did not, however, develop in a vacuum, and the realities of global trade could not be ignored. The British had long been aware of the threat Brazil posed to their economic dominance, and from the inception of the empire, Britain pressured Brazil to cease the importation of African slaves. Although British arguments against the slave trade were publicly framed in a social and humanitarian context, it was clear that the use of slaves in Brazil undermined the international competitiveness of British interests in the Americas, particularly those exporting sugarcane and cotton. In 1831, Britain sent a strong signal to Brazil, banning the transatlantic slave trade and outlining consequences for those who persisted in the practice. However, a signal is only as good as its credibility, and the lack of enforcement negated the threat. The profitability of British interests in the Americas continued to erode throughout the 1830s, culminating in 1845 in the passage of the Aberdeen Act, a bill committing both will and resources to the enforcement of the 1831 ban on international slave trade.

This real and credible threat of the eventual demise of slavery is a primary driving force in the development of nineteenth-century Brazil. It was widely understood that the prosperity of the Brazilian enterprise was based on the productivity of slave labor and that any attempt to dismantle the institution of slavery would disrupt fundamental economic processes and threaten the power and status of Brazil's growing upper class.

Further, it was clear that the slave population could not reproduce itself on a scale to maintain existing levels, much less accommodate the evident growth potential for Brazilian output. Particularly among the slave population, both maternal and infant mortality rates were high, and the preference for male slaves eventually created slightly skewed sex ratios. The continued importation of slaves was thus viewed a necessity to maintain and foster continued economic growth.

Coffee and the threat of abolition thus represent primary driving forces, but of two quite different types. The impetus and scope of the growth of the coffee industry clearly exerted a massive and profound influence on Brazil's socioeconomic landscape, and its position as a primary driving force seems unambiguous. The demise of slavery is somewhat more subtle but no less significant, for its role was not to derail Brazilian development, but to redirect its path. Faced with the credible threat against slavery, Brazil's political and economic leaders confronted the challenge of maintaining growth and power in a social structure that would eventually not include slaves.

Immigration and Property Rights

Brazilian independence from Portugal in 1822 ended the formal system of land titling by the crown. Thus, in the absence of legal processes, squatting and the principle of adverse possession—ownership arising from undisputed land use—guided land acquisition in the empire of Brazil. Also, following the Aberdeen Act, when Britain began to enforce an 1831 international ban on slave trade, Brazil was forced to cease the importation of slaves, thus indicating the impending, but not immediate, end of slavery in Brazil. These two facts left the growing Brazilian coffee industry in a potentially difficult situation since the source of labor and collateral (slaves) would be diminishing without a suitable replacement, given land's low value and tenuous claims of ownership. As a direct but not necessarily obvious result, a land law, introduced in 1843 and finally passed in 1850, provided squatters and land grant holders alike the opportunity to register and entitle their land after proper measurement and recording (Coleção das Leis do Império do Brasil 1831–1889).

The neoclassical evolutionary theory of property rights postulates the Brazilian situation as a classic case in point (Alston, Libecap, and Mueller 1999; Alston, Libecap, and Schneider 1994; Mueller, Alston, Libecap, and Schneider 1994; Mueller 1995). As coffee was beginning to emerge as a significant export commodity, coffee producers perceived ever-greater benefits to establishing secure property rights such that the costs of titling and enforcement became worthwhile. In response to increases in coffee demand, suggests the evolutionary theory, coffee producers exercised their substantial political influence to promote the development and refinement of effective property rights.

However, the evolutionary theory minimizes the importance of more nuanced factors (Nugent and Saddi 2004). In particular, the evolutionary theory does not address the failure of the Land Law of 1850 as a mechanism to promote titling or the enforcement of property rights (Guimaraes 1968; Dean 1971). As titling and enforcement required a nontrivial cost in terms of both money and effort with, at the time, relatively little commensurate benefit, few landowners sought enforcement of their legal property rights in the wake of the passage of the law (Coleçao dos Decretos 1843–1889).

Also, the evolutionary theory does not account for the political processes behind the Land Law of 1850 (Saddi 2002). The parliamentary debates leading to the passage of the law demonstrated consistent patterns (Anais do Parlamento Brasileiro 1843–1850): (1) no explicit mention of property rights as a motivation for the law; (2) general agreement on the need to secure a rural labor force base before abolition; and (3) cognizance of and reference to failed attempts in Australia to generate self-sustaining agricultural expansion by financing immigration through land sales.[8]

These facts indeed predict the failure of the 1850 law as a land law and highlight from the beginning the key role of state actions in the attraction of immigrants to Brazil's coffee provinces. One of the explicit goals of the land law was to generate a complete map of private and public lands, and a major provision of the law was that any unclaimed and untitled land was by default public land available for titling to immigrants. In addition, the land law specified the commitment of state funds to support immigration programs, giving both substance and credibility to the effort to attract immigrants to Brazil. The Land Law of 1850 was followed by several updates, refinements, and extensions that broadened the scale and funding levels of immigration programs. In general, however, effective property rights in land were only marginally improved while slavery continued to exist.

Immigration and Property Rights in São Paulo

The experience of the state of São Paulo provides a notable example of the successful development of property rights. The state of São Paulo adopted in 1895 a land law (postabolition) granting generous allowances to squatters—even those who acquired land after 1850—and substantially reduced the bureaucratic process, and thus the cost, of land registration and titling (Coleçao de leis e decretos do Estado de São Paulo 1892–1927). The ensuing marked rise in land titling in São Paulo altered the business of coffee cultivation, especially as compared to other states. Titles allowed the mortgaging of land for the purpose of obtaining agricultural credit, a particularly important opportunity given the relatively large number of small, cash-poor, immigrant-owned farms in São Paulo. The São Paulo land law of 1895 coincides with a gross inflow of over 750,000 migrants to the state during the decade of the 1890s, nearly 17 percent greater than the total inflow to all of Argentina during the same period.

It is worth noting that no other coffee-producing state took similar action to reduce the cost and expand the scale of land titling following the formation of the republic,[9] and the activity in São Paulo stands in contrast to that in Minas Gerais, a neighboring coffee-producing state. Despite a similar set of incentives suggested by rising coffee prices and export volume, Minas Gerais did not enact a land law until 1900, and even then, still required a somewhat lengthy bureaucratic process to register and title land. The result was much slower development of land markets in Minas Gerais and a lagging proportion of immigrant labor flowing to that state.

Two additional major land laws were passed in São Paulo in 1907 and 1921. These served primarily to enhance the complementarities between São Paulo's land laws and immigration policies by expanding programs and funding to facilitate land acquisition by immigrants and further recognizing the claims of squatters.

The connection between São Paulo's land and immigration policies and its emergence as the leading coffee-producing state during the republic is difficult to ignore and signals a key transformation of the landscape. Immigration policies and the land-for-service schemes resulted in the propagation of small, efficiently run, immigrant-owned farms that gave São Paulo an edge in production. The marked decrease in average farm size signaled the decline of the *latifundia* system well in advance of the Depression, the traditionally postulated culprit, as smaller producers made evident the diseconomies of scale in coffee production. While the physical landscape began to reflect the trend toward widespread, small-scale, intense cultivation, it was perhaps the social and cultural landscape of Brazil that was most profoundly affected. These immigrant producers represented the first substantial home-grown middle class, and the foci of new wealth generation, political power, and artistic innovation moved toward this growing entrepreneurial and well-networked group.

Immigration, Inequality, and Instability

A crucial and often overlooked aspect of the immigration programs in Brazil is the explicit decision to commit state funds to bringing European immigrants rather than offering incentives (like land ownership) to freed slaves. Emancipation did not make former slaves less available as workers, but in promoting immigration incentive programs, Brazilian leaders appear to have deliberately excluded the majority of the black and mulatto population from growth opportunities afforded to immigrants (Andrews 1988; Prado 1945). In particular, the Land Law of 1850 and its updates did not seek to extend to the native population (free or not) the offer to obtain titled land in exchange for a period of service in agricultural labor, thus limiting the wealth-accumulation potential of the majority of Brazilians.

On the surface, the logical argument appears valid: European immigrants, relative to slaves, brought substantial human capital as artisans and craftsmen that might contribute to the creation of a "modern" Brazil. Bringing in immigrants would be a quick and easy way to develop the presence of a skill set that was scarce in the Brazilian environment. Further, agricultural producers were keenly aware that the development of a strong labor market would drive up labor costs and would be detrimental to their interests, and a primary focus of much of the legislative debate surrounding the land laws and their updates was the desire to generate an oversupply of workers such that wages would remain low.

However, while governments are, admittedly, rarely forward looking or efficient in an economic sense, the immigration scheme has the tone of a particularly short-run solution. Struggling businesses will often seek infusions of new capital to bolster immediate performance and complement long-term plans for retooling and retraining; however, investors undertake such risky ventures only if long-term plans suggest positive returns into the future. The Brazilian immigration programs instead resemble short-term tactics that do not reside within the context of a long-term strategy. For example, had the land laws allowed freed slaves to participate in the land-for-service scheme offered to immigrants, it seems likely that the economic disparities between freed slaves and immigrants at the turn of the century might have exhibited both lesser magnitude and lesser variation. To the extent that economic inequality is associated with cultural tension and social strife, any policies that might have mitigated Brazil's turbulence during the twentieth century would seem worthy of reflection. And while it is perhaps unfair to decompose historical events in the context of strategic management theory, the point is meant to be illustrative and not definitive: immigration was by no means costless, was not the only option available to policymakers, and served to strengthen the black-white socioeconomic status quo. Economic rationale thus seems to offer only an incomplete justification of the need for Brazil's immigration programs.

The role of racism in the formulation of Brazilian policy cannot be ignored. However, racism is, in general, an argument of exclusion—once the argument is put forth, other approaches may be categorically discarded—

and it is methodologically necessary to have considered racism only after having accounted for more direct influences such as the economic argument presented above. Only having found fault with the completeness of the economic explanation does it seem appropriate to include racism.

Certainly, it would be logically contradictory to regard as equals individuals over whom one holds legal rights of ownership, and racism thus seems necessary to the functioning of a slave society.[10] After generations of slavery in Brazil, racist beliefs were typically expressed as social Darwinism and the *ideologia da vadiagem* (Andrews 1988): the idea that blacks (or, more precisely, traits of blackness) reflected a lack of capacity for higher-order thought or noncoerced labor. While justifying the persistence of slavery, this attitude also reduced dramatically the probability that blacks might have been expected or anticipated to play a significant role in the postabolition development of Brazil.

The immigration scenario thus becomes more focused. Beyond lacking nonagricultural skills, freed slaves were perceived to be unable to acquire a desirable set of modern urban or industrial skills. Immigrants, predominantly recruited from southern Europe, generally had the desired qualifications, but perhaps more importantly, also brought a social, cultural, and religious background that overlapped substantially with Portuguese society. Further, as part of the immigration programs, immigrants were dispersed over a relatively wide geographic area, and, intentionally or not, they contributed to the spread of European culture and a more significant white presence in Brazil.

The result, the culmination of the driving force process, is the overarching picture of Brazil at the dawn of the twentieth century. For several decades after the extinction of slavery in 1888, firsthand memories of slavery remained widespread, and perceptions were slow to change. Neither former slaves nor slave owners transitioned easily to traditional employee-employer relationships as long-established cultural boundaries were only gradually modified. Perhaps most significantly, the majority of former slaves are unlikely to have experienced substantial improvements in their day-to-day quality of life.

Many former slaves remained at the *fazendas*, but others with an entrepreneurial spirit sought to strike out on their own to pursue the dream of becoming their own *fazendeiro*. However, more often than not, they found that most of the profitably arable land was already occupied by immigrant farmers running small but highly efficient operations; indeed, these farmers begin the next chapter in Brazil's transformation, representing a shift in economic and political power away from traditionally entrenched interests to Brazil's nouveau riche. Faced with few options, many former slaves sought out the urban centers, and São Paulo and Rio de Janeiro experienced large inflows to both their urban cores and the surrounding *favelas*. Again, most urban services and the nascent industrial concerns were primarily under the direction of enterprising immigrants, and the large black and mulatto influx ensured that urban wages remained low.

The instability of the situation seems difficult to overestimate. The traditionally entrenched Portuguese elite found its economic power eroding as labor costs crept up and an increasing proportion of the nation's export production was being provided by small, organized immigrant farmers—ironically, those who were brought to stave off the elite's demise. These economic tensions translated directly to the public arena as immigrants sought greater representation and influence in policymaking spheres while traditional interests retreated to a more opaque method of government. And in the background remained the impoverished and disenfranchised majority.

Conclusion

The goal of this work is to offer a unique perspective on history, not by relating historical endpoints, but by focusing on intermediate, pivotal events that influence the trajectory to the result. The legacies of coffee and slavery are an intimate part of the Brazilian cultural identity, but the intermediate vehicles that served to reinforce those values and perceptions are seldom mentioned. The recruitment of immigrant labor and the associated switch from property rights in people to property rights in land represented reactions to the growth of the coffee industry and the potential demise of slavery that significantly altered Brazil's physical, social, and economic landscape. Immigration programs increased the European presence in Brazil and created a new category of agricultural landowner that directly reduced the economic opportunities for freed slaves or native Brazilians. The extinction of slavery marked a moral victory, but its tangible effects were not obvious. Thus, the robust economic growth evidenced in Brazil during the nineteenth century should not necessarily be associated with commensurate widespread improvements in real well-being.

The use of a generalized concept of landscape also provides a useful lens through which to view the interactions of heterogeneous influences across broad expanses of space and time. Sociocultural differences between slaves and Europeans stand in stark contrast to the growth of a significant mulatto population in Brazil, and the influx of large numbers of immigrants during the latter half of the nineteenth century clearly altered that landscape and influenced the development of the modern Brazilian identity. Similarly, the north-to-south shift in economic power altered the physical landscape as many northeastern *fazendas* fell into disrepair, were parceled among family members, or were sold, often to enterprising immigrant families. The southern landscapes equally saw a transition from traditional, primary crops to the near-total domination of profitable coffee plantings.

Two avenues for further work seem particularly relevant. The analysis presented here reaches across large time frames and a wide geographical space; however, specific regions of Brazil followed unique paths in their historical development in relation to agricultural exports and the slave system. In particular, deeper comparative studies of the experiences of São Paulo, Rio de Janeiro, and Minas Gerais in the context of driving force analysis are required to elucidate their differentials in economic progress and unique cultural developments during the nineteenth century. Also, as every end is a new beginning, the driving force process should be taken to its logical conclusion. Urbanization, the rise of immigrants to political and economic prominence, and the frustration of the masses provide fertile ground, well rooted in historical context, to explain the intimately linked social and economic turbulence in Brazil during the twentieth century.

Notes

I acknowledge my enormous debt of gratitude to Jeffrey Nugent and Vitória Saddi, whose pioneering work forms the basis of this analysis. Many thanks to the participants at the 2005 Society for Economic Anthropology Annual Conference. Any errors are, of course, my own.

1. Although not explicit, Graham (1966) applies a genre of driving force analysis to the Brazilian case postulating coffee and urbanization as primary forces.

2. For example, algebraically, if $a = f(b)$ and $b = g(c)$, then the relationship between a and c may be fully specified as $a = f(g(c))$, and the intermediate variable b plays no significant role.

3. While the broad facts of nineteenth-century Brazilian history are well known and easily uncovered, Skidmore (1999) provides a thorough yet compact treatment.

4. To this day, color remains an important feature of the Brazilian system of categorization, as the national census asks individuals to self-identify as white, black, brown, or yellow.

5. This is not entirely true. Although some markets for land did exist, implying that land did have value, their prevalence varied widely by state in Brazil and, in most cases, focused on urban, nonagricultural land.

6. The assumption of agricultural economies of scale was based on the mercantilist philosophy, but smallholder production, which proved to be more efficient, did not become widespread until the twentieth century.

7. Martin (1933) provides a dated but rich treatment of slavery in Brazil and the processes leading to abolition.

8. The Australian failure informed much of the parliamentary debates, particularly in the context of immigration to the United States, where land could be obtained at virtually no cost, and resulted in the 1850 Land Law's provision of land to immigrants at very low prices.

9. Other non-coffee-producing states farther south did seem to strengthen property rights for the purpose of attracting immigrants.

10. Racism is perhaps not the correct term here. While there have been examples of slave societies where master and slave are culturally and genetically similar, the irrational perception of the slave population as generally inferior seems pervasive.

References

Alston, Lee J., Gary D. Libecap, and Bernardo Mueller. 1999. *Titles, Conflict, and Land Use.* Ann Arbor: University of Michigan Press.

Alston, Lee J., Gary D. Libecap, and Robert Schneider. 1994. "The Determinants and Impact of Property Rights: Land Titles on the Brazilian Frontier." *Journal of Law, Economics and Organization* 12 (1): 25–61.

Anais do Parlamento Brasileiro. Câmara dos Senhores Deputados. 1843–1850.

Andrews, George Reid. 1988. "Black and White Workers: São Paulo, Brazil, 1888–1928." *Hispanic American Historical Review* 68 (3): 491–524.

Coleção das Leis do Império do Brasil. Rio de Janeiro: Imprensa Nacional, 1831–1889.

Coleção de leis e decretos do Estado de São Paulo, 1892 a 1927. Diário Oficial do Estado de São Paulo.

Coleção dos Decretos do governo do Império do Brasil. 1843–1889.

Dean, W. 1971. "Latifundia and Land Policy in Nineteenth-Century Brazil." *Hispanic-American History Review* (November): 606–25.

Folha de São Paulo. 1994. FHC Nega Ter Dito Que Tem Um "Pé na Cozinha." June 1.

Forman, Richard T. T., and Michael Godron. 1986. *Landscape Ecology*. New York. John Wiley and Sons.

Graham, Richard. 1966. "Causes for the Abolition of Negro Slavery in Brazil: An Interpretive Essay." *Hispanic American Historical Review* 46 (2): 123–37.

Guimaraes, Alberto Passos. 1968. *Quatro Séculos de Latifundio*. Rio de Janeiro: Paz e Terra.

Hanley, Anne G. 1997. "Capital Markets in the Coffee Economy: Economic Growth and Institutional Change in São Paulo, Brazil, 1850–1905." *Journal of Economic History* 57 (2): 493–96.

Klijn, Jan. 2002. "Driving Forces Behind Landscape Transformation in Europe: From a Conceptual Approach to Policy Options." In *The New Dimensions of the European Landscape, Proceedings of the Frontis Workshop on the Future of the European Cultural Landscape*, 201–18. Wageningen, the Netherlands.

Martin, Percy Alvin. 1933. "Slavery and Abolition in Brazil." *Hispanic American Historical Review* 13 (2): 151–96.
Mueller, B. 1995. "The Political Economy of Agrarian Reform in Brazil." PhD diss., University of Illinois, Urbana-Champaign.
Mueller, B., L. Alston, G. Libecap, and R. Schneider. 1994. "Land Property Rights and Privatization in Brazil." *Quarterly Review of Economics and Finance* 34:261–80.
Nugent, Jeffrey B., and Vitória Saddi. 2004. "When and How Do Land Rights Become Effective? Historical Evidence from Brazil." Manuscript.
Prado, Caio. 1945. "Distribuição da Propriedade Fundiária Rural no Estado de São Paulo." *Boletim Geográfico* 29 (August): 692–700.
Saddi, Vitória. 2002. "The Role of Coffee in the Creation of Institutions in Brazil (1830–1930)." PhD diss., University of Southern California.
Skidmore, Thomas E. 1999. *Brazil: Five Centuries of Change*. New York: Oxford University Press.

III

POLITICAL ECONOMY AND INSTITUTIONAL INTERACTIONS

10

Unsettled Landscapes
Settlement Patterns and the Development of Social Inequality in Northern Iceland

DOUGLAS J. BOLENDER, JOHN M. STEINBERG, AND E. PAUL DURRENBERGER

IN RECENT WORK, DOREEN MASSEY HAS CALLED ATTENTION to a contemporary emphasis in the social sciences on process, movement, and the "rejection of settledness," supplanting the analysis of formal spatial features, such as borders and territories (Massey 2006: 40). The notion of landscape provides a means to negotiate the tension between the formal territories and places that have real political and economic significance (Dodgshon 1998; Massey 2005) and the underlying unsettledness of social process. It encompasses a range of meanings from the highly subjective, multifaceted, and transient experience of individuals (Bender 2002, 2006; Ingold 1993) to the structured products of these individual perspectives in spatial practice and the built environment (Bourdieu 1977; Lawrence and Low 1990; Lefebvre 1991). One of the strengths of the landscape is its potential to see these as complementary, as opposed to contradictory, positions in which environment (natural and manufactured), social practice, and subjective experience all play a part. From this perspective landscape can be simultaneously structured and unsettled.

The Viking age settlement of Iceland reveals tensions between the ordering of landscape in the creation of farmstead properties and the changing circumstances of the households that occupied them. In the late ninth century the previously uninhabited island was rapidly settled and a new society created. The process of land claim and farmstead establishment had an enduring impact on Icelandic society. Throughout Iceland's history farmstead location has been highly stable and many farmsteads established a millennium ago remain today. The first farmsteads were established by independent colonists from Scandinavia and the British Isles but systematic inequalities soon emerged, resulting in landowning and tenant households. By the end of the seventeenth century, when the first systematic surveys of landownership were conducted, over 95 percent of Icelandic households lived on tenant properties (Lárusson 1967). The emergence of institutionalized interhousehold inequality was tied to the dynamics of land division in the century following the initial settlement as an unsettled island became a propertied landscape.

The majority of Iceland is uninhabitable wasteland, and settlement was, and remains, restricted largely to the more fertile lowland fjords, valleys, and coastal plains where the first settlers and their descendants established their homes. Circumscribed by rivers, steep mountain slopes, and rocky moraines, these lowland areas comprised a bound space in which households competed for land and resources. Iceland was never an egalitarian society. The first settlers imported a highly stratified household organization divided between the landowning family and household dependents, such as servants and slaves, and the concerns of the landowning elite disproportionately shaped the developing landscape. While there is little evidence to suggest institutionalized inequalities among the initial settlement households, power and authority were not evenly distributed among landowners either. In the absence of state institutions the defense of land claims fell to the landowners and whatever support networks they could muster.

In the process of land division following the initial settlement of Iceland it is clear that not all farmsteads were created as equals. In the early eleventh century land-division practices changed from a pattern of large, dispersed farmsteads to small farmsteads neighboring the earlier, larger farmsteads. We argue that landowners settled dependent labor at the margins of their property, thus creating a new class of subordinate tenant farmsteads. In doing so, they fundamentally altered the dynamics of household production by allowing landowners to benefit from labor outside the household.

What altered in the household and landscape that motivated landholders to subdivide their properties and establish subordinate farmsteads? The early Icelandic landscape was far from stable. Land use, environment, and population were all subject to rapid transformation as farmsteads were established, land cleared, and new generations born. Landowners had to maintain a balance between household production and the defense of property claims in these changing circumstances. We turn to the work of A.V. Chayanov (1966) and the role that marginal returns on labor and land play in household production to explain the changing motivations of Icelandic landowners and how they manifested themselves in the process of land division and farmstead creation.

At first glance, Chayanov may appear an odd complement to a landscape perspective and the analysis of economic transformation. Chayanov used the theory of marginal returns, embodied in the household consumer-to-worker ratio, to explain stagnation in the Russian peasant economy. Nonetheless, Chayanov and the consumer-to-worker ratio provide insights into the internal logic of household production and the forces that drive household composition. The Icelandic settlers were actively shaping their households and the landscape. Behind the apparent stability of farmstead location was an unsettled landscape of changing social and environmental pressures. Chayanov's studies were motivated by the goal of changing the dynamics of peasant production—Icelandic landowners also were aware of these dynamics and actively worked to manipulate them.

The Settlement of Iceland

Iceland was one of the last large landmasses in the world to be settled. It is said in the sagas that the first settlers, Viking chieftains and wealthy farmers, were fleeing state consolidation in Norway between ca. AD 870 and 930. These individuals, prosperous enough to own a ship, brought over family, livestock, and dependent workers and slaves. Iceland's settlement was a rapid migration into a previously uninhabited landscape and the settlers established large, stratified households on independent farmsteads. Later, landowners subdivided farmsteads to create tenant properties resulting in institutionalized inequalities *among* households.

The settlement and early history of Iceland has long been a focus of literary, historical, and archaeological research, both within and outside Iceland (Andersson 1964; Friðriksson 1994; Kristjánsson 1992). The period is witnessed by a corpus of literary texts, primarily the Family Sagas (Viðar 1997) and the Book of Settlements (Pálsson and Edwards 1972). These texts vividly describe the political, economic, and social interactions of chieftains, farmers, household dependents, and slaves. Written primarily in the thirteenth and fourteenth centuries, hundreds of years after the events they chronicle, they nonetheless provide critical insights into the social dynamics of the new society (Byock 1988; Durrenberger 1992; Turner 1971). Property plays a prominent role in the sagas. Rights to land were regularly challenged, and property disputes often precipitated the feuds that form the principal narrative of the sagas. However, from the stories alone, no coherent chronology of changing settlement patterns emerges that can be used to explore the development of property relationships in early Iceland.

From the Settlement until its incorporation into the Norwegian state in 1262, Iceland was a stratified society without state institutions, a situation that Fried (1967) identifies as unstable and transitory. Disputes among highly ranked people were heard at annual assemblies. In the absence of state institutions the only way to enforce an assembly decision was through a sufficiently large support group to compel compliance, or the support of someone with such a group. The Icelandic chieftains had coalitions of followers who provided the support necessary to enforce decisions. A chieftain's ability to enforce decisions depended on the size of his following, and the size of his following depended partially on generosity, especially feasting. The same need to maintain support networks was true of any landowning household because without significant support, it risked losing its property.

Recent work by the Skagafjörður Archaeological Settlement Survey (SASS) in northern Iceland documents the process of land claim, farmstead division, and the first appearance of a new class of subordinate farmsteads in the late ninth through eleventh centuries (Steinberg 2002, 2004; Steinberg and Bolender 2005). By augmenting the archaeological record of settlement pattern changes with the sagas' descriptions of early Icelandic politics and household organization, we can begin to understand the process of land division that gave rise to interhousehold stratification. Specifically, we contend that increases in the productivity of large farmsteads reached an upper limit because of the seasonal nature of Icelandic agropastoralism and marginality of the environment.

The limits on farmstead production were superseded by the movement of farmstead labor out of the household to small tenant farmsteads at the edges of the primary farmstead properties. The shift from internally stratified households to interhousehold stratification, controlled via inequalities in land tenure, was a critical step in institutionalizing revenue streams to the elite—thereby creating the conditions for an expansion of political power and the development of regional hierarchies and finally an island-wide hierarchy. The elite resettlement of subordinate labor onto marginally utilized land purposefully altered the economic and physical landscapes in tandem.

A Model of Settlement and Land Division

The settlement of Iceland has been viewed alternatively as a gradual process of expansion (Lárusson 1967) or as a relatively rapid process encompassing both lowland and productive highland regions, resulting in a hierarchically organized system of farmsteads born out of inequalities in the initial settlement (Durrenberger 1991; Herschend 1994; Smith 1995; Vésteinsson, McGovern, and Keller 2002). Based on systematic survey data from the Langholt region in northern Iceland, we propose an alternative to an extended open landscape with a slow progression of independent farm establishment and the rapid concretization of a hierarchical property system. Instead we see stages of farmstead establishment, each reflecting the landowning elite's control over productive land and, after the initial settlement, dictating the terms of subsequent farmstead establishment. The alternative model is predicated on a series of developments from the settlement through the end of the eleventh century:

1. During initial settlement, ca. AD 870–930, land was readily available and farmsteads could be established with minimal consideration for neighboring farmers. Land may have continued to be available for some time after the arrival of the first settlers and there was little resistance to the establishment of new farmsteads. The availability of land and difficulty of exerting control over other farms would have favored large properties and complex servant and slave-owning households as the principal means of increasing production. Households were the locus of social stratification, from slave to chieftain.
2. By the second half of the tenth century, productive lands were under the control of specific households as lawfully recognized farmstead property. Major immigration to the island ceased in AD 930 when the land was said to be "fully settled" and all productive lands claimed (Þorgilsson 1930). Afterward, new farmsteads could be established only by dividing an existing farmstead property. These new farmsteads were widely dispersed and had many of the same characteristics as the initial farmsteads.
3. In the eleventh century we see a significant shift in the location and size of new farmsteads. They were smaller, closer, and likely subordinate to the preexisting farmsteads. The sagas describe many smaller farms started by freed slaves or former servants of the primary household on land provided by the landowner. We suggest that these farms were established as dependent properties belonging to the primary farm. Landowners shifted direct control over labor and productivity to indirect control in the form of rents and, possibly, continued labor obligations.
4. The final stage in the establishment of interhousehold inequality comes at the end of the eleventh century. Now subdivided, some primary landowning farmsteads reorganized. On Langholt these shifts would have improved intervisibility with outlying farmsteads. After the conversion to Christianity in AD 1000, churches appeared at many of these farms that would have served as central places for the outlying tenant farms. The hierarchical structure of land tenure

appears to have been firmly established by the end of the eleventh century: a landscape of landowners and tenants. Within the study region, there were no significant changes in farmhouse location from this period until the twentieth century. The development of institutionalized inequalities in land tenure provided one of the essential bases of the expanding political economy and regional consolidation that characterized the next two centuries of Icelandic history.

The Settlement of Iceland

Isolated in the North Atlantic, Iceland was settled late in the first millennium, ca. AD 870, primarily from Scandinavia and the northern British Isles. The historical accounts describe a rapid emigration and extensive settlement of the island, a picture generally supported by the archaeological evidence. Colonizing expeditions included a leader or group of leaders, household members, servants, and slaves (Karras 1988).

The Book of the Icelanders, the earliest preserved Icelandic history, reports that the settlement lasted until AD 930, about the same time that the general assembly was established at Þingvellir to embody an islandwide legislative and judicial, but not executive, authority (Þorgilsson 1930). After this it is said that there was little additional immigration. This claim is all but impossible to verify archaeologically but it does serve as a potential, and at present uncontested, model for the settlement: a couple of generations of immigration followed by a period of land division based on the dynamics of the indigenous population and society. Settlement Age farmsteads tended to do well in later centuries. They are often the wealthiest farms in the region in the late seventeenth- and early eighteenth-century land surveys. Various authors have argued that expedition leaders exercised significant influence over subsequent settlements within their claims by granting land to expedition members or later settlers to set up their own farmsteads (e.g., Durrenberger 1991; Herschend 1994; Smith 1995). While first comers probably did influence later settlers, the settlement pattern from our study region reveals only a few large, highly dispersed farmsteads through the first half of the tenth century. We see little support for the idea that the Settlement itself resulted in institutionalized inequalities *among* households. The research in the Langholt region does not support the model of a relatively dense and hierarchical settlement of Iceland but instead indicates that the Settlement and secondary land divisions resulted in independent farmsteads (fig. 10.1).

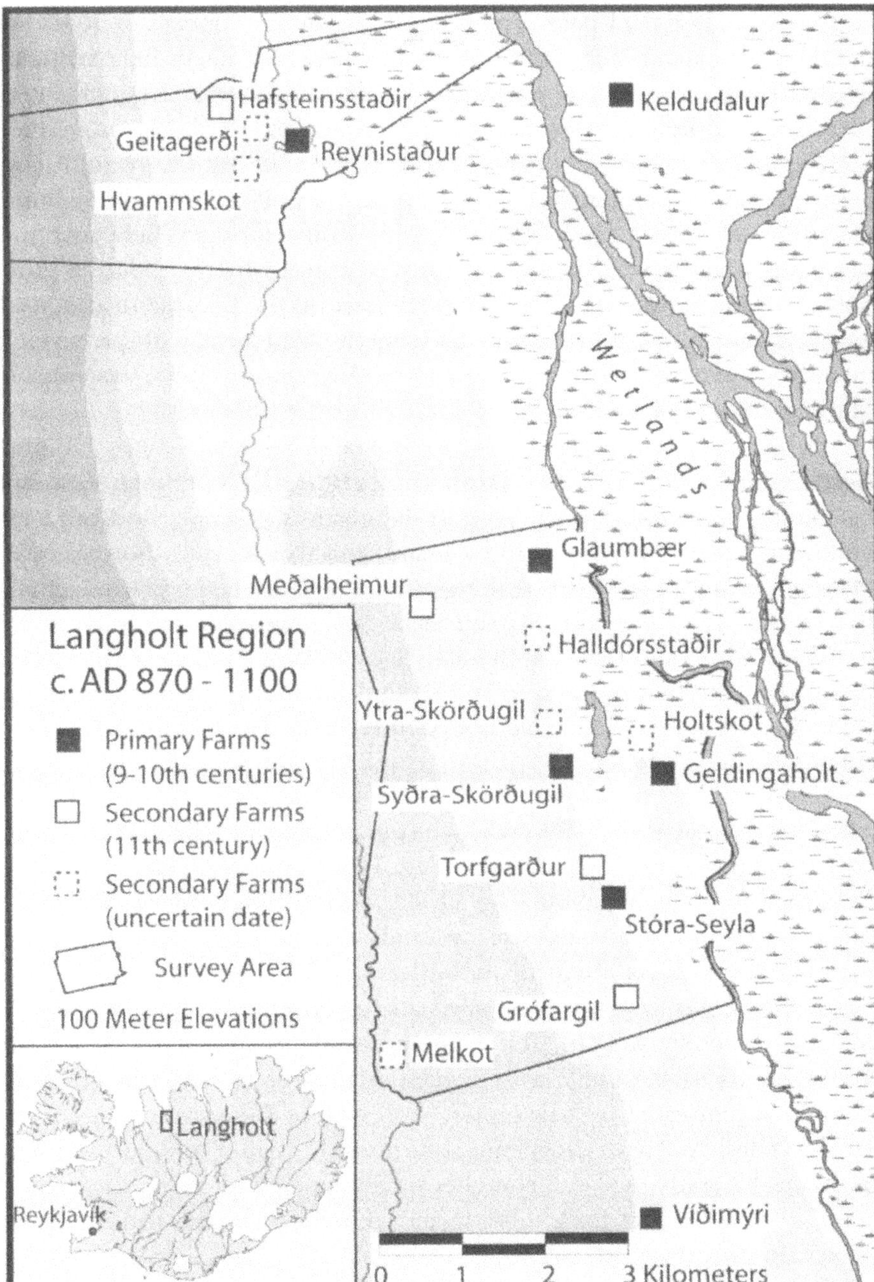

Figure 10.1 Langholt, on the western side of Skagafjörður in northern Iceland, with indications of the locations of early farmsteads dated by archaeological work.

The first settlers brought with them domestic animals, primarily cattle, sheep, horses, pigs, and goats, and also nonproductive animals such as cats and dogs (Buckland 1988). One of the most pressing needs for newly arrived farmers was access to grasslands to support livestock. Livestock could be grazed at a distance from the occupation but settlers also had to gather hay for winter fodder for their animals. Initial herds' stocks would have been low due to limited space on ships, and a well-fed herd throughout the winter was critical to increased fertility in the spring. Where cow and hay barns have been identified on early farmsteads they are only a short distance from the domestic buildings (Berson 2002). Because of the need for grass, site choice was likely to be biased toward areas with preexisting meadows and wetlands at the settlement (Vésteinsson 1998; Vésteinsson, McGovern, and Keller 2002).

Settlement and Land Division in Langholt, Northern Iceland

Langholt is located in Skagafjörður in the north of Iceland. Most of Langholt has good access to low-lying wetland areas that probably boasted open grassland at the time of the settlement. The Settlement Age farms identified in the survey, Reynistaður and Stóra-Seyla, were located in relatively low-lying areas close to rivers. Similarly located early Viking age farmsteads have been identified at Víðimýri and Keldudalur, south and northeast of the study area, although these have not been securely dated to the Settlement Age itself (Zoëga 2004).

Within the survey area three additional farms appear during the late tenth century, after AD 930 when historical sources report that significant immigration to Iceland had ended. These farms—Glaumbær, Syðra-Skörðugil, and Geldingaholt—are all located at a significant distance from the primary farmsteads and are on lands that probably were used only marginally, if at all, by the primary settlers (fig. 10.1).

At Glaumbær excavation revealed a large farmhouse approximately 40 m long (Bolender 2006b). Test excavations and coring at the other late tenth-century farms, while only suggestive, are consistent with substantial domestic occupations in their earliest phases. All of these farms have characteristics consistent with independent farmsteads. Glaumbær and Geldingaholt both had early medieval churches and became parish seats, an extremely unlikely development for a subordinate property. They also had their own subtenant properties, Meðalheimur and Holtskot. Syðra-Skörðugil also has a small neighboring farm, Ytra-Skörðugil, located immediately to the north, although by the time the two farms appear in the historical record in AD 1295 the original relationship between them is unclear.

These late tenth-century farms are evidence for a process of secondary land division following the Settlement. The new farmsteads were established on lands claimed by the original settlers and presumably belonged to one farmstead or another, although property boundaries may have been less defined than they were in later periods. The most likely candidates for establishing the new farmsteads are members of the landholding families who already held rights to the land and its inheritance, although the sagas also relate instances of land sales (often under coercion) for this period. Land division would have put pressure on extensive farm production as the landscape filled in and pasturelands became smaller and closer together. At the same time, the increasing proximity of farmlands would have encouraged a more concrete and definite system of property ownership.

The eleventh century saw major changes in patterns of land division and the relationships among farms in the Langholt region as a new class of farms appeared. At the beginning of the century, the surveyed area had five farmsteads. By the end of the century, at least four (and possibly eight or more) new farms were established on lands immediately neighboring the earlier farmsteads. At least one new farm appears in the immediate vicinity of each primary farm. Unlike the independent farmsteads established at the end of the tenth century, these new farms are all smaller than the earlier farms (table 10.1). Medieval historical records show that many of the new small farms were subordinate to the principal farms. Some are historically identified as subtenancies, which were not distinct farmstead properties but instead continued to be considered part of the primary farm's land. Systematic records of farm value that become available in the late seventeenth century show that all of these farms are of lesser value than the earlier farms (Lárusson 1967; Magnússon and Vídalín 1930). It is clear that the farms established during the eleventh century represent a new dynamic of land division.

If early farmers successfully maintained large and productive households, why would households subdivide or allow new farms to be created on their own properties? Three scenarios can be proposed: (1) the early farms could not, in fact, control or protect their own lands from encroachment and were forced to cede or sell portions of their property to other households; (2) farmers willingly gave up portions of their land, presumably either to family members or in exchange for payment or support, essentially a continuation of the process of secondary land division described for the late tenth century; and (3) early landowners maintained property rights over the new farmsteads and were willing to give up direct control of portions of their farmlands in exchange for indirect exploitation of the lands through rents.

Table 10.1. Dates for First Occupation with Midden Size from Archaeological Survey

Farm	Site #	Estimated area of midden and structures (m2)	Earliest occupation	Abandoned
Hafsteinsstaðir	SK-071-001	≈650	Between 1000 & 1104	1954
Geitagerði	SK-064-010	≈225	Before 1713	1948
Torfgarður	SK-106-002	≈400	Between 1000 & 1104	1964
	SK-106-100	≈225	Between 1000 & 1104	Before 1300
Grófargil	SK-089-001	≈400	Between 1000 & 1104	After 1900
Hafsteinsstaðir	SK-071-001	≈400	Between 1000 & 1104	After 1900
Meðalheimur	SK-111-201	≈400	Before 1300	1701
Víðimýri (†)	SK-092-010	?	Before 1104	After 1900
Glaumbær (†)	SK-111-010	3,300	Before 1000	Before 1104
	SK-111-010	6,400	After 1104	1952
Skörðugil	SK-107-001	2100	Before 1000	After 1900
Geldingaholt	SK-102-001	1800	Before 1000	After 1900
Stóra-Seyla (†)	SK-104-100	3,500	Before 1000	Before 1104
	SK-104-001	3,900	After 1104	1957
Reynistaður (†)	SK-063-009	2,025	Before 1000	Before 1300
	SK-063-010	10,000	Before 1000	After 1900

The first scenario is simply implausible as it is difficult to imagine that a small household could effectively encroach on the lands of the large and established households. A new generation of landowners, each contending for a piece of the family property in an increasingly crowded landscape, could result in the new settlement pattern. Early on, farmlands could be divided evenly among multiple heirs without adversely affecting the productivity of the farmstead because available labor limited the amount of land a household could effectively use. This dynamic probably accounts for many of the new farms established in the late tenth century. In fact, the division of land among related households may have been both an economic and a political boon to families who could stay close together for support while more effectively exploiting their extensive lands and reducing the risk of encroachment by outsiders.

Estates could not be indefinitely divided without negatively impacting the household. Hayfields, extensive pastureland, and fuel sources such as woodland or peat bogs were all critical to farmstead production. As lands became more crowded the dynamics that encouraged the partition of marginally utilized lands would have been replaced with practices that preserved the estate. This appears to be exactly what occurred. Normally, family inheritances were separated into land and movable wealth with one son taking the land while the other children divided the movable wealth (Byock 2001: 271; Hastrup 1985: 190–92). Nonetheless, as population increased with each new generation, pressure to create more farms would have increased. Some children might have accepted smaller properties or even the status of tenant in order to begin a new household.

Lowland areas were under additional demographic pressures during the eleventh century. Settlement and grazing had damaged the fragile highlands (Amorosi et al. 1997; McGovern et al. 1988). In Skagafjörður, lowland soil histories show the significant accumulation of aeolian material corresponding to highland erosion during the eleventh century (Carter 2003; Guðbergsson 1975). This environmental degradation in the highlands corresponds to the first wave of highland abandonment (Sveinbjarnardóttir 1992). It seems that the highlands were no longer able to support the same density of settlement. Some highland farmers would have sought land in the lowlands areas and may have been willing to rent land or be available for wage labor when no other options were available.

Displaced farmers and second sons could have contributed, and probably did contribute, to the process of farm subdivision in the eleventh century but we argue that it is the third scenario that typifies the transformation in the Langholt region. Based on changes in household labor status and the reorganization of the primary farms in the eleventh century, the main source for subordinate tenants came from within the existing stratified household. Former slaves and household labor were moved out of the households and settled on subordinate farms where they paid rents to their landlords. Direct control over household labor was spread from large households on to the landscape and regulated through increasingly enforceable unequal property rights.

Household Production and Incentives for Farmstead Subdivision

We see the internal dynamics of household organization and land division as best explained by a Chayanovian model (Durrenberger and Tannenbaum 1992, 2002). A.V. Chayanov (1966) argued that household production units are different from capitalist ones because the household units limit their production to what it is worth their effort to produce. To understand what the judgment of "worth the effort" amounted to, Chayanov imagined the intersection of a geometrically declining curve of marginal utility of the values produced with a geometrically increasing curve of the disutility of labor. In other words, the more households produce, the less they need to produce any more to meet their consumption needs. At the same time, the more effort they expend in production, the less inclined they are to expend any more. He argued that other things being equal, the higher the ratio of consumers to workers, the greater the expenditure of labor per worker required to support that household. He also argued that other things are not equal. Other factors that affect the curve of marginal utility include any other demands on the household budget aside from feeding its members—demands such as paying taxes or rents as well as any debts, interest, and levies of labor such as corvée (Durrenberger 1980).

The main factor that affects the curve of drudgery, as Chayanov calls the inclining curve, is the productivity of labor. The greater the value a unit of labor produces, the greater its productivity. If productivity doubles, drudgery halves (fig. 10.2). He conceives of productivity and drudgery as direct inverses of each other. Factors that he identifies as affecting the productivity of labor include fertility of soil, distance to markets where products were sold, technology, and scheduling conflicts of various tasks and crops.

The medieval Icelandic economy depended on grass. Sheep and cattle had to be housed during the winters and fed hay. Sufficient grass collection required the concentration of labor in the summer for cutting, turning, gathering, and storing hay for the winter. The more labor a household could provide for haymaking, the more livestock it could maintain, and the greater its store of dairy, meat, and woolen products for consumption and exchange and the larger the group of supporters it could muster to enforce ownership claims.

The marginally productive environment set limits on the effective size of the farmstead. Summer pastureland was available in the highlands but hay for winter fodder had to be cut, dried, and stored during the relatively short harvest period. The production of winter fodder was the most significant limit on herd and, in turn, household size. Hay was cut from both small homefields surrounding the farmhouse and scattered outfield areas. Homefields provided some opportunity for households to intensify production but were nonetheless constrained by available labor at harvest. Hay was cut from outfield areas over a longer period of time at the end of the summer but was also limited by available labor and increasing transportation costs as workers moved away from the farm center.

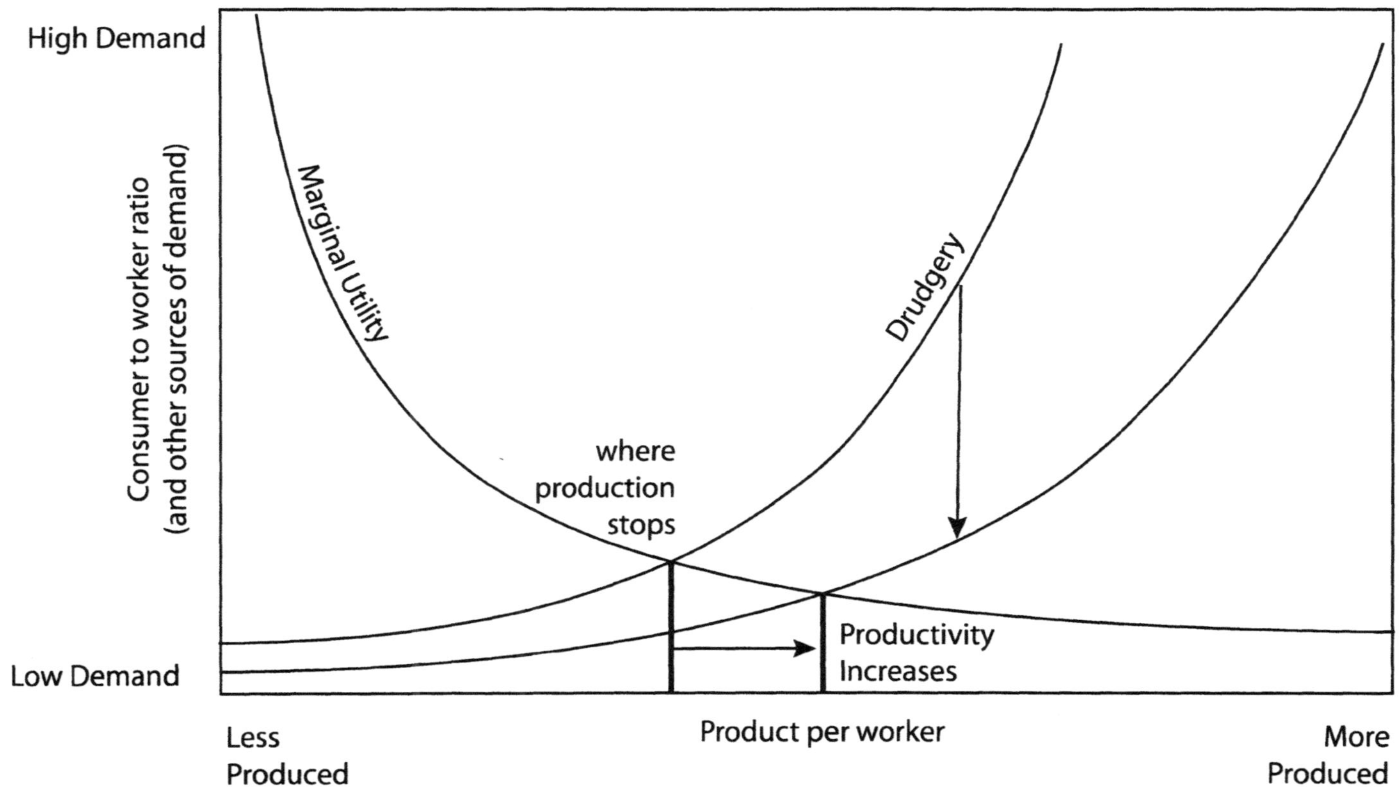

Figure 10.2 Increase in productivity per worker causes the drudgery curve to shift downward.

The sagas indicate that slavery was on the decline at the end of the tenth century in Iceland (Karras 1988). This interpretation is consistent with the archaeological record in Langholt described above. We interpret this shift in terms of the dynamics of household economies. In agriculturally marginal Iceland the productivity of slaves was not much more than they consumed because household labor had to be supported through the long winter (Durrenberger 1992; Gelsinger 1981). Labor productivity compared to the consumption costs would have diminished on large farmsteads as labor inputs to gather hay from distant areas increased. Thus slaves did not significantly change the ratio of consumers to workers in a household.

Landowners preferred wage labor when it was available because its cost was only a portion of that of supporting equivalent slave or dependent labor (Durrenberger 1992). This was an economic incentive to free slaves. The saga literature describes two fates for freed slaves: they could hire themselves out as laborers or establish new farmsteads on lands given to them by landowners, usually land belonging to the household to which they had belonged. It is unlikely that newly freed slaves owned enough movable wealth or livestock to buy land and equally unlikely that landowners would willingly give up control of their own land without some assured return in the form of rent and/or labor obligations.

Marshall Sahlins (1971) presents a simplified version of Chayanov based on the consumer/worker ratio. He suggests that the production per worker should increase as the consumer/worker ratio increases—the more consumers each worker must support, the more each worker must produce. He suggests representing the "Chayanov line" as a straight-line graph of increasing production on the horizontal axis against consumer/worker ratios on the vertical one (fig. 10.3).

He further suggests graphing empirical data on volume of household production against this theoretical line to determine how well the two fit. If each household were producing for its own needs, each household would fall along the Chayanov line. If some households were producing more than they needed and some less, the question would be by what means were the differences distributed from surplus-producing households to those with deficits.

In the period following the settlement of Iceland, each large internally stratified household was producing primarily for its own needs. Thus we would expect the households to fall on the Chayanov line. If primary households subdivided their properties, placing former household labor or slaves on the new tenant properties, they could lower their own household subsistence costs while maintaining, or potentially increasing, their income and developing a dependable revenue stream to effectively increase the

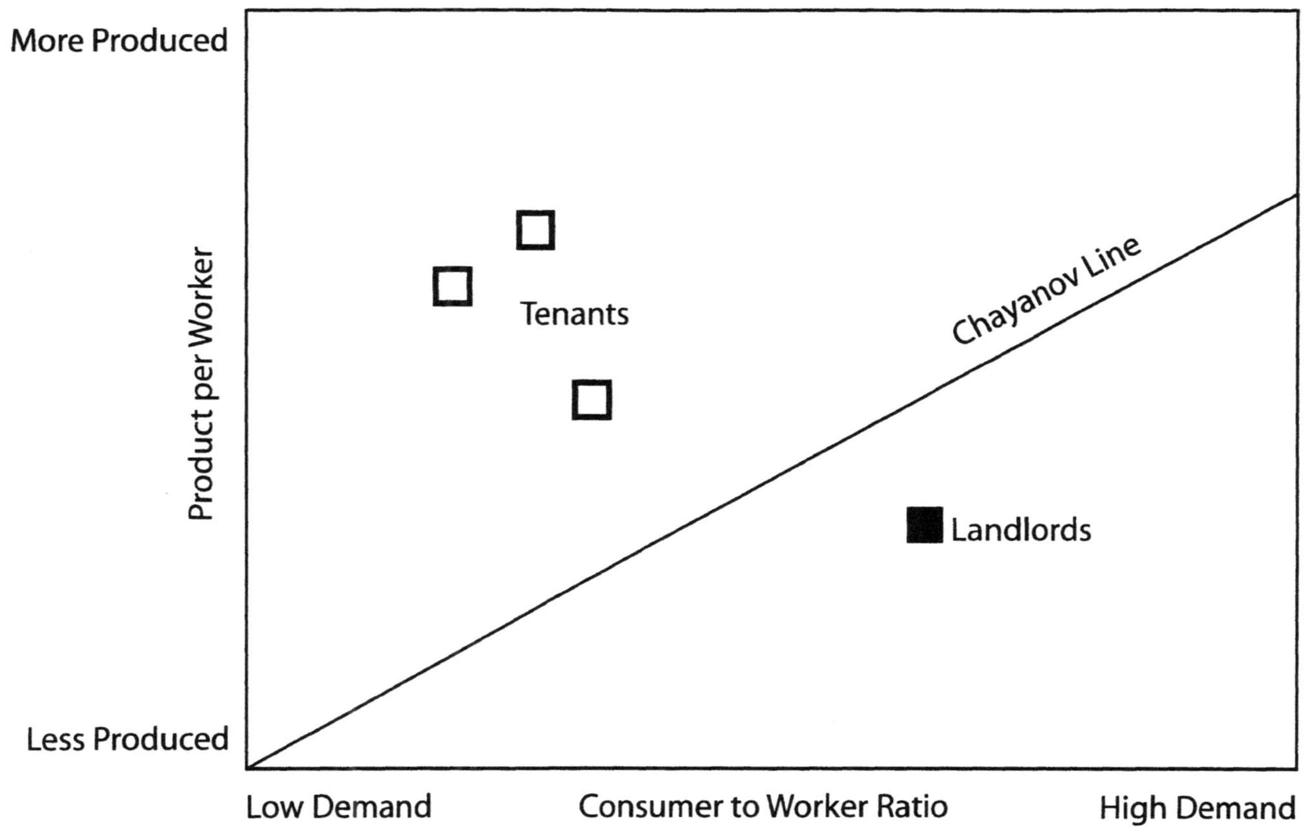

Figure 10.3 Sahlins's Chayanov line with tenant and landlord farmsteads represented.

funds for prestige expenditures. Such a household would fall below the line as household productivity would be lower than expected by the consumer-to-worker ratio while former slave and dependent households, producing more than they needed for household subsistence to fulfill labor or rent obligations, would fall above the line (fig. 10.3).

If the first farmers could control labor only inside their households there would have been pressure to maintain farmsteads up to a certain point of diminishing labor productivity. Lands beyond the limit of marginal productivity would have been alienable to other farmers without a real loss to the productivity of the farm, either to later settlers or eventually to later generations of farmers, probably from the same family, as is seen in the later tenth-century farmstead divisions. Eventually properties were reduced to the point that the cost of labor maintenance was matched by the productivity of the land. The only incentive to further divide farmlands would be if farmers could still benefit from the land. At this point, any additional members to the household would become a burden as their marginal productivity would lessen the average productivity, creating an incentive to free some slaves and other dependents.

This is exactly what we see happening in the eleventh century when existing farmsteads subdivided, presumably creating subordinate tenant properties. In the process they could effectively increase the productivity of the old estate by spreading out the effective limits on household size, each new farmstead with its own labor, homefield, farm buildings, and winter storage for livestock and hay. The increase in the overall productivity of the land would have supplied the rents for the new tenant farmers (Bolender 2006a).

For landowning farmers the substitution of indirect control over land for direct control over household labor transformed the ratio of consumers to workers in the household as household production was augmented by rents. With the same curve of drudgery but reduced ratios of consumers to workers combined with contributions in labor or rent from extrahousehold labor, the curve of marginal utility for large landowners would have decreased (fig. 10.4).

Institutionalizing a Propertied Landscape

Rent taking requires the ability to enforce effective control over properties that are not immediately occupied by the landowner. We argue that by the mid-eleventh century primary farms were sufficiently confident in their control of the land to subdivide their own productive lands with the expectation of benefit from rents and/or labor obligations. The small size of the new farmsteads suggests that landowners would have had difficulty

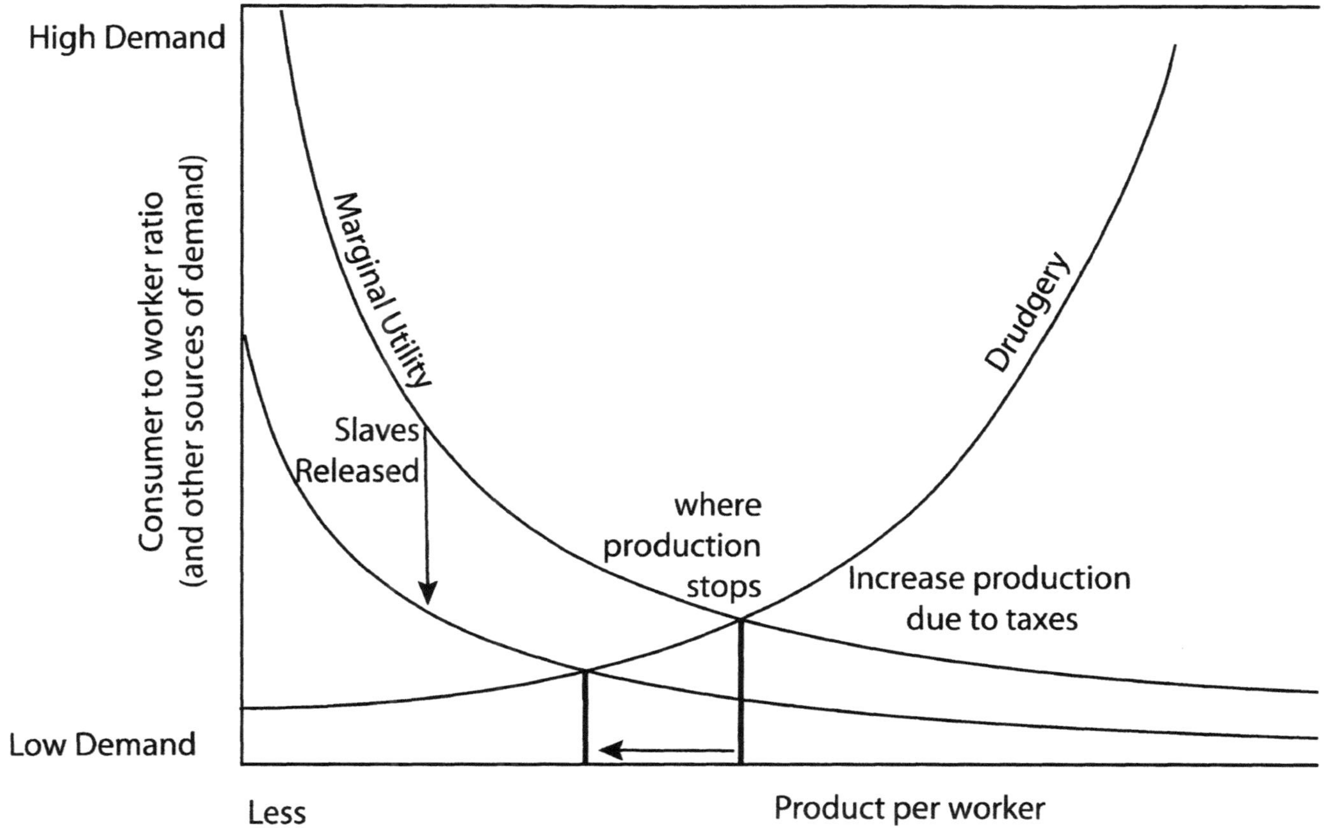

Figure 10.4 Marginal utility decreases; productivity constant.

asserting a claim to independence if this were not supported by the primary household. Primary farms could extract rent and quite possibly labor obligations at key moments in the productive calendar as well as political support at times of conflict.

The ability to extract rents from tenant and subordinate farms dramatically changed the dynamics of household production. This change laid the basis for an effective expansion of the political economy beyond the limits of single-household production by allowing some farmsteads to benefit from labor outside their households. The appearance of small dependent households would also have introduced new possibilities to political networks. Tenant farmers would have been easier to force into supporting the political aims of their landlords than independent neighbors would have been.

The final transformation of the landscape involved the reorganization of the earliest farmsteads. At Glaumbær and Stóra-Seyla the original occupations were abandoned sometime before the end of the eleventh century and relocated a short distance away. On Langholt these movements were upslope and away from wetland areas. While environmental and land-use considerations may have influenced the choice of the new sites, the pattern of relocating early farmhouses is not restricted to the Langholt region and reflects more than a local set of conditions. Farmhouses in Iceland rarely relocated prior to the twentieth century.

The reorganization of the primary farmsteads provided an opportunity for new landlords to assert control over their new tenants. Where farmhouses were relocated, the new buildings were placed in situations with better visibility of their tenant farms. This symbolic prominence was augmented institutionally. Each one of the farmsteads that reorganized also became a church farm. The early churches were closely associated with the farmhouses and landholding households (Vésteinsson 2000).

Glaumbær is the only farm with a history describing the building of its first church—in the Saga of the Greenlanders (Viðar 1997) it is said that Snorri, the son of Guðriður, had the church erected when his mother returned from a pilgrimage to Rome ca. AD 1020—but it is likely that the churches at Stóra-Seyla, Geldingaholt, and Reynistaður also were built sometime in the century following the conversion. These churches would have formed the center of each local community, a visible and active integrator where neighboring householders would have been baptized, married, and eventually buried, coinciding with the location of the landlord farm. Although former slaves may have become tenant farmers they remained symbolically tied to their landlord's household (Bolender, 2007).

Churches provided more than ideological control over neighboring farms. In AD 1097 the Icelandic assembly passed the tithe law, the first of its kind in Scandinavia. At first it seems surprising that farmers would have willingly instituted a tax on their own lands for the church but the reasons for the farmers' acceptance of the tithe make more sense in light of the weakly centralized early church in Iceland.

The tithe was divided into quarters for the maintenance of the local church, the priest, the poor, and the bishop. Churches were built on private land and belonged to the local landowner who could also serve as priest or hire someone to fill that function. Poor relief was also administered locally. Ultimately, this meant that up to three-quarters of the tithe stayed in the hands of the local church owner (Vésteinsson 2000). Lands donated to the church were not subject to the tithe but continued under the management of the donor, including the transfer of usufruct to heirs. Church-owning farmers could donate their own lands to the church to avoid the tithe, while maintaining control over production, and benefit from additional revenue from other farms.

Conclusion

The creation of formal landscape features such as land claims, farmsteads, fields, and pastures was an essential component of the Icelandic settlement. Later, land division and the reorganization of household labor played a critical role in the institutionalization of inter-household inequality. The settlement of the Icelandic landscape was not a simple imposition of society on an unsettled island. The processes that gave rise to the system of highly stable farmstead properties were closely tied to household dynamics in evolving political and environmental circumstances.

We turn to Chayanov to understand how landowners organized land and labor to increase household production and retain control over productive lands while balancing marginal returns on household size and land use. The resulting balance manifests itself in stages of settlement and land division, each reflecting the changing ability of landowners to control labor and land. At the Settlement large households were an important factor in defense and production in the relatively open landscape. At the same time, marginal returns on land and labor placed effective limits on household and farmstead size, leading to a dispersion of independent farmsteads. In the eleventh century, landowners subdivided their estates, resituating household dependents as tenant farmers. Splitting off lower-status farms had the dual effect of reducing early large farmstead consumption and creating a physically separate class that could be further exploited in an expanding political economy.

The remarkable stability of the Icelandic settlement system after the eleventh century was not complemented by stability in Icelandic society. The following centuries saw continued changes in household dynamics, in part responses to climatic change, the rise of a landowning aristocracy, and the eventual submission of Iceland to foreign rule. In particular, the institution of tenancy expanded beyond subdivided farmsteads to incorporate many formerly independent farmsteads. In the Langholt region almost all the farmsteads were tenant occupied by the end of the fourteenth century. Within these now-stable formal landscape features—farmhouse location, fields, and boundaries—households continued to adjust their organization and production in response to changing political and environmental circumstances. In many ways, Iceland remained an unsettled landscape.

Acknowledgments

We would like to thank the National Science Foundation, the Wenner-Gren Foundation, and Byggðasafn Skagafirðinga for their generous support of this research.

References

Amorosi, Thomas, Paul Buckland, Andrew Dugmore, Jon H. Ingimundarson, and Thomas H. McGovern. 1997. "Raiding the Landscape: Human Impact in the Scandinavian North Atlantic." *Human Ecology* 25:491–518.

Andersson, Theodore M. 1964. *The Problem of Icelandic Saga Origins: A Historical Study*. New Haven, CT: Yale University Press.

Bender, Barbara. 2002. "Time and Landscape." *Current Anthropology*, Suppl. no. 43: 103–12.

———. 2006. "Place and Landscape." In *Handbook of Material Culture*, ed. C. Tilley, W. Keane, S. Kuechler-Fogden, M. Rowlands, and P. Spyer, 303–14. London: Sage Publications.

Berson, Bruno. 2002. "A Contribution to the Study of the Medieval Icelandic Farm: The Byres." *Archaeological Islandica* 2:34–60.

Bolender, Douglas J. 2006a. "The Creation of a Propertied Landscape: Land Tenure and Intensification in Medieval Iceland." PhD diss., Northwestern University.

———. 2006b. *Excavations at Glaumbær, 2005: Report of the Skagafjörður Archaeological Settlement Survey*. Sauðárkrókur, Iceland: Byggðasafn Skagafirðinga.

———. 2007. "House, Land, and Labor in a Frontier Landscape: The Norse Colonization of Iceland." In *The Durable House: Architecture, Ancestors, and Origins*, ed. R. A. Beck. Vol. 33, 400–21. Carbondale: Center for Archaeological Investigations, Southern Illinois University.

Bourdieu, Pierre. 1977. *Outline of a Theory of Practice*. Cambridge: Cambridge University Press.

Buckland, Paul C. 1988. "North Atlantic Faunal Connections: Introduction or Endemics?" *Entomologica Scandinavica 1988*, Suppl.:8–29.

Byock, Jesse. 1988. *Medieval Iceland: Society, Sagas, and Power*. Los Angeles: University of California Press.

———. 2001. *Viking Age Iceland*. New York: Penguin.

Carter, Tara Dawn. 2003. "Land Productivity and Social Collapse in Medieval Iceland." MA thesis, California State University, Northridge.

Chayanov, Alexander V. 1966. *The Theory of Peasant Economy*. Homewood, IL: Richard D. Irwin.

Dodgshon, Robert A. 1998. *Society in Time and Space: A Geographical Perspective on Change*. Cambridge: Cambridge University Press.

Durrenberger, E. Paul. 1980. "Chayanov's Economic Analysis in Anthropology." *Journal of Anthropological Research* 36:133–48.

———. 1991. "Production in Medieval Iceland." *Acta Archaeologica* (Copenhagen) 61:14–21.

———. 1992. *The Dynamics of Medieval Iceland: Political Economy and Literature*. Iowa City: University of Iowa Press.

Durrenberger, E. Paul, and Nicola Tannenbaum. 1992. "Household Economy, Political Economy, and Ideology: Peasants and the State in Southeast Asia." *American Anthropologist* 94 (1): 74–89.

———. 2002. "Chayanov and Theory in Economic Anthropology." In *Theory in Economic Anthropology*, ed. J. Ensminger, 137–54. Walnut Creek, CA: AltaMira.

Friðriksson, Adolf. 1994. *Sagas and Popular Antiquarianism in Icelandic Archaeology*. Aldershot: Avebury.

Gelsinger, Bruce E. 1981. *Icelandic Enterprise, Commerce and Economy in the Middle Ages*. Columbia: University of South Carolina Press.

Guðbergsson, Grétar. 1975. "Myndun Móajarðvegs í Skagafirði." *Íslenzkar Landnúnaðarrannsóknir* 7 (1–2): 20–45.

Hastrup, Kirsten. 1985. *Culture and Society in Medieval Iceland*. Oxford: Clarendon.

Herschend, Frands. 1994. "Models of Petty Rulership: Two Early Settlements in Iceland." *Tor* 26:163–91.

Ingold, Tim. 1993. "The Temporality of Landscape." *World Archaeology* 25 (2): 152–74.

Karras, Ruth Mazo. 1988. *Slavery and Society in Medieval Scandinavia*. New Haven, CT: Yale University Press.

Kristjánsson, Jónas. 1992. *Eddas and Sagas: Iceland's Medieval Literature*. Reykjavík: Hið Íslenska bókmenntafélag.

Lárusson, Björn. 1967. *The Old Icelandic Land Registers*. Lund: C. W. K. Gleerup.

Lawrence, Denise L., and Setha M. Low. 1990. "The Built Environment and Spatial Form." *Annual Review of Anthropology* 19:453–505.

Lefebvre, Henri. 1991. *The Production of Space*. Oxford: Blackwell.

Magnússon, Árni, and Páll Vídalín. 1930. *Járðabók Árna Magnússonar og Páls Vídalíns I–XIII*. Copenhagen: Hið íslenska fræðafélag.

Massey, Doreen. 2006. "Landscape as a Provocation." *Journal of Material Culture* 11 (1–2): 33–48.

———. 2005. *For Space*. London: Sage Publications.

McGovern, Thomas H., Gerald Bigelow, Thomas Amorosi, and Daniel Russell. 1988. "Northern Islands, Human Error, and Environmental Degradation: A View of Social Ecological Change in the Medieval North Atlantic." *Human Ecology* 16:225–70.

Pálsson, Hermann, and Paul Edwards. 1972. *The Book of Settlements: Landnámabók*. Trans. H. Pálsson and P. Edwards. Manitoba: University of Manitoba Press.

Sahlins, Marshall. 1971. "The Intensity of Domestic Production in Primitive Societies: Social Inflections of the Chayanov Slope." In *Studies in Economic Anthropology*, ed. G. Dalton, 30–51. Washington, DC: American Anthropological Association.

Smith, Kevin P. 1995. "Landnám: The Settlement of Iceland in Archaeological and Historical Perspective." *World Archaeology* 26 (3): 319–46.

Steinberg, John. 2002. *Interim Report of the Skagafjörður Archaeological Settlement Survey, 2001*. Los Angeles: Cotsen Institute of Archaeology, University of California.

———. 2004. *Report of the Skagafjörður Archaeological Settlement Survey, 2004*. Los Angeles: Cotsen Institute of Archaeology, University of California.

Steinberg, John, and Douglas Bolender. 2005. "Rannsóknir á búsetuminjum í Skagafirði" [Settlement pattern analysis in Skagafjörður]. *Árbók hins íslenzka fornleifafélags*, 2002–2003, 107–30.

Sveinbjarnardóttir, Guðrún. 1992. *Farm Abandonment in Medieval and Post-Medieval Iceland: An Interdisciplinary Study*. Oxford: Oxbow Press.

Þorgilsson, Ari. 1930. *The Book of the Icelanders [Íslendingabók]*. Trans. H. Hermannsson. Vol. 20. Ithaca, NY: Cornell University Library.

Turner, Victor Witter. 1971. "An Anthropological Approach to the Icelandic Saga." In *The Translation of Culture: Essays to E. E. Evans-Pritchard*, ed. T. O. Beidelman, 349–74. London: Tavistock Publications.

Vésteinsson, Orri. 1998. "Patterns of Settlement in Iceland: A Study in Prehistory." *Saga Book (Viking Society of Northern Research)* 25 (1): 1–29.

———. 2000. *The Christianization of Iceland: Priests, Power, and Social Change, 1000–1300*. Oxford: Oxford University Press.

Vésteinsson, Orri, Thomas McGovern, and Christian Keller. 2002. "Enduring Impacts: Social and Environmental Aspects of Viking Age Settlement in Iceland and Greenland." *Archaeological Islandica* 2:98–136.

Viðar, Hreinsson, ed. 1997. *The Complete Sagas of Icelanders, Including 49 Tales*. Reykjavík: Leifur Eiríksson Pub.

Zoëga, Guðný. 2004. *Greining mannabeina úr kirkjugarðinum í Keldudal, Hegranesi*. Sauðárkrókur, Iceland: Byggðasafn Skagfirðinga.

11

The Decentralized Landscape
Regional Wealth and the Expansion of Production in Northern Tanzania before the Eve of Colonialism

N. THOMAS HÅKANSSON

THIS CHAPTER EXAMINES THE PANGANI REGION IN NORTHERN Tanzania where, for millennia, human communities have shaped a landscape dominated by an arc of highlands that stretch from Usambara to Arusha, and which surrounds a great plain (see fig. 11.1).[1] In this region, ecotonal variations in environments have shaped, and were, in turn, shaped by political and economic forces. I contend that the environmental gradient that extends from the highlands to the lowland plains was as much a result of human activity as of such natural forces as temperature and rainfall. Economic activities in the region varied from pastoralism to intensive cultivation, interspersed with foraging, iron manufacturing, salt making, and exchange networks. The regional interaction of exchange of goods was paralleled by movement of people between communities and economic specializations. The maintenance of landesque capital and sustainable livelihoods in marginal environments was possible because wealth was retained and circulated within the region. This leads to the observation that the driving forces behind land use must be analyzed in relation to the effective political and economic scales at which human and environmental exploitation take place. In the noncapitalist regional economy the character of land use was determined by political factors aimed at building large followings and wealth in people. When the area was incorporated into the capitalist world-system, land use became geared to the profit-making interests of the core nations in the world-system. While this process has been fairly well documented, less attention has been paid to explaining the productivity of the precolonial economy. A theoretical understanding that is not based on assumed subsistence production and ecological adaptation may also contribute to solving contemporary problems of food shortage and environmental degradation in sub-Saharan Africa.

The benefit of the landscape concept (see introduction to this volume) to the study of human-environmental relationships is inclusiveness and ability to overcome the dualistic nature-culture divide that has plagued research in human ecology (Crumley, forthcoming). However, in order to apply such a broad concept to actual research problems, more precise operationalizations must be formulated. In this chapter, I analyze region and landscape as mutually constitutive, that is, the landscape is both the result of human regional interaction and a force that shapes land use over time (McGlade 1999). For analytical purposes, I use region as a spatial extension of economic and social interactions that, at a particular scale, differentiates it from other areas in time and space. The regional landscape, then, is both the result of regional interactions and the environmental resource for such interactions. I will attempt such an analysis based on ongoing research on archeological, linguistic, and historical sources for the Pangani region.

My central hypothesis is that land use in both capitalist and noncapitalist contexts is shaped primarily by institutions and strategies directed toward the production and accumulation of wealth, rather than by subsistence considerations (cf. Hayden 1995; Sahlins 1974). As Douglas (1982 [1966]: 141) noted in another context long ago, "Human groups . . . are more often inspired by concern for scarce social resources, for objects giving status and prestige, than by concern for dwindling basic resources." This does not imply that concerns for food security and subsistence were not important to the households and farm managers. In this chapter I am highlighting the regional political-economic parameters that conditioned and affected the way farm managers pursued food production, rather than the local conditions of everyday household provisioning.

The landscape as a resource built by human activity is usefully enshrined in the idea of "landesque capital" developed by Brookfield (1984), who defines it as "any investment in land with an anticipated life well beyond that of the present crop, or crop cycle" (see also Blaikie and Brookfield 1987: 9). This concept has been further elaborated by Widgren (forthcoming), who emphasizes the durability of certain types of landesque capital and their capacity to reach through time in social and economic contexts vastly different from those that influenced their development.

The analysis of production and land use in kin-ordered modes of production is unfortunately still influenced by theories that privilege the emergence of political and economic hierarchies as the driving forces of economic diversification and surplus production (e.g., Chase-Dunn and Hall 1997; Downs and Reyna 1988). Conversely, where hierarchy is absent, many Marxists and non-Marxists alike are similarly locked in a

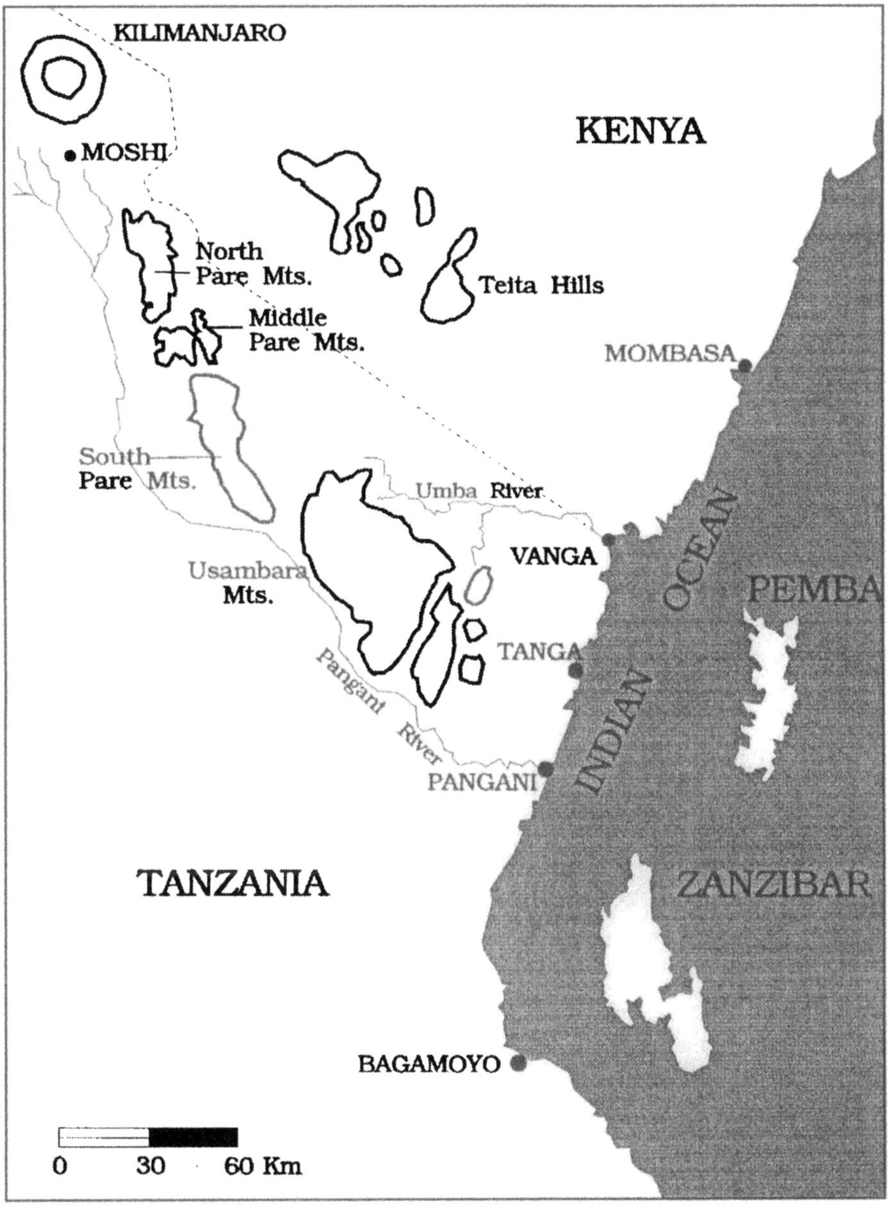

Figure 11.1 Northeastern Tanzania and the Pangani region.

view of production as the sole result of local subsistence requirements and use values. This inability theoretically to conceive of an exchange-based economy, together with the construction of a precolonial-colonial duality of use values versus commodities, still permeates many anthropological and historical analyses (Sluyter 2002). For example, the precolonial economy in the Pangani region is regarded by several historians as primarily having been oriented toward subsistence production and use values, and regulated by culturally defined "spheres of exchange" (Glassman 1995: 45; Sheriff 1987). Accordingly, this economy was then destroyed and human land use changed by the penetration of merchant capital in the nineteenth century (Glassman 1995: 42).

Although the precolonial societies surely were not capitalist, it does not follow that their economies were local and were not geared toward the accumulation of wealth. As early as the beginning of the twentieth century, Mauss (1990 [1950]: 32–33) recognized that gift-based economies were capable of producing large surpluses that flowed through wide regional exchange networks. In accordance with this perspective, I argue that the colonial transformation of the landscape was not caused by a change from an autonomous production of use values into commercial commodity relations per se. Rather, I contend that it was the result of the incorporation of a regional economy of circulating prestige goods and labor values into the extractive economy of the capitalist world-system.

The Landscape

The Pangani River has its source in the glaciers of Kilimanjaro approximately 300 km inland from its mouth at the coastal town of Pangani. It flows through the dry, level Maasai plains at approximately 800 m to 1,300 m above sea level. The savanna that stretches here southeast from Kilimanjaro and Meru receives less than 600 mm of rain per year. Around 100 km from the Indian Ocean the climate changes and annual rainfall exceeds 800–1,000 mm (fig. 11.2).

The area is dominated by thorn-bush vegetation and limited grasslands. Precipitation is too low for cultivation but provides good grazing for cattle and is today inhabited by Maasai pastoralists. Pastoral settlements have historically been mainly south of the highlands where the Pangani River provides water all year around. The area north of the mountain ranges is deficient in water and pastoralist presence was sparse and seasonal.

Along the northern rim of the valley lies a chain of mountains with high rainfall, fertile soils, and a benevolent climate; this area has been inhabited by iron-using and cattle-keeping cultivators for at least two thousand

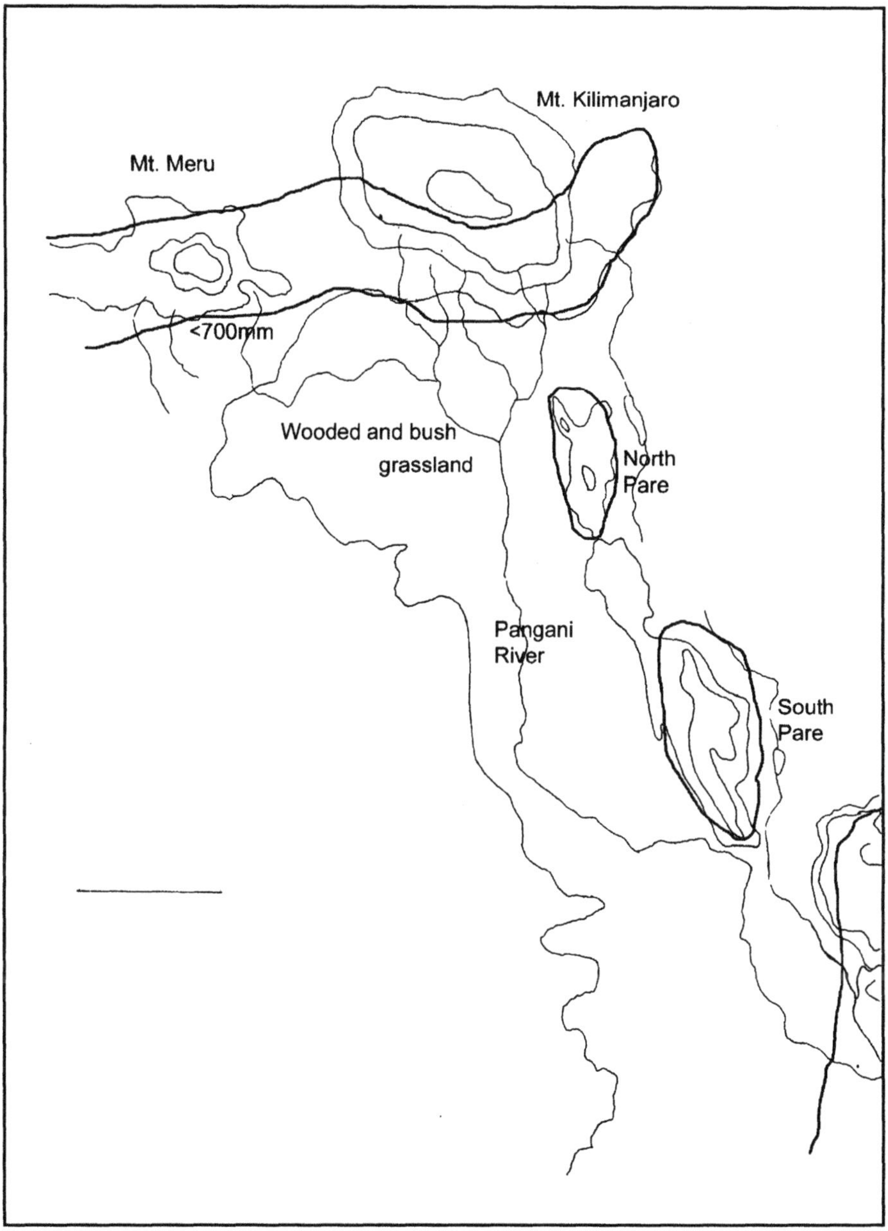

Figure 11.2 Simplified map of environment and rainfall in the Pangani region. The map outlines the limits of average annual precipitation over and below 700 mm. This is an approximate boundary between areas where rainfed agriculture can be undertaken with success and those where rain is generally deficient for cultivation. Most of the highland areas receive over 1,000 mm of rain per year and some over 2,000 mm. The plain is a dry savanna suitable for cattle herding.

years. Rising to 5,895 m, Kilimanjaro is the highest mountain in Africa. Its higher elevations are covered with rainforest, alpine vegetation, and snow. Farther southeast lies the broken range of North, Middle, and South Pare with rocky and forested plateaus at the height of 1,200–2,000 m. Farther east, around 60 km from the coast, rise the Usambara mountains with the highest peaks reaching slightly over 2,000 m in elevation. From Usambara eastward, the Bondei hills follow, and then the coastal region (see fig. 11.1) where the increase in rainfall makes cultivation possible in the lowlands.

During the second half of the nineteenth century, numerous European visitors described agriculture in the highlands in glowing terms, impressed by luxuriant plantations, orderly fields, and irrigation furrows. Their detailed descriptions of crops and agricultural techniques (e.g., Krapf 1860; Kersten 1869; Johnston 1886; Baumann 1891; Widenmann 1899) portray complex and highly productive agricultural systems that provided reliable subsistence and a continuous surplus. In the nineteenth century, agriculture in the highlands, as well as in a few well-watered spots on the plains, was mainly intensive permanent and semipermanent cultivation, although in many areas it was combined with fallow cultivation on the plains and foothills near the mountains. These intensive systems of cultivation were not the result of high population densities but were used to produce a sizeable surplus of crops for exchange within the region (Håkansson 1995, 1998; Sheridan 2002; Widgren 2004; Börjeson 2004).

I have attempted to sketch the extent of settlements with irrigation in the map in figure 11.3. The shaded areas were of course not uniformly inhabited and cultivated. The furrow systems covered most of the surface in the inhabited areas but because of comparatively low overall population densities there were stretches of uncultivated land (Håkansson 1995; Sheridan 2002). Thus, the irrigated landscapes on the mountains consisted of several square kilometers of discontiguous assemblages of fields separated by swaths of uncultivated land. The main outtake furrows extended from a couple of hundred meters to ten kilometers (Dundas 1924: 262; Warburg 1894) and several could run parallel across uninhabited mountainsides. On Kilimanjaro the main furrows branched out into secondary and even tertiary channels in an intricate system covering most of the inhabited southern slope (Stahl 1964: 25). Except for Usambara, the highland settlements were not nucleated but consisted of dispersed farms situated in banana groves. The irrigated fields were normally located some distance from the farmsteads on slopes along the hillsides and in the valley bottoms, and could extend for several kilometers with uninterrupted cultivation (Johnston 1886: 120; Meyer 1893: 185). One observer (Karasek 1911: 175) noted that

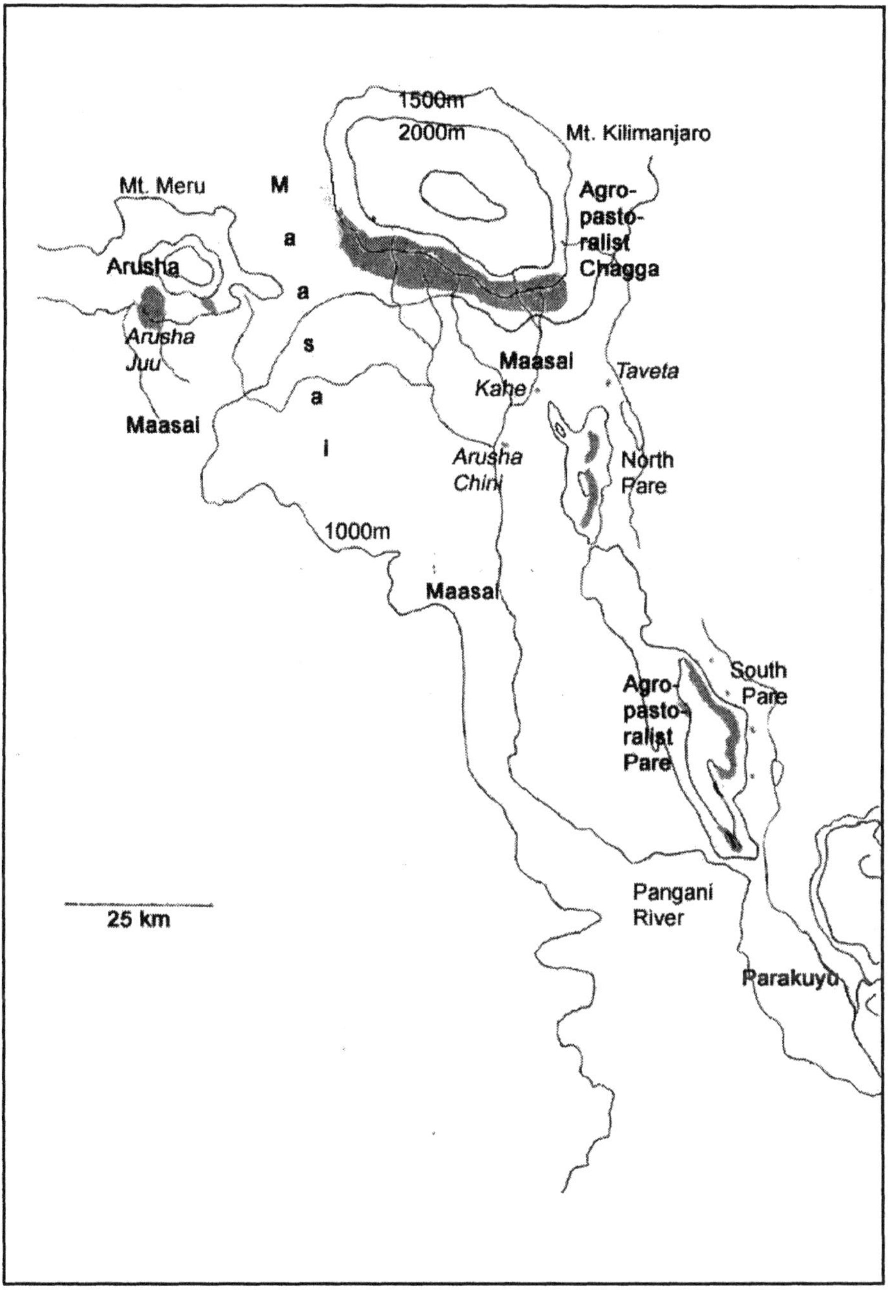

Figure 11.3 Intensive cultivation and the Maasai expansion, ca. 1850. The shaded areas denote irrigation and banana cultivation. Bananas were grown mainly in the highland systems. Ethnic groups or peoples are in bold and place names in italic. Geographical features are written in normal font.

in West Usambara, "on every hillside furrows run several hundred meters in length and thousands of hectares were watered."

Along the Pangani River, close to the highlands, there were several smaller communities of intensive cultivators, that is, Kahe, Arusha Chini, and Taveta. By the middle of the nineteenth century they were multiethnic enclaves with close trade connections to both the surrounding pastoralists and the mountain farmers. These settlements are at least two hundred years old and consist of a core population and refugees from economic difficulties and political conflicts in the nearby region (Waller 1985). Although maintained by a multiethnic core, the communities functioned as economic oases where destitute people could build up cattle herds through trade. They produced a wide variety of crops on irrigated fields and, together with iron implements, honey, and salt, exchanged the surplus with neighboring pastoralists and cultivators (Spear 1997: 38). Substantial iron manufacturing, smelting, and blacksmithing had existed on the Pare Mountains since the early second millennium and seem to have increased during the nineteenth century due to expanded cultivation and demand for weapons generated by the escalation of conflicts. By the second half of the nineteenth century, North Pare had been largely denuded of trees to fuel the furnaces that supplied iron to the whole region (Kersten 1869: 2:19; Meyer 1893: 223). In addition, foraging groups lived interspersed with pastoralists and cultivators providing products such as honey, game meat, and ivory in exchange for livestock, crops, milk, metals, and coastal goods.

The regional specialization of production into cultivation, pastoralism, and craft industries cannot be accounted for by a simple barter for use values or scarcity of land. There was no shortage of agricultural land in the area and, as I will show below, each specialization represented a strategy of investment and exchange designed to optimize access to cattle. Iron production was geared toward exchange for foodstuffs and cattle. Agropastoral and pastoralist populations attempted to increase their access to cattle through herd management. Finally, the farmers used the pastoral sector to obtain cattle through trade. These productive strategies were integrated into a political economy in which agricultural production enabled local elites to extract resources from the regional exchange system.

Although quantitative information about the volume of trade is sparse, I have endeavored to calculate a rough estimate of the crop trade. Based on early colonial population figures and the fact that specialized pastoralists require an annual supply of 30–35 percent of their caloric intake in the form of crops to complement pastoral foods, it is possible to reach a minimum figure for the amount of agricultural products exchanged in the region. In the 1880s, a minimum of 13 percent, but more realistically, probably at least 20 percent, of the annual harvests in the highlands was produced for exchange.[2] At this time the pastoral population was at least 50,000 and the cultivators numbered about 140,000, excluding Usambara.[3] To this should be added agropastoralists, foragers, and semispecialized groups of iron smelters, blacksmiths, and salt makers. Considering these volumes of grain and other crops produced for exchange against livestock only, it is not possible to view the precolonial economies as subsistence and use-value oriented. In addition, foodstuffs also entered into barter for iron and other goods, and were converted into beer that was consumed in large but unknown quantities.[4] It is worth repeating here that while such exchanges were also directed to the management of household needs and the viability of farming, the intensive cultivation systems themselves were not necessary for a subsistence-oriented economy.

Landscape Transformation

From the relatively sparse source material it is possible to reconstruct how the landscape was transformed and further effected changes in the regional political economy. Here I attempt to link the transformation of land use over time to the political economy of agriculture and pastoralism. These activities were tied together in a positive feedback relationship of mutually reinforcing processes.

The Political Economy of Cattle

In East African patrilineal societies cattle were (and to a great extent still are) essential to social reproduction (Schneider 1979; Håkansson 1994). Without cattle the basic social institutions of families, households, and kin groups could not, and cannot, be formed. Hence, cattle were constantly sought after and functioned as the objects of control and allocation by elders.[5] All economic activities were ultimately connected through cattle as the primary prestige good and investment. Agricultural production and land use can therefore be traced to political and economic strategies directed toward access and control of cattle. In this region other goods also entered into exchanges—for example, goats, iron, glass beads, and cloth.

Thus, every family had to obtain cattle in order to build new households and to establish vital networks of kinship and affinity. There was a tension between tendencies toward pastoralism as successful cultivators accumulated enough cattle to move into a pastoral economy, and toward cultivation by those who failed. The two productive specializations were not exclusive but represented the ends of a continuum along which members of different communities moved. Parts of predominantly agricultural societies often developed semipastoral sections of households that were in close contact with Maa-speaking neighbors (Waller 1985).

As droughts and cattle epidemics struck, the pastoralists migrated into the cultivating areas, expanding the agricultural population, and as the cattle numbers increased successful accumulators moved from cultivation to cattle keeping. However, as I will discuss below, changing from pastoralism to farming was not a completely reversible process. Participation in the farming economy also entailed a commitment to social and economic institutions that made cattle accumulation difficult. As a community of cultivators expanded, new economic and social constraints and opportunities emerged. Because of the central role of cattle in social reproduction, political power became dependent on securing agricultural production for the exchange of crops for livestock.

In addition, the kinship- and neighborhood-based highland communities were organized into chiefdoms of varying sizes and degrees of stratification. The ability of a chief to maintain his[6] administration, and the elites' possession of wealth in the form of livestock, rights in persons, and rights in land, depended partly on the elites' access to the fruits of others' labor. A social surplus was transmitted from the farmers to the chief as tribute in the form of crops, livestock, and beer. The most valued part of the tribute was cattle, which the chief needed to build a large family, to obtain debt clients, and to offer as gifts to lineage heads and the young men who served as warriors (Kimambo 1969: 109–10; Moore 1986: 63). The political cohesiveness of the chiefdoms was dependent on the chief's ability to control the flow of cattle and to supply them to local lineage heads and subchiefs. The importance of cattle as the lifeblood of political relationships was brought to the fore during the nineteenth century when increased political turmoil, caused by participation in the coastal trade, resulted in amplified demand for cattle that had to be satisfied through increases in tribute demands, trade, raiding, and warfare (Moore 1986: 37; Håkansson 1998).

On Kilimanjaro the continuity of settlement indicates continuity in the importance of cultivation in the economy. Throughout the second millennium, settlements were basically restricted to the zone of habitation and cultivation observed in the nineteenth century, that is, at an elevation of 1,050–1,800 m (Kersten 1869: 1:271). Archaeological data, oral traditions, and linguistic evidence all show a concentration of settlement in the southeastern region of Vunjo in the eleventh century (fig. 11.4) and a slow spread throughout the rest of the southern slope until the nineteenth century (figs. 11.5 and 11.3) (Stahl 1964; Odner 1971; Spear 1997: 17). Until the middle of the nineteenth century grazing was plentiful on the lower slopes where

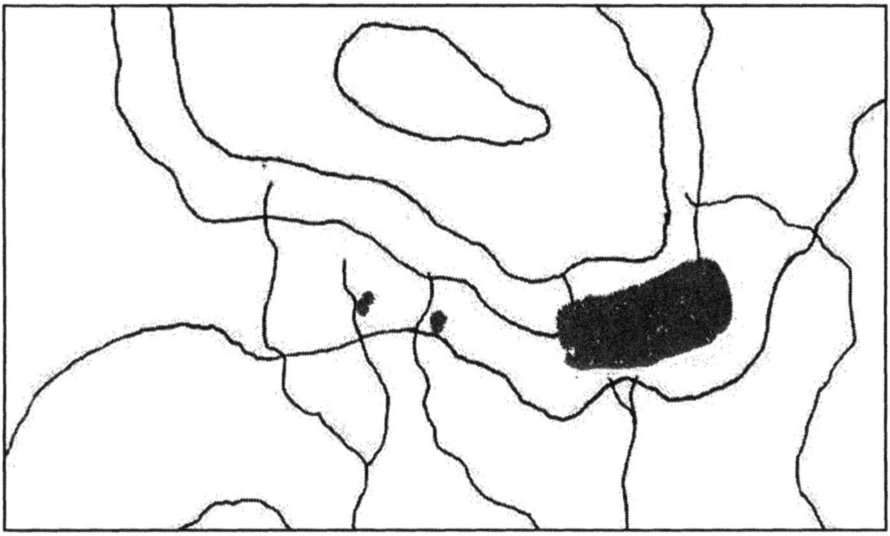

Figure 11.4 Main areas of agricultural settlements on Kilimanjaro, ca. AD 1100. The density of settlement is unknown. Sources: Nurse 1979; Odner 1971; Stahl 1964.

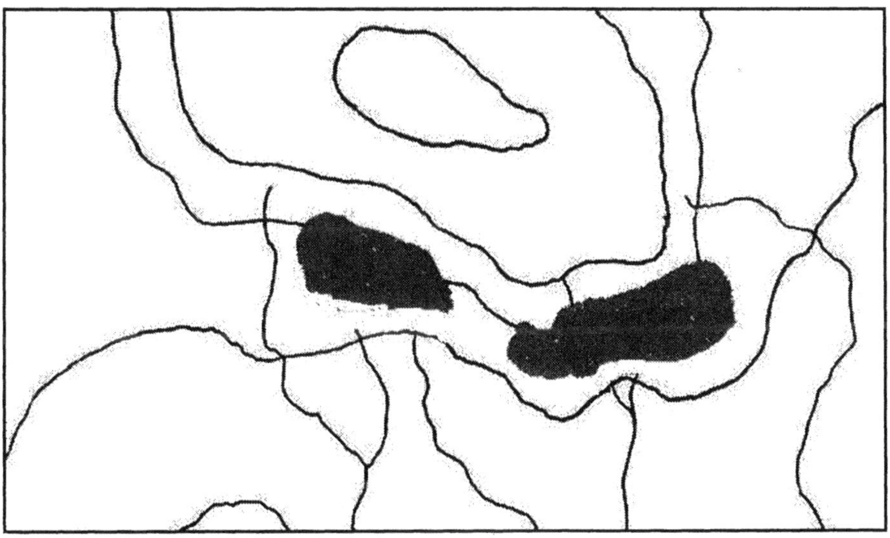

Figure 11.5 Main areas of agricultural settlement on Kilimanjaro, ca. AD 1700. Sources: Nurse 1979; Odner 1971; Stahl 1964.

the farmers pastured their animals. The density of cattle varied between areas, and in the early nineteenth century, and probably earlier, the largest holdings were found in Rombo on the eastern side of Kilimanjaro.

Unfortunately, there are no useful archaeological records from the eastern slopes. Historical linguistics shows that in the early second millenium, the area was occupied by an agropastoralist Maa-speaking population, the Ongamo, who raised livestock and cultivated sorghum and finger millet (Nurse 1979: 330; Ehret 1984). During the second millennium, Chaga speakers expanded westward, absorbing the Ongamo, but retained an agropastoral economy through the nineteenth century. The eastern slopes are well suited for cattle raising but not for irrigated agriculture. There were no chiefs. Rather, people lived scattered in clan-based communities under the leadership of big-men[7] who were rich in cattle and excelled as warriors. In addition to cultivation and herding, the nineteenth-century population trapped elephants and traded ivory with the coast (Stahl 1964: 248).

It is probably no coincidence that the earliest settlements in the intensive cultivation zone emerged high up on the southeastern slopes. These communities practiced irrigation, and herded cattle on the lower slopes. This area is the easternmost part of the high rainfall zone and is situated close to the cattle-rich agropastoral area of Rombo from where the settlers could obtain livestock in exchange for crops. Although the farming communities on the rest of the southern slopes kept cattle, oral traditions stress that they were scarce before the arrival of the pastoralist Maa (Stahl 1964).[8] By the late 1600s, two areas of widespread agricultural settlements are visible on the southern slopes (fig. 11.5). The subsequent centuries, especially the nineteenth century, would see a doubling of the area of settlement and intensive cultivation that paralleled, in time, the influx of pastoralism (fig. 11.3).

It is difficult to provide an exact account of the mutually reinforcing interaction between specialized pastoralism and intensive cultivation in the highlands, especially before the late nineteenth century. However, oral traditions pertaining to the eighteenth century indicate substantial migration from the plains to the mountains, and an expansion of irrigated land (Stahl 1964; Kimambo 1969). On Kilimanjaro, the importance of putting more land under irrigation both at that time and later is emphasized by oral traditions that preserve the names of furrow engineers whose skills were in great demand (Stahl 1964: 26, 226). Another aspect of land use, overlooked by researchers, was the consequences of large-scale accumulation of cattle in the highlands before the 1880s. Contemporary informants and early European travelers agree that there were large herds on all the mountains before the 1870s, after which the slave raiding and political turmoil caused by the caravan trade began a process of large-scale extraction of cattle from the Pare Mountains (Weishaupt 1913: 126; Baumann 1891: 216; Fischer 1882–1883; Kimambo 1969: 140–41).[9]

Centuries of cattle accumulation transformed parts of the forested mountains into grazing and grasslands. For example, a part of the central plateau on South Pare that today is covered with forest was probably grassland before the 1880s. Baumann (1891: 206) observed young regrowth forest in the northern part of the plateau in an area that used to be important pastureland. Remains of human habitations, cattle tracks, and an old marketplace were still visible. In North Pare, where iron smelting was another factor responsible for deforestation, he noted patches of young forest between the cultivated fields (Baumann 1891: 215). Hence, human interference with forests in this region is not of recent date and the current tree cover on the Pare Mountains may actually be more extensive than in the nineteenth century.

By the late nineteenth century, cattle on the southern slopes of Kilimanjaro were kept in stalls, and former pastures had been transformed into agricultural land. Prior to this time, however, Chagga politics had centered around cattle accumulation on a grand scale. Around 1800, one Chagga chief amassed cattle in such large numbers that he had to open up grazing lands on the plains and had to construct two furrows to provide water from Kilimanjaro for his herds. At about the same time, in Rombo on the eastern side of the mountain, a legendary big-man gained political control over half of the inhabited area of Kilimanjaro by initially using cattle gained from ivory trading as gifts to build strategic alliances. His military exploits were further fueled by raiding, which transferred most of the cattle to him on the eastern side on the mountain where he had large stone enclosures built to protect his herds. The grazing needs for these immense herds made it necessary to expand into the Maasai territory on the plains and to repeatedly fight the most renowned warriors in East Africa on their own territory (Dundas 1924: 74). Throughout most of the nineteenth century the expanding ivory trade led to accelerated competition between chiefs on Kilimanjaro and the proliferation of cattle raiding, which in turn must have changed the landscape in ways that still await investigation.

The expansion of specialized pastoralism was undertaken by the forebears of contemporary Maasai and their culturally associated communities in Kenya and Tanzania. By the seventeenth century, Maa-speaking pastoralists from central Kenya had migrated to northern Tanzania. They assimilated to and accommodated their predecessors and neighbors. In the eighteenth century, other Maasai sections had moved to the rich Sanya corridor between Meru and Kilimanjaro in northern Tanzania (Galaty 1993). In the 1830s a prolonged and severe drought sparked conflicts and migrations among the Maasai and other Maa speakers that would continue during the rest of the century (Waller 1985). These factors stimulated migrations to Kilimanjaro and other highland areas with subsequent expansion of settlement and cultivation. At this time, before the end of that century, the earlier Maa speakers, forebears of contemporary Parakuyu, had been pushed near South Pare and Usambara east of the Pangani River (Kimambo 1969: 137).

The increase in the pastoralist population in the nineteenth century was accompanied by conflicts between different Maa-speaking groups.[10] Pastoralism in the Pangani area had by then reached the limits of available grazing. The new larger and powerful coalitions of Maasai sections that moved into the Pangani area displaced their predecessors, took their cattle, and absorbed parts of these populations. Remaining destitute pastoralists migrated into the highlands and took up cultivation (Waller 1985). The overall effect of the Maasai expansion in Tanzania seems to have included a transfer of people from the northern part of Maasailand and the absorption of successful cattle accumulators from other agropastoral and agricultural populations from Kenya to the Pangani valley. As the pastoralist population expanded so did cultivation and the building of landesque capital in the highlands and in enclaves on the plains. According to several authors, the spread of pastoralism on the plains stimulated the formation of a managed landscape of grasslands and reduced bush and tree vegetation (Kjekshus 1977; Giblin 1992). The farmers and pastoralists burned the vegetation and killed wild ungulates in order to exterminate tsetse flies and maintain a landscape suited for cattle.

The pastoralists' increased demand for crops was met partly by the establishment of annual fields for cereal production on the lower foothills of Kilimanjaro (Gutmann 1926: 275, 307), Pare (Baumann 1891: 229), and Usambara (Maddox 1986). Production on these fields was especially designated for exchange with pastoralists (Maddox 1986)[11] who met with cultivators for barter of livestock and livestock products for crops and iron implements at particular marketplaces (Farley 1882; Fischer 1882–1883: 45, 97). Prior to the end of the nineteenth century, sorghum seems to have been the predominant crop, but before the end of that century it was replaced by maize. The increase in the pastoral populations in the nineteenth century led to an expansion in cultivation in the enclave communities of Arusha Juu and Taveta in particular (Waller 1985). Around the turn of the nineteenth century, Maa speakers began migrating to Meru, where they established communities practicing irrigation and banana cultivation. This group, known as Arusha, grew in size during the century through immigration both from neighboring Bantu-speaking areas, and from destitute

Maasai. As the population grew and agricultural productivity increased, the cattle numbers multiplied to the extent that numerous Arusha had accumulated herds on the plains, replacing Maasai from the pastures around the mountain (Spear 1997: 53).

The Caravan Trade

In the 1840s, coastal caravans from the northern Tanzanian coast towns of Pangani, Mtangata, and Tanga took control of much of the trade with northern Tanzania and the interior of East Africa. By the 1850s, Arab and Swahili traders from the central coast of Tanzania had established communities at Lake Tanganyika, and caravans reached as far as western Kenya and Uganda (Sheriff 1987). These caravans could number around 2,000 people for which food had to be obtained along the route. General estimates by German travelers give a number of around 100,000 porters passing yearly through the central caravan route. The number for the Pangani is smaller, but judging from the amount of ivory transported through this path in the 1880s, food for around 10,000 persons per season had to be produced. The coastal caravan trade represented a significant quantitative increase in the number of people transporting ivory to the coast.[12] The demand for food by the caravans contributed to an increase in production over and above the volumes already bartered to the pastoralists and others. This would have amounted to about 400 metric tons annually and caused an increase in the cultivated acreage, notably along the eastern foothills of South Pare, but also in other places.

The lowland settlements of South Pare began as camping and supply points for the caravans. The farmers came down from the mountain with provisions but did not reside in these places (Kimambo 1969: 127). The caravan trade had contradictory effects on cultivation and food security. On one hand, food production was increased and new irrigation was developed in some areas. On the other hand, in some areas slave trading and political competition wreaked havoc on communities and destroyed cultivation systems. Independent local big-men soon established stockaded villages to obtain tolls and to sell slaves, and some ivory, to caravans in exchange for cloth, beads, and livestock. These plain communities grew under the production of the big-men who also raided the surrounding mountains for slaves and cattle, destroying communities and food production (Kimambo 1969: 152, 184; Håkansson 1998). These settlements grew into small towns that still dot the lowlands. These villages attracted numerous people from the Pare Mountains who seem to have been primarily responsible for the extension of intensive cultivation for their own gain rather than accumulation by local elites (Kimambo 1969: 185–86). The sale of food to caravans therefore was under the control of households that maintained sustainable intensive agriculture.

Although I will not treat here the subject of the slave trade, which began to take on importance in the second half of the nineteenth century, it must be mentioned as another aspect of the political ecology of the region. In contrast to their activities in Kenya, the ivory caravans in Tanzania also searched for slaves. The traders extended capital and guns to local leaders that emerged as regionally important big-men and big-women (Giblin 1992: 55). The passage of the caravans removed not only food from regional circulation, but also people. The slave raids devastated production systems and contributed to population movements to areas of trade and to where protection and patronage could be obtained.[13]

The caravan trade generally led to political unrest and competition between existing chiefs and new trade big-men/big-women. During the nineteenth century several chiefs expanded grazing to the plains and had irrigation furrows built to provide water for their herds along the foothills of Kilimanjaro (Stahl 1964: 301). The grazing needs for their immense herds made it necessary to expand into the Maasai territory on the plains and to repeatedly fight the most renowned warriors in East Africa (Dundas 1924: 74).

Development of Landesque Capital

In the absence of extensive archaeological investigations, the origins of many cases of extensive developments of landesque capital, such as on Kilimanjaro and the Pare Hills, cannot yet be determined. Despite this shortcoming in the source material we can use comparative material from several historical instances in the nineteenth century where the connection between the building of sustainable intensive cultivation is clearly related to exchanging foodstuffs for wealth. The established areas of irrigation provided a sustainable cultivation landscape in which productivity was projected through time. The built or engineered environment of the highlands thus provided a stable resource that made the fluctuating pastoral economy possible.

Two sets of interrelated conditions are likely to have been involved in the origins and maintenance of the highland cultivation landscape: first, the pattern and character of regional and external exchange, and second, self-reinforcing local institutional and economic developments related to the intensive system itself (cf. Börjeson 2004: 169–70). This is a recursive process akin to what some authors call "self-organization," that is, a self-reinforcing trajectory of change resulting from the complex interaction of social processes independent of the original cause (Adams 1988: 4; McGlade 1999). A regional division of labor that absorbs surpluses is a precondition for the emergence of landesque capital, but while exchange can be said to be the primary driving force, it does not relate to agricultural management in a linear fashion (Håkansson and Widgren, forthcoming). For example, short-term fluctuations in the flow of wealth did not cause abandonment of soil conservation methods, nor did the decline in the exchange rates for food in Pare during the colonial period lead to an immediate decline in their irrigation system. Farmers showed great resilience and adaptability in the face of declining prices and male labor migration from the mountains. However, it was probably the introduction of cash crops, especially coffee, that provided incentives to maintain the irrigation system, albeit at a reduced capacity.

Maintaining Intensive Cultivation in the Pare Mountains

The cattle-crop exchange nexus was central to the maintenance of landesque capital. However, to assume that profitable exchange of agricultural products automatically leads to sustainable intensification is an oversimplification. The growth of agricultural communities in the Pare Mountains entailed the development of social relations of production and an integrated set of institutions through which labor was mobilized in a sustained fashion. In addition, settlements and economic diversification provided another set of incentives and constraints that affected the farmers. First, studies (see Håkansson 2003) have shown that agropastoral and mixed farming leads to lower herd growth than optimal pastoralism. This effect probably derives from the conflict of labor demands between herding and cultivation, and a shortage of pasture. In addition, fear of theft must have contributed to a desire to keep the livestock close to the settlements. Second, in South Pare, and elsewhere in East Africa, the herds of cultivators were frequent targets for raids by the Maasai, and by rival big-men/big-women. These conditions contributed to a chronic shortage of cattle.

Economic diversification was encouraged by intensive cultivation. For example, already in the beginning of the first millennium, large-scale iron smelting and toolmaking were established. Semispecialized smelters and blacksmiths in turn required food and livestock in exchange for their products. Pottery and salt were other commodities that circulated in the region as well. Ritual specialists, especially rainmakers, and irrigation engineers were in demand.

The basic social organization of Pare society consisted of the family household, and lineage. Although overlaid by a chiefdom political organization that impinged on land tenure and economic organization (Kimambo 1969; Maghimbi 1994; Håkansson 1998), the local kinship groups retained considerable independence and control over their resources and activities. In the early 1800s, the mountain communities were integrated into chiefdoms of different complexities and powers. According to Kimambo (1969), all of North Pare was unified under the Ugweno paramount chief in the seventeenth and eighteenth centuries. There were about ten districts, each ruled by a hereditary chief (Kimambo 1969: 55). The territorial extents and populations of these districts were quite small and comprised at most 30 km^2 and a few thousand people. In South Pare, the political units were smaller, and some chiefs counted less than one thousand subjects. Nowhere was the political hierarchy involved in the construction or management of irrigation, although chiefs and their retainers did have more and larger fields under irrigation and access to more labor than the majority of farmers. The powers of the chiefs differed between the two mountains. In the north, the chiefs demanded tribute in the form of agricultural products, cattle, and beer, but the chiefly clans were exempt from such contributions. In the south, the chiefs' claims to tribute were much weaker and more intermittent, and usually did not involve cattle.

The means by which labor was recruited and organized were based on a particular form of lineage structure and political/religious hierarchy. The ultimate sources of cattle wealth were the permanent banana plantations and irrigated land owned by the polygynous extended families. Cattle were necessary for bride wealth and controlled by the elders who decided about their allocation for sons' marriages. The exchange of grain for livestock with the Maasai was also enclaved[14] by the elders. Such exchanges did not take place at regular marketplaces but through arrangement between individual household heads and their Maasai counterparts.[15] The irrigation system itself was a collective asset that constituted the vein that brought water, the lifeblood of the crops (Håkansson 2003). Both the management of and control over these assets were ultimately lodged with the senior male elders of the water-using community. The male elders of the patrilineage allocated the use rights of plots and assured their fertility through rituals designed to propitiate ancestral and other spirits.

The development of landed resources made cooperation between family households necessary, and the power to transmit and to allocate such resources was, at least ideally, transferred to all men and women as they aged. This placed young men in a dependency relationship until their fathers and mothers died. Women, who generally did not inherit land, had to marry, and they became dependent on their husbands, although their ability to control resources increased by age and the development of their sons' families. Parallel to the building of landesque capital, the ritual primacy of elders, especially old men, as responsible for the generative powers of the land was strengthened as well. Thus, the economic calculus of labor expenditure was differentiated according to age, gender, and kinship so that those in control of resources did not bear the brunt of the work.

Intensive cultivation was also necessary for full community integration in rituals and formal gatherings that supported the social order. Beer from sugarcane grown on irrigated fields was used whenever elders gathered, at ritual occasions, and as gifts or tribute from clients to chiefs and other patrons. Rituals in turn were part and parcel of the cosmology of economic production built around the cultivation system itself (Sheridan 2002; Håkansson 2003). Once embarked on, intensive cultivation led to a constellation of institutional conditions and economic incentives that directed household labor to the management of landesque capital. The importance of institutional control of cattle exchange by elders for the mobilization of labor is revealed by the impact of the caravan trade. The increase in sources of wealth not controlled by elders, in the form of cloth and beads, enabled young men to accumulate cattle on their own, which in turn resulted in an increase in the number of married men and women who established themselves as pastoralists and agropastoralists on the plains (Kimambo 1969: 185).[16]

Discussion

Historical landscapes are not only of theoretical interest. Understanding the conditions that led to sustained high levels of crop production in the precolonial period has direct relevance for food security in contemporary Tanzania and sub-Saharan Africa. Although sustainable intensive cultivation expanded in the nineteenth century, the intensification of the pastoral sector led to high densities of people and cattle, which, in turn, facilitated a series of bovine and human pandemics. First, the Rinderpest epidemic of the early 1890s devastated Maasai herds, reducing their size by 90 percent. The East Coast fever added more dead animals. This led to starvation among the pastoralists, which was accompanied by a smallpox epidemic, which resulted in a reduction of the Maasai population by three-fourths to four-fifths (Iliffe 1979: 124). It should be mentioned that these epidemics were not simply the result of human and livestock densities but were carried along the expanding networks of trade and violence that connected the region to the rest of eastern Africa and the world economy.

A basic precondition for the maintenance of landesque capital and sustainable agricultural production was the circulation of wealth in the form of cattle and other livestock. Exchange rates between crops and livestock were set regionally and depended on growth and decline in cattle herds (cf. Spear 1997: 52). When the pastoral economy expanded, cattle became worth less in terms of crops and presumably other products such as iron and salt. Hence, any households with surplus crops or other goods could obtain cattle, which in turn allowed communities everywhere to accumulate some cattle and survive in areas marginal to agriculture. When cattle herds declined through droughts and diseases, the pastoralists could take up cultivation. Food security remained high due partly to flexibility in movement of people between different economic activities and parts of the landscape. However, another important factor in the maintenance of landesque capital was that labor time was directed to investment in regional production. That is, even during the caravan trade, only low amounts of labor value, in the form of time spent in production, were extracted from the region. Long-term investments in intensive sustainable agriculture were also made possible by the control of the labor of young men and women by the elders of the landowning lineages.

The character of the precolonial regional system can be contrasted with the impact of colonialism. Space does not permit a detailed treatment of this subject and in the following sketch I oversimplify in order to highlight particular features of the new economy that were going to have repercussions for coming changes in land use. It is probably wrong to consider the advent of colonialism as a sharp break in social and economic relationships from the immediate precolonial period. However, new political and economic factors came into play as communities and individuals continued to adapt and retain previous economic and political networks as well as develop new regional ties. Nevertheless, the advent of colonialism, first through the Germans from 1884 to 1914, and then the British from 1916 to1961, drastically changed many aspects of the regional economy. While labor value had previously been retained to a great extent in the region, the Germans started to extract forced labor for the building of roads, railroads, and porterage. After a few years, the labor demands increased through the establishment of settler plantations that used both forced labor and "voluntary" workers. Taxation and money were introduced to further pressure Africans into work. These developments removed labor from farms and led to disinvestment in agriculture and the degradation of landesque capital. The regional economy was further undermined by the introduction of money, livestock, and food from other areas inside and outside the colony. Finally, the permeable political and ethnic boundaries between communities were replaced by rigid borders through the establishment of settler estates around

Meru and Kilimanjaro and the creation of a reservation for the Maasai away from the highlands. As a consequence, food shortages began to appear at the end of the German colonial period (Koponen 1995: 611). Areas such as Usambara, which had previously exported large amounts of food from their irrigated fields to the coastal towns and the plains dwellers, experienced large reductions in crop production and widespread degradation of their field systems (Feierman 1993).

Conclusion

In contrast to the theories of cultural evolution that link political complexity and high population densities with intensive cultivation, economic specializations and high levels of production in the Pangani region, from at least the 1600s to the 1890s, were not enshrined into states and market hierarchies.[17] Rather, they were organized into a number of independent communities and a geographical division of labor (cf. Widgren 2004). Although markets existed, economic integration was also achieved through other forms of exchange such as personal trade relationships, blood-siblinghood, social transactions, tribute, and patron-client ties. To borrow a popular term in archaeological landscape studies (Crumley 1994; Ehrenreich, Crumley, and Levy 1995), this was a heterarchical system of overlapping political and economic relationships with great flexibility that was part of the landscape as a continuously evolving precondition for further economic and political processes. The landscape of grassland savanna, irrigation furrows, fields, and marketplaces was a human construction that represented assets not necessarily only for subsistence but also for the accumulation of wealth. It was this human-made landscape that provided the preconditions for expansion of pastoralism through the presence of the intensive agricultural systems that, once developed, continued and remained unaffected by the fluctuations in the pastoral economy.

The seemingly sustainable nature of the agricultural economy was not caused by environmental adaptation but was rather a consequence of the particular political economy and the flexibility that it entailed. By focusing on the spatial and structural conditions for wealth accumulation, rather than subsistence considerations, it also becomes possible to understand why the pastoral sector was unstable and the subject of violent fluctuations. This approach to human-environmental relationships shows the utility of a political-economic perspective for the analysis of nonstate societies and economies. The landscape perspective allows us to comprehend the complexity of nonhierarchical relationships and directs us from privileging states in political-ecological analysis.

The inception of colonialism entailed a shift to a landscape of deterioration and declining resources. The scale of effective transfers of value changed from the region to the capitalist world-system in which local production was directed toward the profit interests of Europe. With this quantitatively and qualitatively paradigmatic shift in resource extraction, as in many parts of the world-system periphery, landesque capital in parts of the Pangani region deteriorated or became oriented toward cash-crop production. These developments have unfortunately led to declining levels of food production and a loss of food security in Tanzania and elsewhere in Africa.

Notes

1. Research for this chapter was funded by the Swedish Research Council and the Swedish International Development Authority (SIDA) as part of an ongoing project—Northeast Tanzania, 1850–2000: The Political Ecology of Trade Networks, Food Production and Land Cover Change, with Dr. Mats Widgren and Dr. Lowe Börjeson (Stockholm University, Department of Human Geography). I would like to thank Monica Udvardy, Chris Pool, and Lowe Börjeson for comments on the manuscript.

2. It is of course extremely difficult to estimate how much food was exchanged. I have used colonial population figures for the Maasai in 1919. These numbers were then considered to be an underestimation. Several sources estimate a reduction of the Maasai population by about 75 percent between 1889 and the mid-1890s due to disease and starvation. Using an annual population growth of 2 percent pertaining to Maasai in the 1950s (Molnos 1972) I have reached a figure of about fifty thousand inhabiting the Pangani region in 1888. To this must be added an unknown number of pastoralists and agropastoralists amounting to several thousand in the area. I have used modern dietary research on pastoralists that show that their diet consists of approximately 30 percent vegetable food, mainly grain (Galvin, Coppock, and Leslie 1994; Schneider 1979: 64). Colonial studies (Brantley 1997) of Maasai caloric intake and FAO (Food and Agriculture Organization of the United Nations) estimates of general human calorie needs provide a point of departure to calculate the amount of calories needed for the population per year. Although grain was the most common food, the Maasai also obtained beans and bananas. For the sake of simplicity I have used only the caloric values of maize and sorghum. From these figures I have attempted to reach a gross estimate of the amount of crops that must have been consumed by the healthy pastoralists and agropastoralists reported by travelers before the 1890s (e.g., Fischer 1882–1883). Let me also add that the Maasai did not hunt or gather, and they shunned game meat.

3. Population estimates are based on calculations made by Håkansson (1995), Sheridan (2002), Moore (1986), and Spear (1997).

4. Beer was the common lubricant in most social occasions, formal meetings, and rituals.

5. Both male and female elders controlled livestock. However, as a category, men had more power than women. For more detail on gender roles in Pare, see Håkansson (2003).

6. While there were no female chiefs on the Pare Mountains, some women held such positions on both Kilimanjaro and Usambara.

7. Only big-men, not women, are noted by Stahl (1964).

8. Oral traditions from the southern slopes often refer to immigrations of "Maasai" who brought cattle into areas with few cattle. In contrast, the traditions from the southeastern area close to the agropastoral eastern slopes emphasize the long-standing existence of cattle and herding (Stahl 1964).

9. While the slave trading and its associated cattle raiding had declined by 1890, the catastrophic bovine Rinderpest epidemic bankrupted the Maasai, who then started to steal the remaining Pare cattle.

10. It is important to note again that the increase in the Maasai population was not only due to natural increase but was caused by political-economic processes that at certain times enabled people to shift from cultivation or foraging to pastoralism.

11. Field notes from North Pare, 1995.

12. Ivory trade in northern Tanzania before ca. 1840 was in the hands of the interior peoples. They did not organize large caravans. Instead, ivory percolated to the coastal towns through "relay trade" moving in small amounts and short distances. The 1800s also saw a significant increase in the volume of trade.

13. The slave trade in the Pangani region was important during the 1870s and 1880s. The total number of people taken as slaves was low, but raiding and fighting caused depopulation in several areas on the plains and in the Pare Mountains. Probably several thousand people were taken as slaves or died in the turmoil (Kimambo 1969; Giblin 1992).

14. This concept is defined by Robbins and Akin (1999: 24) as "the erection of barriers to protect reproductive institutions from disruption by money and commoditization." I think we should extend it to cover the social and political strategies, often by the powerful, designed to protect and control the flow of wealth in favor of those with power in any society.

15. Blood brotherhood and blood sisterhood were a common vehicle for institutionalizing long-term trade relationships (Dannholz 1989 [1912–1918]); field notes North Pare 1995).

16. Field notes, South Pare, 1995.

17. The political character of the chiefdoms varied in time and space with respect to complexity and centralized exercise of power. The received anthropological typology of political centralization is often difficult to apply in the East African context. The power of chiefs in small chiefdoms, such as in the Pare Mountains, was often less than that exercised by the big-men/big-women or, "chieftains," as they are called by historians.

References

Adams, Richard N. 1988. *The Eighth Day*. Austin: University of Texas Press.

Baumann, Oscar. 1891. *Usambara und Seine Nachbargebiete*. Berlin: Dietrich Reimer.

Blaikie, Peter, and Harold Brookfield. 1987. *Land Degradation and Society*. London: Methuen.

Börjeson, Lowe. 2004. *A History Under Siege. Intensive Agriculture in the Mbulu Highlands, Tanzania, 19th Century to the Present*. Acta Universitatis Stockholmiensis / Stockholm Studies in Human Geography 12. Stockholm: Stockholm University.

Brantley, Cynthia. 1997. "Kikuyu-Masaii Nutrition and Colonial Science: The Orr and Gilks Study in Late 1920s Kenya Reconsidered." *International Journal of African Historical Studies* 30 (1): 49–86.

Brookfield, Harold C. 1984. "Intensification Revisited." *Pacific Viewpoint* 25:15–44.

Chase-Dunn, Christopher, and Thomas D. Hall. 1997. *Rise and Demise*. Walnut Creek, CA: Westview Press.

Crumley, Carole. 1994. "Historical Ecology: A Multidimensional Ecological Orientation." In *Historical Ecology*, ed. Carole L. Crumley, 1–16. Santa Fe: School of American Research.

———. Forthcoming. "Historical Ecology: Integrated Thinking at Multiple Temporal and Spatial Scales."

Dannholz, Jacob. J. 1989 [1912–1918]. *Lute luvivi-lwedi* [The curse and the blessing]. Bishofweisen: Erika Dannholz.

Downs, R. E., and S. P. Reyna. 1988. Introd. to *Land and Society in Contemporary Africa*, ed. R. E. Downs and S. P. Reyna, 1–22. Hanover, NH: University Press of New England.

Douglas, Mary. 1982 [1966]. "Population Control in Primitive Groups." In *In The Active Voice*, ed. Mary Douglas, 135–47. London: Routledge & Kegan Paul.

Dundas, Charles. 1924. *Kilimanjaro and Its People*. London: H. F. & G. Witherby.

Ehrenreich, Robert M., Carole M. Crumley, and Janet E. Levy, eds. 1995. *Heterarchy and the Analysis of Complex Societies*. Archaeological Papers of the American Anthropological Association, No. 6. Washington, DC: American Anthropological Association.

Ehret, Christopher. 1984. "Between the Coast and the Great Lakes." In *The UNESCO General History of Africa, 12th–16th Centuries*, ed. D. J. Niane, 481–97. Berkeley: University of California Press.

Food and Agriculture Organization of the United Nations. 2003. "Human Energy Requirements." *Food and Nutrition Technical Report Series 1*. Rome: FAO.

Farley, J. P. 1882. "Native Routes in East Africa from Pangani to the Masai Country and the Victoria Nyanza." *Proceedings of the Royal Geographical Society* 4:730–53.

Feierman, Stephen. 1993. "Defending the Promise of Subsistence: Population Growth and Agriculture in the West Usambaras." In *Population Growth and Agricultural Change in Africa*, ed. B. L. Turner II, Goran Hyden, and Robert Kates, 114–40. Gainesville: University of Florida Press.

Fischer, Gustav A. 1882–1883. "Bericht uber die im Auftrage der Geographischen Gesellschaft in Hamburg unternommene Reise in das Massai-Land." *Mittheilungen der Geographischen Gesellschaft in Hamburg*, 36–99; 189–279.

Galaty, John. 1993. "Maasai Expansion and the New East African Pastoralism." In *Being Maasai*, ed. Thomas Spear and Richard Waller, 61–86. London: James Currey.

Galvin, Kathleen A., Layne D. Coppock, and Paul W. Leslie. 1994. "Diet, Nutrition, and the Pastoral Strategy." In *African Pastoralist Systems*, ed. Elliot Fratkin, Kathleen A. Galvin, and Eric Abella Roth, 113–32. Boulder, CO: Lynne Rienner.

Giblin, James L. 1992. *The Politics of Environmental Control in Northeastern Tanzania, 1840–1940*. Philadelphia: University of Pennsylvania Press.

Glassman, Jonathon. 1995. *Feasts and Riot*. London: James Currey.

Gutmann, Bruno. 1926. *Das Recht der Chagga*. Munich: Beck'sche Verlagsbuchhandlung

Håkansson, N. Thomas. 1994. "The Detachability of Women: Gender and Kinship in Processes of Socio-economic Change among the Gusii of Kenya." *American Ethnologist* 21:516–38.

———. 1995. "Irrigation, Population Pressure, and Exchange in Precolonial Pare, Tanzania." *Research in Economic Anthropology* 16:297–323.

———. 1998. "Rulers and Rainmakers in Pre-Colonial South Pare, Tanzania: The Role of Exchange and Ritual Experts in Political Fragmentation." *Ethnology* 37:263–83.

———. 2003. "Rain and Cattle: Gendered Structures and Political Economy in Precolonial Pare, Tanzania." In *Gender at Work in Economic Life*, ed. Gracia Clark, 19–40. Walnut Creek, CA: AltaMira.

Håkansson N. Thomas, and Mats Widgren. Forthcoming. "The Political Economy of Landesque Capital: Northeastern Tanzania in the 19th Century." Geografiska Annaler, Ser B.

Hayden, Brian. 1995. "Pathways to Power. Principles for Creating Socio-Economic Inequalities." In *Foundations of Social Inequality*, ed. T. D. Price and Gary M. Feinman, 15–86. New York: Plenum Press.

Iliffe, John. 1979. *A Modern History of Tanzania*. Cambridge: Cambridge University Press.

Johnston, H. H. 1886. *The Kilimanjaro Expedition*. London: Kegan, Paul, and Trench.

Karasek, A. 1911. "Beiträge zur Kenntnis der Waschambaa, Pt. 1." *Baessler-Archiv* 1:155–222.

Kersten, Otto. 1869–1879. *Von der Deckens Reisen in Ost-Afrika in den Jahren 1859 bis 1865*. Vols. 1 and 2. Leipzig: C. F. Winter.

Kimambo, Isaria N. 1969. *A Political History of the Pare of Tanzania, c. 1500–1900*. Nairobi: East African Publishing House.

Kjekshus, H. 1977. *Ecology Control and Economic Development in East African History*. Berkeley: University of California Press

Koponen, Juhani. 1995. *Development for Exploitation*. Helsinki: Finnish Historical Society; Hamburg: LIT Verlag.

Krapf, Johann Ludwig. 1860. *Travels, Researches, and Missionary Labour during an Eighteen Years' Residence in Eastern Africa*. London: Trubner.

Maddox, Gregory. 1986. "Njaa: Food Shortages and Famines in Tanzania." *International Journal of African Historical Studies* 19 (1): 17–34.

Maghimbi, Sam. 1994. "Pre-capitalist Modes of Production in Tanzania: Reference to Modes of Production in the Old Ugweno State of North-Eastern Tanzania." *Utafiti* (New Series): 1, 20–35.

Mauss, Marcel. 1990 [1950]. *The Gift*. London: Routledge.

McGlade, James. 1999. "Archaeology and the Evolution of Cultural Landscapes: Towards an Interdisciplinary Research Agenda." In *The Archaeology and Anthropology of Landscape,* ed. Peter J. Ucko and Robert Layton, 458–82. London: Routledge.

Meyer, Hans. 1893. *Across East African Glaciers*. London: George Philip and Son.

Molnos, Angela. 1972. *Cultural Source Materials for Population Planning in East Africa*. Vol. 1. Nairobi: East African Publishing House.

Moore, Sally. F. 1986. *Social Facts and Fabrications*. Cambridge: Cambridge University Press.

Nurse, Derek. 1979. *Classification of the Chaga Dialects: Language and History on Kilimanjaro, the Taita Hills, and the Pare Mountains*. Hamburg: Buske.

Odner, Knut. 1971. "A Preliminary Report on an Archaeological Survey on the Slopes of Kilimanjaro." *Azania* 6:131–49.

Robbins, Joel, and David Akin. 1999. "An Introduction to Melanesian Currencies." In *Money and Modernity*, ed. David Akin and Joel Robbins, 1–40. Pittsburgh: University of Pittsburgh Press.

Sahlins, Marshal D. 1974. *Stone Age Economics*. London: Tavistock.

Schneider, Harold. K. 1979. *Livestock and Equality in East Africa*. Bloomington: Indiana University Press.

Sheridan, Michael. 2002. "An Irrigation Intake Is Like a Uterus: Culture and Agriculture in Precolonial North Pare, Tanzania." *American Anthropologist* 104:79–92.

Sheriff, Abdul. 1987. *Slaves, Spices & Ivory in Zanzibar*. London.

Sluyter, Andrew. 2002. *Colonialism and Landscape*. Lanham, MD: Rowman & Littlefield.

Spear, Thomas. 1997. *Mountain Farmers*. London: James Currey.

Stahl, Kathleen M. 1964. *The History of the Chagga People of Kilimanjaro*. The Hague: Mouton.

Warburg, O. 1894. "Die Kulturpflantzen Usambaras." *Mittheilungen von Forschungsreisenden und Gelehrten aus dem Deutschen Schutzgebiet*, no. 7:131–98.

Waller, Richard. 1985. "Economic Relations in the Central Rift Valley: The Maa-Speakers and their Neighbours in the Nineteenth Century." In *Kenya in the Nineteenth Century*, ed. Bethwell A. Ogot, 83–151. Nairobi: Bookwise.

Weishaupt, Martin. 1913. *Ostafrikanscher Wandertage durch das Gebiet des Leipziger Mission in Deutsch Ostafrika*. Leipzig: Verlag Evengelischer-Lutherischen Mission.

Widenmann, A. 1899. *Die Kilimanscharo Bevölkerung*. Petermanns Mitteilungen, suppl. 129.

Widgren, Mats. Forthcoming. "Pre-colonial Landesque Capital: A Global Perspective." In *Rethinking Environmental History: World Systems History and Global Environmental Change*, ed. A. Hornborg, J. Martinez-Alier, and J. R. McNeill. Walnut Creek, CA: AltaMira.

Widgren, Mats. 2004. "Towards a Historical Geography of Intensive Farming in Eastern Africa." In *Islands of Intensive Cultivation in Eastern Africa*, ed. Mats Widgren and John Sutton, 1–18. London: James Currey.

Maya Handicraft Vendors, Crime, and the Social Re/construction of Market Spaces in a Tourism Town

12

WALTER E. LITTLE

"One such irony is the way the indigenous embrace of multiculturalism turns out to be quite compatible with neoliberalism, peculiar though such a notion initially appears to many progressive and left-leaning individuals, indigenous and nonindigenous alike"

Warren and Jackson (2002b: 24).

The interrelationship between political and economic practices of street vendors[1] contributes to the social reconstruction of space in Antigua, Guatemala. For these vendors space is both economically and politically constituted through the physical occupation and use of public space in Antigua, in relation to ideological conceptualizations of that space by Maya vendors working there and non-Mayas living there. I use Kay Warren and Jeane Jackson's comments about how neoliberalism has positively changed power relations for indigenous people as a point of departure to question whether this is the case for handicraft vendors with regard to their economic conditions and in their political dealings with Antigua's city government.

Warren and Jackson (2002b: 24) observe that "neoliberal tenants such as decentralization and political and ethnic pluralism permit indigenous communities to strike their own bargains with national and international corporations and NGOs [nongovernmental organizations], bypassing paternalistic regional and state agencies." This condition has allowed indigenous people throughout the Americas to renegotiate their political power within their respective regional and state governments. As Warren (1998) and others (Bastos and Camus 2003; England 2003; Fischer 2001; Nelson 1999) illustrate, Maya activists have successfully altered power relations within the state. Charles Hale (2002) makes a similar case in his argument that neoliberalism allows for the recognition of cultural rights. Although power still rests primarily in the hands of a few non-Maya elite, more political spaces in Guatemalan society have opened for Maya voice and participation. In the government Mayas occupy key cabinet positions, and in the media they hold editorial columnist positions in the country's two major daily newspapers. Despite such positive changes with regard to political participation and opening for human and cultural rights advocacy, economic conditions in Latin America under neoliberalism continue to decline.[2]

In contrast to the indigenous activists described in Warren and Jackson's (2002a) volume, I discuss Maya street vendors in Antigua, Guatemala, whose perceptions of neoliberalism are tempered by deteriorating local economic and social conditions. Neoliberal political and economic policies are not easily correlated with street vendors' experiences. There are no policies that are directly aimed at them. However, the discourse of free markets and open borders that the Maya learn about in the media is especially attractive to these small-scale salespersons. As street vendors contend with economic decline and increasing violent crime, they relate these conditions to neoliberalism. In particular, when they talk about crime, they spatialize their experiences and contextualize crime within the economic and political spheres in which they work. This contributes to an ongoing social reconstruction of Antigua's public spaces.

Interestingly, Matejowsky (in this volume) presents a case in which neoliberalism has not had such a negative economic impact. In both the case presented here and that of Matejowsky, what constitutes the urban landscape is related to the particular places and actors engaged in economic exchanges. Like Matejowsky, I am interested in how neoliberal policies impact urban retail outlets and the people who buy and sell in them. Where he puts greater emphasis on the physical transformation of San Fernando's retail districts, I place more emphasis on the role of a type of person, the Maya handicraft vendor, in constituting the urban landscape of Antigua.

In this chapter, I elaborate on Warren and Jackson's thesis that ironies of power emerge through neoliberal economic policies, which may not necessarily lead to more positive social, political, or economic conditions, as is argued here. As June Nash (2001: 217) states, and as Warren and Jackson imply, indigenous activism "is more adapted to the emerging global ecumene than the neoliberal program that relies on militarized nation-states and a growing gap between rich and poor." This chapter is situated within a context in which economic and social conditions come about because of these power shifts.

I also draw on Colloredo-Mansfield's (2002: 114) point that "the competitive dynamic [of capitalism] is frequently not go-it-alone individualism but positioning, and, consequently, competition is better understood as a vital relationship among competitors than as discrete acts of identification of winners and losers." My goal here is to illustrate the social and political dimensions of Maya street vendors' economic strategies in order to elaborate on Colloredo-Mansfield's thesis that "competing in the production and sale of commodities consolidates cultural identities and community commitments." As argued by Colloredo-Mansfield (2002), and as will be discussed here, regarding the street vendors, the market impacts identity formations and the socially constructed landscape.

The politics of space is well documented by ethnographic research. Most studies, among them Low's (2000) analysis of the Latin American plaza, Cross's (1998) research on Mexico City street vendors, Stoller's (2002) analysis of the political conflicts between the city of New York and African street vendors, Caldeira's (2000) discussion of crime and fortified (gated) communities in São Paulo, and others (see Certeau 1984; Low 2004), take place within the context of neoliberal ideologies and economic reforms. Ironically, these studies tend to downplay or disregard economic factors. A great deal of research (Cross and Stoller above; Babb 1998; Castañeda 1997; Clark 1988, 1994; Field 1999; Kapchan 1996; Little 2004a; Meisch 2002; Weismantel 2001) has been fruitfully used to discuss identity politics as it unfolds in the marketplace. This research has not adequately shown the linkages between the politics of space and economics, a point that Harvey (1990: 201) also makes with respect to Marshall Berman's (1982) theories of modernity and space and Frederic Jameson's (1984) conditions of postmodernity and space.

The case I present here aims to show the connections between economics and space. In this volume, Matejowsky also not only notes these linkages, but he shows how the physical urban landscape of San Fernando City, Philippines, has changed without the conflicts described by Cross, Stoller, and my case here. Although Maya street vendors do not construct large retail venues, their presence—especially because of the colorful traditional clothing they wear and the goods they sell—make the urban landscape what it is. In the Antigua case, I consider landscape to be constituted, in part, by the particular actors who occupy the place and the exchanges—economic and political—that they have with each other. It is the socioeconomic context and long history of Maya vendors in Antigua that lends to how they and tourists conceive of the place. Certainly, this is not to deny that there is physicality to it: Spanish colonial architecture and cobblestone streets, the Cerro de la Cruz to the north, and the looming volcanoes—Agua to the south and Fuego to the southwest. Of course, these natural and human-made phenomena also contribute to Antigua's particular urban landscape that is conceptualized.

By attending to street vendors' comments and conversations about crime, the case study here contextualizes the vendors' economic practices within the local politics of Antigua to better understand both the physical and conceptual landscape. How street vendors talk about crime provides insight into their concepts of how economic practices relate to identity and space, as well as how these are inextricably linked. It is here that local understanding of landscape can be delineated. Vis-à-vis their experiences with crime and the municipal government—selling clandestinely to tourists to avoid fines, protecting themselves from thieves, and avoiding local police officers—vendors are rethinking their economic relationship with public places.

Ethnographic Context: Street Vendors in Antigua

In various capacities—fixed stall vendors, plaza periodic marketplaces, ambulatory vendors, and peddlers—street vending has been a part of Antigua life since the founding of the city in 1541 (Lutz 1994; Swetnam 1975). Like the colonial buildings and rustic cobblestone streets in which they sell their colorful handicrafts, the presence of Maya vendors defines this urban landscape. Their identities are tied to both place and vending, and tourists, too, conceive of these Maya vendors as part of this landscape.[3]

This chapter focuses on street vendors, *ambulantes* (ambulatory street vendors, peddlers, mobile retailers) of handicrafts. The vast majority of these vendors are women. The number of *ambulantes* working in Antigua has grown dramatically over the past three years. Roughly one hundred *ambulantes* from Maya (Kaqchikel, K'iche', and Ixil) and Ladino ethnic groups peddled handicrafts on Antigua's streets in 1999. Seventy Kaqchikel Maya *ambulantes* at that time represented the largest group (Little 2002), while Ladinos (non-Mayas) comprised the smallest group with only a few vendors. As of July 2004, the number of vendors increased to more than three hundred, all of whom are Mayas. With such an increase, it is not surprising that *ambulante* relations with the city government and other businesspeople have become contentious. Even vendors themselves agree that they are too numerous.

Over the past thirty years, the nature of ambulatory handicrafts sales has changed significantly because of changes in the Guatemalan and world economy, as well as changes in tourists' and collectors' tastes. Up until the late 1970s, there were few *ambulantes*. Most were Maya women who maintained a vending circuit that included the residences of textile collectors, retail outlets that sold Maya handicrafts, and the hotels in which collectors and wealthy tourists stayed. Since the 1970s, *ambulante* sales to collectors have gradually declined and vendors have changed their sales strategies and product lines to attract new clients. Vendors attribute the decline to the changing tastes of collectors and tourists alike, as well as changes in the types of tourists that visit Guatemala. Compared to earlier tourists, many tourists today, according to one older female, "don't know how much time and work it takes to weave. They don't know how much thread costs. They think they can buy *típica* for cheap like clothes from China." Indeed, Michael Chibnick (2003) explains that overall interest in Latin American handicrafts has declined in recent years. Maya *ambulantes* today sell far fewer textiles than they did four years ago. Like good salespeople everywhere, they try to sell items that appeal to their customers. Their inventories contain fewer traditional textiles (*po't* [blouses] and *su't* [utilitarian and ceremonial cloths]) and more inexpensive jewelry, key chains, change purses, and simple woven decorations that are easily transported by U.S., Salvadoran, and Mexican consumers.

Ideologies of Public Space Use

Within this always-changing handicraft market, Maya and Ladino concepts of how to use public space—plazas and streets and sidewalks—come into conflict. How vendors use municipal public space relates to a long historical memory about the function or role of public spaces, notably the Central Plaza. As Setha Low (2000) explains regarding Mesoamerica and the Caribbean in general, the plaza serves as an important physical/spatial locus of indigenous culture, despite Spanish colonialism and the imposition of Spanish, and lingering colonial concepts of the built environment. At stake are ideological differences between Maya vendors and Ladino politicians about both the place of the market and use rights to public streets. Although there are no laws officially prohibiting street vending, Mayas are fighting for rights to use common property that help perpetuate their and tourists' concepts of landscape. Their ideological conflicts with Ladinos, particularly politicians and some businesspeople, have led to physical conflict.

From the Maya vendors' ideological perspective, the Central Plaza, or *ruk'u'x tinamït* (literally, "the heart of the city"), is where commercial, ceremonial, and political power should be located. For them, markets, physically situated in the plaza, are in the heart and the lifeblood of the city. To be excluded from the plaza—prohibited from selling and buying handicrafts, pushed outside city politics, discouraged from worshipping in the Catholic cathedral, and shooed off benches by local police officers—is to be cut off from an important means of livelihood, religious practice, and social and political participation. At times when the police force them out of the plaza, vendors describe themselves and the plaza as sad (*b'is*) because it lacks the vibrant social and economic bustle of buying and selling. For Mayas, plazas and public spaces, in general, require the ongoing use by people. This interaction of people and place allows not only for the social construction of place, but also for the social construction of identity. As John Watanabe (1992) and I (Little 2004a) demonstrate elsewhere, being Maya is living, working, socializing, and worshipping in a particular place with others mutually identified as part of the same sociocultural group. To not be intimately involved in that place with other people is not only "sad" according to Maya vendors, it threatens to undermine one's identity and sense of self.

Maya vendors complement these traditional ideologies of how to conceive of and use public space with more contemporary rationalizations based on economic contexts. For roughly the past eighty years, Maya handicraft vendors from nearby towns, San Antonio Aguas Calientes, Santa Catarina Barahona, and Santa Maria de Jesus, have sold handwoven textiles and other crafts to tourists from the United States, Europe, and other Latin American countries. Some vendors have literally grown up within this tourism site, accompanying their mothers and grandmothers as children and then taking their own children and grandchildren to Antigua to sell. These vendors and their extended families conceive of Antigua as a meeting ground for tourists and Mayas, a place of economic and cultural exchange.

Maya vendors have also come to view themselves as tourism subjects/objects, as traditional adornment to Spanish colonial ruins and other public spaces. This attitude parallels their representation in the popular media—travel guidebooks, advertising, tourism trade journals, and postcards, for example[4]—and is expected by international tourists visiting Antigua. Ideally, vendors maintain ambulatory routes that follow paths from one historical monument or plaza to a church or hotel, entering when permitted. More stationary street vendors try to sell in front of or inside these same places. Unlike the invasions of large numbers of handicraft vendors at the Chichén Itzá ruins in Mexico, which Quetzil Castañeda (1997) describes and characterizes as a theater of war, Maya *ambulantes* and semistationary vendors occupy touristic spaces in Antigua only in small numbers. According to Michel de Certeau (1984), part of the *ambulantes*' strategy to occupy public spaces, but to avoid the authorities' attention, is to be in and around the places tourists visit, but not to be conspicuous. I confirmed through observations and interviews with tourists that vendors themselves hold that tourists are more receptive to two or three *ambulantes* than they are to large groups. In other words, framed in Colloredo-Mansfield's (2002) terms, within the context of the tourism market, *ambulantes* collectively agreed to limit their numbers and avoid competition. In small numbers, this allows them to appear to be more a part of the site and establish rapport with tourist consumers. Establishing rapport with tourists, which in the de Certeauian (1984) sense is tactical, reduces the chances that the police will fine or arrest them for selling because the arrests would be an embarrassment to the city. *Ambulantes* take advantage of international tourists' desire to see colorfully dressed Mayas because arresting peaceful Maya *ambulantes* offends tourists.

The Ladino ideological perspective of public spaces and the use of those spaces contrast with those of Mayas. For Ladinos the plaza and the city center and public/common spaces should be orderly and "clean." As Goldín (1987) and Swetnam (1975) have explained, in the 1930s and again in the 1970s, Ladino-run municipalities removed periodic and daily marketplaces from city centers. The general argument has been that markets, which are disorderly and unsanitary, should be relegated to the outskirts of town—or at the very least away from the Central Plaza—and put into buildings and regulated. From the Ladino perspective, the Central Plaza represents order, cleanliness, and tranquility, which Maya *ambulantes* are perceived to threaten.

Many Ladino businesspeople, residents, police officers, and city officials commonly characterize *ambulante* vendors as "dirty" and "unruly," attributing a range of unfounded negative behaviors to them: littering, urinating in public, stealing, harassing tourists and residents, blocking legitimate businesses, fighting, and engaging in public drunkenness. *Ambulantes* contend that behaving in such ways would diminish their sales, since it would alienate them from their primary consumers, international tourists. In fact, when vendors engage in any of these behaviors, other vendors step in and sanction them. Over the years, I have watched vendors themselves castigate the occasional peer who behaved inappropriately and apologize to the offended person, even giving him a small, inexpensive key chain or bracelet.

Conflicts over Use of Public Space

The different ideological orientations of public space and how to use that public space have resulted in conflicts between Maya vendors and the municipal government dating back to the 1970s, according to vendors and Ladino residents. Since then, against the wishes of government officials, vendors have sold their handicrafts in the plaza and in other public areas. Over the years, local police have periodically expelled them, seized their merchandise, or fined them.

The history of struggle between Maya handicraft vendors and the municipality is addressed in Little (2004a, 2004b). The contentious relations between street vendors and city officials in Antigua are similar to those faced by vendors in other areas of the world (Bromley 2000; Cross 1998, 2000; Dannhaeuser 1989; Stoller 2002), in which street vendors are accused by the government officials and taxpaying businesspeople of blocking public streets and squares, failing to pay taxes, lacking vending permits, and selling contraband.

In general, Ladino residents are ambivalent about street vendors. This has to do with the contradictory ways in which they relate to Mayas, not just vendors. Those who work in the tourism industry recognize that international tourists expect to see and interact with Mayas. However, those who do not work in the tourism industry or sell competing products are far more adamant about removing vendors from the city. These practical market-based concerns are reinforced by racist attitudes (see Smith 1990; Carey 2001; and Casaús Arzú 1998 for Guatemala in general), in which Mayas are perceived of as subhuman. This is most evident in the ways that Ladinos tend to describe Maya languages as "grunts" or "just sounds." After more than a decade of cultural and linguistic activism (see Cojtí Cuxil 1998; England 2003; Fischer and Brown 1996; Warren 1998), Ladinos and even Mayas themselves, whose culture and languages have been devalued for more than five hundred years, are slow to change their attitudes.

Since the 1980s, street vendors have been subject to police crackdowns, which can take the form of arrests, seizures of merchandise, and fines. Municipal officials have been cautious about levying fines or arresting vendors in the presence of tourists, not wanting to tarnish the city's image.

The municipality intensified its actions regarding vendors after opening of a new handicrafts market in February 1998 and an annex in March 2003, located on the outskirts of the city. When the annex was opened all other public places (the Central Plaza, church courtyards, the Tanque de la Unión, Spanish colonial ruins, and street sidewalks in front of hotels and Spanish language schools throughout the city) in which vendors sold were closed. The tourism police forcibly removed vendors of handicrafts from public places. It is difficult to gauge the reasons why the city took such a position, but police worried less about arresting vendors and seizing merchandise in front of tourists during the high tourism seasons in the summers of 2003 and 2004. Maya vendors and Ladino residents speculate that it had to do with keeping order, racist attitudes against Maya vendors, shop owners wanting street vendors out of the city to reduce competition, and efforts to improve Antigua's visual image. To put it another way, Ladino officials and businesspeople were reorganizing the urban landscape so it conformed to their perceptions, not those of tourists or Mayas. Like the chapters in this volume (those by Crothers and Rivera, for example) that show how changing property rights can lead to changes in the landscape, changes in access to public vending space influence changes in both the physical and imagined urban landscapes of Antigua.

Maya vendors viewed these actions by the city government as a direct assault on their livelihood. They used traditional strategies (described elsewhere in Little 2004a, 2004b with regard to fixed, marketplace vendors) to protest. They went en masse to the Central Plaza and protested in front of city hall. They initiated petition drives by collecting signatures from tourists and foreign students of Spanish at tourism sites, restaurants, hotels, and language schools. They also made alliances with vendor-friendly businesses (hotels, restaurants, and Spanish language schools) to allow them to sell in the entryways or to meet patrons at mutually agreed-on times. In December of 2002, immediately before the city relocated handicraft vendors to the new marketplace annex or expelled them from the city, they formed an organization (Asociación Comité Representativo de Artesanos del Altiplano de Guatemala [CORAGUA]), became members of a national-level vendor organization (Frente Nacional Vendedores Mercados de Guatemala [FENVEMEGUA]), and affiliated with a national workers' organization (Centro de Trabajadores de Guatemala [CGTG]). They also filed grievances with the United Nations Office of Human Rights and the Presidential Commission Against Discrimination and Racism Against Guatemalan Indigenous Peoples. They even commissioned a Ladino lawyer, who specialized in human rights, to argue their case on a pro bono basis. Basically, where one sells is economically significant and to occupy optimal places must be defended in political spheres. Hence, economic exchange, politics, and space are interrelated and contested, which then leads to new conceptualizations of and physical changes in the landscape (again this in part is what Crothers and Rivera show).

As the vendors took action, their arguments remained consistent: Street vending is a historically established tradition. As colorfully dressed Mayas, they attract tourists. And as citizens they have a right to work and practice their livelihood. This can be seen in the recording of CORAGUA in the Civil Register on December 19, 2002. The organization's objectives include the following:

- Stimulate the production, promotion, preservation, and sale of handmade crafts
- Contribute to the preservation of Antigua's historical center and to help keep the city clean and stimulate sustainable local tourism

- Promote the culture, traditional customs, and folklore of the municipality
- Help maintain peaceful relations among vendors, local authorities, and others

These objectives were aimed at addressing problems between vendors and the municipality, but can be interpreted as an attempt to formally establish handicraft vendors as an economically and socially necessary part of Antigua's historical and touristic landscape.

Despite these alliances and the registration of CORAGUA, beginning in March 2003, vendors have been subjected to periodic wholesale expulsions from the city—usually during lulls in tourism—and increased random fining and seizing of merchandise. By May 2004, the central issue for handicraft vendors, especially street vendors, other local businesses, the municipal government, and residents was where *ambulantes* and other vendors would sell.

The proposed locations, Plaza Isabel (the location recommended by city officials) and the Predio or Tanque de la Unión (the vendors' preferred locations), highlight the different conceptualizations of public space held by Maya vendors and Ladino city officials. The debates between vendors and city officials are taken up below. From within this contested urban landscape, vendors expressed their frustrations that Guatemala was not becoming the more open economic and political society it was heralded to be following the 1996 Peace Accords.

The Promise and Failure of Neoliberalism

Throughout the 1990s, Maya handicraft vendors in Antigua embraced what they understood was neoliberalism. Basing their interpretations on newspapers and television, vendors expected the opening of international borders that would facilitate their ability to travel. They embraced the rhetoric of free, unfettered trade, imagining expanding their markets far beyond Guatemala. Older vendors, who in the 1970s traveled to and sold handicrafts in Mexico, other Central American countries, the United States, and other distant places, anticipated rebuilding their businesses, long negatively impacted by the thirty-six-year war. They watched indigenous people throughout the Americas, including Guatemala, win more freedom to express their languages and culture and make gains in political and cultural and human rights.

For vendors, neoliberalism held the promise of connecting them to the greater world that would reduce state control over them (see Little 2004a).

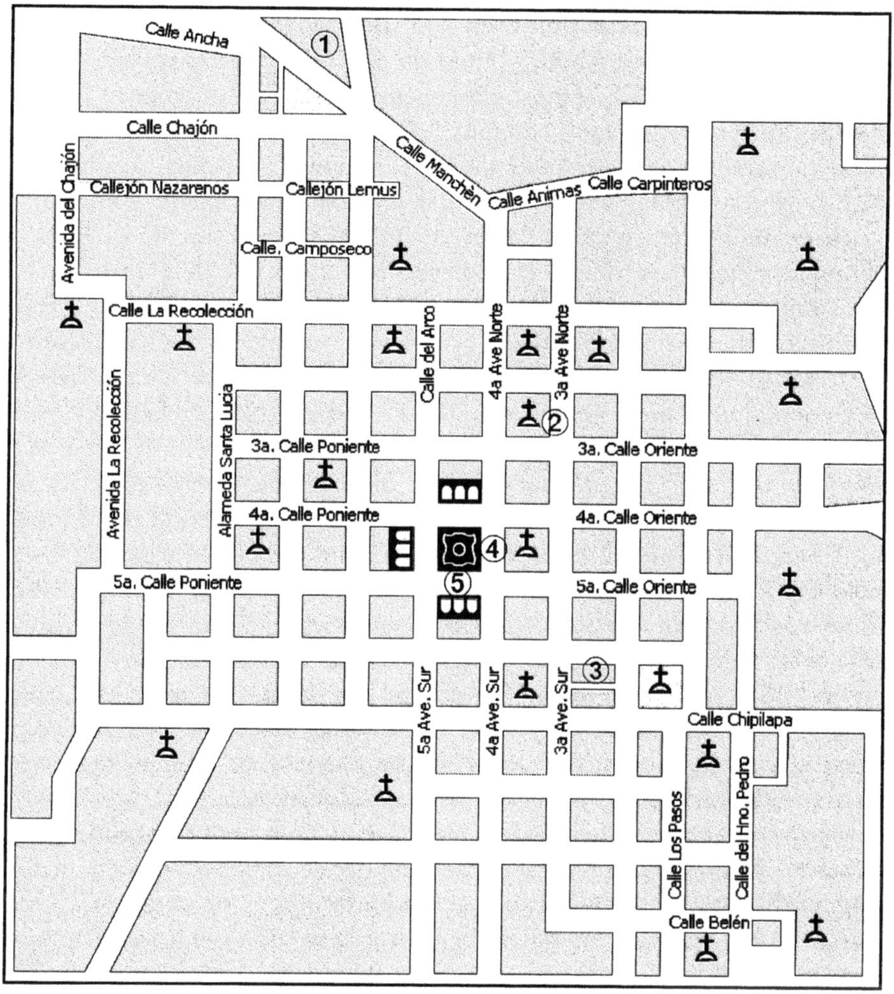

Figure 12.1 Antigua Guatemala: 1. Plaza Isabel, 2. Plaza del Carmen, 3. Tanque de la Unión, 4. Plaza Central and cathedral, 5. Predio. All crosses represent churches and missions. Source: Walter E. Little.

Vendors perceive that commodity exchange and mutual appreciation of Maya history and culture link them to tourists. And like international tourists, vendors would travel transnationally, the former for reasons of leisure and the latter for reasons of commerce. Throughout the 1990s, handicraft vendors commented, "The [local handicraft] market was part of the world market," that they and their "artisan products will travel freely around the world." Maya vendors from San Antonio Aguas Calientes, the town from which most handicraft vendors in Antigua come, cheered for the San

Antonio Spurs NBA basketball team and said that through "television and basketball and the Saint Anthony, the two San Antonios are united." Such comments are illustrative of the complementary process that Stephen Gudeman describes as localization and globalization, which "instantiates the dialect of community and market or the tension between keeping identity and the base, and spreading ties to others and accumulating capital" (2001: 20).

Given their interpretation of the neoliberal rhetoric in the mass media, what vendors experienced, however, was not what they anticipated. The Philippine merchants, whom Matejowsky describes elsewhere in this volume, by contrast have positively experienced neoliberal change. According to Maya vendors, instead of a wide-open social and economic world, they encountered more restrictions. Most complained of facing increased travel restrictions. This was based on their unsuccessful attempts to get visas to Mexico, the United States, Canada, and Europe. Central America is, however, more open, since residents of Central American countries do not need visas. In fact, since 1998, Central American tourists to Guatemala have increased from 208,145 persons to 442,889 persons. For the first time, the number of Salvadoran tourists, 317,108, surpassed U.S. tourists to Guatemala, who numbered 220,540[5] (Banco de Guatemala 2005).

An additional complaint of vendors is the decline of sales. This data, coming from vendors, is very suspect, especially since they try to avoid showing any signs of success to avoid the jealousy of their peers. Even more so than handicraft vendors in permanent marketplaces (Little 2004a), *ambulantes* and other street vendors are self-conscious about flaunting their successes. Envy, a classic divisive element in small-scale Mesoamerican communities (see Foster 1979), can wreak havoc among street vendors. Not only do street vendors downplay their economic successes, they also support one another informally by protecting themselves from thieves, sharing food, and passing on whatever information they gather about police sweeps to clear vendors from public places (see Little 2002).

Colloredo-Mansfield's (2002) thesis offers another way of looking at the street vendors' complaints about the closing of international borders and the difficulty of getting visas. His thesis is that within the neoliberal economy subordinated classes, wage laborers and street vendors, are not necessarily reduced into competition wars among themselves that lead to a winner-take-all position. In the case presented here, competition in the neoliberal economy does not necessarily weaken vendors in the face of the Ladino-run municipal government's anti-street-vending policy. To be clear, handicraft vendors do want to make money, but they rationally try to balance the quest for profit with the social and political conditions in which they sell.

Police repression (described above) and victimization by criminals are other complaints that street vendors have about the "neoliberal world" in which they work. Robberies of vendors are not reported in the press, nor are the authorities responsive to vendors who file theft reports. This was the case when masked thieves driving a pickup truck robbed a Kaqchikel Maya family of street vendors of all their merchandise. When the family reported it to the police, they were told that they should not have been selling on the street. Sensational crimes against tourists are also reported. For example, on August 24, 1997, the newspaper *La Prensa Libre* published the first of several reports about Antigua's roles as cocaine and marijuana distribution and sales centers. On June 14, 1998, a Chilean tourist on an organized tour was shot to death in La Merced church in broad daylight. And a January 16, 2004, Warden Message from the U.S. Embassy warns that "armed individuals have robbed a hostel, a restaurant, and a private home. These crimes may be an anomaly in Antigua, but should be considered during any visits." Over the years, these reports of violent crimes have contrasted with the tourism industry's image of Antigua as a quiet town, not a city struggling with theft, gangs, assault, rape, and other crimes.

Thieves affect how vendors use Antigua. Instead of being composed of different zones, based on economic potential, places in the city are reconceptualized according to how safe they are for tourists and vendors themselves. As *ambulantes* walk from tourism sites to hotels and restaurants to hawk their handicrafts, they vigilantly watch out for thieves. The Spanish colonial church ruins on the outskirts of Antigua are viewed apprehensively as dangerous places. The Cerro de la Cruz (Hill of the Cross), which overlooks Antigua and is a popular place for locals and tourists to look at the city and picnic, is considered so dangerous by vendors that they do not sell on the hill or the path leading to it.

The tourism police have also delineated the hill as a dangerous place, but will now accompany groups of tourists electing to go there. Even though the police-accompanied tours to the Cerro de la Cruz make the trip significantly safer, vendors do not sell on the hill or along the path to it, since they do not enjoy police protection from thieves. Moreover, vendors who cross paths with these police officers and tourists have been fined and some have been arrested, accused of being thieves themselves.

Another failure of neoliberalism, according to vendors, is the loss of public vending spaces, described above. For them, this loss contradicts the open-market ideology of neoliberalism. With the city officials' view that public space should be devoid of vendors has also come the labeling of handicraft vendors as criminals. Even worse, as vendors explain it, has

Figure 12.2 Plaza del Carmen. Cerro de la Cruz is the hill in background to the north. Source: Walter E. Little.

been that the police have increasingly targeted street vendors as criminals or suspected criminals who have to be removed from Antigua in order to reestablish order and tranquility. There are no records of police arrests of vendors. Vendors, who have been jailed for theft, have later been released with no charges pressed. For example, as one man spent three weeks in jail, his family contacted human rights lawyers and had me take notes and food to him because they were afraid that they too would be arrested. In the end, he was released without any explanation or apologies. Many vendors report that tourism police pickup trucks pull up behind them and grab their merchandise. To recover it, they must report to the police station and pay a 300 quetzal (roughly $40) fine. Vendors claim that they rarely receive all their merchandise—some do not recover any of it.

Negotiations with City Hall

Since the formation of CORAGUA, *ambulantes* and other street vendors have worked through legal channels. Alliances are formed with a national-level vendor (FENVEMEGUA) and labor/worker (CGTG) organizations to improve collective-bargaining leverage. The vendors' organizing efforts culminated with a series of letters to the mayor, the United Nations in Guatemala Office of Human Rights and the Guatemalan Congress in May and June 2004, and several meetings with Antigua's mayor, Cesar Antonio Siliesar, in June and July 2004.

On May 11, vendors wrote to Mayor Siliesar, explaining that their human rights were being violated according to the national constitution and that they wanted to schedule a meeting. Among the letters that followed this one were those written to the United Nations in Guatemala Office of the Human Rights attorney on May 21 and two letters to the congressman who heads the Municipal Affairs Committee. The letter to the human rights attorney describes that the municipality and tourism police treat them like animals, take their merchandise, and "hit them brutally." The letter denounces the countrywide practice of incarcerating vendors and the government's manipulation of the mass media to negatively portray vendors, oppose the threats, seizures of merchandise, removal from vending locals, and fines. Two other letters followed. On June 2, vendors complained that the municipality treats them as delinquents and foreigners, when many of their families are from the area and have sold handicrafts for years. Some vendors reported that municipal police and other officials had physically attacked them and that their merchandise was taken and not returned. In a June 11 letter, vendors complained that they were being forced to sell near trash cans, treated as "obstinate and stubborn *indios*."

In the May 21 letters to the congressman vendors complained of nationwide abuses by municipal police, fines, loss of merchandise, violent assaults, and murders, and wrote that in Antigua the mayor ordered tourism police to remove vendors, fine them, and seize merchandise. When recovering merchandise, the police increased the fines and the vendors discovered missing merchandise, which they later saw worn or used by police officers' family members.

Quite possibly these letters had an impact on the mayor and motivated the city council's decision to agree to meet with the vendors. The meetings, however, between the mayor and street vendors was unprecedented in the memories of the oldest vendors, who were elderly women sixty years of age and older. None of these women recalls an Antigua mayor meeting and negotiating with vendors about the city's policies on street vending. At the first meeting on June 12, the mayor proposed that the vendors establish a permanent, open-air marketplace on the edge of the city in Plaza Isabel. After the meeting the vendors went en masse to the plaza and planned their strategies for the next meeting, in which they would reject the Plaza Isabel marketplace. In the meetings that followed on June 19 and 27 and July 10, vendors countered that they rejected the Plaza Isabel location, preferring either the Tanque de La Unión or the Predio, which was where the Guatemalan National Guard had been stationed. The latter is located in the Governor's Palace, along with the national police department offices, and across the Central Plaza from City Hall and the tourism police office. The mayor, countering that the Tanque de la Unión was unacceptable and that only the governor could make any decisions regarding the Predio, offered that the vendors sell on weekends in the Plaza del Carmen, after the city had expelled the unauthorized food vendors selling there. He reiterated that the Plaza Isabel could still be used.

In response to the mayor's meetings, from June through September, vendors held regular planning meetings in the Spanish colonial ruins, La Recolación, in order to discuss two interrelated issues. The first regarded public space in Antigua, who has rights to use it, and how it can be used. The second regarded how to keep Antigua safe and clean. Vendors also argued that the Plaza Isabel is too far from the center of the city and, even worse, it is located next to administrative offices of the Guatemalan Social Security Office and the Ministry of Health, two places that tourists never visit. They argued that the busy road makes it difficult for tourists to cross on foot and that even if they come they risk being pickpocketed or mugged because the police do not patrol that area regularly. Vendors explained that they too were worried about thieves operating in that area.

They agreed that the Plaza del Carmen is an acceptable location and one that tourists will visit. However, they are allowed to sell only two days per week, which is not enough for them to support their families. They agreed to lobby the municipality to permit them to sell as ambulatory vendors the other days of the week. Maintaining the traditional arguments, described in the sections above, they offered to limit their numbers, carry official identification, and pay the city for a reasonably priced monthly permit. In addition, they would respect the times and places that they and the municipality agreed to, just as long as they could sell Monday through Friday in locations frequented by tourists.

Economics of Public Space

In order to better understand the negotiations between vendors and city hall, it is necessary to review the economic conditions of street vending in Antigua. Although all Maya handicraft vendors have historically appealed to the city that their role is a "traditional" part of Antigua and tourists have come to expect them, the vending locations under negotiation are not economically or ideologically neutral.

For street vendors, daily earnings vary dramatically from nothing to several hundred quetzals (US$1 = 7.8 quetzales). My observations of vendor earnings and interviews with vendors indicate that most monthly average earnings ranged in 2004 from $90 to $375. Vendors also have a number of expenses, including bus fare to Antigua, rent or hotel accommodations, and food. Vendors from nearby Kaqchikel Maya towns pay roughly $0.15 one-way bus fare, while those from more remote areas of the country will pay $1 or more for the one-way ticket. These vendors also have to pay rent for the nights they spend in Antigua, since sleeping in the street is too dangerous. Rent in a budget traveler hotel, for only space in the corridor, is $1 per night, compared to an average of $112 per month for a small apartment that can be shared with family members and friends. Food expenses average about $3 per day or less if the vendor makes no sales. Their costs for the merchandise they sell are relatively low, because most of it is on consignment. Vendors also include merchandise that they themselves and members of their extended families weave or fabricate.

The mayor's proposal to establish a handicraft marketplace in the Plaza Isabel would have dire economic consequences. The optimal selling area for street vendors is roughly a three-block radius from the Central Plaza. This space has the greatest concentration of tourism-oriented businesses (hotels, restaurants, curio shops, Spanish language schools) and Spanish colonial ruins. Plaza Isabel falls three blocks out of this optimal selling zone. Unlike the handicrafts market and its annex, which are located behind a popular fried chicken restaurant, next to the utilitarian marketplace, and en route to the municipal bus station, there are no such places near the Plaza Isabel that would attract tourists. Street vendors were cognizant that conceding to the city's proposal would effectively reduce their now meager earnings to nothing. The compromise with the city to use the Plaza del Carmen on weekends places vendors firmly within the tourism zone. In fact, this location represents a space that conforms nicely to tourist, Maya, and Ladino sentiments about the use of public space, and even to conceptualizations of landscape. From the vendors' perspective, it is in a location where tourists pass when going to the plaza, hotels, and restaurants, and it is on the route that the tourism police use to escort tourists to the Cerro de la Cruz. From the Ladino politicians' perspective, it removes the vendors from the Central Plaza and allows for better surveillance of them. Vendors argue, however, that being restricted from weekday ambulatory sales prohibits them from their best selling opportunities, which are to Spanish students and independent tourists who stay in midpriced and more expensive hotels.

Scholarship on the social construction of space (Bourdieu 1977; Castells 1983; Harvey 1990; Lefebvre 1991; Low 2000, 2004; and others), as Low (2000: 36) points out, has focused on "linking political economic theory with the social production of the built environment." Although Low adds to this analysis a discussion of "spatializing culture," socially constructed space of touristic Antigua cannot be understood without taking into consideration the economic consumption of that space. When vendors make ideological arguments about their tradition of handicraft selling and their relationship with Antigua and its Spanish colonial architecture, they are demonstrating what they know about how Antigua is consumed. Consumption correlates with a clearly demarcated geographic area that has been socially constructed through the processes of international tourism.

When city officials made a sweep of Antigua in September 2004, removing vendors from public streets and plazas, fining them, and seizing merchandise, the vendors were given a final ultimatum to contain their sales to the official handicraft marketplace (which was and is full), and to sell weekdays at Plaza Isabel and weekends at Plaza del Carmen, or to cease selling in Antigua entirely. This event caused vendors to reevaluate their negotiation strategies with city hall and their street-selling tactics.

Self-Representation and the Reconceptualization of Public Space

In light of the increased vigilance of the tourism police, street vendors now sell clandestinely to tourists, always keeping an eye out for the police. The younger vendors pose as high school and university students, keeping their goods in backpacks. Women pretend they are en route to the market to buy food or other goods, hiding their merchandise under their *su't* (rectangular cloth used to carry items, including babies). Men, too, carry smaller amounts of goods in backpacks and small cases, as they act as if they are going to work or to the bank.

Vendor-friendly businesspeople note the furtive sales tactics that street vendors employ and consider the city's restrictions unfair and harmful to the general economic health of the city. These individuals allow street vendors to enter their businesses to escape the police. I consider this to be one of those ironies of neoliberalism that Warren and Jackson note allow indigenous people to escape local paternalistic power structures. Recognizing the consumptive interests of international tourists, competitors join together and attempt to thwart the local government's policies, hence supporting Colloredo-Mansfield's thesis about neoliberalism and competition.

There is, however, an additional irony with regard to the effects of neoliberalism, as street vendors interpret it. When vendors realized that they were going to have limited success convincing the mayor and city councilors that they were part of an important ongoing tradition and were a powerful economic resource that drew tourist consumers to Antigua, they developed a new argument for staying and selling in the city. Since the mid-1990s vendors have complained to me about crime and confided about being victims of it. In July 2004 and since then (as of February 2005), vendors have played on local concerns about petty and more violent crime. When they meet with the mayor, they agree with city officials and both vendor-friendly and vendor-unfriendly businesspeople that Antigua has become a dangerous place. Public space—the Spanish colonial ruins, the plazas and parks, and the streets—is reconceptualized as unsafe. Vendors argue that the tourism police are stretched too thin and cannot possibly protect Antigua's residents and tourist guests. The irony here is that for decades vendors have sold the handicrafts in a city that was defined by them and by tourists as safe, which sometimes contradicted the non-Maya municipal government's perception of them as nuisances or petty criminals who threatened the cleanliness or order of the city.

The vendors' interpretations of neoliberal discourse, the effects of crime, and the place within local power structures and international tourism have contributed to their social reconstruction of public space and their new identity within that space. In a strategy to change the opinions of city officials, tourism police officers, and unfriendly businesses, Maya street vendors have devised a new role, a new identity: *protector* of Antigua's residents and guests. They argue that Antigua is less safe because the vendors are not present. Allowing them to sell in public places will once again make the social space of Antigua safe. The vendors offer to work with the police and businesses to aid tourists and catch criminals. Hence, within a competitive economic field, competitors themselves are creating a new collective identity to contend with what they perceive of as the negative effects of neoliberalism and a repressive local government. This new identity and social role, like their traditional identity and economic role, works within a specific, socially constructed space that is tied to the physical places of Antigua, effectively transforming the conceptual landscape held by Mayas, Ladinos, and tourists.

Conclusion

Mayas, Ladinos, and even tourists have different perspectives about how to use Antigua. In comparison with the kinds of places that have been discussed by Setha Low, the Latin American plaza in Costa Rica (2000) and gated U.S. communities (2004), and most other scholars of the social construction of space (Bourdieu 1977; Castells 1983; Harvey 1990; Lefebvre 1991),[6] these distinct social groups conceive of Antigua as a place that is architecturally stuck in time, a Spanish colonial city that was ravaged by earthquakes. Municipal and vendor ideologies of public space and corresponding economic uses of that space—as practiced social, economic, and political space, where vendors are part of the landscape—are what give the Antiguan landscape its unique character.

Maya handicraft vendors in Antigua, Guatemala, sell within a highly ambiguous and often contradictory socioeconomic space that is multiply layered by local and international economic and political interests. Being a successful vendor depends on much more than being a good salesperson because of the complex economic and political context in which the vendors sell. The places—marketplaces, public parks and plazas, and streets—where these vendors sell to thousands of tourists over the course of a year are highly contested by street vendors themselves, shopkeepers, hotel and restaurant owners, tourists, and local residents. Over the last ten years, amid growing violent crime, two city administrations have reorganized Antigua's public spaces in ways that contradict both neoliberal ideologies and Maya concepts of how public spaces are conceived of and used. This social re/construction of public space negatively impacts the economic success of vendors and confuses tourists. At the same time, it has opened new ways for vendors to organize and speak of their use of public spaces.

Vendors see the city administrators' policies regarding street selling and the regulation of public spaces as distinctly anti-indigenous and antineoliberal. Vendors also see neoliberal discourses of free markets, open borders, and deregulation as mere fantasies that have undermined their personal and economic security. Rather than argue that street vending is an indigenous tradition that is more than five hundred years old or that within an open neoliberal state vendors should have access to public spaces, the vendors use discourses on crime and safety to convince city officials and merchants they should be allowed to sell in the parks and on the streets of Antigua, because they can make the city safer for residents and tourists. The vendors' focus on crime and safety reflects a new strategy to oppose the city administrators' policies of public-space use. Hence, within the social reconstruction of Antigua's public spaces and neoliberal politics, vendors develop new discourses and strategies that evade traditional and economic justifications in order to sell in more lucrative public places. By redefining their roles as protectors and by reconceptualizing public space, they hope to obscure their economic motivations and secure their traditional selling places. In effect, they are trying to maintain a particular conceptualization of Antigua that corresponds with their ideal places to sell and their idealizations of their place and economic activities in this urban landscape.

Notes

1. This chapter is based on ongoing ethnographic research that began in 1992 and has continued annually to the present. It has been funded by the Wenner-Gren Foundation, Fulbright IIE, and the University at Albany, SUNY. Data was collected through participant observation, tape-recorded interviews and conversations with vendors, tape recording of public municipal meetings, and photographing vendor-related events. The author is responsible for all translations from Kaqchikel Maya and Spanish into English.

2. According to United Nations and World Bank economic indicators, overall economic conditions have generally declined throughout Latin America since 1990 (unstats.un.org/unsd/). The situation in Guatemala is one of the worst in the Western Hemisphere. The United Nations' 2004 *Human Development Report* ranks Guatemala 121 out of 177 countries worldwide, while its neighbor Mexico merits a rank of 53 with regard to quality of life. In Guatemala, 56.2 percent of the population lives in extreme poverty. The Human Development Sector Manage-

ment Unit (2003: 33) report of the World Bank explains that Mayas comprise "58% of the poor and 72% of the extreme poor. Over three-quarters of the indigenous population live in poverty, as compared with 41% of the non-indigenous. Poverty is also deeper and more severe among the indigenous."

3. For a decade, I have been surveying tourists (610 people between 1997 and 2006) about their perceptions of Antigua, and have found that tourists invariably consider Maya vendors part of the scenery and expect to see them, even if they do not particularly like their selling techniques.

4. For instance, the Lonely Planet guidebooks, *Guatemala* by Conner Gory (2001) and *Guatemala, Belize & Yucatan: La Ruta Maya* by Tom Brosnahan (1994), as well as other guidebooks; the travel industry trade magazine *Recommend* (October 1998); advertisements, such as those for Marriott Hotels and DHL; and dozens of postcards and picture books associate Maya vendors with Antigua's Spanish colonial architecture.

5. Tourism statistics for Guatemala are controversial among handicraft vendors and those who run tourism-related businesses (travel/tour agencies, Spanish schools, restaurants). Since 1998 the total number of reported tourists entering the country has gradually increased from 632,683 persons to 890,167 persons in 2004 (Banco de Guatemala 2005).

6. Notable exceptions are Marc Augé (1995) and Michel de Certeau (1984), who treat places as consumable and focus on how places are used. As Antigua is a tourism site, its residents and workers are especially oriented to presenting the place in terms of something that can be consumed.

References

Augé, M. 1995. *Non-places: Introduction to an Anthropology of Supermodernity*. London: Verso.

Babb, F. E. 1998. *Between Field and Cooking Pot: The Political Economy of Marketwomen in Peru*. 2nd ed. Austin: University of Texas Press.

Bastos, S., and M. Camus. 2003. *Entre el Mecapal y el Cielo: Desarrollo del Movimiento Maya en Guatemala*. Guatemala: FLACSO and Cholsamaj.

Berman, M. 1982. *All that Is Solid Melts in Air*. New York: Penguin.

Banco de Guatemala. 2005. Boletín Estadístico. At www.banguat.gob.gt/estaeco/boletin/.

Bourdieu, P. 1977. *Outline of a Theory of Practice*. Cambridge: Cambridge University Press.

Bromley, R. 2000. "Street Vending and Public Policy." *International Journal of Sociology and Social Policy* 20 (1/2): 1–29.

Caldeira, T. 2000. *City of Walls: Crime, Segregation, and Citizenship in Sao Paulo*. Berkeley: University of California Press.

Carey Jr., D. 2001. *Our Elders Teach Us: Maya-Kaqchikel Historical Perspectives: Xkib'ij Kan Qate' Qatata'*. Tuscaloosa: University of Alabama Press.

Castañeda, Q. E. 1997. "On the Correct Training of Indios in the Handicraft

Market at Chichén Itzá: Tactics and Tactility of Gender, Class, Race and State." *Journal of Latin American Anthropology* 2 (2): 106–43.

Casaús Arzú, M. E. 1998. *La Metamorfosis del Racismo en Guatemala*. Guatemala: Editorial Cholsamaj.

Castells, M. 1983. *The City and the Grassroots*. Berkeley: University of California Press.

Certeau, M. de. 1984. *The Practice of Everyday Life*. Berkeley: University of California Press.

Chibnick, M. 2003. *Crafting Tradition: The Making and Marketing of Oaxacan Wood Carvings*. Austin: University of Texas Press.

Clark, G., ed. 1988. *Traders versus the State: Anthropological Approaches to Unofficial Economies*. Boulder, CO: Westview Press.

———. 1994. *Onions Are My Husband: Survival and Accumulation by West African Market Women*. Chicago: University of Chicago Press.

Cojtí Cuxil, D. 1998. *Ri Maya' Moloj pa Iximulew (El Movimiento Maya en Guatemala)*. Guatemala: Editorial Cholsamaj.

Colloredo-Mansfeld, R. 2002. "An Ethnography of Neoliberalism: Understanding Competition in Artisan Economies." *Current Anthropology* 43 (1): 113–37.

Cross, J. C. 1998. *Informal Politics: Street Vendors and the State in Mexico City*. Stanford, CA: Stanford University Press.

Cross, J. 2000. "Street Vendors, and Postmodernity: Conflict and Compromise in the Global Economy." *International Journal of Sociology and Social Policy* 20 (1/2): 29–51.

Dannhaeuser, N. 1989. "Marketing in Developing Urban Areas." In *Economic Anthropology*, ed. S. Plattner, 222–53. Stanford, CA: Stanford University Press.

England, N. 2003. "Maya Language Revival and Revitalization Politics: Linguists and Linguistic Ideologies." *American Anthropologist* 105 (4): 733–773.

Field, L. W. 1999. *The Grimace of Macho Ratón: Artisans, Identity, and Nation in Late-Twentieth-Century Western Nicaragua*. Durham, NC: Duke University Press.

Fischer, E. F. 2001. *Cultural Logics and Global Economies: Maya Identity in Thought and Practices*. Austin: University of Texas Press.

Fischer, E. F., and R. M. Brown, eds. 1996. *Maya Cultural Activism in Guatemala*. Austin: University of Texas Press.

Foster, G. 1979. *Tzintzuntzan: Mexican Peasants in a Changing World*. Prospect Heights, IL: Waveland Press.

Goldin, L. 1987. "De plaza a mercado: La expresión de dos sistemas conceptuales en la organización de los mercados del occidente de Guatemala." *Anales de Antropología* 24:243–61.

Gudeman, S. 2001. *The Anthropology of Economy: Community, Market and Culture*. Oxford: Blackwell.

Hale, C. 2002. "Does Multiculturalism Menace?: Governance, Cultural Rights, and the Politics of Identity in Guatemala." *Journal of Latin American Studies* 34:485–524.

Harvey, D. 1990. *The Condition of Postmodernity*. Blackwell.
Jameson, F. 1984. *Postmodernism, or the Cultural Logic of Late Capitalism*. Durham, NC: Duke University Press.
Kapchan, D. 1996. *Gender on the Market: Moroccan Women and the Revoicing of Tradition*. Philadelphia: University of Pennsylvania Press.
Lefebvre, H. 1991. *The Production of Space*. Trans. D. Nicholson-Smith. London: Blackwell.
Little, W. E. 2002. "Selling Strategies and Social Relations among Mobile Maya Handicrafts Vendors." *Research in Economic Anthropology* 21:61–95.
———. 2004a. *Mayas in the Marketplace: Tourism, Globalization, and Cultural Identity*. Austin: University of Texas Press.
———. 2004b. "Outside of Social Movements: Dilemmas of Indigenous Handicrafts Vendors in Guatemala." *American Ethnologist* 31 (1): 43–59.
Low, S. 2000. *On the Plaza: The Politics of Public Space and Culture*. Austin: University of Texas Press.
———. 2004. *Behind the Gates: Life, Security, and the Pursuit of Happiness in Fortress America*. New York: Routledge.
Lutz, C. 1994. *Santiago de Guatemala, 1541–1773: City, Caste, and the Colonial Experience*. Norman: University of Oklahoma Press.
Meisch, L. 2002. *Andean Entrepreneurs: Otavalo Merchants and Musicians in the Global Arena*. Austin: University of Texas Press.
Nash, J. 2001. *Mayan Visions: The Quest for Autonomy in an Age of Globalization*. New York, Routledge.
Nelson, D. 1999. *A Finger in the Wound: Body Politics in Quincentennial Guatemala*. Berkeley: University of California Press.
Smith, C. A. 1990. *Guatemalan Indians and the State: 1540–1988*. Austin: University of Texas Press.
Stoller, P. 2002. *Money Has No Smell: The Africanization of New York City*. Chicago: University of Chicago Press.
Swetnam, J. 1975. "The Open Gateway: Social and Economic Interaction in a Guatemalan Marketplace." PhD diss., University of Pennsylvania.
Warren, K. B. 1998. *Indigenous Movements and Their Critics*. Princeton, NJ: Princeton University Press.
Warren, K. B., and J. E. Jackson, eds. 2002a. *Indigenous Movements, Self-Representation, and the State in Latin America*. Austin: University of Texas Press.
———. 2002b. "Introduction: Studying Indigenous Activism in Latin America." In *Indigenous Movements, Self-Representation, and the State in Latin America*, ed. K. B. Warren and J. E. Jackson, 1–46. Austin: University of Texas Press.
Watanabe, J. 1992. *Maya Saints and Souls in a Changing World*. Austin: University of Texas Press.
Weismantel, M. 2001. *Cholas and Pishtacos: Stories of Race and Sex in the Andes*. Chicago: University of Chicago Press.

13

The Commercial Transformation of a Philippine Cityscape
A Case from San Fernando City, La Union

TY MATEJOWSKY

URBAN LANDSCAPES THROUGHOUT THE DEVELOPING world are increasingly exposed to the transformative influence of Western market forces. As the macroprocesses of neoliberalism and globalization take root in less developed countries (LDCs), the built morphology of many towns and cities begins to take on a more contemporary edge (Miller 1997). Central to this change is a proliferation of large trade facilities such as supermarkets, fast-food outlets, warehouse clubs, shopping malls, department stores, and giant discount chains (Dannhaeuser 1997; Matejowsky 2006; Watson 1997). The emergence of these new retail forms in the provincial regions of advanced LDCs works to reshape the physical growth of urban centers, alter prevailing land use patterns, and transform the sensibilities of local inhabitants (Dandekar 1998). Moreover, it poses a mounting threat to the viability of many of the small-scale trade institutions that have traditionally defined municipal commerce (Collins and Wingard 2000).

Until recently, modern retail outlets were viewed as incompatible with the socioeconomic realities of trade life outside major LDC urban centers. It was noted that local commerce could only marginally accommodate Western-style commercial enterprises (Kaynak 1982). Factors such as fragmented market supply channels, weak public infrastructure, and poor sanitation conditions worked against these types of ventures (Kaynak 1982). Moreover, an overall lack of purchasing power and the need for flexible credit arrangements by consumers favored small-scale trade operations (e.g., market vendors, hawkers, and small street stores) over large retail facilities (Davis 1973; McGee and Yeung 1977). As advances in global marketing, technology, consumer choice, and mass communication expand beyond major LDC cities, the viability of modern commercial operations in outlying communities takes on new relevance.

To shed light on how the spread of contemporary trade establishments affects the physical and commercial landscapes of provincial cities within a developing context, this chapter examines the recent experience of San Fernando City, the Philippines. The Asia-Pacific region, in general, and the Philippines, more specifically, presents an ideal setting for this type of research. A growing body of work compiled by anthropologists and others has documented the remarkable rise of urban East and Southeast Asia over the last few decades (Bishop, Phillips, and Yeo 2003; Drakakis-Smith 2002; Terry 2002; Yeung 2000). The advance of globalization and the rapid economic growth that it engenders have created conditions across the Far East favoring the emergence of a middle class and scale economies. This market climate has, in turn, facilitated the spread of large retail ventures. In the Philippines, the presence of mega-malls, twenty-four-hour convenience stores, and fast-food restaurants has been most conspicuous in Metro Manila (Tiglao 1994). By the mid-1990s, enterprises of this type had begun to dot the landscapes of medium-range cities. The encroachment of modern commercial facilities onto the Philippine hinterland has presented both challenges and opportunities for local communities looking to balance economic growth with quality-of-life concerns (Cohen 2004; Matejowsky 2000).

This chapter provides a microlevel account of (1) how state-of-the-art retail facilities emerge within a developing setting and (2) how their spread redefines the physical and commercial landscapes of LDC urban centers. Information collected through household surveys, participant observation, street surveys, archival research, and other field methods adds ethnographic depth to a process that is transforming communities worldwide.

After presenting a community profile of San Fernando City, I will describe the contemporary organization of local commerce. Next, I will detail the move toward retail modernization in San Fernando over the past thirty years and feature background information about those developments at the forefront of this trend. I will then examine the effects of retail modernization on the city's built character and entrenched trade community of independent street stores and market vendors. Finally, I will summarize the findings of this chapter and offer critical commentary on how San Fernando's cityscape experienced this new expansion of modern retail forms.

Two general points should be made before addressing these issues in more detail. First, for the purposes of this chapter, I conceive of landscape as the natural and man-made surroundings that provide the setting for day-to-day human experience, whether physical or ideational. In this respect, landscapes are not static, but rather dynamic domains shaped by myriad environmental, socioeconomic, and political forces. Specific attention focuses on the evolving nature of landscapes as they relate to global market influences much like Little's contribution to this volume. Here, however, transformations to the physical landscape, land use patterns, and built forms are emphasized over changing public space concerns or perceptions by local inhabitants. Second, to avoid unnecessary repetition, I use the terms *cityscape*, *urban landscape*, and *built environment/morphology* interchangably as generalized synonyms to describe the densely constructed and man-made formations within the natural environment that provide the context for everyday human interaction and exchange. Similarly, *commercial landscape* refers to the linked commercial activities, institutions, and patterns that define trade life in a given locale.

San Fernando City: A Community Profile

San Fernando City lies along the Lingayen Gulf some 300 km north of Metro Manila on the main Philippine island of Luzon (see fig. 13.1). It occupies a west-central section of La Union province with a topography characterized by coastal lowlands and a mountainous interior. Most of San Fernando's 100,000 residents live in one of the twenty low-lying *barangays* (precincts) paralleling the north-south shoreline. Given its seaside locale and white beaches, the city serves as a popular destination for foreign tourists.

San Fernando's *población* (urban center) inhabits a harbor area along La Union's coastal plain. Thanks to a strict enforcement of the municipal code and intense feelings of civic pride, San Fernando presents an ideal model of urban living in the northern Philippines (Cruz 1988). During the week, downtown bustles with activity as streams of pedestrians and vehicles move along the Manila North Road (MNR). Many of San Fernando's more prominent family-run street stores are found on this busy roadway. The *población*'s western edge looks out onto Poro Point (233 ha), a semi-industrialized peninsula that is home to the Wallace Air Station (167 ha). The base has been occupied by the U.S. military on a more or less permanent basis from the early 1900s to 1991.

Taking up an entire city block at the heart of downtown is the pedestrian-friendly San Fernando Supermarket. The bilevel public marketplace serves as the town's primary center for local vending and small-scale trade. With a total sales area of 4,000 m^2, the complex is subdivided into approximately four hundred trader spaces that are regulated by the municipal government. The top level accommodates small-scale enterprises like beauty salons, repair shops, dress boutiques, and dry-goods merchants. Wet dealers selling fish, meat, fruit, vegetables, and groceries are housed on the more

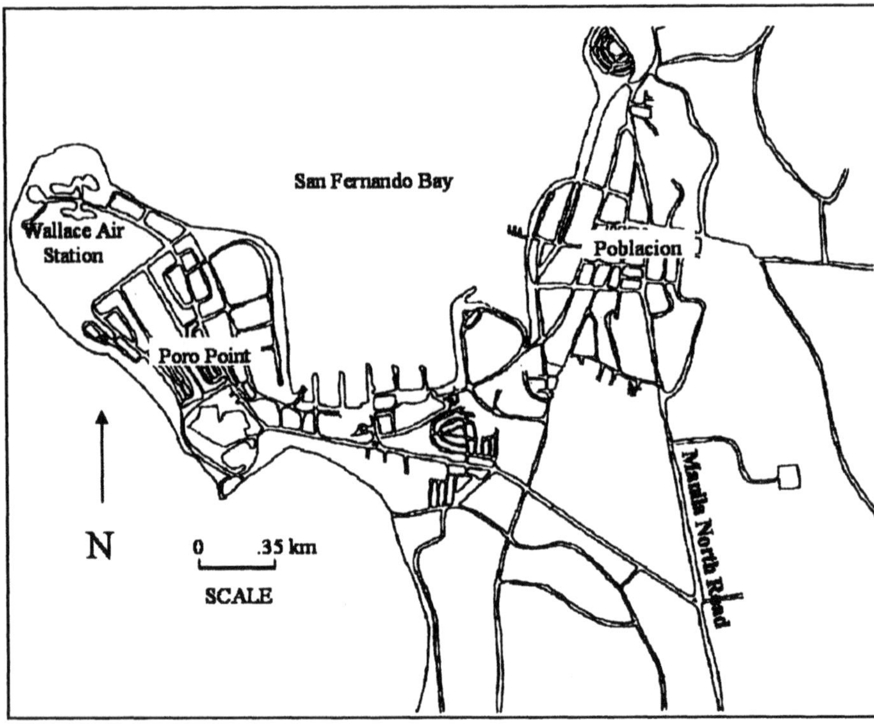

Figure 13.1 San Fernando City. Source: Ty Matejowsky.

accessible first floor. Offering few consumer amenities, the marketplace's interior is often dark, hot, and reeking of unrefrigerated food.

The basic organization of urban commerce in San Fernando generally corresponds to the dual-sector economic model (Dannhaeuser 1989; Smith 1989). Locals rely on small trade outlets to meet everyday employment and consumption needs. Over the years, the vendors, microenterprises, and small shops housed in and around the downtown San Fernando Supermarket have profoundly shaped area commerce. In contrast, more expensive and durable items come from the town's larger and highly capitalized retail ventures. While fewer in number, these more sophisticated enterprises remain competitive through the integrated supply linkages they maintain with corporate firms headquartered in Metro Manila.

Broadly speaking, most small trade ventures in San Fernando are controlled by native Filipinos with an Ilocano ancestry. Ilocanos represent the third-largest ethnic group in the Philippines and are recognized for their hardworking and enterprising tendencies (Pertierra 1992). Aside from the local grocery trade, the majority of San Fernando's larger retail enterprises have ethnic Chinese owner-operators. This tight-knit minority group has never made up more than 5 percent of the total population yet it has remained a dynamic force in local commerce since the mid-nineteenth century.

Retail Modernization

San Fernando's experience with retail modernization has been characterized by the limited encroachment of vertically integrated market supply channels and large shopping facilities. Until recently, the local cityscape was defined by several blocks of unassuming, low-rise commercial buildings. Storefronts were minimally adorned beyond some basic signage. Interiors were poorly lit and reflected a no-frills, utilitarian approach to retailing. This traditional character was altered somewhat in the mid-1970s as a few subsectors of local commerce developed official linkages with outside manufacturers and distributors. The move by some appliance and electronics retailers to serve as exclusive brand dealers for national companies represented San Fernando's first step toward increased trade modernization.

The 1980s witnessed the arrival of a new multilevel department store and several modern grocery superettes in the downtown. Most of these large and air-conditioned ventures were operated by local ethnic Chinese firms formally linked to Manila-based suppliers. Their success soon attracted the attention of several national and multinational chains. A number of outside companies opened branch and franchise operations in the *población* in the late 1980s. Downtown San Fernando came to include a chain drugstore (Mercury Drug) and three modern fast-food eateries (Cindy's, Mister Donut, and Dunkin' Donuts). While these new outlets had managerial and service formats similar to their chain counterparts in Manila, they were relatively modest in terms of floor space and number of employees.

Collectively, the modern retail ventures that opened in San Fernando during the 1980s added a new texture to the *población*'s commercial fabric. Their contemporary design, service style, and name brands stood out against what was offered by the San Fernando Supermarket and independent merchant community. Notably, these new enterprises introduced many locals to consumer experiences heretofore available only in Metro Manila.

In many ways, however, these operations represented something less than the sum of their individual parts. Modern retail expansion in the 1970s and 1980s did little to alter the traditional dynamics of local commerce. Small-scale trade institutions remained vital, in part, because modern sector operations were unable to establish a major physical presence in the *población*. The best downtown retail spaces were already occupied by the Supermarket and established street stores. The city's jagged coastline and abruptly mountainous terrain also limited the availability of commercial real estate in and around the *población*. Further hindering the encroachment of modern commercial enterprises was the fact that these new ventures depended significantly on the patronage of nonlocal groups like foreign tourists and American military personnel from Wallace Air Station. Most San Fernandians still shopped for essential items at the conveniently located public marketplace or street stores. This reliance on nonlocal customers raised questions about how San Fernandians would respond to more ambitious commercial undertakings like shopping malls and giant discount chains. While residents would almost surely visit these new enterprises, it remained unknown if they had the purchasing power to support them.

Poro Point Special Economic Freeport Zone

Modern retail operations had an established but limited presence in San Fernando at the end of the 1980s. Over the next few years, however, many of the preconditions for increased commercial innovation took shape. First, by 1990, the community possessed an increasingly affluent middle class. Their newly realized prosperity contributed to a rise in the number of privately owned vehicles in San Fernando. As locals were able to get around more easily, properties outside of the *población*, especially those along the MNR, came to be reevaluated in terms of their commercial potential. Second, retail developers were now reasonably assured that large-scale retail ventures would prosper in San Fernando. This observation was based on the growing number of national and multinational firms that had successfully opened modern trade facilities in other provincial cities in recent years (Dannhaeuser 1997; Matejowsky 2002).

More than anything, however, it was the 1991 withdrawal of the U.S. military from its bases in the Philippines, including the Wallace Air Station on Poro Point, that marked a turning point for San Fernando's modern retail sector. While the American departure effectively sounded the death knell for local economies near the sprawling Subic Bay Naval Facility (Olongapo City, Zambales) and Clark Air Field (Angles City, Pampanga), San Fernando was spared an abrupt economic dislocation by the U.S. exit from the smaller Wallace installation (Kirk 1998). Unlike other base communities, San Fernando's economy was diversified enough to withstand the U.S. military's departure. Ultimately, it was the planned increase of investment activity along the recently demilitarized Poro Point that set the stage for a transformation in San Fernando's commercial and physical landscape.

In the summer of 1993, the Philippine government announced plans to redevelop the peninsula and reclaimed sections of San Fernando Bay into a specialized investment zone known as the Poro Point Special Economic Freeport Zone (PPSEFZ). This mixed-use economic area would include an eighteen-hole golf course, a casino, a seaport for cruise ships, and an upscale shopping center (Mendoza 1996). Families living along Poro Point were alarmed by the project because it called for their eventual resettlement. Downtown shopkeepers were concerned that the PPSEFZ would precipitate a major consumer exodus from the *población* as it was being hyped as greater San Fernando's new center of commercial growth.

For a time, a hollowed-out urban core seemed imminent. Yet, the prospect of the PPSEFZ's supplanting the *población* as the commercial heart of San Fernando appeared less and less certain as the months and years passed. Although never officially abandoned, work on the PPSEFZ became bogged down by a series of false starts and bureaucratic interruptions during the 1990s. These delays ultimately worked to the advantage of San Fernando's established trade community of store owners and independent merchants. They not only kept local retail life centralized in downtown, they also provided local interests a head start in gearing up for whatever new competition emerged within the PPSEFZ. In a very real sense, government plans to redevelop Poro Point sparked a new series of retail developments in and around San Fernando that reshaped aspects of the local cityscape without greatly undermining its traditional commercial character.

Retail Modernization (Mid-1990s)

San Fernando experienced an upsurge of retail modernization soon after the PPSEFZ proclamation of 1993. For the most part, this expansion took the form of ribbon development on the MNR. This growth did not so much reflect a coordinated effort on the part of local interests to preempt the PPSEFZ, but rather entailed individual firms' or groups' capitalizing on favorable market conditions. By 1994, a number of modern commercial projects were either under construction or in the planning stage for sites along the national highway. In terms of scale, design, accessibility, and innovations, these undertakings differed from most other downtown trade operations. The circumstances behind their development provide a backdrop against which the preliminary effects of retail modernization on the local landscape can be most accurately assessed.

The KC Mall

The first venture to gain local attention was the KC Mall—a multistory consumer facility to be located halfway between Poro Point and the *población* along the MNR. The mall was conceived as San Fernando's most complete one-stop shopping venue with two cinemas, a supermarket, and various high-end shops and boutiques. This ambitious project was the brainchild of the Lee brothers—four second-generation mestizo Chinese traders with backgrounds in the local construction and furniture trades. A rift developed among the Lees as one brother tried to seize control over the mall venture soon after the project was made public in 1994. Rather than emerging as the crowning achievement of local trade expansion in the mid-1990s, the never-completed KC Mall came to symbolize San Fernando's largely untapped commercial potential.

Fiesta Supermarket Chain

While many San Fernandians were put off by the infighting that ultimately derailed the KC Mall, such feelings quickly subsided with the successful start-up of Fiesta Supermarket. This grocery store chain was owned and operated by Flores-Bolong Ltd.—a family-run corporation with diverse business holdings in La Union. An important commercial player since the mid-1980s, Flores-Bolong Ltd. stood apart from other similar-sized companies in that its owners were not ethnic Chinese but rather native Ilocanos.

Fiesta Supermarket's flagship store opened in 1994 at a downtown site along the MNR. With a total floor space of 900 m^2, the Fiesta Supermarket stood apart from other groceries by offering innovations like air conditioning, a contemporary decor, automatic doors, and advanced checkout lanes. Not surprisingly, the store did a brisk business in its first few years of operation with roughly four thousand customers passing through its doors each day. In 1995, an additional Fiesta grocery was opened in downtown San Fernando. The new branch was smaller than its sister store but possessed nearly all the same consumer conveniences.

The opening of the Fiesta Warehouse Club in 1996 further consolidated the influence of Flores-Bolong Ltd. over the local grocery trade. The giant supermarket complex was situated a few kilometers north of the *población* along the MNR and maintained a sales area of some 2,000 m^2. Its modish facade concealed an array of new amenities like spacious aisles, track lighting, and bar-code scanners. The warehouse club catered primarily to wholesale customers with a clientele of over two hundred small neighborhood groceries spread throughout La Union. Although located some distance from the *población*, many urbanites were willing to journey out to the warehouse club because it promised a new type of retail experience.

Altogether, Fiesta Supermarket maintained a work force of approximately two hundred employees and was ranked as one of San Fernando's top taxpayers. The chain's success prompted other downtown groceries to follow its lead. Many of Fiesta's competitors began adopting those strategies and techniques that had proved effective for the company. This new approach to selling groceries was most conspicuously manifested in the structural improvements made to existing store facilities. By early 1997, there was a flurry of activity in the local supermarket trade as rival firms undertook renovations to their downtown operations. In most cases, these upgrades entailed the installation of new decors and increased floor space. As the *población*'s commercial character became increasingly modern, Fiesta began contemplating even grander schemes. Notably, its future development projects included a multilevel shopping mall on a 30 ha lot near Poro Point. The giant retail complex was to compete directly with the upscale mall planned for the PPSEFZ. As the effects of the 1997 Southeast Asian economic crisis made their way to San Fernando, however, the Fiesta mall project was indefinitely postponed.

Christ the King College Commercial Center

By far the most unanticipated modern retail development along the MNR in the mid-1990s was the bilevel strip mall established near the turnoff to Poro Point. Notably, this ambitious project was developed exclusively by San Fernando's Catholic diocese under the auspices of its local university: Christ the King College (CKC). Known collectively as the CKC Commercial Center, the mall became a focal point for modern retail-sector expansion at the local level.

The circumstances leading up to the opening of the retail strip in early 1997 were unusual, to say the least. As in many towns and cities in the Philippines, San Fernando's diocese controlled a large share of area real estate. Church properties were used mainly for religious and/or charitable purposes such as the construction of chapels, schools, and hospitals. While small tracts of land had been previously rented out for petty commerce and vending, few could have anticipated the local diocese moving so boldly into commercial retailing.

As local market conditions appeared primed for major retail investment in the early 1990s, many church holdings came to be seen as commercially underexploited. This new outlook came to light in late 1993 when word leaked out that the local diocese planned to redevelop a sizable parcel of church land just outside of the *población*. The project entailed the construction of a new branch campus for CKC and, more ambitiously, a two-story shopping center. A rather morbid note was that the property slated for strip mall development had served as San Fernando's main cemetery since the late nineteenth century and contained thousands of interred bodies.

Oddly enough, the diocese's plan met with little or no public resistance. In fact, it drew scant attention from local or national media outlets. The lack of controversy surrounding the project is perhaps best explained by the fact that it was the Catholic Church, an institution enjoying tremendous influence on the local level, developing the mall. Church officials imposed a two-year grace period for relatives to remove their kin from the cemetery. Families who could afford it began transferring their loved ones' remains to new locations for reburial. By 1995, all unclaimed bodies were exhumed by bulldozer and collectively reburied just north of the *población*.

Enough of the cemetery had been cleared by January 1996 so that primary work on the CKC Commercial Center could begin. The main structure of the strip mall was divided into twenty-six individual retail spaces. Each of the units shared identical dimensions (total floor space of 50 m^2) and a basic layout whereby business operations were housed on the first floor with office and storage facilities above. The bilevel structure sported a clean facade and was fronted by a sizable parking area. Because the asking monthly rent for each two-story space was $375, the local diocese stood to take in approximately $9,800 each month ($117,600 annually) in rental fees.

As construction progressed, church officials met with a number of local and nonlocal firms about leasing retail spaces within the CKC Commercial Center. Securing rental agreements initially proved difficult because store owners were hesitant about setting up shop outside the *población*. It was not until commitments from two Manila-based fast-food companies—Mister Donut and Giacomino's Pizza and Pasta—were secured that other firms followed suit and lease agreements for all the rental spaces were negotiated.

The CKC Commercial Center opened for business in early 1997. Given its prime location along the MNR and proximity to many of San Fernando's universities and holiday resorts, many of the commercial establishments in the strip mall catered to students, tourists, and highway travelers. Aside the from the sleek, new fast-food outlets, the shopping center also included a twenty-four-hour convenience store, a copy center, a video rental shop, several fashion boutiques, and shoe stores. The incongruity of the local Catholic Church's putting up a state-of-the-art shopping center on a converted cemetery notwithstanding, the CKC Commercial Center became one of San Fernando's most popular consumer attractions in the late 1990s.

Fast-Food Expansion

Following the lead of the Fiesta Supermarket chain and CKC Commercial Center, several other cutting-edge trade facilities began operations along the MNR in the mid-1990s. These new ventures were competing for a share of the community's burgeoning fast-food market. Within the span of two years, three of the country's most popular restaurant chains established outlets along or near the community's main business thoroughfare.

By 1997, San Fernando's commercial landscape had come to include outlets of McDonald's, Jollibee, and Chow King (Chinese fast food). The three restaurants were similar in terms of consumer services and amenities. One major difference was that the Jollibee was established not as a franchise enterprise like McDonald's and Chow King but as a branch outlet owned and operated by the company. The McDonald's franchise was secured by an ethnic Chinese family firm with diverse business holdings in San Fernando including groceries, electronics, and tobacco. Two brothers from a politically prominent Filipino family held the Chow King franchise. Another difference was that the McDonald's was situated just beyond the urban periphery across from the CKC Commercial Center while the Chow King and Jollibee were more centrally located within the *población*. Differences in operational style and location helped create distinctive clientele for each restaurant. McDonald's appealed more to highway travelers, foreign tourists, and college students, while Jollibee's customer pool was comprised mainly of urbanites and downtown office workers. Because it fronted a movie theater and bus depot, the twenty-four-hour Chow King was most popular among night owls and those arriving or departing from San Fernando via passenger line.

The impact of these modern eateries on the local character of urban life cannot be overstated. Their sleek design and splashy color schemes added a modern touch to the aesthetics of San Fernando's built environment. Their standardized service format and distinctive menu had an appeal that immediately resonated with San Fernandians (Matejowsky 2006). Popular not just for their food but also for their clean and cheerful atmospheres, McDonald's, Jollibee, and Chow King became trendy hangouts for local youth and families. So successful were the eateries, in fact, that within a few months of operation both McDonald's and Jollibee began plans to open additional restaurants in San Fernando.

Modern Trade Sector and Street Store Growth (Late 1990s)

Notwithstanding the KC Mall's failure, the opening of major consumer ventures like the Fiesta Supermarket chain, the CKC Commercial Center, and fast-food restaurants along the MNR in the mid-1990s did much to augment the presence of modern retail outlets within San Fernando's commercial landscape. This growth becomes apparent when quantitative factors such as changes in aggregate floor space and sales personnel among urban stores are taken into consideration.

Prior to the arrival of the supermarket chain, strip mall, and quick-service eateries, most of the *población's* independently owned shops were rather unassuming in terms of decor and operating style. These modest enterprises had only a few employees and limited floor space. Figures from the Department of Trade and Industry in San Fernando (DTI 1997) provide some indication of how this component of local commerce was structured.

The official data suggests that before 1996 the dimensions of San Fernando's independent merchant community broke down as follows: approximately three hundred street stores situated along downtown's primary and secondary commercial thoroughfares occupying an aggregate floor space of 14,950 m^2 (50 m^2 per store) that was supported by a total service personnel of some 1,800 individuals. Operating within this retail trade structure were twenty-seven commercial outlets (9 percent of all street stores) that could be considered distinctly modern in management style and consumer amenities. This specialized sector encompassed a total floor space of 1,600 m^2 (11 percent of the aggregate sales area) and had an average size of 59 m^2 per individual store. In addition, these more innovative enterprises were maintained by a staff of 202 employees (11 percent of all street store personnel).

By January 1998, as the most recent wave of retail modernization took effect, a somewhat different picture began to emerge. Based on data collected through a comprehensive street survey, it becomes apparent that San Fernando's street store community underwent significant growth inside the span of just two years. The opening of major ventures like the CKC Commercial Center, Fiesta Supermarket chain, and various fast-food outlets

Table 13.1. Dimensions of San Fernando City's Street Store Operations (1996 and 1998)

	1996—total	1996—modern sector	1998—total	1998—modern sector
Number of stores	299	27	330	56
Aggregate floor space	14,950 m2	1,600 m2	18,400 m2	3,450 m2
Aggregate sales force	1,794	202	2,012	414

contributed to this expansion. During this time, the number of street stores in San Fernando grew by some 10 percent to 330, and the sales area by a remarkable 23 percent to 18,400 m^2. What is more, the average size of local retail outlets increased to 56 m^2, up from 50 m^2, and the total number of sales personnel operating within this trade sector expanded to 2,012, a 12 percent increase from the aforementioned period.

More noteworthy is the effect these recent developments had on that sector of the local economy classified as modern. By January 1998, 17 percent of all street stores (56 outlets) fell into this category, up from 9 percent. Such ventures accounted for 19 percent of San Fernando's total sales area (3,450 m^2) with the average size per retail outlet standing at 62 m^2. Moreover, 21 percent of all street store personnel, 414 individuals, were employed in these more high-profile facilities. Certainly, the addition of those outlets at the cutting edge of commercial innovation in the mid-1990s did much to elevate San Fernando's modern retail sector as an integral part of the local trade scene.

Vendor Growth (Late 1990s)

New commercial growth in San Fernando during the 1990s was not limited to the private sector. Several public trade projects were also implemented during this time. Most significant was the new vendor facility established one city block west of the San Fernando Supermarket. Dubbed the Auxiliary Wet Market, the commercial complex was composed of seven interconnected market sheds that housed 355 vendor stalls spread over a total sales area of 1,900 m^2. The wet market was built to accommodate an overflow of meat, fish, and fruit vendors within the supermarket and to help the city's dry-goods sellers remain competitive as downtown commerce took on an increasingly modern edge.

After 355 traders were relocated to the new Auxiliary Wet Market, the more centralized supermarket became the exclusive domain of small-scale dry-goods sellers. Seemingly overnight, the supermarket's top level devolved from a thriving center of vending into a retail space virtually devoid of activity as dry-goods sellers occupied the newly uninhabited ground floor. The town government's decision to split up the local vendor community into two distinct trade zones precipitated a name change for the San Fernando Supermarket. Despite its drab condition and sparse amenities, the supermarket was paradoxically renamed the San Fernando Shopping Mall. Some vendors cynically viewed the name change as the first step toward its commercial redevelopment by outside corporate interests (e.g., Shoe Mart, Robinson's, Ever-Gotesco—all three shopping mall developers owned/

operated by Chinese Filipino retail magnates). The fact that the marketplace occupied the most central and commercially viable location within the *población* for a giant shopping mall was not lost on most vendors.

Like recent changes to San Fernando's independent merchant community, the opening of a second downtown marketplace altered the dimensions of trade in terms of aggregate floor space and sales personnel. When operations at the newly renamed San Fernando Shopping Mall and Auxiliary Wet Market are considered together—assuming that they are functioning at full capacity—755 vendor spaces are found occupied by 1,510 vendors and their hired personnel (an average of two persons per vendor stall) with a cumulative sales area of 5,900 m^2. Based on these figures, San Fernando's market vendor community experienced an unprecedented 48 percent increase in available floor space.

While such growth suggests a flourishing vendor population, this description is somewhat misleading as it fails to take into account the fact that by 1998 only a third of the San Fernando Shopping Mall's 1,800 m^2 second level remained occupied. The relocation of San Fernando's wet vendors to the Auxiliary Wet Market precipitated a move by dry-goods dealers to the mall's more accessible first floor. In the years since, the mall's downstairs area has operated at full capacity while the top level has never been fully replenished with new vendors.

When the top-floor vacancy is taken into account, a slightly less robust profile of the local vendor community emerges. Dimensions of San Fernando's small-scale trade sector in the *población* sector break down as follows: 635 market spaces comprising a total sales area of 4,700 m^2. While this translates into a 20 percent reduction in aggregate sales area from the aforementioned figure of 5,900 m^2, the *población*'s nonmodern trade economy still grew by an impressive 28 percent in terms of square meters with the opening of the Auxiliary Wet Market. These findings, coupled with the fact that small-scale downtown traders had by the late 1990s not suffered any major losses in terms of total number of vendors or sales personnel, suggest that San Fernando's nonmodern trade sector has remained vital in the face of recent retail innovation.

Discussion

Prior to 1990, modern retail ventures had a minimal presence in San Fernando. The commercial life of the *población* was defined almost exclusively by modest-sized street stores and small vendor operations. The built character of downtown, although quaint, possessed few of the qualities associated with a thriving provincial urban center of some 100,000 inhabitants. A shift in local commerce, precipitated by state-sponsored conversion efforts on Poro Point, set in motion a transformation in San Fernando's physical and commercial landscape in the mid-1990s.

The success of several modern supermarkets, chain restaurants, and a two-story strip mall along the MNR increased the presence of global consumer culture on the local level. Thanks in part to these new retail facilities, national and international consumer brands became increasingly familiar to local urbanites. This success also added to San Fernando's overall aesthetic appeal as many of downtown's preexisting stores underwent refurbishing in the wake of these larger ventures. Remodeled shop fronts, glassed facades, increased floor space, and new color schemes were all features of this commercial revitalization. Collectively, these architectural enhancements gave the *población* a decidedly more cosmopolitan feel.

Other aspects of local life beyond urban aesthetics were affected by the emergence of modern retail outlets in the 1990s. Notably, prevailing land use patterns were reconfigured to accommodate new large-scale commercial growth. The PPSEFZ called for changes in residential patterns along Poro Point and the reclaiming of parts of San Fernando Bay, while the CKC Commercial Center necessitated the removal of thousands of interred bodies from the century-old Catholic cemetery. These redevelopment efforts illustrate how previously utilized properties in greater San Fernando came to be reassessed in terms of their dormant commercial potential. What is more, the city's move toward increased retail modernization extended the geographical scope of local commerce. Sites peripheral to the *población*, especially those out of walking distance, were now subject to commercial development. The CKC Commercial Center, Fiesta Warehouse Club, and McDonald's were all established along stretches of the MNR beyond downtown. For those without private vehicles, these new retail ventures could be reached only by passenger jeepney, bus, or tricycle (motorcycle with covered sidecar), all of which require modest fares of a few pesos.

The launching of new large-scale trade facilities also affected local consumption patterns in the late 1990s. Data about the purchase of consumer goods like shoes, clothing, and groceries was collected in a household survey in March 1998 (Matejowsky 2002: 334–35). Despite an overwhelming reliance on the modern retail sector for groceries—by 1998, almost nine out of every ten local households bought groceries from one of the city's chain supermarkets—the majority of area households still turned to market vendors for clothing and footwear. By a margin of more than two to one, San Fernandians patronized outlets within the San Fernando Shopping Mall for shoes and dress apparel. Notwithstanding the dominance of modern chains over the local grocery trade, small-scale trade operations continued to exert a powerful influence over the selling of basic wares like clothing and shoes.

Conclusion

In assessing the incipient influence of globalization and mass consumerism on San Fernando's physical and commercial landscape, it is useful to consider the community's recent experience within the context of modernization/development theory. The viability of this theoretical perspective as a model or strategy for social change and poverty reduction has generated considerable debate among anthropologists and others over recent decades (Hill 1986; Mair 1984). Most recognize this paradigm as seriously flawed (Arce and Long 2000). Among other things, it has been criticized as being excessively optimistic, ethnocentric, unduly concerned with the macro-level, and many times detrimental to local populations (Gardner and Lewis 1996: 12–25).

The idea that all LDC communities will achieve an improved standard of living through a linear trajectory of socioeconomic development that is identical to the experience of the West is something that has been shown to be empirically incorrect (Gardner and Lewis 1996). If anything, the effects of modernization and development processes on local communities are highly varied. Neoliberalism and other market processes rooted in Western economic theory can generate positive outcomes at the local level just as they can produce negative ones. The muted impact of retail modernization on the political economy of San Fernando illustrates that the encroachment of Western market forces into provincial LDC communities need not destabilize core aspects of urban life. Unlike Little's findings in Antigua, Guatemala, San Fernando's small-scale trade community and traditional cityscape were not significantly undermined as global market forces began to take root at the local level. The difference between San Fernando and Antigua indicates how the impact of development processes on LDC landscapes can vary from place to place.

What is more, as the case of San Fernando illustrates, large retail outlets are no longer endemic to the major metropolitan areas of LDCs. Over the past two decades, provincial communities throughout the developing world have become increasingly subject to these modern commercial forms as conditions favoring economies of scale and a new middle-class have emerged. These ventures can create an imposing presence on the urban landscape by virtue of their physical size, sleek architecture, and economies of scale. Though their encroachment into medium-range LDC cities invariably brings about changes in land use patterns, consumer preferences, and urban aesthetics, it does not necessarily spell the end for established trade operations at the local level.

Although it is still too early to assess the full impact of retail modernization on San Fernando's urban landscape, it appears that by the late 1990s the community had not experienced many of the trend's more destructive effects. This is true for a number of reasons. First, commercial activities have remained concentrated within the *población* and have not reached a massive scale. Even though new development efforts along the MNR and Poro Point have raised the stakes as far as the economic hegemony of downtown is concerned, the intensification of commercial development beyond the urban core has yet to lure large numbers of shoppers away from the main business district. Second, market vendors and shop owners continue to play an important role in defining downtown municipal life. Besides representing an important voting bloc, San Fernando's small-scale trade community also controls, via the town government, two of downtown's largest and most strategically valued commercial properties—the San Fernando Shopping Mall and the Auxiliary Wet Market. The future of small-scale traders should remain secure as long as this advantageous position in the local political economy is upheld. Third, the equilibrium underlying the town's trade structure has persisted more or less intact through this recent surge of retail modernization. The municipal trade community has yet to confront a situation whereby the modern retail sector or its more traditional counterpart could dramatically augment its influence over municipal commerce at the expense of the last. Fourth, San Fernando's move toward retail modernization has been driven primarily by local interests. Both ethnic Chinese and Ilocano family firms, not to mention the local Catholic diocese, have been at the forefront of this trend. These groups are more likely interested in preserving the quality of urban life in San Fernando than are outside corporate developers with no deep ties to the community.

Postscript: The Coming of the Megamalls (Late 1990s and Beyond)

At the turn of the new century, outside commercial interests have continued to make inroads into San Fernando. Most notably, national and regional shopping mall developers have stepped up efforts to engage the local market. The renaming of the San Fernando Supermarket to the San Fernando Shopping Mall illustrates the degree to which modern shopping malls captured the local imagination in the late 1990s. During that time, it was widely rumored that representatives from the Philippines' most successful retail firm—Shoe Mart—had secretly visited San Fernando to scout out locations for a megamall complex within the *población*. The company had embarked on an ambitious plan in the mid-1990s to penetrate midsize Philippine cities with a new shopping mall to be opened each year until 2000 (Tiglao 1994).

In July 2004, San Fernando City's first ever megamall was opened. The giant shopping center was developed not by Shoe Mart but rather by one of the northern Philippines' most powerful ethnic Chinese firms—City Super Market Inc. (CSI). Based out of neighboring Dagupan City, CSI operates a chain of malls, warehouse clubs, and supermarkets throughout the region. Their San Fernando undertaking was inaugurated as the CSI City Mall La Union on a 3 ha lot several kilometers north of the *población*. The bilevel facility sports a strikingly modern design and a parking lot capable of accommodating over six hundred vehicles. With its numerous upscale shops and restaurants, the mall represents a new stage in San Fernando's experience with retail modernization in that it is the first major commercial development to successfully open well beyond the reach of downtown. To what extent the new CSI mall affects the socioeconomic vitality of San Fernando's urban landscape is a question that warrants further research.

Acknowledgments

The material presented in this chapter was collected in the Philippines between 1997 and 1998. Part of the research was supported by a fellowship from the Leland T. and Jessie W. Jordan Institute for International Awareness, Texas A&M University. My research was also sponsored by the Institute of Philippine Culture, Ateneo de Manila University, Quezon City.

References

Arce, Alberto, and Norman Long. 2000. "Reconfiguring Modernity and Development from an Anthropological Perspective." In *Anthropology, Development, and Modernities: Exploring Discourses, Counter-Tendencies, and Violence*, ed. Alberto Arce and Norman Long, 1–31. New York: Routledge.

Bishop, Ryan, John Phillips, and Wei Wei Yeo, eds. 2003. *Postcolonial Urbanism. Southeast Asian Cities and Global Processes*. New York: Routledge.

Cohen, Margaret. 2004. "Mighty Malls." *Far Eastern Economic Review*, July 1, 5; 38.

Collins, Thomas W., and John D. Wingard, eds. 2000. *Communities and Capital: Local Struggles against Corporate Power and Privatization*. Athens: University of Georgia Press.

Cruz, Elpia R. 1988. "Multi-faceted La Union." *Manila Times*, March13.

Dandekar, Hemalata C., ed. 1998. *City Space and Globalization: An International Perspective. Proceedings from an International Symposium. College of Architecture and Urban Planning. The University of Michigan. February 26–28, 1998.* Ann Arbor, MI: College of Architecture and Urban Planning.

Dannhaeuser, Norbert. 1989. "Marketing in Developing Areas." In *Economic Anthropology*, ed. Stuart Plattner, 222–52. Stanford, CA: Stanford University Press.

———. 1997. "The Malling of Dagupan." *Philippine Studies* 45 (2): 151–73.

———. 2004. *Chinese Traders in a Philippine Town. From Daily Competition to Urban Transformation.* Quezon City, Philippines: Ateneo de Manila University Press.

Davis, William G. 1973. *Social Relations in a Philippine Market Place. Self-Interest and Subjectivity.* Berkeley: University of California Press.

Department of Trade and Industry (DTI). 1997. *Registered Businesses Alphabetized, 1988–1997, San Fernando.* San Fernando City, Philippines: Department of Trade and Industry.

Drakakis-Smith, David W. 2002. *Pacific Asia: Routledge Introductions to Development.* New York: Routledge.

Gardner, Katy, and David Lewis. 1996. *Anthropology, Development and the Post-Modern Challenge.* Chicago: Pluto.

Hill, Polly. 1986. *Development Economics on Trial: The Anthropological Case for Prosecution.* Cambridge: Cambridge University Press.

Kaynak, Erdener. 1982. *Marketing in the Third World.* New York: Praeger.

Kirk, Donald. 1998. *Looted: The Philippines after the Bases.* New York: St. Martin's Press.

Mair, Lucy. 1984. *Anthropology and Development.* London: Macmillan.

Matejowsky, Ty. 2000. "The Privatization of Public Plazas in the Philippines. Three Cases from Pangasinan." *Philippine Quarterly of Culture and Society* 28:263–300.

———. 2002. "Globalization and Retail Development in the Post-Disaster Context. A Comparison of Two Philippine Communities." In *Social Dimensions in the Economic Process. Research in Economic Anthropology.* Vol. 21, ed. Norbert Dannhaeuser and Cynthia Werner, 311–41. Amsterdam: Elsevier-JAI Press.

———. 2006. "Global Tastes, Local Contexts: An Ethnographic Account of Fast Food Expansion in the Provincial Philippines." In *Fast/Slow Food. The Cultural Economy of the Global Food System*, ed. Richard Wilk, 145–59. Lanham, MD: AltaMira.

McGee, T.G., and Tue-man Yeung. 1977. *Hawkers in Southeast Asian Cities. Planning for the Bazaar Economy.* Ottawa: International Development Research Centre.

Mendoza, Felipe M. 1996. *The Poro Point Special Economic and Freeport Zone Master Development Plan: Final Report.* Quezon City, Philippines: Base Conversion and Development Authority.

Miller, Daniel. 1997. *Capitalism: An Ethnographic Approach.* Oxford: Berg.

Pertierra, Raul, ed. 1992. *Remittances and Returnees: The Cultural Economy of Migration in Ilocos.* Quezon City, Philippines: New Day Publishers.

Smith, M. Estelle. 1989. "The Informal Economy." In *Economic Anthropology*, ed. Stuart Plattner, 292–317. Stanford, CA: Stanford University Press.

Terry, Edith. 2002. *How Asia Got Rich: Japan, China and the Asian Miracle.* Armonk, NY: M. E. Sharpe.

Tiglao, Roger. 1994. "Strength in Numbers." *Far Eastern Economic Review* 7 (21): 60–61.

Watson, James, ed. 1997. *Golden Arches East: McDonald's in East Asia.* Palo Alto: Stanford University Press.

Yeung, Yue-man. 2000. *Globalization and Networked Societies: Urban Regional Change in Pacific Asia.* Honolulu: University of Hawaii Press.

Index

Note: The letter *t* following a number denotes a table; the letter *f* following a number denotes a figure.

About the Editors

Lisa Cliggett (PhD, Indiana University) is associate professor of anthropology at the University of Kentucky. She has carried out ethnographic fieldwork in Zambia since 1992, focusing on issues of household economy, intergenerational relations, and most recently migration and environmental change in a Game Management Area bordering a national park. Her book, *Grains from Grass: Aging, Gender, and Famine in Rural Africa*, was published in 2005. She is also coauthor with Richard Wilk of the new edition of *Economies and Cultures: Foundations of Economic Anthropology*.

Christopher A. Pool (PhD, Tulane University, 1990) is associate professor of anthropology at the University of Kentucky. He has studied ceramic production and exchange in southern Veracruz, Mexico, since 1983 and has directed archaeological investigations of long-term change in political economy at Tres Zapotes, Veracruz, since 1995. He is editor, with George J. Bey III, of *Pottery Economics in Mesoamerica and Ceramic Production and Distribution: An Integrated Approach* and author of *Olmec Archaeology and Early Formative Mesoamerica*.

About the Contributors

Douglas J. Bolender received his doctorate in anthropology in 2006 from Northwestern University, where he is currently a visiting assistant professor. His research examines the role of land tenure in household production strategies in Iceland, where he has done extensive fieldwork. He is codirector with John M. Steinberg of the Skagafjörður Archaeological Settlement Survey.

George M. Crothers is director of the William S. Webb Museum of Anthropology and assistant professor of anthropology at the University of Kentucky. He received his PhD from Washington University in St. Louis in 1999. His research interests include the archaeology of hunting and gathering populations and early agricultural societies. He has worked extensively in the southeastern and midwestern United States, and currently has long-term research projects in Mammoth Cave National Park and the middle and lower Green River valley of Kentucky. He was a visiting scholar at the Center for Archaeological Investigations at Southern Illinois University in 2000–2001, which resulted in the edited book *Hunters and Gatherers in Theory and Archaeology* (2004).

David E. Doyel received his PhD from the University of Arizona in 1977. He has directed archaeological research projects throughout much of the American Southwest and has numerous publications on the region. Currently he is an archaeologist for Luke Air Force Base in Glendale, Arizona, and an adjunct faculty member in the School of Human Evolution and Social Change at Arizona State University in Tempe. His research interests include cultural ecology, political economy, technology, exchange, community organization, and the history of archaeology.

E. Paul Durrenberger is professor of anthropology at Pennsylvania State University. He has done ethnographic work with highland and valley rice and opium producers in northern Thailand as well as work on industrial fishing and farming in Iceland, commercial fishing in Alabama and Mississippi, industrial swine production in Iowa, and labor unions in Chicago and Pennsylvania. He has written extensively about the political ecology of medieval Iceland, including his book, *The Dynamics of Medieval Iceland: Political Economy and Literature* (1992). He has worked with Doug Bolender and John Steinberg on the archaeological survey of northern Iceland. His most recent book is an introduction to anthropology, *Anthropology Unbound: A Field Guide to the 21st Century* (2006), which he wrote with his wife and collaborator, Suzan Erem. Durrenberger is also a founding member of the Society for Economic Anthropology (SEA).

Timothy Earle is a professor of anthropology at Northwestern University. He received his PhD from the University of Michigan in 1973. His field research has included major archaeological projects in Hawaii, Peru, Argentina, Denmark, and now Hungary. Earle's *How Chiefs Come to Power* (1997) looks at the economic strategies used by emerging elites to gain control over military and ideological power. In *Bronze Age Economics* (2002), he discusses the nature of non-market-based political economies in early chiefdoms and states, and how they served as alternative ways to finance political centralization and social stratification.

Juliet S. Erazo is an assistant professor of anthropology at Florida International University. She received an interdepartmental PhD in anthropology and natural resources from the University of Michigan in 2003. Early drafts of her chapter were written during an S.V. Ciriacy-Wantrup Postdoctoral Fellowship in Natural Resource Studies at the University of California, Berkeley, which she held from 2003 to 2005. Her research interests include indigenous political movements, state/society relations, international development, and political ecology.

Elliot Fratkin is professor of anthropology and director of the African Studies Program at Smith College in Northampton, Massachusetts. His research focuses on social organization, health, and change among Ariaal, Rendille, and Samburu pastoralists of northern Kenya. He is author of *Ariaal Pastoralists of Northern Kenya* (2004) and coauthor of *African Pastoralist Systems* (1994) and *As Pastoralists Settle: Social, Health, and Economic Consequences of Pastoral Sedentarization in Marsabit District, Kenya* (2005).

N. Thomas Håkansson is an associate professor in the Division of Human Ecology at Lund University, and an adjunct associate professor in the Department of Anthropology at the University of Kentucky. His recent work has focused on the political ecology of agricultural intensification in nonstate societies. He is currently collaborating with human geographers in a research program that aims to develop regional models of long-term changes in land use in northeastern Tanzania. Håkansson's work on regional economies and land use in East Africa has been published in *Human Ecology*, *Ethnology*, *World Development*, *Geografiska Annaler*, and other journals.

Walter E. Little is an assistant professor of anthropology at the University at Albany, SUNY, who focuses on the political economy of Maya handicraft vendors and Maya spirituality. He is the author, with R. McKenna Brown and Judith M. Maxwell, of *La ütz awäch? Introduction to the Kaqchikel Maya Language* (2006); *Kaqchikel Tijonïk Oxlajuj Aj: Curso de Idioma y Cultura Maya Kaqchikel* (with Judith M. Maxwell; 2006); and *Mayas in the Marketplace: Tourism, Globalization, and Cultural Identity* (2004). In addition, he was guest editor of a special issue of *Latin American Perspectives*, "Maya Livelihoods in Guatemala's Global Economy" (2005).

Carol MacLennan is associate professor of anthropology in social sciences at Michigan Technological University. She teaches in the environmental policy and the industrial heritage and archaeology graduate programs and works with anthropology undergraduates. Her long-term interests encompass the histories of sugar and mining industries and their environmental consequences. She is currently completing a manuscript on the history of the sugar industry in Hawaii titled *Sovereign Sugar: Industrialization of the Hawaiian Landscape, 1840–1930*. Her research and fieldwork on mining landscapes is ongoing in Silver City, New Mexico, and the Lake Superior district, where she is examining the historical and political ecology of mining and pollution.

Ty Matejowsky is an assistant professor of anthropology at the University of Central Florida. He received his PhD in anthropology from Texas A&M University in 2001. His research focuses on fast food, retail globalization, migration, and urbanization in the Philippines. Publications include "SPAM and Fast Food 'Glocalization' in the Philippines" (2007) in *Food and Culture*; "Global Tastes, Local Contexts: An Ethnographic Account of Fast Food in San Fernando City, the Philippines" (2006) in *Fast Food/Slow Food: The Economic Anthropology of the Global Food System*; and "Overseas Contract

Labor, Remittances and Household Consumption: A Case Study from San Fernando City, the Philippines" (2006) in *Markets and Market Liberalization: Ethnographic Reflections*. He is currently working on a book about fast-food globalization in the Philippines.

Verónica Pérez Rodríguez is an assistant professor of anthropology at Northern Arizona University. She received her PhD in ecological and environmental anthropology from the University of Georgia in 2003. Her research focuses on human-environment interactions, landscape transformation, and its relationship to social complexity in the Mixteca Alta, Oaxaca, Mexico. Her latest work has appeared in the journal *Latin American Antiquity* (2006).

Paul A. Rivera received his doctorate in economics from the University of Southern California in 2002, and currently is a professor of economics at California State University, Channel Islands. His primary research addresses labor and migration and remittances between Latin America and the United States, although his published articles span a variety of topics: Central Bank reform in Venezuela, educational investment in Taiwan, the effects of oil price shocks on economic policy, and the development of property rights in nineteenth-century Brazil.

John M. Steinberg is a senior scientist at the Fiske Center for Archaeological Research at the University of Massachusetts Boston. His research involves developing archaeological methods to answer questions concerning the economics of human social evolution. He has been directing the Skagafjörður Archaeological Settlement Survey, along with Douglas J. Bolender and E. Paul Durrenberger, since 2000. He works in Iceland and in the Northeast United States.

Paul Trawick, a cultural anthropologist, is a senior lecturer in applied sociology at Cranfield University in Silsoe, Bedfordshire, United Kingdom. His work has focused on the theory and practice of water management for irrigation and socioeconomic development in Peru and Latin America and recently in Spain and Europe. Trawick is the author of *The Struggle for Water in Peru: Comedy and Tragedy in the Andean Commons* (2003). He has published more than twenty articles in journals on anthropology and environmental and development studies, has received research grants from the Fulbright Association, MacArthur Foundation, and National Science Foundations in the United States, and has worked as a consultant on water policy for the World Bank and the InterAmerican Development Bank in Washington.

Christa Walck is dean and professor of organizational behavior in the School of Business & Economics at Michigan Technological University and a member of MTU's Sustainable Futures Institute. Her current research investigates organizational impacts on the natural environment from a land use and place-based perspective. She is currently working on historical studies of land use on Cape Cod and in the Gila National Forest in New Mexico, and applying Aldo Leopold's concept of land health to environmental management. She serves on the editorial review boards of *Management Learning*, the *Journal of Organizational Change Management*, and the *Journal of East-West Business*; is past president of the Keweenaw Land Trust; and cochaired Common Ground, a citizens' group encouraging sustainable development and land use planning in Michigan's Upper Peninsula.